POLITICAL PARTIES
IN
NEW ZEALAND

POLITICAL PARTIES
IN
NEW ZEALAND

BY

R. S. MILNE

OXFORD
AT THE CLARENDON PRESS
1966

Oxford University Press, Ely House, London W. 1

GLASGOW NEW YORK TORONTO MELBOURNE WELLINGTON
CAPE TOWN SALISBURY IBADAN NAIROBI LUSAKA ADDIS ABABA
BOMBAY CALCUTTA MADRAS KARACHI LAHORE DACCA
KUALA LUMPUR HONG KONG

© *Oxford University Press 1966*

PRINTED IN GREAT BRITAIN

Professor Brookes and was financed by the New Zealand
University Grants Committee, to whom I wish to record my
thanks. Dr. Robinson kindly answered numerous last-minute
queries on recent political events. The responsibility for any
errors is, of course, my own.

I must also pay tribute to the patience, and visual acuity, of
those who typed the manuscript, notably Mrs. Diana Ng,
Mrs. Lilian Wong, and my Wife.

R. S. MILNE

University of British Columbia, Vancouver

NOTE

EARLY in December 1965, in accordance with the new procedure
mentioned on page 144, the Labour Party caucus elected Mr. N. E.
Kirk as its Leader in preference to the existing Leader, Mr. A. H.
Nordmeyer. This was the first time that an existing Leader had
stood for re-election and been defeated. Mr. Kirk entered Parliament in 1957, and was elected President of the Party in 1964.
In his career in the Labour Party Mr. Kirk has enjoyed substantial support from the industrial side of the movement. Some
of Mr. Nordmeyer's difficulties with the industrial side are described on pages 110–12.

PREFACE

I T is said that one New Zealand political figure seriously considered writing reminiscences entitled, *Bastards I have met.* In writing this book, perhaps because I was not myself actively engaged in politics, my experience was quite otherwise. I was repeatedly astonished by the willingness of politicians and others to give up their time cheerfully in order to talk about New Zealand politics. It is not possible to list all the people who helped me, but among those who had already retired from active politics when I interviewed them, my special thanks are due to the following: Sir Walter Broadfoot; Colonel S. J. E. Closey; Mr. J. H. Furniss; Mr. Alex. Gordon; Mr. F. Jones; Mr. Frank Langstone; Mr. J. A. Lee; Mr. A. A. McLachlan; Mr. J. T. Paul; Sir William Polson; Mr. T. E. Y. Seddon; Mr. A. C. A. Sexton; Mr. C. A. L. Treadwell; Mr. C. Morgan Williams; Mr. Ormond Wilson.

At the headquarters of the parties and of the Federation of Labour I was helped on many occasions by: Mr. K. McL. Baxter; Mr. J. E. Colechin; Mr. Fraser Colman; Mr. Cyril Hester; Mr. Alan McDonald; Mr. Ian Main; Mr. Martin Nestor; Mr. Ken Richards; Mr. Ralph Wilson. Other party officials who provided useful information included divisional secretaries of the National Party and divisional area representatives of the Labour Party.

My indebtedness to some other persons engaged in politics who do not come into either of these two categories will be evident from references in the book.

I am also grateful to a number of academics and public servants, notably: Professor R. H. Brookes; Mr. Bruce Brown; Professor J. B. Condliffe; Dr. P. J. O'Farrell; Mr. W. J. Gardner; Mr. Douglas Law; Miss Therese May; Mr. R. J. Polaschek; Mr. John Roberts; Dr. Alan Robinson; Dr. J. L. Robson; Professor Keith Sinclair; Miss Whetu Tirikatene.

Much of the material on which the book is based was collected while I taught at the Victoria University of Wellington, 1956–9. A visit to New Zealand in April and May 1964 was arranged by

CONTENTS

I

THE SOCIAL AND POLITICAL SETTING

NEW ZEALAND's history is short and its inhabitants few. European settlements of any size date from 1840, while the country's present population is about 2½ million. Its importance on the world scene, judged objectively, is small. Unless the Great Powers become suddenly more concerned with the Antarctic, New Zealand is probably of less strategic interest than most other countries on earth, except perhaps Monaco and Andorra.

In spite of all this, the number of general books published about New Zealand is huge, perhaps excessive.[1] This introductory chapter does not attempt to reproduce, even in miniature, what has already been written in these books: to be, in effect, a 'short white cloud'. It seeks merely to provide a social and political background for the analysis of New Zealand political parties. This subject is one which perhaps is still 'underwritten' rather than 'overwritten', at least as far as published material is concerned.[2] Yet party politics in New Zealand is of some

[1] Among those which could *not* be dispensed with are: W. P. Reeves, *The Long White Cloud* (London, 4th edn., 1950); H. D. Lloyd, *A Country Without Strikes* (New York, 1900); A. Métin, *Le Socialisme sans Doctrines* (Paris, 1901); A. Siegfried, *Democracy in New Zealand* (London, 1914); W. P. Reeves, *State Experiments in Australia and New Zealand* (London, 1923); L. C. Webb, *Government in New Zealand* (Wellington, 1940); H. Belshaw (ed.), *New Zealand* (Berkeley and Los Angeles, 1947); L. Lipson, *The Politics of Equality* (Chicago, 1948); F. L. W. Wood, *This New Zealand* (Hamilton, 1958); K. Sinclair, *A History of New Zealand* (London, 1959); J. B. Condliffe, *New Zealand in the Making* (London, 1959); W. H. Oliver, *The Story of New Zealand* (London, 1960).

[2] There is relevant material on parties in the above references, particularly in Lipson. Other general references to parties since 1890 include: J. Drummond, *The Life and Work of Richard John Seddon* (Christchurch, 1906); J. T. Paul, *Humanism in Politics* (Wellington, 1946); J. Thorn, *Peter Fraser* (London, 1952); R. M. Burdon, *King Dick* (Wellington, 1955); W. Downie Stewart, *Sir Francis H. D. Bell, His Life and Times* (Wellington, 1957); Bruce Brown, *The Rise of New Zealand Labour* (Wellington, 1962); R. N. Kelson, *The Private Member of Parliament and the Formation of Public Policy, a New Zealand Case Study* (Toronto, 1964); John A. Lee, *Simple on a Soapbox* (Auckland, 1963); J. Penfold, 'The New Zealand Labour Party: its Formal Structure', *Political Science*, vol. vi, no. 1 (1954); R. N. Kelson, 'The New Zealand National Party', *Political Science*, vol. vi, no. 2 (1954); Louise Overacker,

intrinsic interest, as an illustration of what becomes of parties
and politics in a small egalitarian country with a high degree of
consensus and few burning political issues. The New Zealand
parties are also worth studying from the point of view of comparisons, particularly with Great Britain and Australia.

Three basic features are of chief importance in determining
New Zealand's social setting: her size; her historical, family,
and sentimental links with Britain; the structure of her economy
and the fact that her external trade has been carried on mainly
with Britain. Although New Zealand's area is slightly larger
than that of Great Britain, the population is only one-twentieth
of Britain's; roughly two-thirds of the population live in the
North Island, the remainder in the South Island. New Zealand's
problems are therefore different in scale from those of larger
countries. When a New Zealand Prime Minister illustrated his
references to the country's rapid development by speaking of
the tramping feet of the 'third million', the footsteps must have
sounded rather louder in Wellington than they would have in
Delhi or Djakarta.[1] A British commentator[2] has referred to the
'intimacy' of New Zealand politics, while an eminent local
public servant, more crudely, once described them as a 'tin-
pot show'. The implications are considerable. Because of the

'The New Zealand Labor Party', *American Political Science Review*, vol. xlix, no. 3
(1955); P. Campbell, 'Politicians, Public Servants, and the People in New Zealand',
Political Studies, vol. iii, no. 3 (1955), and vol. iv, no. 1 (1956); Louise Overacker,
'The British and New Zealand Labour Parties: A Comparison', *Political Science*,
vol. ix, nos. 1 and 2 (1957); W. J. Gardner, 'The Rise of W. F. Massey, 1891–
1912', *Political Science*, vol. xiii, no. 1 (1961); and 'W. F. Massey in Power', *Political
Science*, vol. xiii, no. 2 (1961). The forthcoming *New Zealand Encyclopaedia*, edited
by A. H. McLintock, will contain articles on the parties by B. M. Brown, B. J.
Foster, W. J. Gardner, M. J. S. Nestor, and A. D. Robinson.

The following unpublished university theses are particularly useful: L. C. Webb,
'The Rise of the Reform Party' (Canterbury, 1928); R. M. Chapman, 'The Signi-
ficance of the 1928 General Election' (Auckland, 1949); R. T. Shannon, 'The
Decline and Fall of the Liberal Government' (Auckland, 1953); B. J. Foster,
'Development of Unity and Organization in the New Zealand Political Parties of
the Liberal Era' (Victoria, 1956); A. D. Robinson, 'The Rise of the New Zealand
National Party, 1936–49' (Victoria, 1957); J. R. S. Daniels, 'The General Election
of 1943' (Victoria, 1961).

A fuller bibliography may be found in Josephine F. Milburn and Taylor Cole, 'Bibliographical Material on Political Parties and Pressure Groups in Australia, New
Zealand, and South Africa', *American Political Science Review*, vol. li, no. 1 (1957).

[1] Aided by immigration, the annual rate of increase of the population, 1956–
1961, was 2·1 per cent (*New Zealand Official Yearbook 1963* (Wellington), p. 55).

[2] Campbell, art. cit. (1955), p. 193.

relatively face-to-face nature of politics in New Zealand, it may be possible to avoid some of the oligarchic tendencies which exist in large organizations in bigger countries. Similarly, it may be feasible to allow personal appeals to ministers by members of the public, which would just not be practicable in many other countries. If only for this reason, the 'style' of New Zealand politics may be distinctive and incapable of successful imitation, unless substantially adapted, by larger countries.

New Zealanders are overwhelmingly of British stock,[1] with the exception of the Maoris, who form less than 10 per cent. of the population. Racial problems are as nothing compared with South Africa's, and affect politics much less than in Canada. There are relatively few inhabitants of Irish origin, which partly accounts for the low proportion of Roman Catholics, about one-seventh, as compared with almost a quarter in Australia. Even the climate is a milder version of Britain's, and, although the proportion of the land which can easily be brought into cultivation is popularly over-estimated, there is no counterpart of the vast arid central region in Australia. Because of their British origins and the ties of sentiment, culture and trade that bind New Zealand to Britain, 12,000 miles away, it might be too hastily assumed that New Zealanders unreservedly identified themselves with Britain. This belief would be strengthened by the constant references to Britain as 'home' or 'the old country' and by statements of the 'where she [Britain] stands, we stand' variety.[2] It would also gain support from the intense desire New Zealanders have to visit Britain (at least for the first time). Many young New Zealanders save up for years in order to be able to see Britain; and some time ago it was reported that a retiring Cabinet minister was 'compensated' for his resignation by being given a trip to London.[3] But this is not an accurate picture. Curiosity about Britain and the recognition of links with 'home' do not rule out ambivalent feelings. A growing number of New Zealanders, and especially the small band of intellectuals, are searching for a new identity and are not content to follow Britain, as if they were British provincials at the end of rather

[1] But not quite so British as is sometimes imagined (Sinclair, op. cit., p. 297).
[2] By Prime Minister Savage at the start of the Second World War.
[3] After the National Party came into power in 1949, because of the sensitivity of public opinion (and the party's previous propaganda on the subject), overseas trips by public servants required Cabinet approval.

long lines of communication. To develop this argument fully
would entail exploring the prospects for a distinctive New Zealand culture. Some of the ways in which New Zealanders'
attitudes differ from British ones will be apparent a little
further on. Here, it may be enough to mention that there has
been a perceptible change during the last twenty or thirty years
in New Zealand's views on external relations and defence,
expertly traced in the early chapters of *The New Zealand People
at War*.[1] In the beginning New Zealand's position was adequately reflected by J. E. FitzGerald's address to the Queen,
submitted to Parliament in 1854. 'This colony, young and
feeble, situated in so remote a portion of the globe, can, unfortunately, add but little to the expression of the unalterable
attachment and true and faithful allegiance to your Majesty's
throne and person.'[2] Towards the end of the century an 'imperialist' phase followed, marked by New Zealand participation
in the Boer War and the First World War and by ambitious
schemes for Imperial Federation[3] and annexations in the
Pacific. From this period New Zealand inherited the minute
Cook Islands (and Niue), a United Nations trusteeship (which
was relinquished in 1961) for Western Samoa, and the Ross
Dependency in the Antarctic. More recently New Zealand has
been taught by the last world war that she is no longer safe from
invasion, and that the United States is now her first and last
best hope against a Pacific enemy. This led to the conclusion of
the ANZUS pact (between Australia, New Zealand and the
United States) in 1951. New Zealand is also a member of
SEATO. At the same time New Zealand has continued to
develop, in the United Nations, the independent role of a
spokesman for the small powers,[4] which, from 1936 on, she had
already begun to play in the League of Nations. This has been
accompanied, rather belatedly, by greater interest in Asia,
shown by increased diplomatic representation in Asian countries and by participation in schemes such as the Colombo
Plan.[5] When the Prime Minister, Mr. Holyoake, left for a

[1] By F. L. W. Wood (Wellington, 1958).
[2] Quoted in *Cambridge History of the British Empire*, vol. vii, part ii (1933), p. 199.
[3] See K. Sinclair, *Imperial Federation* (London, 1955).
[4] See K. J. Cunningham, 'New Zealand as a Small Power in the United Nations', *Political Science*, vol. ix, no. 2 (1957).
[5] J. B. Condliffe, *The Welfare State in New Zealand* (London, 1959), ch. viii.

SEATO ministers' meeting in April 1964 he said that it was impossible to stress too much New Zealand's close and vital interest in Southeast Asia.

New Zealand's economy and her standard of living, which is among the highest in the world, are based on agriculture. She is able to produce at low cost because of a favourable soil and climate and through the industry and initiative of her farmers, shown, for instance, in the extensive adoption of aerial top-dressing. Her dependence on a small range of agricultural exports is indicated by the fact that about three-quarters of her export revenue is derived from butter, meat, and wool. The world prices of these primary products are subject to great fluctuations, and these economic disturbances have political repercussions. A fall in the prices of these products inevitably leads to import and exchange controls and to higher taxation in order to cut down internal demand. So the New Zealand tax-payer is quickly made aware of a decline in the revenue from exports. In addition the marketing schemes, which exist to stabilize some agricultural prices and thus shield producers from bearing the full weight of a drop in world prices, have their political effects. Being human, many farmers are grateful for protection against 'adverse' fluctuations, but do not press with the same intensity for 'protection' against fluctuations which bring them windfall gains.

New Zealand's revenue from exports is especially precarious because over half of it is derived from exports to a single country —the United Kingdom. The possibility of Britain's entry into the European Common Market was therefore a source of serious concern to New Zealand in case her exports might lose the pre-ferences which they had hitherto enjoyed. For some time before Britain's entry into the Common Market was definitely pro-posed, New Zealand had been attempting to increase her ex-ports to other countries, but, although recognized as clearly desirable in principle, this has proved to be a slow process. She has also tried to widen the range of items exported, and has, for instance, increased her timber and paper exports. The problem has also been tackled from another angle—attempting to cut down the bill for imports by increasing local production of manufactured goods.[1] These efforts were stimulated by the

[1] Between 1938–9 and 1961–2 the value of 'factory' production increased by

negotiations over Britain's entry into the Common Market in 1963.

Although New Zealand is so dependent on agricultural exports only about a seventh of the labour force is engaged in agriculture. A higher proportion than this is engaged in each of the categories, 'manufacturing', 'commerce', and 'service trades'. Politically, however, farmers have an importance far greater than these figures would suggest. The reasons for this will be examined in a later chapter, but it may be remarked that there is no urban-rural division, almost to the point of a dichotomy, such as is sometimes alleged to exist in Australia. The biggest New Zealand towns do not contain so great a proportion of the population as the largest Australian towns. To be sure, in the New Zealand backblocks (backwoods) Wellington is resented as an unfriendly place where applications to government departments are often turned down. And Auckland, whose 500,000 inhabitants are sometimes known as 'Rangitoto Yanks', is often regarded as the big city, full of slickers and espresso bars. But the large towns do not give the impression of dominating the country as they do in Australia, and consequently the country does not react violently against this real or imagined domination. Similarly, with one or two notable exceptions, it is not so easy in New Zealand as it is in Australia to rouse country dwellers to oppose the trade unions on the ground that they represent an aspect of big-town ascendancy.

The Social Background

These observations are grounded on history, geography, and economics. But attempts to assess the 'social climate' of New Zealand, or to portray the 'New Zealand character', must rest on a more slender foundation. Nevertheless, there is widespread agreement that an outstanding feature of New Zealand life is its tendency toward equality—indeed Leslie Lipson chose for his book the title, *The Politics of Equality*. This is not to say that class distinctions are completely absent in New Zealand. But it seems evident that, although they exist, they are not nearly so rigidly defined as in Britain.[1] Extremes of wealth are less than

more than eight times. The value of farm production was only four and a half times as high (*New Zealand Official Yearbook*, 1963, p. 410).

[1] A. A. Congalton, 'Some Aspects of Social Stratification in New Zealand' (Victoria unpublished thesis, 1947).

in Britain, and there are smaller differentials between the wages of the skilled and the unskilled. There is certainly resentment against inherited status, privileges, or wealth. As in Australia,[1] there are no institutions corresponding closely to Oxford and Cambridge, the public schools, the City, the armed forces, the landed aristocracy, the established Church, or the Foreign Office in Britain. In other words, there is no equivalent of the 'Establishment'. Hatred of inequality in New Zealand extends further than this: it is also directed against inequality resulting from superior *achievement*, on the ground, perhaps, that to strive after achievement shows a lack of dedication to equality. However, mere inequality of circumstance, *provided that it is patently accidental*, would probably not be resented. The winner of a lottery would not come under attack, although he had become much more wealthy than his neighbours. The explanation, presumably, is that plainly the win has not resulted either from special privileges (such as inheritance) or from special achievement (arising from a desire to be superior). Siegfried, Lipson, and many others have pointed to the ways in which this love for equality, piled on top of New Zealand's smallness and isolation, has tended to blight culture, original thinking, and research. Gradham Wallas, in making a comparison with Norway, thought that New Zealand 'may still have to learn that the Extreme as a personal ideal for those who are called by it is a necessary complement of the Mean in public policy'.[2] And it has often been remarked that the concept of equality, which benefits from being loosely equated with 'democracy', has often been pursued in New Zealand at the expense of liberty.[3] Less familiar is the fact that there are strong undercurrents concealed by this apparent devotion to equality. Siegfried observed that underneath the surface the colonial is a snob.[4] Unwilling to defer to privilege and status on the part of his fellows, the New Zealander with social pretensions still seeks honours conferred from London ('the crumbs of nobility which England is good enough to let fall from her table'), and when visiting England one of his chief concerns is to be invited to royal garden parties. In New

[1] J. D. B. Miller, *Australian Government and Politics* (London, 1959), p. 30: cf. Oliver, op. cit., p. 273.
[2] *The Great Society* (New York, 1914), pp. 368–9.
[3] Lipson, op. cit., pp. 7–9.
[4] op. cit., p. 46, also pp. 270–9.

Zealand itself the attentions of the socially ambitious are directed towards an imported temporary 'monarch' in the person of the Governor General.

Another prominent New Zealand characteristic is pragmatism, corresponding to what Siegfried called the lack of 'principles, convictions, reasoned beliefs'.[1] Adapting Siegfried, one might say that New Zealand was 'doubly pragmatic'. On the continent of Europe the British have acquired the reputation of being pragmatic; this trait has been intensified among the (largely British) New Zealanders by the original need to develop the land, leaving little time for intellectual pursuits, by the country's smallness and remoteness, and by the prejudice against theorizing associated with insistence on equality. Pragmatism perhaps is the key to what, viewed from any other angle, appear as opposing tendencies in New Zealand; on the one hand New Zealand's invocation of the State to conduct experiments, as if the country were a social laboratory, and on the other hand the 'social conservatism' of New Zealanders. The 'social laboratory' view of New Zealand is relevant only for rather limited periods of time. Broadly speaking, it applied, under Liberal governments, from 1890 for a maximum of some sixteen years, marked by the introduction of compulsory arbitration, old-age pensions, and other strikingly novel social legislation.[2] It was also applicable, under Labour, from 1935 to 1939, when legislation created the equivalent of a welfare state in New Zealand. The actual 'social experiments' attempted during these two periods will be discussed later. It is enough to say that the great attention given to them (especially to the first by such brilliant writers as Siegfried, Métin, Pember Reeves, Lloyd, and others) has produced a misleading picture of New Zealand history as one protracted non-stop social experiment. Perhaps attention should be drawn, however, to some recent reforms in a particular field. Since 1961 there has been some pioneer legislation originating in the Justice Department—for instance as regards compensation for the victims of crimes and in the use of detention centres.

On the other hand, it is not difficult to find evidence of social conservatism in New Zealand. On two occasions when the Bank of New Zealand, a private bank, was in difficulties, the

[1] Op. cit., p. 62.   [2] See Ch. II, below.

Government declined the opportunity of taking it over, even although the second occasion (1894–5) occurred during the great 'experimentation' period. Indeed, a picture of New Zealand could be drawn in terms of its being 'Victorian'[1] in its architecture, respectability, culture, attitudes towards women, slow recognition of Britain's decline as a world power, and puritanically joyful acceptance of import cuts affecting *other people's* 'luxuries'. Another telling description, by a labour leader well versed in Marxist terminology, is that New Zealand has always been the land of the petty bourgeoisie.

It would seem that 'social conservatism' is the prevailing attitude, but that on two occasions, 1890 and 1935, under the spur of an economic crisis, the electors have voted-in a Government prepared to undertake extensive reforms. Once these Governments began to carry out reforms they were probably less inhibited by the 'accepted theories' of the times than Governments in less 'pragmatic' countries would have been. Perhaps, so to speak, it took a greater effort to overcome 'inertia' in the first place, but, once reforms had been initiated, they tended to be more far-reaching. In any case, as Siegfried pointed out, once the State has been made use of in order to carry out reforms, New Zealanders become almost conservative because they have been given something to conserve.[2]

Other observations agree with this view of New Zealand as predominantly socially conservative. No one has discovered a 'new frontier' to fire the enthusiasm of New Zealanders. The tempo of business life is slow. National party leaders found to their astonishment that, when the Labour Government cut imports in 1958, some importers and retailers made only routine and perfunctory protests. They lost some business but did not need to work as hard as before and now had two extra days a week in which to play golf. It would be wrong to argue that New Zealanders had become 'soft'. Their energy and competitiveness have simply been transferred to other spheres. Although New Zealand's exports are an example of extreme specialization, the internal arrangements for house repairs and gardening are not. Consequently many New Zealanders work harder at home, on Saturday and Sunday, than they do in the course of their

[1] Sinclair, *A History of New Zealand*, p. 299.
[2] Op. cit., p. 91.

employment on the remaining days of the week. The closing of most shops two whole days a week is another symptom of a preference for 'strenuous leisure' rather than for work. Sport, particularly rugby football and horse-racing, is a ruling passion, not to say religion, with most New Zealanders. Indeed it might almost be regarded as their perpetual frontier. It is significant that when the Prime Minister appealed for volunteers for home defence in May 1939 he took care to promise that the normal Saturday's sport would not be interfered with by military duties.[1]

One expression of 'social conservatism' is a concentration on retaining existing advantages. To choose a well-known metaphor, there is a tendency to take the size of the national 'cake' as fixed, and to be preoccupied with dividing it fairly. There is less concern about taking steps to ensure that the cake will remain large enough to meet *future* needs. 'Stabilization' is one example of this, both in its narrow sense of ensuring that the return to certain agricultural producers does not fluctuate too rapidly over time, and also in broader senses, such as that returns to farmers should bear some fairly constant relation to the returns to other sections of the community.[2] It has been justly remarked that the notion of stability cut at the root of the traditional Labour 'assumption of indefinite progress'.[3] But in practice many post-war Labour supporters seem to have been willing to settle for whatever 'progress' had actually been achieved since 1935. The concept of 'insulation' is perhaps an even more striking illustration of the wish to preserve *situations acquises*. Of course, 'insulation' may be intended simply to cushion New Zealand against the worst effects of sudden changes in world prices. But some conceptions of 'insulation' have gone far beyond this, and have amounted almost to wishfully thinking that New Zealand could 'contract out' of trade relations with the rest of the world and still remain as prosperous as before. The tariff is, of course, an attempt at 'one-way' insulation, as Siegfried saw when he remarked that a free-trade New Zealand

[1] Wood, *The New Zealand People at War*, p. 82.

[2] See R. S. Parker (ed.), *Economic Stability in New Zealand* (Wellington, 1953), especially, L. C. Webb, 'The Making of Economic Policy'; J. B. Condliffe, *The Welfare State in New Zealand* (London, 1959), pp. 103 ff.; C. Westrate, *Portrait of a Mixed Economy, New Zealand* (Wellington, 1959), ch. vi.

[3] Wood, *The New Zealand People at War*, p. 241.

could not long afford the luxury of its social legislation.[1] One root of the desire for insulation is the wish to convert New Zealand's disadvantage of geographical isolation into a positive advantage. The other root is a naïve belief in what the 1935 Labour Party's election manifesto referred to as 'the wonderful resources of the Dominion'. As a Labour M.P. put it three years later, 'If the sun still shines in New Zealand, if the rain still falls, sheep will be raised and butter made. We will be in a position to maintain a wonderfully good standard of comfort even though prices do fall.'[2] The Prime Minister, Savage, was equally confident three years later, 'We have always stated that it is possible to insulate the New Zealand economy from the effects of any world depression. . . . It is largely a money problem.'[3]

An American visitor to New Zealand, Professor David P. Asubel, has claimed that authoritarianism is an outstanding national trait, particularly in the context of secondary school education.[4] This is not a unique opinion. An English psychiatrist working in New Zealand has written: 'In his dealings with authority . . . the New Zealander knows only two manœuvres— flat disregard when unseen, and passive compliance otherwise. Typically, he seldom questions authority, and he never opposes it head on, but if its back be turned, he follows his own inclinations.'[5] However, Professor Asubel greatly overstates his case. The attitudes towards authority which he describes are surely to be found in many other places as well as New Zealand. Some of the 'authoritarian' traits he has discovered, such as strict party discipline, do not belong exclusively to New Zealand, but are, in the broadest sense, British. And when Professor Asubel seeks to derive certain features of New Zealand political life from 'authoritarianism', he is sometimes factually in error, for instance on candidate selection and on the consultation of public opinion by the Government. In the emphasis on equality and in the impatience of authority[6] (however expressed) New

[1] Op. cit., p. 158. On the 'insulation' of New Zealand manufacturers see 'How to Progress Backwards', *The Economist*, 9 Mar. 1963.
[2] C. H. Chapman, M.P., *Dominion*, 26 Sept. 1938.
[3] *Auckland Star*, 28 Feb. 1938.
[4] *The Fern and the Tiki* (Sydney, 1960).
[5] H. Bourne, 'Authority and the New Zealander', *New Zealand Listener*, 4 Oct. 1957.   [6] Dr. Findlay, *Our Man in the Street* (Dunedin, 1909), pp. 4–5.

Zealanders are less authoritarian, though less polite, than the British.

The Political Framework

In a comprehensive survey of the New Zealand social setting these topics should be treated at greater length, and many others should be dealt with as well. Notably, there should be descriptions of New Zealand literature, art, and the mass media, and also of the social position of the Maoris (good by comparison with other countries but less good than is suggested in the orthodox view that complete racial equality exists).[1] However, in this book it is now time to turn from the social setting to the political background.

New Zealand is a fully self-governing member of the British Commonwealth.[2] It is a member of the United Nations and has diplomatic representation in some countries overseas. Many of the ingredients in New Zealand's political style are 'British',[3] although the resulting flavour is unique. Like Britain, its constitution is unitary, and even before 1876, when there was a system of 'provinces', these did not constitute a true federation. The constitution is 'unwritten',[4] like the British, although there has recently been some propaganda activity for a written constitution. The counterpart of the Queen is the Governor General, usually appointed for five years. Apart from his social functions he corresponds to the Queen in the designation of Prime Ministers and the granting or refusal of requests for a dissolution of Parliament.[5]

The legislature has a single house of eighty members. Until 1950 there was also an upper, appointed, chamber. At the time of its abolition it was understood that it would be replaced by a chamber composed on a different principle, although this has

[1] See Oliver, op. cit., ch. xv. The second part of Asubel's book concerns the Maoris, as does his *Maori Youth* (Wellington, 1961). More balanced, but less recent, is I. L. G. Sutherland (ed.), *The Maori People Today* (Wellington, 1940).

[2] For this and for other points of constitutional law, see J. L. Robson (ed.), *New Zealand—the Development of its Laws and Constitution* (London, 1954).

[3] But on U.S. and Australian influences see Lipson, op. cit., pp. 9–10, and Sinclair, *A History of New Zealand*, pp. 295 ff.

[4] The Electoral Act, 1956, had some features of a written constitution (K. J. Scott, *The New Zealand Constitution* (Oxford, 1962), pp. 6–10).

[5] For a Governor General's view of his functions see Viscount Cobham, 'The Governor-General's Constitutional Role', *Political Science*, vol. xv, no. 2 (1963).

not yet been done. Some legally minded persons, both in the National Party and outside it, have pressed for its restoration, but there is as little popular appeal in this proposal as there is in the agitation for a written constitution.[1]

Four of the seats in the House of Representatives have been filled by the votes of the Maoris since 1868. The remainder, which now number seventy-six, are redistributed at intervals of five years by a 'Representation Commission'. There used to be a 'country quota' by which greater representation (latterly 28 per cent.) was given to the rural areas, but this was abolished by the Labour Government, to its own advantage, in 1945. The system of election is the 'simple majority' one, as in England, although at the elections of 1908 and 1911 preferential voting was used and previously there had been multi-member constituencies in the four large cities. The term of Parliament is three years, although its life has been prolonged during both world wars (1914–19 and 1938–43) and also from 1931 to 1935, and there was an early dissolution in 1951 after only two years. There was manhood suffrage in New Zealand by 1879 (although plural voting persisted for ten more years), and women received the vote in 1893. In spite of the fact that voting is not compulsory (although registration to vote *is* compulsory), a high proportion of the electors, usually over 90 per cent, vote at general elections. Since the end of the nineteenth century referenda have been held at regular intervals on liquor licensing, nowadays at the same time as general elections. There have also been special referenda on such subjects as betting on horse-racing and on compulsory military training.[2] There is no need to hold a referendum in order to change the constitution, as is the case in Australia.

There are usually between fifteen and seventeen ministers in the Cabinet, and possibly two or three parliamentary under-secretaries who are not Cabinet members. This is a high proportion of the total Government strength in the House, roughly between 30 and 40 per cent., whereas the corresponding figure in Britain (even if parliamentary secretaries are taken into account) is only about 12 or 15 per cent. The number of

[1] The New Zealand Constitutional Society has pressed for both a Second Chamber and a written constitution. A body with the specific purpose of restoring a Second Chamber, the 'Legislature Reform League', was founded in 1957.

[2] See N. C. Phillips, 'The Referendum—a retrospect', *Landfall* (Christchurch, Dec. 1949).

government departments (forty or so) is much larger than the number of ministers. Consequently one minister may be given several portfolios, sometimes not very closely related in their subject-matter. The judiciary and the civil service conform to established British standards of impartiality and incorruptibility. One feature to note is the absence of an exact equivalent of the British 'administrative class' in the New Zealand civil service.

The extent of Government activity is impressive. The social security system and other welfare legislation are extensive, although state dental and optical services are not so complete as in Britain. Government departments or corporations are engaged in operating the railways, air flights internally and between New Zealand and Australia, broadcasting, the Reserve Bank and the Bank of New Zealand, life insurance, fire insurance, plants for generating electricity, pulp and paper production (in co-operation with private enterprise), and a number of other activities.

Many of the conventions which condition British political life are to be found, subject to qualifications introduced later, in much the same forms in New Zealand. The use of the veto by the Governor General has fallen into disuse as New Zealand gained full independence from Britain. In this century there has been only one instance of a dissolution being requested before the life of Parliament had ended (1951), and this request was granted by the Governor General. The convention of ministerial responsibility has been accepted verbally by New Zealand politicians, although some have not learned their lines very well, and have produced ministerial statements accepting 'responsibility' but putting most of the blame on permanent officials.[1] In practice the convention seems to impose only the weakest of sanctions, as is the case in Britain.[2]

The Parties and Public Opinion

In this framework there operates a party system broadly on the British model. In both countries a two-party system developed,

[1] K. J. Scott, op. cit., pp. 118 ff. It is significant that when it was proposed to introduce the Ombudsman in New Zealand there were no objections (as there were in Britain) on the ground that it would weaken ministerial responsibility.

[2] See S. E. Finer, 'The Individual Responsibility of Ministers', *Public Administration* (London), vol. xxxiv, no. 4 (1956).

but was complicated by the rise of a Labour Party, resulting after a time in a return to two main parties, one Labour, one anti-Labour. Again as in Britain, 'Independents' have disappeared from Parliament, and within each party there is strict internal discipline. The broad lines of the relationships between parties and pressure groups are also familiar. In both countries the trade unions are, by their constitutions, linked to the Labour Party. But the farmers' and business groups, which largely support the Conservative and National parties, are related to these parties in a much looser way. This similarity of structure conceals significant differences in political atmosphere and style. Some of these result directly from the small scale of New Zealand politics. For instance, there is no need to have (as in Britain) a special Liaison Committee to bridge the gap between the front benches and the back benches of the New Zealand Labour Party, because the number of members in the parliamentary party is unlikely to exceed fifty. Nor at party conferences is there a need to squeeze delegates into 'overflow' meetings because they cannot be accommodated in the main conference hall. In both New Zealand parties' conferences there are usually seats to spare. Quite apart from this, the New Zealand parties operate in a more bread-and-butter context. The important pressure groups with which they have to deal are more blatantly concerned with economic questions; they are, in fact, the local equivalents of Professor J. D. B. Miller's Australian 'syndicates'.[1] There is naturally less discussion of world politics than in Britain, and, for instance, there is less interest in nationalization, because there are few, if any, local industries large enough to be nationalized. It has already been argued that New Zealanders are willing to engage in social experiments only in order to overcome great and immediate evils. At the present moment no such evils are apparent.

No comprehensive study has yet been made of the relations between politics and public opinion or the mass media.[2] In spite of the high figures for voting and party membership, the

[1] J. D. B. Miller, op. cit., p. 65.
[2] On the Press see E. Warburton, 'A Study of the Press', *Landfall*, Sept. 1954; K. J. Cunningham, 'City Newspapers and the 1957 Election', *Political Science*, vol. xi, no. 2 (1959). On radio see T. H. Qualter, 'Political Propaganda as broadcast by the National Stations of the New Zealand Broadcasting Service' (Victoria unpublished thesis, 1951).

hypothesis, or perhaps 'hunch', may be put forward that interest in politics as such is not very great. Voting may be largely the result of habit, a social act rather than a political one. The membership figures are the result rather of the activity of organizations than of consuming interest in politics on the part of individuals. More significant is the fact (admittedly based on a survey in an urban area with a partly transient population) that few electors seem to listen to parliamentary broadcasts. When Parliament sits its proceedings are broadcast twelve hours a week in the evenings, as well as for a longer period during the day. But in one area in 1957, 59 per cent. of the voters for the two major parties did not listen at all, and another 25 per cent. listened for less than three hours a week.[1] A diminished interest in politics may also be inferred from the recent lack of activity on the part of the New Zealand Fabian Society. It is possible that much of the apparent interest in elections is not political but sporting. The election is viewed as a contest, and the interest lies in spotting the winner. During the 1957 election in one constituency 60 per cent. of the electors were asked 'political' questions by relatives or friends, but in two-fifths of these cases the questioner had simply asked who would win the election.[2]

When there is a direct conflict between politics and sport there is not too much difficulty in spotting the winner. When the first New Zealand rugby team visited Britain the news of the tour was cabled direct by the High Commissioner in London to the Prime Minister in New Zealand, and he sometimes interrupted debates in the House to read the results aloud.[3] A few years ago the annual conference of the National Party was partially disrupted by the broadcast of a rugby international.

From the moment the conference started the chairman (Mr. Alex. McKenzie) was under pressure to adjourn the conference and bring in a radio to broadcast the commentary. Firmly, but with good humour, he refused the demand. But speaker after speaker (including Mr. Holland) [Party Leader and Prime Minister] urged that something should be done about it. Finally Mr. McKenzie compromised. He read out progress scores, and finally did adjourn the

---

[1] R. S. Milne, 'Voting in Wellington Central, 1957', *Political Science*, vol. x, no. 2 (1958), pp. 45–46. The results of a more recent survey on election listening are included in A. D. Robinson and A. H. Ashenden, 'Mass Communications and the 1963 Election: a Preliminary Report', *Political Science*, vol. xvi, no. 2 (1964).
[2] Ibid., p. 43.   [3] Burdon, op. cit., p. 288.

conference for the final 35 minutes or so. Long before this, however, several delegates had surreptitiously disappeared to listen to a portable radio ensconced behind the scenes.[1]

Press and radio help to mould public opinion on politics. The Press attempts to cover world news and provide the necessary background information for it. Unfortunately in each of the four main towns there is only one morning and one evening paper. Although the average level of political reporting is probably rather better than in Britain, there is no New Zealand paper which gives as complete coverage as the best British papers. There is a good deal of local complacency on the quality of New Zealand papers, mainly on the negative ground that they do *not* include lurid crime reports or many comic strips. Political reporting is fair and usually accurate, and at elections most papers are careful to give equal space to speeches by the two major parties,[2] and proportionate space to other parties. But in editorials and cartoons, there is a strong tendency to favour the National Party. There is only one definitely pro-Labour paper in New Zealand, the 'Grey River Argus', which has a very limited circulation, just over 4,000 a day. The attempt to support a daily Labour Party paper, the *Southern Cross*, persisted for only five years (1946–51). Even the weekly *Standard* (formerly the *New Zealand Worker*) and before that the *Maoriland Worker*) ceased publication in 1959; it has since been replaced by the monthly *Statesman*, produced in Auckland, with a circulation much greater than *Standard*'s.[3]

Politics on the radio consists mostly of the broadcasts of Parliament previously referred to. These broadcasts were actually begun by the Labour Party, soon after it came into power in 1935, in an endeavour to correct the 'anti-Labour bias' of the Press. There is also political news contained in news bulletins and political party broadcasts at election times—some of them broadcasts from political meetings which may last as long as two hours. The first political television broadcasts occurred in 1963. In news bulletins the Government of the day tends to receive more publicity than the Opposition, just because its

---

[1] *Evening Post*, 20 Aug. 1956.   [2] Cunningham, art. cit., (1959).

[3] *Standard*'s National rival, *Freedom*, became a monthly in 1961. Television has hit the sale of weekly periodicals. It is planned to increase *Freedom*'s circulation by making subscriptions to the party include a subscription to the paper, now renamed the *National Observer*.

members are functioning as the Government and their activities have more publicity value.

New Zealand Governments have been less than scrupulous in allocating radio time so as to give all main sections of opinion a fair hearing. At the 1935 election a notorious incident occurred when a Labour Party broadcast was jammed by the Government. The National Government during the watersiders' strike of 1951 ensured that the 'news' bulletins were devoted largely to government propaganda. The Social Credit Political League was given broadcasting time when it contested the 1954 election, but it had to press hard to get it and was dissatisfied with its allocation. Institutionally something might be done to remedy these defects, for instance by taking the allocation of time for election broadcasts away from the Government and entrusting it to some body independent of politics. Looking below the surface a little, the events just quoted seem to form part of a pattern. Taken in conjunction with other circumstances, such as the postponement of the general election which should have been held in 1934 until 1935, and the restrictions placed on the Press during the 1951 strike, they indicate a certain unscrupulousness on the part of governments and a tendency to slight the rights of minorities.[1] In one sense New Zealand governments are highly sensitive to 'public opinion'. Richard Seddon won five consecutive general elections as Prime Minister, and his views on this subject are entitled to respect: ' . . . ascertain what the desire of the people really is, and then I say it is the duty of the Government or whoever is on these benches to give to the people what they ask for or desire and through the ballot box establish a claim to.'[2] This approach is still followed both in the attractive 'offers' which parties sometimes make at elections and in the use of the referendum on certain matters. But in these instances sensitivity to public opinion often pays a dividend in the form of votes. When it is a question of safeguarding minorities or the rights of other political parties, there may be no such dividend or even a negative 'return'. To be sure, the substantial amendments made to the Police Offences Amendment Bill of 1951 to meet the substantial criticism voiced by the Opposition, in the Press, and before the Statutes Revision

---

[1] For a discussion of such instances, see Campbell, art. cit., 1956, pp. 27–28.

[2] *N.Z.P.D.*, vol. cxxxiv, p. 687 (14 Sept. 1905).

Committee, was a major victory for civil liberties in New Zealand.[1] But it is significant that the battle needed to be fought at all. It should also be noted that during the last war New Zealand Press censorship was more drastic than in Britain in some important respects.[2] This lack of regard for civil rights and liberties is probably largely due to the fact that, in the New Zealand scheme of values, such questions are not regarded as of much importance.

The Quality of Politicians and Political Life

Recent research by Austin Mitchell gives some evidence about the age, occupation, and education of Members of Parliament.[3] There is nothing very remarkable about the age figures. For the twenty-five years up to 1960 the average age of members, calculated at the time of a new Parliament, had varied from just over 51 to just over 55. In earlier years it was generally lower. In 1854, in the first House of Representatives, it was only 40, in 1911 only 49. Over the last few years there has been hardly any age difference between members of the two parties—unlike Britain where the Labour members have been definitely older. There has been a recent tendency for the average age of *newly elected* members to fall since 1949.

At the 1957 election unsuccessful candidates for each major party were roughly seven or eight years younger than successful ones. Social Credit candidates were slightly older than other unsuccessful candidates.

TABLE I[4]

Average Age of Candidates, 1957 Election

	Labour	National	S. Credit
Successful	52	54	—
Unsuccessful	44	47	48

In 1960 Labour candidates were slightly younger than

[1] Shirley Smith, 'The Police Offences Bill, 1951', *Political Science*, vol. iv, no. 2 (1952).

[2] Wood, *The New Zealand People at War*, pp. 271–6.

[3] 'The New Zealand Parliaments of 1935–1960', *Political Science*, vol. xiii, no. 1 (1961). Where not stated otherwise the figures quoted below come from this article. Comparable figures for ministers are given in P. Campbell, 'New Zealand Ministers, 1935–1957', ibid., vol. x, no. 2 (1958).

[4] Data on candidates were collected for the writer by Mr. Douglas Law.

National or Social Credit candidates. Successful candidates in each major party were older than the unsuccessful; but the age-gap between successful and unsuccessful was smaller in the National Party.[1]

Changes in the broad categories of members' occupations may be seen in the following table:

TABLE II[2]

Occupations of Members

Occupation	*1896–1902*	*1911–35*	*1935–49*	*1949–60*
Law	24 (10%)	78 (14%)	16 (10·7%)	11 (9·1%)
Professional . .	8 (3%)	35 (6%)	15 (10%)	26 (21·5%)
Commerce, trade and manufacturing .	60 (26%)	112 (20%)	35 (23·4%)	25 (20·7%)
Journalists . . .	23 (10%)	26 (5%)	4 (2·7%)	2 (1·6%)
Farmers . . .	95 (40%)	192 (34%)	47 (31·3%)	36 (29·8%)
Workmen and trade union secretaries . .	10 (4%)	79 (14%)	31 (20·7%)	19 (15·7%)
No information . .	16 (7%)	33 (6%)	2 (1·3%)	2 (1·6%)

The decline in the proportion of farmers and of journalists may be noted. However, the figures for farmers should be used with caution. They do not distinguish between various categories, not even between 'big' and 'small' farmers. And farming is particularly likely, in New Zealand, to be combined with some other occupation, or to be taken up after another occupation has been discontinued, which makes classification difficult. It should also be noted that the proportion of farmers in the whole populations is now only about a third of what it was in 1896.[3] On the other hand, there has been a marked rise in the proportion of professional men, the only group which has shown consistent increases over the whole period. There were increases, until recently, in the 'workmen and trade union secretaries' category (almost invariably consisting of only Labour members)

[1] B. M. Chapman, W. K. Jackson, and A. V. Mitchell, *New Zealand Politics in Action* (London, 1962), p. 141.

[2] 1896–1902 figures adapted from Siegfried, op. cit., pp. 86–87. 1911–35 figures adapted from Webb, op. cit. (1940), p. 47, quoted by Mitchell. 1935–49, and 1949–60 figures adapted from Mitchell. Note that percentages do not total 100 in Mitchell.

[3] *New Zealand Official Yearbook*, 1963, pp. 1002–3 and *Statistics of the Colony of New Zealand*, 1896, 'Summary of Results of 1896 Census'.

but this has now been replaced by a decline. At the last few elections only between a quarter and a third of the new Labour members come into this group. Contrary to what might have been expected, there has *not* been an increase in the broad category, 'commerce, trade and manufacturing'.

Mitchell's calculations provide some further details. Among Labour members the proportion of small businessmen has fallen, while that of larger businessmen has increased. The proportion of teachers and civil servants has also gone up. Changes in the occupations of National Party members have not been so marked, but their 'new men' show an increasing tendency to be accountants or teachers.[1]

No detailed research has yet been done on the occupations of unsuccessful candidates. The figures below relate only to the 1957 elections.

TABLE III[2]

Successful and Unsuccessful Candidates, 1957

Occupation	Successful		Unsuccessful	
	National	Labour	National	Labour
Business	5	7	18	6
Farming	23	4	12	11

For other occupations there is little difference between the proportions of successful and unsuccessful candidates in each party, although there were slightly more successful than unsuccessful workmen and trade-union secretaries among the Labour Party candidates. The 'Business' and 'Farming' figures arise from the fact that most of the safe National seats are rural, while most of the safe Labour seats are urban, and because most candidates are local men. A National candidate who is a businessman had less than one chance in four of being elected, while a Labour farmer has just over one chance in four. Presumably the odds on Labour businessmen are only a little better

[1] For comparisons with Britain see J. F. S. Ross, *Elections and Electors* (London, 1955), ch. 26; D. E. Butler, *The British General Election of 1955* (London, 1955), ch. iii; D. E. Butler and R. Rose, *The British General Election of 1959* (London, 1960), pp. 124 ff.
[2] Data from Mr. Law. 1960 figures do not differ substantially (Chapman, Jackson, and Mitchell, op. cit., p. 145).

than even (7–6), because 'workmen' or 'trade unionists' are chosen as Labour candidates for some of the safest seats.

During the last fifty years there has been a steady rise in the educational qualifications of members. Thirty-one per cent. of all members who served in Parliament, 1949–60, and 40 per cent. of the members first elected during that period, had a university education. In the 1959 British Parliament 52 per cent. of the members had had a university education.[1] When the Labour Party was first represented in Parliament, its members had received much less formal education than other members, but this gap is gradually closing.

There is a limit, however, to what statistics can tell us about New Zealand politicians and the standard of politics which they practise. In analysing the House of Representatives after the 1949 election, the earnest researcher would find that one Labour member was in his middle sixties, had been a post-office worker and labourer, and had received only a primary education. But such a statistic, suggesting an ageing political wheelhorse, would in fact conceal the person of Peter Fraser, wartime Prime Minister and figure of international importance at the San Francisco Conference of 1945. On the other hand, the recruitment into Parliament of professional men with university degrees may improve the quality of members 'statistically', but some of them may make hopeless politicians.

Turning to a more impressionistic, but perhaps more illuminating, line of approach, a good starting-point might be Reeves's opinions on the three main types of men in public life in the colonies sixty years ago.[2] One was the politician with strength and staying power; another consisted of brain workers, notably the lawyer-politicians; the third was composed of the 'new' parliamentarians of his time, the labour leaders, tenacious but not brilliant, with an appetite for details and burning with loyalty to their class. Like all simplifications this is in some respects an *over*-simplification. And some of the conditions of political life in the colonies on which Reeves founded these observations, the rough-and-tumble nature of politics, and the unstable party organizations, are no longer so marked in New Zealand. But it is remarkable how the first group has tended

[1] Butler and Rose, op. cit., p. 128. See also Ross, op. cit., ch. 25.
[2] Reeves, *State Experiments in Australia and New Zealand*, vol. i, pp. 53–55.

to produce Prime Ministers, Seddon, Massey, and (perhaps not with the same scale of 'bull neck' and 'big stomach'[1] but with great staying power), S. G. Holland, Mr. Nash, and Mr. Holyoake. A party leader must be 'tough'. As Reeves said elsewhere, 'He may dispense with eloquence, but must be a debater; whether able or not to arouse public meetings, he must know how to conduct wearisome and complicated business by discussion; he must not only have a grasp of great principles, but readiness to devote himself to the mastery of uninteresting minds and unappetizing details.'[2] Politicians with less politically desirable qualities and attitudes are destined never to reach the top. The Labour Party Leader, H. E. Holland died before the party came to power, but a man who protested against the adjournment of the House in order to watch an All-Black (rugby) game[3] was clearly not the right type to guide New Zealand's destinies. Reeves himself was so innocent of the facts of political life that he used to ride past cheering factory workers on his bicycle without making any adequate acknowledgement.[4]

If Reeves's three types of politician were ever clearly distinct, they do not appear to be so today. An outstanding impression of the New Zealand Parliament is that it is decidedly homogeneous. This is obvious when it is compared with, say, the Parliament of India which contains representatives widely different in their ethnic origins, language, and dress. But the New Zealand Parliament is also more homogeneous than the British. This arises not only from the whole population being more homogeneous than in Britain, because New Zealand is smaller and because of the emphasis on 'equality'. It is also partly because politics in New Zealand is more humdrum and less idealistic and theoretical than in Britain, and this rules out certain types of intellectuals from the New Zealand Parliament. Of the two best political thinkers in the Labour Party during the last thirty years, Mr. Ormond Wilson never acquired a safe

---

[1] Rolleston referred to these necessary characteristics of successful politicians when encouraging Massey to stay in political life (G. H. Scholefield, *The Right Honourable W. F. Massey, Prime Minister of New Zealand: a Personal Biography* (Wellington, 1925), p. 16).

[2] Reeves, *The Long White Cloud*, p. 249.

[3] *N.Z.P.D.*, vol. clxxxvii, p. 208 (18 Aug. 1920).

[4] *Interview*, Mr. T. E. Y. Seddon, Dec. 1958.

seat, and his parliamentary career was short. For fourteen years, Dr. A. M. Finlay was out of Parliament (before returning to it in 1963), although he had been prominent in the party outside Parliament, and had become Labour Party President in 1960. But, as an exercise in pure fantasy, it is unlikely that a New Zealand equivalent of Mr. Michael Foot, if he existed, would ever want to sit in the House of Representatives, implausible that he would ever be selected as candidate by a major party for a winnable seat, and inconceivable that, if elected, he would survive more than, at most, one term. Some potential candidates may be deterred from trying to enter Parliament because of the low salaries, although it is almost meaningless to speak of high or low salaries except by comparison with the alternatives open to particular individuals.[1]

The atmosphere in Parliament at the end of the last century was stigmatized by a high authority as one of 'complete vulgarity'.[2] Some recent writers have thrown doubt on whether things were ever any better—even in the 1850's, the so-called 'golden age in politics'.[3] A commentator writing in 1919 gives the impression that the proceedings were desultory rather than vulgar. 'Members themselves are commonly indifferent listeners. Sometimes a debate rather seems to be a series of monologues than a discussion—only a few speakers, by their status in the House, by a galvanic utterance, or by comicality, can command the politeness of a wide hearing. The average speaker beholds generally a large proportion of his 'audience' reading newspapers or documents, or writing letters. There is usually good excuse, in such cases, for these occupations.'[4] Since the introduction of parliamentary broadcasting members have been more attentive to the proceedings; indeed there has been some playing to the wider 'gallery', and an appeal is often made

---

[1] May 1964 salaries were £1,550 p.a., plus tax-free allowances of between £370 and £550 p.a. plus £2. 10s. a day attendance money and travel and other allowances. Contributions to constituency causes may cost up to £250 p.a. The strain on a member and his (unpaid) wife can be heavy (H. J. Walker, 'A Government Back-Bencher', *Political Science*, vol. xv, no. 2 (1963), p. 43).

[2] By Sidney Webb, quoted in Siegfried, op. cit., p. 75. Siegfried himself went only so far as to say that the general tone of the debates was 'rather vulgar'.

[3] Gardner, op. cit., vol. xiii, no. 1 (1961), referring to D. G. Herron, 'Alsatia or Utopia, New Zealand Society and Politics in the Eighteen-Fifties', *Landfall*, Dec. 1949, p. 330.

[4] L. S. Fanning, 'Bills in the Mills', *Politics and the Public* (1919).

specifically to radio listeners. One member may also act as a 'feed' to another of the same party to help to drive home a point into the head of the densest listener. Thus a member making a speech complaining that potatoes are being exported when there is a potato shortage inside New Zealand may be interrupted by a colleague, who helpfully inquires, 'Exported?', thus giving him the opportunity to repeat, 'Yes, exported'.

It is true that there is a distinct lack of intellectual interest and curiosity on the part of most Members of Parliament. One estimate, made recently by a person in a position to know the reading habits of Labour members, was that only about 15 per cent. of them ever read serious overseas weeklies, such as the *New Statesman* or *Economist*. M.P.s in either party who do not keep themselves informed about what is happening in the world are obviously quite unready to meet the challenge to New Zealand which might result from Britain's entry into the Common Market. But this is not the whole story. Sometimes politicians may seem to be 'vulgar' partly because they are conforming to what they think is the popular view of what a New Zealand politician *ought* to be like. When the National Party Leader was heckled at an election meeting in 1957, he claimed that he was a worker because of the size of his hands, and challenged his interrupter to come up and measure hands at the end of the meeting. A Labour member, a few years ago, when in his own constituency, did not advertise the fact that he had a university degree, and deliberately modified his accent so as to convey the impression of the 'common touch' to his constituents. On the other hand, perhaps criticism of the low standard of politicians has gone too far. If politicians are criticized unreservedly and undeservedly, this will prevent good men from coming into politics and so lower the standard still further. Perhaps the time has arrived for a truce both to intemperate attacks on politicians by the public and also to excessive deference by politicians to the public? Of course, a critic of the standard of New Zealand politicians may be asked what qualifications and abilities they ought to possess. It is possible only to indicate, very roughly indeed, what the desirable limits might be. They should certainly in some respects be above average. Bryce believed that the New Zealand House was 'in one sense too representative, for its members are little above the average of the electors in knowledge or ability.[1] A legislative assembly should be more than an average sample of 'ordinary men'.[2] If the main function of such an assembly is to discuss, criticize, and amend current issues and current measures, clearly its members should be better qualified than the average in such matters. In some respects, of course, such as skill in archery, knowledge of Chinese cookery, or ability to dance the tango, they may be well *below* average without inviting national calamity. Additional above-average qualities will be required from those members (a high proportion in New Zealand) who may become ministers and from others who have special duties in the parliamentary party. A more-than-average amount of tact, for instance, should be possessed by a party whip. This argument is not destroyed by the fact that one of the favourite quotations of a recent Prime Minister (Sir Sidney Holland) was Theodore Roosevelt's 'I am only an average man, but by George, I work harder at it than the average man.'[3] When the epigrammatic element is removed, this clearly means just the opposite of what it appears to say. Theodore Roosevelt was far from being an average man; so, in his less flamboyant way, was Sir Sidney Holland.

To some extent, individual deficiencies in politicians are made up for by the New Zealand characteristic of being able to work well as a team. Any dozen New Zealanders taken at random will rise to the occasion if they are given a job to do—even the job of running New Zealand as a Cabinet. Co-operation may break down at times, as it did in the Labour Cabinet during the late 1930's, but in general good teamwork raises the level of government in New Zealand above what might have been expected from looking at politicians as individuals.

It should also be borne in mind that, in any country, politicians should not be so outstanding that they lose touch with the people they represent. It is the function of parties and politicians to 'aggregate', or synthesize, the demands voiced by individuals and groups.[4] In order to perform this part of the political

[1] Lord Bryce, *Modern Democracies* (New York, 1921), vol. ii, pp. 318–20.
[2] Cf. Mitchell (quoting Laski), op. cit., p. 31. For comment see J. F. S. Ross, *Parliamentary Representation* (London, 2nd edn., 1948), pp. 178–80.
[3] Quoted by Campbell, *Political Science*, art. cit., p. 65.
[4] G. A. Almond and J. S. Coleman, *The Politics of the Developing Areas* (Princeton, 1960), especially pp. 16–18.

process they need to stand a little way 'above' their constituents, but not so far as to lose touch with them. They should not be 'too bright or good for human nature's daily food'. A sensible, though imprecise, conclusion would be that New Zealand politicians are above the national 'average' in certain necessary respects, but that the country would be better served if they were somewhat further above it.

II

THE COURSE OF NEW ZEALAND
POLITICS SINCE 1890

FOR some readers any historical introduction may be un-
necessary. Others might prefer that Lipson's example were
followed, and that the course of New Zealand politics
should be traced from 1840. Perhaps a compromise may be
attempted; it is proposed to sketch the main events in the
development of political parties since 1890, not in detail but
rather as an introduction to the analytical treatment of certain
political problems.

From 1890 dates 'the emergence of clearly defined, unified,
logically organised, truly national political parties. Political
parties were organised for the first time on a national basis,
between 1890 and 1912, and their impact was both immediate
and decisive.'[1] 'After 1890', says Reeves, 'policies become more
definite and interesting and party divisions more permanent,
clear and justifiable.'[2] The three great political issues with which
politicians in early New Zealand had concerned themselves
were dead: a constitution had provided for representative
government (1852); struggles between the provincial governments and the central government had been ended by the
abolition of the provincial governments in 1876, and by that
date the Maori wars, though not their consequences, were over.
By the 1880's another set of problems was on the stage. There
was the question of large landholdings, mostly in the South
Island and largely devoted to the production of wool, New
Zealand's chief export at the end of the nineteenth century. The
existence of these estates was defended by the 'oligarchy'[3] which
formed the dominant political class up to 1890. The 'oligarchy'

---

[1] Foster, op. cit., p. viii. See also K. Sinclair, 'The Significance of "the Scare-
crow Ministry", 1887–1891', in R. Chapman and K. Sinclair (eds.), *Studies of a
Small Democracy* (Auckland, 1963).
[2] *The Long White Cloud*, p. 270.
[3] Ibid., ch. xxii.

consisted of the 'early colonial gentry, with their public school or university background, their Latin tags and cultivated English speech, their sheep-runs and their clubs'.[1] There was the issue of free trade and protection, brought into prominence in the late 1880's.[2] There was also the question of the welfare of the urban population, hit by a long depression and low wages. In addition, there were less 'materialist' issues, such as prohibition, the extension of the franchise, and the emancipation of women.

Underlying all this were certain economic factors which were bound to affect politics in the future. Among these was the distribution of New Zealand's population. In 1891 more than 55 per cent. of the population was living in the South Island, but by 1901 the North Island was slightly in the lead. The end of the Maori wars was followed by the development, by the Europeans, of new land in the North Island areas of Taranaki, the Waikato Plains, and the hinterlands of Wanganui. Much of this land was ideal for dairy-farming, and with the possibilities opened up by refrigeration, which had already encouraged the export of meat in the 1880's, dairy exports, negligible in 1890, soon greatly increased.

The Liberal Era

At the 1890 election the Liberal Party, under its new Leader, Ballance, defeated the incumbent Conservatives, and put a decisive end to the already twice-interrupted 'Continuous Ministry'. Essentially the Liberals won by appealing successfully to two important unsatisfied sections of the population, the small farmers who were now so numerous that there was not enough available land for them, and the urban workers, who, after several years of depression and the unsuccessful Maritime Strike earlier in 1890, were persuaded by the Liberals to seek a political remedy. The basis of the Liberals' victory was recognized by their opponents, and denounced in terms as strong as similar denunciations of the New Zealand Labour Party in 1935, or of Franklin D. Roosevelt in 1931: '. . . the election was indeed a mere class fight—a struggle between the poorer and the less poor. What matter to the victors that they were restricting their own freedom by invoking legislative interference with

[1] Sinclair, *A History of New Zealand*, p. 168.
[2] Condliffe, *New Zealand in the Making*, pp. 178–9.

. . . liberty of action and liberty of ownership? Their interests lay in higher wages and less work. They voted for the plausible demagogues who promised these things.'[1]

After the election the Liberals passed laws to satisfy both these groups of 'clients'. The Minister for Lands and Agriculture, Jock McKenzie, used graduated taxation to keep the large estates in check, and legislation such as the 1894 Advances to Settlers Act promoted closer settlement on the land. For the urban workers it passed a succession of 'industrial' measures, for preventing 'sweating', for setting up of a system for industrial conciliation and arbitration, and for old-age pensions. This second group of laws, which so impressed visitors to New Zealand at the turn of the last century, has sometimes been described in exaggerated terms. This is partly because it suited Richard Seddon, who, as Prime Minister after the death of Ballance (1893–1906) so dominated New Zealand politics that he was known as 'King Dick', to maintain the 'fiction' of a deep gulf between the parties. He did his utmost to make capital out of the fact that whatever remnant of the old Conservatives and the large landowners still existed was to be found in the ranks of the Opposition.[2] This approach, allied to the publicity given to the Liberals' reforms, has tended to obscure the fact that men like Atkinson, Rolleston, and Hall, who held office before 1890, had introduced far-from-reactionary legislation.[3] The notion that there was a clear ideological distinction between pre-1890 and post-1890 Governments is not tenable. It seems to have resulted from Liberal attempts to create a contrast in party images, rather similar to Sir George Grey's attempt to convey the image of his followers as 'radicals' a few years earlier.[4]

Commentators who think it of extreme importance to demarcate 'Socialism' from 'non-Socialism' have been sorely perplexed about whether or not the expression, 'State Socialism' may justly be applied to the Liberals' industrial legislation. It seems

[1] Norwood Young, 'The Labour Party in New Zealand', *The National Review*, July 1892.

[2] W. Downie Stewart, *William Rolleston* (Christchurch, 1940), p. 196.

[3] See Ruth Allan, review of Lipson's *The Politics of Equality* in *Historical Studies, Australia and New Zealand*, vol. iv, no. 15 (1950), p. 282.

[4] Edmund Bohan, 'The 1879 General Election in Canterbury', *Political Science*, vol. xii, no. 1 (1960). See also T. C. Wilson, *The Grey Government 1877–9* (Auckland, 1954) and *The Rise of the New Zealand Liberal Party, 1880–1890* (Auckland, 1956).

a little unreasonable to expect precision on this point when, even in the 1960's, Labour parties in many countries have not reached anything like unanimity on what 'Socialism' is. Reeves, who was in a position to know more about it than most people, has surely said the last word on this subject. The Liberal Government's policy was socialistic, 'if we are to admit that every measure is socialistic that enlarges the scope of state interference in social life, extends the State's functions and arms administration with fresh powers. . . . But if real socialism means the discouragement and repression of private enterprise and the reduction of its energy and total volume, then that was not the intention of New Zealand experimental legislation.'[1] Reeves himself and a few other Liberals had doctrines, although they were not doctrinaires.[2] To the extent that this variety of socialism had any 'doctrinal' basis, it derived mainly from writers like Arnold, Ruskin, John Stuart Mill, Henry George, Bellamy, and *Fabian Essays in Socialism*.[3] But, as far as the majority of New Zealand politicians were concerned, in the sense that they had no direct contact with theory, it was indeed 'Socialism without doctrines'. Most of the members of the Liberal Government of 1890 'did not know what Socialism was, and if they had studied it, would not have agreed with it'. Prime Minister Seddon, a practical humanitarian, simply picked up his ideas as he went along.[4] As Bryce observed, some years later:

Here is the answer to those Europeans who ask, after reading of New Zealand's experiments in legislation, 'Are the New Zealanders all Socialists, and if so, what has become of the Individualists?' They are in principle no more Socialists than Individualists. The great majority do not think in abstractions: they have no use for theories. If the most obvious way to avert some evil or obtain some good seems to be in invoking the State's action, they invoke it. 'What is the State but ourselves? It is ours to use; why be jealous of it.'[5]

[1] *The Long White Cloud*, p. 282. For bibliographical material see Josephine F. Milburn 'Socialism and Social Reform in Nineteenth-Century New Zealand', *Political Science*, vol. xii, no. 1 (1960).

[2] Sinclair, *A History of New Zealand*, pp. 171–2 and 184. See also his 'The Legislation of the Liberal Party' in R. M. Chapman (ed.), *Ends and Means in New Zealand Politics* (Auckland, 1961).

[3] Condliffe, *New Zealand in the Making*, pp. 182 ff. See also Frank Rogers, 'The Influence of Political Theories in the Liberal Period, 1890–1912: Henry George and John Stuart Mill' in R. Chapman and K. Sinclair (eds.), op. cit.

[4] Reeves, op. cit., pp. 282 and 301.

[5] Bryce, op. cit., vol. ii, pp. 323–4.

The period of 'legislative experiments' was at its height from 1890 to 1898. The chief architect of these experiments was Pember Reeves, who, in his grasp of theory, was quite untypical of his colleagues in the Government. After he left for London, eventually to become Director of the London School of Economics, there was a slackening off, and an 'imperialist' phase followed, marked by New Zealand's participation in the Boer War and by Seddon's Roman triumphs in London. The party was now held together largely by the personality of Seddon, aided, his opponents alleged, by the judicious use of patronage.[1] After his death in 1906 the Liberals retained power for another six years, but were subjected to severe stresses and strains. Ward, the new Prime Minister, had a reputation as a financial wizard, only temporarily dimmed by his bankruptcy in 1896. But he was not built on the same titanic scale as Seddon, and, as a Roman Catholic, he was increasingly subjected to sectarian political attacks.

Electorally, the Liberals improved their majority in 1893, and thereafter, with some fluctuations, obtained majorities until the election of 1905, when they won 55 out of the 76 European seats. But by then the party was facing attacks from two directions. A somewhat right-of-centre Labour politician has written that in the 1890's no clear dividing line could be drawn between Liberalism and Labour principles.[2] But when the Liberal programme of social reform slowed down there were demands for a separate Labour Party. In reply to these Seddon founded the 'Liberal and Labour Federation' in 1899 which he contrived to carry, Atlas-like, largely on his own shoulders. His interpretation of 'Liberal-and-Labour' may be inferred from his telling one of the Federation's conferences that the delegates gathered in the room were 'good and true Liberals'.[3] On the other flank the support of the small farmers could no longer be relied on. The popular Minister for Lands and Agriculture, McKenzie, had resigned in 1900. And a demand had grown up that farmers should be enabled, not merely to lease land, but to own it, on freehold tenure. This issue was taken up by the

[1] e.g. the vitriolic *An Impeachment of the Seddon Administration* by T. E. Taylor (Christchurch, 1905).

[2] J. T. Paul, op. cit., p. 28.

[3] *Report of Proceedings of the Conference of Delegates of the Liberal and Labour Federation of New Zealand, 1903* (Wellington, 1903), p. 4.

Opposition, and was particularly injurious to Liberal solidarity because the Government included both leaseholders and free-holders.

Before the 1908 elections the Liberals took action to try to secure both flanks.[1] The new Prime Minister, Ward, introduced provisions for a second ballot where no candidate had secured an absolute majority at the first ballot. By this means he hoped to prevent losses of votes from Liberal to Labour candidates and to reduce the danger of a 'split' Liberal vote resulting from there being more than one Liberal candidate. At the same time he declared a legislative 'holiday', guaranteeing a pause in social legislation and possibly implying some concessions on the free-hold issue. This was a move to persuade electors who were unsympathetic to the problems of urban workers that the Liberals were really just simple agrarian reformers. As it hap-pened, the second ballot made hardly any difference to the 1908 election result. Unfortunately for the Liberals, solely through the vagaries of the electoral system, a gain in votes was accom-panied by a loss of eight seats. By the next election, 1911, the position was worse. Two prominent left-wing Liberal members had resigned from the party; and compromise provisions on land tenure, introduced but not passed into law in 1909, antago-nized both freeholders and leaseholders. At the 1911 election the Liberals lost heavily both in votes and in seats (30 instead of 47). The second ballot proved to be actually disadvantageous to them in some seats. In the South Island there were many Liberal–Labour agreements, but in the North Island a number of agreements were reached between Reform and Labour. The net consequence of the second ballot in 1911 seems to have been that, compared with what would have happened under the simple majority system, Labour won 3 seats, the Liberals lost 2 and Reform lost 1. With the support of Labour members and some Independents the Liberals were still able to form a Government after the 1911 election. But, after a series of policy manœuvres tending towards the left, Ward resigned, and a new Liberal Government was formed. It lasted only a few months, because in July 1912 sufficient Liberals and Independents

---

[1] On the following section see R. T. Shannon, op. cit. On the Liberal 'break-up' in the Waikato see B. D. Graham, 'Waikato Politics' (Auckland unpublished thesis, 1954), pp. 156 ff.

supported Reform to vote out the Liberals and put a Reform Government into power.

The Reform Party

The Reform Party had a long and arduous climb to power. Some writers believe that its organization outside Parliament derived from the 'National Association', founded in Auckland in 1891 to 'resist the socialistic tendency of the present legislation'.[1] Others trace it back only as far as the Political Reform League, formed in Christchurch in 1905 but with roots going back a year or two earlier.[2] Also of importance outside Parliament was the Farmers' Union, founded in 1899. Ostensibly this was a non-political body; and so it actually was, in the senses that its members came from both political parties, that it tried to influence both parties, and that it helped to return candidates from both parties who favoured its policies.[3] But many of its leading members were prominent in Opposition circles, and the policies it advocated had decidedly political implications. One of these was the abolition of the protective tariff.[4] Another was its advocacy of the freehold stated at its annual conference of 1905. One is inclined to agree with the eminent New Zealand trade unionist who said that more 'bunk' had been talked about leasehold and freehold than anything else. The freehold agitation was not carried on by oppressed peasants anxious to escape from rapacious landlords by acquiring a little corner of land. Those who wanted to purchase land were principally concerned to buy at low prices and benefit from (what they hoped would be) rising land values. It was also easier to borrow money to improve one's land if it were held on freehold tenure and not merely leased.[5] Even in the North Island the number of persons in a

[1] Brand, op. cit., pp. 51 and 79–80. For the rise of the Reform Party, see also Webb, 'The Rise of the Reform Party' (p. 1, n. 2); Foster, op. cit.; Graham, op. cit.; B. S. E. Bellringer, 'Conservatism and the Farmers; a study in the political development of Taranaki and Wanganui between 1899 and 1925' (Auckland unpublished thesis, 1958); W. J. Gardner, art. cit., vol. xiii, no. 1. Note the claim that the League was founded in Auckland, *Reform Party Year Book* (Christchurch, 1913), pp. 41; *Light and Liberty* (Journal of the Reform Movement), 27 May 1913, p. 23.

[2] Gardner, art. cit., pp. 10 and 25.

[3] Graham, op. cit., p. 110.

[4] Ibid., p. 49; Sinclair, *A History of New Zealand*, p. 200.

[5] This was one reason for farmers' opposition to the Liberals' land bill in 1907: cf. *The Land Bill* (issued by the Farmers' Union, 1907).

position to benefit from freehold was comparatively small.[1] Perhaps the demand for 'freehold' made such a powerful appeal because it symbolized independence and individualism and opposition to 'Socialists' and land nationalizers. One interpretation was that, particularly in the North Island, farmers who had been helped by the Liberal Government were turning conservative because they now had something to conserve.[2] This is a well-known theme, but its force is perhaps driven home by an extract from a newspaper in 1902, complaining of the small farmer's ingratitude. It was the Liberals who cut up the big estates and put the farmers on the land. At first they were grateful. 'But the miserable little cockie whom the Ballance and Seddon governments took from being the squatter's serf and made an independent farmer, became prosperous and arrogant.' He looked down on the town artisan and opposed socialistic legislation, although it was 'socialistic legislation' that put him on the land with cheap land and cheap money.[3]

Inside the House of Representatives the Opposition endured a season of demoralization. For a time it had no name other than 'the Opposition', and for some years it did not even face the Government as an organized group, but rather as individual guerillas. It had a number of *potential* leaders, but no actual leader, prepared to devote all his time to politics, until 1903 when this position was filled by 'Bill' Massey, a stolid and pertinacious North Island farmer. Even then the Opposition's policy was in doubt. Was emphasis to be laid on continuity with the party's pre-1890 history, and the claim made, in the face of the prevailing Liberal 'myth', that it had not all been reactionary? Or were the 'old gang' to be repudiated, and new aspects of the party's policy stressed? Eventually themes were found which, combined with some degree of organization, were good enough to defeat a debilitated Liberal Party. The parliamentary party started consistently to refer to itself as the 'Reform Party' in 1909, and outside Parliament it worked in loose conjunction with the Political Reform League. It adopted the freehold as part of its platform, and promised reform of the

---

[1] Graham, op. cit., pp. 147 and 149, and Sinclair, *A History of New Zealand*, p. 201. See also Sinclair, ibid., p. 231, and Condliffe, *New Zealand in the Making*, p. 240, on the small number who converted into freehold after 1912.
[2] W. Downie Stewart, Introduction to Siegfried, op. cit., p. xi; Métin, op. cit., p. 268.   [3] *Sydney Bulletin*, 18 Oct. 1902.

public service by ending the patronage and irregularities which, it claimed, had existed since the time of Seddon. Otherwise Liberal reforms were to be left intact, and the party ceased to attack the tariff. In the towns at the 1911 election it sought support largely as an opponent of 'Socialism'. In 1911, however, the party was, in essence, a 'sectional' farmers' party, and received fairly explicit support from the Farmers' Union.[1] It would not have come within striking distance of success in 1911 if its rural vote had not been 'inflated' in terms of seats by the country quota. Even then Reform failed to win the 1911 election outright, although it placed itself in a position of strength to heave itself into office less than a year later.

At the 1914 election the Reform Party increased its share of votes and seats. It had put its proposals for freehold tenure and civil service reform into effect; at the same time Massey had drawn nearer to the Liberal centre by adopting and administering Liberal measures.[2] This section of Liberal opinion was now perhaps closer to 'Masseydom' than to 'progressive' Liberalism. By breaking the waterside workers' strike of 1913, Massey had proved that Reform was an effective shield against 'Socialism' and 'lawlessness'. As recommended by the itinerant American Labour publicist, 'Professor' Mills at the Lyttelton by-election of 1914 the Liberals tried to 'do business' with the rising political Labour movement at the 1914 election; and agreements were reached not to put up rival candidates for certain seats. But the Liberals must have been uncomfortably aware that the professor had advised them to do this only in order to pass the time while they were waiting for their own funeral.[3] In addition to proposing an increase in the graduated land tax and cheap-money facilities for farmers, they threw in proportional representation, a scheme for making basic foods cheaper, and £5 in the bank for each newly born child. But, in spite of these ingenuities, they failed to win the 1914 election.

The Rise of the Labour Party

For some years before 1914 the Liberals had been facing danger from the left, from the threat of an independent Labour

[1] The Executive of the Auckland Province of the Union announced that the interests of the Union were parallel with those of the Reform Party (Graham, op. cit., p. 205).   [2] Sir John Findlay, *New Zealand Times*, 6 Feb. 1914.

[3] Quoted in *General Election Campaign, 1914*, No. 1 (Reform Party, 1914), p. 1.

Party. It is true that this threat did not appear, at least in a co-ordinated form, so early as in some other countries. New Zealand Labour was not politically united until 1916, while Australia had had a Federal Labour Government for a short time in 1904. This delay is understandable. New Zealand was less indus-trialized than Australia and less exposed to external ideologies. Outside the main towns trade unions were small and scattered, and some weight must be given to the 'braking' influence of Seddon. But the two threats to the Liberals soon reinforced each other, like the two jaws of a vice. The fact that Liberal–Labour contacts still persisted enabled the Reform Party to charge that the Liberals were guilty, by association, of being socialists and 'reds'.

The exact train of events by which an independent Labour Party was founded is too tangled to explore in detail.[1] Under-lying the struggle was a wish to follow the example of Britain and Australia, dissatisfaction with the slowing-down of Liberal measures of reform and, more specifically, reaction against decisions by the Arbitration Court which had become less favourable to the workers. Throughout the whole process there was one persistent element, the efforts of some members of the

[1] See Paul, op. cit.; Brown, op. cit.; R. F. Paddock, 'Labour as a Force in Politics in New Zealand up to 1919' (Auckland unpublished thesis, 1932); F. M. J. Irvine, 'The Revolt of the Militant Unions', (Auckland unpublished thesis, 1936); D. W. Crowley, 'The Labour Movement in New Zealand, 1894–1913' (Otago unpub-lished thesis, 1946), printed in shorter form as 'An Outline History of the New Zealand Labour Movement', *Historical Studies, Australia and New Zealand*, May 1951; J. Y. Hunt, 'The Development of the Labour Party in New Zealand as a Political Organisation from 1913–1919' (Auckland unpublished thesis, 1947); R. T. Newman, 'The Genesis of the Labour Movement' (Christchurch unpublished thesis, 1948); Josephine F. Milburn, 'Socialism and Social Reform in Twentieth-Century New Zealand', *Political Science*, vol. xii, no. 2 (1960); P. J. O'Farrell, 'The Formation of the New Zealand Labour Party', *Historical Studies, Australia and New Zealand*, vol. x, no. 38 (1962). Overacker deals with the topic more briefly, *American Political Science Review*, art. cit., and *Political Science*, art. cit.

As a political force, the Communist Party has never had more than a curiosity value in New Zealand. See J. R. Powell, 'The History of a Working Class Party 1918–1940' (Victoria unpublished thesis, 1949); New Zealand Communist Party, *New Zealand Communism, 1946* (Auckland, 1946); S. W. Scott, *A Reply to Robert Semple* (Auckland, 1948); New Zealand Communist Party, *New Zealand Communists Present Their Case* (Auckland, 1949); New Zealand Communist Party, *New Zealand's Road to Socialism* (Auckland, 1955); S. W. Scott, *Retreat from Moscow* (Wellington, 1957); S. W. Scott, *Rebel in a Wrong Cause* (Auckland, 1960); V. G. Wilcox, *New Zealand versus Big Business* (Auckland, 1961); New Zealand Communist Party, *The Differ-ences in the World Communist Movement* (Auckland, 1963). The party has a weekly newspaper, *The People's Voice*.

Trades and Labour Councils in the main cities to found a separate party.[1] These men were evolutionary and Fabian in their approach, and differed from many reforming Liberals chiefly in their desire for 'independence'. In the last years of the century the Trades and Labour Councils began to put forward candidates at general elections who were independent of the Liberals.[2] In 1904 they passed a resolution for an independent Labour Party with a platform including some nationalization proposals and a State Bank. A deputation was charged with the unenviable task of conveying this decision to the formidable Mr. Seddon.[3] For the 1905 election a short-lived Political Labour League was formed, without electoral success, though in 1908 one candidate put forward by one of a number of Trades and Labour Council 'Labour Representation Committees' was elected.

A more militant strain was provided by the Federation of Labour (originally known as the Miners' Federation), founded in 1908 in Greymouth. The change of name made little difference, because in any case it came to be known generally as the 'Red Fed'.[4] Its chief figure, Pat Hickey, had belonged, when in the United States, to a miner's union controlled by the syndicalist IWW (Industrial Workers of the World), and it adopted the IWW cry of 'The World's Wealth for the World's Workers'. Earlier in 1908 Hickey had been responsible for starting a strike at the Blackball Mine. The 'Red Fed' was remarkable in many respects. In the New Zealand context it stood out as 'extremist' in its reliance on the strike weapon and in its disdain for the hitherto almost sacrosanct arbitration system.[5] Its leaders included a high proportion of Australians, and also seven of the thirteen members of the first New Zealand Labour Cabinet of

[1] Paul, op. cit., p. 29 and also in interviews with the writer, 1959.

[2] For details of 'Labour' and 'Socialist' candidates put forward at elections up to 1916 see Norman D. Stevens, 'Labour Candidates for the New Zealand House of Representatives, 1890–1916', *Political Science*, vol. vii, nos. 1 and 2 (1955), vol. viii, no. 2 (1956), and vol. ix, nos. 1 and 2 (1957).

[3] Paul, op. cit., pp. 31–32.

[4] See P. H. Hickey, *'Red Fed' Memoirs* (Auckland: New Zealand Worker Print, 1925); H. E. Holland, 'Ballot Box', and R. S. Ross, *The Tragic Story of the Waihi Strike* (Wellington, 1913).

[5] For a description of the arbitration system see N. S. Woods, *Industrial Conciliation and Arbitration* (Wellington, 1963), chs. 1–3. This is now the definitive work.

1935. Corresponding to the 'Red Fed' was the Socialist Party.[1] The two had no formal constitutional connexion, but they had some office-holders in common, and the Red Fed's official organ, the *Maoriland Worker*, tended not to distinguish between the two.[2] In the years 1912–16 the drive towards consolidation quickened. In 1910 the Trades and Labour Councils had set up a political Labour Party and in 1911 a 'Federation of Labour'. But in 1912 they joined these two in the 'United Labour Party' with a comparatively mild platform. The socialization of the means of production, distribution, and exchange was advocated only in so far as these 'constitute in private hands instruments of oppression and exploitation'.[3] The new ULP was evolutionary and opposed to anarchism and syndicalism. A Unity Congress, representative of all the factions, was called together in 1913 by the 'Red Fed' leaders, a little chastened after the collapse of the Waihi Mine strike in the previous year. Elections provided an incentive to unity. At the 1911 election four 'Socialist' or 'Labour' candidates of various descriptions had been elected, but in a few electorates (constituencies) rival candidates in these categories had fought each other. At the Unity Congress two new organizations were established, an industrial 'United Federation of Labour' and a political 'Social Democratic Party'.[4] But some moderate delegates, including many from the ULP, were quickly antagonized by what they regarded as the extreme IWW ideas of the militants, and they also objected to a provision enabling the Federation to call individual unions out on strike. Consequently they refused to join the new organizations.

Six Labour candidates were returned in 1914, two of them belonging to the Social Democratic Party. The final impetus to unity may have come from the wartime coalition between Reform and Liberals, which called for a closing of the Labour ranks, and from opposition to the Government's conscription bill in 1916. On the part of the United Federation of Labour there was also a turning towards parliamentary action and

[1] H. Roth, 'The New Zealand Socialist Party', *Political Science*, vol. ix, no. 1 (1957).
[2] Newman, op. cit., p. 124.
[3] *Constitution and Platform* (The United Labour Party of New Zealand, Wellington, 1912). It had the unusual feature of combining 'political and industrial machinery in one body' (Paul, op. cit., p. 34).
[4] *Constitution and Platform of the Social Democratic Party* (Wellington, 1913).

away from the direct action which had failed in yet another unsuccessful strike, the attempted general strike in 1913, which Massey had dealt with firmly. The Joint Conference in 1916, with delegates from the United Federation of Labour, the Social Democratic Party, and Labour Representation Committees, resolved to found the New Zealand Labour Party. The objective was 'extreme' and unqualified—the socialization of the means of production, distribution, and exchange. But the individual items in the platform were quite acceptable to the ex-ULP moderates, who were also reassured by the absence of any provisions which would commit the new Labour Party to industrial action.[1]

Coalition and a Three-party System

The wartime coalition (1915–19) between Reform and Liberals led to a comparative lull on the home front, except for the campaign against conscription carried on by Labour and complaints about the rising cost of living. Before the election of 1919 the Liberals left the Coalition, and there was a confused transition period with three parties of roughly equal strength. The Reform Party's long tenure of power, 1912–28, was deceptive, because at no time did it rest on overwhelming superiority. Reform was by no means a 'dominant' party then, in the way that the Liberals had previously been dominant.[2] In none of the elections, 1912–25, did it win as much as 50 per cent. of the vote. From 1919 to 1922 and from 1925 to 1928 it had a majority of seats, thanks to the country quota. From 1923 to 1925 it was saved only by the votes of some defecting Liberals.[3] Nor was the Reform Party free of internal strife. During the war some of the New Zealand officers abroad made an abortive attempt to found a 'Young New Zealand Party', and during the early 1920's Statham, a previous Reform member, tried to start a new party. Some of his parliamentary supporters were won back to Reform by being appointed to the Cabinet, and eventually Statham himself was rewarded, and at the same time politically sterilized, by being made Speaker.

[1] The Official Report of the Joint Conference is reproduced in Paul, op. cit., Appendix A. See also Brown, op. cit., pp. 23–25.
[2] See M. Duverger, *Political Parties* (London, 1954), pp. 307–12 and 417–18.
[3] See H. E. Holland, *How the Liberals Voted* (Wellington, 1928).

Until 1928 the period was one of unrelieved Liberal decline. At each successive election, 1914–25, the party received a lower share of the vote. After the 1925 election it had fewer seats than Labour and the latter became the official Opposition. Its desperation was reflected in its frequent changes of name and Leader, but none of these manœuvres helped. From one point of view the Liberal Party was indeed

> A child crying in the night,
> A child crying for the light,
> And with no language but a cry.[1]

Others might have chosen metaphors drawn from senility rather than from infancy. In any event when the Massey government ran the risk of defeat some Liberals were cruelly racked by cross-pressures, torn between their antagonism to Reform and their fear of Labour and 'socialism'.

There were few sensational developments in party policy up to 1928. Before 1928 the Liberals' most grandiose proposals were those for the 1919 election, which included heavy expenditure on roads, housing, and railways, as well as a State Bank and nationalization of coal mines, flour mills, and the inter-island ferry.[2] The Labour Party seems to have made the calculation soon after the war that, especially with the existing country quota, it could not gain power unless it could win some rural seats. At its 1927 Conference it decided to drop its ambiguous proposals for 'usehold', the party's version of leasehold. In effect it came out for freehold and the individual ownership of land, at the same time stressing more clearly than before that its proposed State Bank would make cheap credit available for primary, as well as for secondary, producers.[3]

In 1919 the Reform Party promised to grant state assistance in the marketing of primary produce, and in 1922 it set up a Meat Board followed by a Dairy Board and boards for other primary products during the next few years. The creation of these boards was in complete opposition to the principles of *laissez-faire*, but the Meat Board, at least, was highly popular

[1] H. E. Holland, *N.Z.P.D.*, vol. clxxxvi, p. 98 (2 July 1920), quoting Tennyson.
[2] See Chapman, op. cit., p. 14 and B. M. O'Dowd, 'The Postwar Years of Massey's Ministry, 1919–25' (Auckland unpublished thesis, 1948), p. 24, quoting *New Zealand Herald*, 22 Aug. 1919.
[3] Brown, op. cit., pp. 85 ff.

with the producers, who chose most of its members. The Government also provided farms for ex-servicemen, as well as advancing them money to buy farms themselves. In its final term, 1925–8, Reform introduced a modest scheme for family allowances. But by then it was finding it hard to hold all its supporters in line. After the immediate post-war boom the small farmers (including newly settled ex-servicemen) clamoured for more credit, and opposed the high import duties which increased the prices of farming implements and consumption goods. Dissatisfaction was particularly strong in the Auckland Branch of the Farmers' Union, and a Country Party was formed which fought several seats in this area unsuccessfully in 1925, but gained one seat in 1928 (Bay of Islands).[1] The farmers campaigned for the creation of an Agricultural Bank, and were not impressed by the Government's statement in its 1928 Election Manifesto that its 1926 and 1927 legislation had assured the farmers of all the advantages of such a bank. But neither was the business community persuaded that Reform had carried out its 1925 election promise of 'less government in business'. The legislation on family allowances, as well as the new producers' boards, were attacked as 'socialist'. The Reform Party was forced, defensively, to argue, 'No sane man would suggest today the abolition of the Meat Board, because the casuist may say it is a form of Socialism, and yet it is being held up as a proof that the Government is playing with socialism and interfering with private business'.[2] A speaker at a 1927 conference of the Associated Chambers of Commerce said that if a Labour Government had attempted half of what the Government had done, there would have been such a storm of opposition that it would have been put out of office.[3]

These conflicts had not assumed serious proportions when Massey died in 1925. After a short stop-gap Administration he was succeeded by Coates, also a North Island farmer but, by New Zealand standards, a sophisticated one. At the 1925 election the new Reform Leader was attractively presented to the public, through such slogans as 'Coats off with Coates' and 'Here is a leader you can trust', by A. E. Davy, a political

---

[1] See Graham, op. cit., pp. 271–382, and pp. 116–18, below.
[2] *Newsletter* (Reform Party), 30 June 1928, p. 5.
[3] 31 October 1937, quoted in *Round Table*, vol. xviii (1927–8), p. 414.

organizer of remarkable talents, which were devoted successively to the service of several parties.

Largely at the expense of the Liberals, Reform increased its vote in 1925, and made a disproportionate gain in seats, securing two-thirds of the European total. Labour's share of the vote went up, although it actually lost five seats, partly, it alleged, because the other two parties did not run candidates against each other in some constituencies. It looked as if a process of 'polarization' was going on round two parties, Reform and Labour, and that the Liberals would disappear as a major party as unobtrusively as in Britain. But, through an extraordinary combination of circumstances, there came a Liberal revival, as swift as a comet, although hardly as brilliant.

The beginnings of this revival were inauspicious. It was hoped that the new United Party (an abbreviation of an originally longer name) would attract members from both non-Labour parties in Parliament, but in fact only Liberal members were willing to join it. A meeting of interested members to choose a leader ended disastrously, because some of the members proved to be *so* interested that, after a ballot had been taken, it was found that two more votes had been cast than there were persons present.[1] Eventually Sir Joseph Ward was persuaded to be Leader, although his health was failing. On the other hand, the party had some decided electoral advantages. Its organizer, indeed one of its founders, was Davy, who had left the Reform Party after helping it to win the 1925 election. The combination of Ward and Davy was a potent one for raising finance. Businessmen, especially in Auckland, had been sufficiently antagonized by the 'socialism' of the Reformers to transfer their contributions to a 'reliable' non-Labour party. To electors who felt that economic conditions were disappointing and that Reform's election promises were unfulfilled, yet who remained afraid of what a Labour Government might do, the United Party was an attractive refuge. United's policy was not remarkable; it offered to spend more money on development, but this was not substantially different from the Liberal proposals at the 1919 election. At least, the policy was not *meant* to be substantially different. But in the opening speech of the campaign in Auckland,

[1] Sir Walter Broadfoot, 'How Political Parties are born and how they die' (unpublished MS.).

Ward, either through failing eyesight or a mental 'blackout', promised to borrow and spend £70 million in a year. A later correction, that this sum was to be borrowed over a period of eight to ten years, never completely caught up with the original 'offer'. The influence of the £70 million at a time of rising unemployment was probably considerable.[1] Reform also lost ground at the election because of rising unemployment and its inept handling of a proposal to introduce religious exercises into state primary schools and of a licensing bill.[2]

After the election the comedy of errors became less amusing. United and Reform had approximately the same number of seats, 27 and 26 respectively. Labour had 19, the Country Party 1, and there were 7 Independents. A United Government was formed, which at first was kept in office by Labour Party support. It attempted to meet rising unemployment by speeding up public works, but, in addition to the troubles suffered by all minority Governments, it had special weaknesses of its own. The majority of the Cabinet were both inexperienced and inept. Ward proved to be physically incapable of carrying out the duties of Prime Minister, and, in quick succession, resigned from that office and died. His successor, George Forbes, a South Island farmer, had the unintellectual qualities of Massey without his political acumen.

Shortly before the 1931 election the United and Reform parties formed a coalition Government, and went to the country as electoral allies. From the short-term point of view 'fusion' was precipitated by the withdrawal of Labour support from United in Parliament. The Government attempted to fight the economic recession in 1931 with economy measures, including a 10 per cent. cut in the wages of public servants, which met with Reform support but Labour opposition. But, from the long-term point of view, 'fusion' between the two non-Labour parties had long been on the cards. It had been canvassed with particular earnestness just after the end of the war, and also from 1922 until 1925, when the Reform Party had no assured majority in Parliament. But a 'fusion conference' of four Reform and four Liberal members, held after the death of Massey in 1925,

---

[1] Chapman, op. cit., pp. 60–73.
[2] A. K. Brady, 'Gordon Coates, Prime Minister of New Zealand, 1925–1928' (Auckland unpublished thesis, 1947), pp. 58–60.

achieved nothing. The large Reform majority, 1925-8, gave grounds to hope that there might be no need for fusion, because the Liberal Party would quickly die anyway. During all this time Reform was in office, and it was the Liberals' objections to fusion which took a high-minded line. In reply to a statement by the Reform caucus in 1923, welcoming 'any equitable arrangements by which those Members of Parliament who are opposed to Communism may be brought together',[1] the Liberal caucus replied, in effect, *noli me tangere*. 'So long as the Reform party continues to represent and to be mainly influenced by owners of large vested interests, large landowners and controllers of monopolies in New Zealand, the opposition of the Liberal Party to the same will be vigorously maintained.'[2] Reform's problems were different. As the larger party they hoped that in fusion they would absorb and assimilate the Liberals. But, to make this process initially attractive, some Liberals would have to be given ministerial jobs. To put it a little less crudely, ' . . . fusion failed because the Liberals insisted, as a condition, on immediate reconstruction of the Government'.[3]

After the 1928 election the situation was different. If fusion took place it would be United members (Liberals) who would be pushed out of the Cabinet by 'reconstruction'. Now it was Reform's turn to be a little self-righteous about its principles: 'The pressure for fusion had come almost entirely from certain city commercial interests, and it was apparent that the proposed new party would be dominated by city interests. This would lead to a direct clash between town and country.' It would, Coates, argued, 'set up a class government and create a definite separation in politics between employers and employed'.[4] More briefly, the greatest pressure for a merger now came from city Liberals 'in a fright'.[5] However, economic conditions worsened during 1931, and businessmen sent petitions to Parliament recommending a coalition. Coates then moved that an inter-party committee be set up to investigate the current economic situation. But when proposals for an all-party Government were

[1] *New Zealand Herald*, 12 Jan. 1923.
[2] Ibid., 7 Feb. 1923.
[3] *Newsletter* (Reform Party), 31 July 1925, Supplement, 'The latest Phase of the Fusion Question', quoting *New Zealand Times*, 31 July 1925.
[4] *Reform Party's Record*, no. 1 (1931), p. 36.
[5] C. A. L. Treadwell, 'The Reform Party' (unpublished MS., 1934), ch. 1.

made, they were rejected by Labour.[1] Eventually, perhaps encouraged to some extent by the British example of a 'National Government', 'fusion' took place between the two non-Labour parties in September 1931. Arrangements were made for sitting members not to be opposed by candidates from the other of the two parties at the 1931 elections and for procedures to choose Coalition candidates to contest seats held by Labour. Although United retained the Premiership for its leader, Forbes, and equal representation in the Cabinet, it put up fewer candidates at the 1931 election than Reform and returned fewer members. The Coalition's net losses to Labour at the election were losses of *United* seats. Yet, considering the Liberals' weakness before 1928 and their continuing fundamental shakiness in 1928–31, they used their temporary ascendancy to drive not too bad a bargain.

The Coalition won the election of 1931, but this merely ensured that, like a British Labour Government and an Australian Federal Labour Government, it would suffer the misfortune of being in office during the depths of the world depression. To be sure, the Coalition could not be charged with inactivity. It set up a committee of economists and also a committee of businessmen to make economic recommendations. It reduced the liabilities of mortgagors and tenants, and also amended the Industrial Conciliation and Arbitration Act so as to make arbitration voluntary. With a rising number of unemployed (altogether about 100,000 in 1933) this contributed to a fall in wage-rates. Conceiving that the basis of the country's prosperity was primary industry, in 1933 it depreciated the exchange to the level of £125 N.Z. to £100 sterling (from £110 N.Z. to £100 sterling) in order to stimulate the export of agricultural products. In the same year a Reserve Bank was set up to secure cheaper credit for the State, and a National Mortgage Corporation was founded to provide cheaper credit for farmers. But all this activity did not do enough to relieve the distress of the population. The depression came too early for New Zealand's economists, or politicians to have read and applied Keynes's *General Theory of Employment Interest and Money*. The Government was committed to 'sound finance', meaning balanced budgets and minimal borrowing. No important section of the population was appreciative of the Government's policy, not the unemployed

[1] Brown, op. cit., p. 148.

'on the dole', not those still in work but at lower wages, not those farmers who were coming to believe that the solution for all their ills lay in cheaper and cheaper credit. Above all, the business community was outraged, notably by the change in the exchange rate which increased the price of imports, and by the ever-accumulating evidence that Coates, Finance Minister since 1933, was introducing 'socialism' at the instigation of his economic 'brains trust' of three *éminences grises* (Drs. Belshaw, Campbell, and Sutch). The Coalition was aware of its own unpopularity, and played for time by passing an Act providing for four-year parliaments, thus postponing the election until 1935. The Coalition also took a further step on the way to complete fusion. It formed a 'National Political Federation', a federation of the two existing parties intended to secure the return of candidates supporting the Government.[1]

In 1935 the National (Government) Party was opposed, not only by the Labour Party and the Country Party, but also by a new 'Democrat Party'. In his election campaign the Prime Minister, Forbes, boldly took the responsibility for the change in the exchange rate. 'We had to face a great deal of opposition and one of our colleagues left our ranks on this account. We then went to the banks and asked them to raise the rate to 25 per cent. What kind of a reception would we have received if we had allowed the banks to dissuade us from assisting the farmers; People would have said, "Who is running the country?".'[2] But the departure of the 'colleague', Downie Stewart, Minister of Finance, left the Cabinet without any representative from a city constituency, and therefore particularly open to attack as a 'farmers' government'. The logical consequence of the Cabinet's boldness was that some city interests backed the new Democrat Party and not the Government. One of the originators of the Democrats, if not *the* originator, was indeed Sir William Goodfellow, prominent in the New Zealand Co-operative Dairy Company and the Auckland Farmers' Union.[3] But he withdrew from the venture, and when the Mayor of Wellington, T. W. Hislop, was chosen as Leader, the emphasis was clearly on the

[1] *Dominion*, 16 May 1935, joint statement on behalf of the two parties by Hamilton and Masters.

[2] *Eketahuna Express*, 14 Nov. 1935.

[3] C. G. Rollo, 'The Election of 1935 in New Zealand' (Canterbury unpublished thesis, 1950), pp. 20–21.

interests of the towns, principally via a return to the 'old' rate of exchange, although the farmers were to be compensated for this by means of subsidies. More generally, the main feature of the Democrats' programme was its 'liberal element' and its opposition to state control.[1] In this emphasis, and in its dependence on city (especially Auckland) finance, the Democrats had something in common with the United Party. They had another thing in common, their chief organizer, A. E. Davy. But one other feature was missing—victory at the election.

The Labour Party in Power

At the 1935 election the National (Coalition) Government also faced the opposition of the Labour Party. Since its foundation the Labour Party had modified its policy and image so as to increase its electoral appeal. The alterations in its land policy did not bring any immediate gains in rural seats at the election of 1928; but in the next three years there was an appreciable shift in the presentation of Labour's policy, which found expression in its 1931 election manifesto. By now its policy had been tailored to fit the existing depression. The financial side of the party's policy was given prominence, including the mobilization of credit and the creation of a State Bank. Reference was also made to the development of secondary industries and to marketing schemes for stabilizing farm prices. On this programme Labour won an increased proportion of both votes and seats in 1931. For the next four years there was no great change in its themes, except that some of them, notably its marketing proposals, were given further consideration inside the party and were spelled out in greater detail. This was done by setting up a 'policy committee' at the 1933 Conference, which produced 'Labour's Plan'. The main heads to this 'plan' were publicized in a series of pamphlets, and formed the basis of the 1935 election programme.[2] The 'permanent' platform with its reference to

---

[1] Interview with T. W. Hislop, Oct. 1958. See also the reports of Hislop's policy speech in Auckland, 1 Oct. 1935, summarized in the *Round Table*, vol. xxvi (1935–6), p. 204.

[2] Brown, op. cit., pp. 156–67. Among the pamphlets were: M. J. Savage, *The Case for Labour* (1935); J. A. Lee, *Labour Has a Plan* (1934) and *Four Years of Failure, a History of the 'Smash-and-Grab' Government* (1935); Ben Roberts, *Labour and the Dairy Farmer* (n.d.); Walter Nash, *Guaranteed Prices, Why and How* (Wellington, 1935), issued at the election as a 'householder' (a leaflet published by a party and distributed by the postal authorities to every house).

the 'socialisation objective' was not formally revised, but it
became inoperative.[1] The emphasis on the provision of credit
was, if anything, intensified, thus enabling the party to benefit
from the general attraction exercised by 'Social Credit' ideas
at this time.[2] More particularly, it benefited from the support
given by farmers to its guaranteed price proposals which had
been generated over a period of years by publicity in favour of
similar schemes by the Auckland branch of the Farmers' Union.[3]
The Labour Party also changed a facet of its image when its old
Leader, H. E. Holland, died in 1934, and was replaced by
Michael Savage. A radical with little flexibility was succeeded
by a man with the image of a Christian humanitarian,[4] although
his 'philosophy bordered on the quaint'.[5] By election time it was
plain to many electors who had never voted Labour before that
a party with a Leader like Savage could never be really 'red' or
really ruthless.

But Labour's overwhelming success at the 1935 election,
when it won fifty-three seats (more than any party had won since
1905), was not solely the result of changes in the presentation of
policy and in leadership. Nor did it result principally from the
intervention of the Democrats, although this perhaps cost the
National Government ten or a dozen seats.[6] It was the depression which was mainly responsible for the big swing away from
the Government. The electors who turned to Labour were
desperate and, in the accepted New Zealand tradition, at the
same time pragmatic. As in 1890 they were giving a mandate
for the relief of economic distress; indeed it has been acutely
pointed out that in New Zealand few 'mandates' have ever been
given for anything else.[7]

The four Maori seats are all held by Labour by large majorities. Two seats were acquired by Labour through an alliance
with the Ratana movement, which led, early in 1936, to the
two sitting Ratana members joining the Labour Party. Even

[1] Brown, op. cit., pp. 171–2; Milburn, op. cit. (Sept. 1960), pp. 175–6.
[2] See R. Clifton, 'Douglas Credit and the Labour Party, 1930–1935' (Victoria unpublished thesis), 1961, especially pp. 267 ff.
[3] Ibid., pp. 302–5.
[4] J. B. Condliffe, 'The Labour Experiment in New Zealand', *The Economic Record*, Aug. 1957, pp. 153–4.
[5] Paul, op. cit., p. 136.
[6] Rollo, op. cit., p. 121.
[7] Chapman, op. cit., p. 85.

before then Mr. Tirikatene, the first Ratana member to be elected (1932), had consistently supported the Labour Party in the House. It had been obvious for some time that the basis for an alliance existed. Both Ratana, which had at first been a religious movement, and Labour were radical and humanist. Both were also parvenu; they were 'minority' parties in the process of turning themselves, each in its own sphere, into 'majority' parties. Apart from any appeal Labour may have made to the Maoris by its programme to help the weak and the poor, as a minority party it may have exercised an attraction for Maoris, a minority race, just as the Democrats won the support of many racial minorities in the United States. The two remaining Maori seats were won, also with Ratana candidates, by Labour in 1938 and 1943, respectively.[1]

The quantity and range of Labour's legislation, 1935–9, can be compared only with the first few years following the Liberal victory of 1890.[2] One series of measures extended the exalting labour legislation by providing for compulsory unionism, the forty-hour week and changes in factory acts, minimum-wage legislation, and so on. These may be viewed as a continuation of the Liberal measures of some forty years before and also as a 'reward' to Labour's most faithful and regular clients, the 'workers'.

Also 'sectional', but addressed largely to more recent converts, was Labour's legislation for the benefit of farmers, in particular the 'guaranteed price'. This was not an unambiguous concept.[3] But when put into practice it took the form of a Primary Products Marketing Department being set up, which purchased all butter and cheese intended for export and then marketed it. The producer was paid a fixed price per pound (with differentials for quality) for the whole season's output. This price was calculated yearly so as to protect the farmer against violent fluctuations in the external prices of the products.

[1] S. F. McClean, 'Maori Representation, 1905–1948' (Auckland unpublished thesis, 1950); J. M. Henderson, *Ratana* (Wellington, 1963); Brown, op. cit., pp. 176–8.

[2] See A. M. Finlay, 'Labour's Legislation', in R. M. Chapman, *Ends and Means in New Zealand Politics*, op. cit.

[3] Mr. Langstone, who is sometimes credited with having first used the term 'guaranteed price' in this context, wrote an earlier pamphlet giving a different sense to the expression. On the origins of the idea see Clifton, op. cit., pp. 280 ff.

From August 1937 onwards an attempt was made to lay down criteria for the calculation of guaranteed prices, but some of the terms used, 'efficient producer', 'usual conditions', and so on, were incapable of being precisely formulated or of resulting in definite uncontroversial answers.[1]

The Government's credit policy was the cause of more dissension within the party than anything else. It was even partly responsible in 1940 for the expulsion of Mr. J. A. Lee, a brilliant but aggressive party member, and for his creation of a splinter party. After the election the Labour members seemed to be divided roughly into those who thought that, although credit creation had been necessary at the depth of the slump, there were strict limits to what purely financial reform could do, and those who, like Lee, subscribed in part to the view of Major Douglas, that the existing monetary system was responsible for a permanent shortage of credit. The former 'orthodox finance' group, headed by Walter Nash, the Minister of Finance, prevailed. Consequently the Reserve Bank was 'nationalized', by replacing the private shareholders with government nominees, but the other banks, including the Bank of New Zealand, were not. And the 'cheap' (that is, low interest) credit was limited in the main to loans for the erection of state housing. The stance of the Prime Minister altered somewhat during his term of office, whether through the influence of Mr. Nash, through reaction *against* Mr. Lee, or simply from a realization that the worst sufferings during the slump had been remedied without recourse to too 'unorthodox' devices. During the election campaign Mr. Savage stated that to finance the building of a railway, instead of borrowing the money 'and paying interest on it for ever', under a Labour Government 'the banker would provide the money just as he does now, but as the Government would control the currency and credit, no public debt would be created'.[2] Some days later Mr. Savage was denunciatory rather than expository. 'The powers of the banks must be wiped out. They have used their powers so badly that they have shown that they are not safe custodians of the money and credit of the country.'[3]

[1] W. B. Sutch, *Recent Economic Changes in New Zealand* (Wellington, 1936). On guaranteed prices generally see A. J. Sinclair, *Guaranteed Prices for Dairy Produce* (Wellington, 1946).
[2] *Bay of Plenty Times*, 18 Nov. 1935.
[3] *Auckland Star*, 22 Nov. 1935.

During the next few years he continued to make statements along these lines, which might have come from the lips of a convinced Social Crediter. But shortly before his death he sometimes expressed himself differently, so that his considered views on the banks were as hard to fathom as (according to Mr. Dooley) were those of Theodore Roosevelt on the trusts in the United States. At the 1939 Labour Party Conference Savage said, 'There are people who think that the short cut to the millennium is by manipulation of the currency.' But he thought that the great bulk of those who attended the Labour Conference would not admit that everything could be brought about simply by such manipulation. On the nationalization of the Bank of New Zealand the main thing was 'to have control of it, whatever happens to the ownership'.[1]

It was also part of Labour's policy to expand New Zealand's secondary industries, and the Industrial Efficiency Act of 1936 provided both for making existing industries more efficient and for promoting new ones. The view that imports should be confined largely to what could not be economically produced in New Zealand,[2] was a logical result of the desire to limit the country's dependence on the variable returns from agricultural exports. In 1938 local manufacturing received encouragement for another reason. The sterling funds held by New Zealand banks dropped heavily between 1936 and 1938, partly because of a high level of imports, partly because of capital transfers. Import control was therefore imposed on a wide range of articles in 1938. The Minister of Finance, Mr. Nash, explained this action in terms of the immediate need to stop the drain on foreign exchange. But, interviewed at about the same time, the Prime Minister said that import controls were part of the Government's plan for 'insulating the Dominion from unfair competition overseas', and expressed the hope that the controls would last 'for ever'.[3] Another outstanding measure of the Labour Government was the Social Security legislation of 1938, which included a forerunner of the British National Health

[1] *Evening Post*, 20 Apr. 1939.
[2] Walter Nash, *Guaranteed Prices, Why and How*, op. cit., p. 16.
[3] Interviews, *Evening Post*, 7 Dec. 1938. See also W. B. Sutch, *New Zealand's Labour Government at Work* (New York, 1940), p. 28. Lee and others in caucus had long been advocating more protection for New Zealand industries against overseas competition (Brown, op. cit., pp. 195–6).

Service of 1948. The Government was united on this as being in the New Zealand tradition of humanitarian legislation. The Opposition did not think it advisable to vote against it, but warned that the costs would be too heavy, that the medical profession would be unhappy, and so on.

Viewed as a whole the Labour Government's legislation, 1935–9, was far from socialist. Many of its measures might have been passed by an intelligent non-Labour Government under a leader like Coates. The path of pragmatism, even of opportunism, was preferred to socialism. At the 1937 Labour Party Conference Savage denied that some of the party's legislation constituted steps in the direction of Socialism; they were rather businesslike and sensible measures to meet immediate problems. 'The Socialisation of the means of production will look after itself if we face the current problems in an intelligent fashion.'[1] In particular the Prime Minister and the Minister of Agriculture, Lee-Martin, were perpetually having to deny reports[2] that Labour intended to nationalize the land. All in all, it seems to be a fair comment that the Government's programme represented a victory for the ideas of the pre-war Trades and Labour Councils rather than those of the 'Red Fed'.[3] 'Humanism', or humanitarianism, had prevailed rather than socialism.

The National (Coalition) reaction to its disastrous defeat in 1935 was first to blame the Democrats, second to improve its organization so as to secure the union of all anti-Labour forces. This was followed by a Conference in May 1936, at which it was decided to found a new party, not just a coalition or federation of existing parties. After some manœuvring the new National Party chose as its Leader a South Island farmer, Adam Hamilton, who had studied theology—but not public relations. His voice lacked appeal, either in person or on the radio, and his attempts at geniality produced only an 'I'll-smile-though-it-hurts-me'

[1] *Round Table*, vol. xxvii (1936–7), p. 887.
[2] Aroused perhaps by articles such as those by R. P. Anschutz and Morgan Williams, M.P. in *Tomorrow*, 28 Apr. and 26 May 1937, respectively. A member of the Cabinet, Mr. Langstone was also believed to be friendly to the idea of State farms. (*Speakers' Notes, Bulletin No. 1* (National Party, 6 Sept. 1938), quoting *The Borer* (official organ of the Amalgamated Society of Carpenters and Joiners) referring to a speech of Langstone's at the 1938 Labour Party Conference).
[3] W. B. Sutch, *The Quest for Security in New Zealand* (London, 1942), p. 125.

expression.[1] When asked questions at meetings he was usually able to think of a good answer next morning. The new party was slow to produce a policy. Hamilton was honest in explaining the delay; the Nationalists were striving to unite the interests of all sections, but it was not easy to get the rural and city interests to see eye to eye.[2]

By the time of the 1938 election the National Party had built up an efficient organization, and had prevented the rise of any substantial rival right-wing party, similar to the Democrats. But trade had improved and unemployment had fallen. The Labour Government reaped the benefits of world recovery just as its predecessor had been swamped by the world depression. The National Party was unable to produce any convincing arguments why those electors who had voted for Labour in 1935 should turn away from it. In fact, for many electors Labour had now the added attraction of being 'respectable', which it had not so obviously been in 1935. Labour stood on its record, as shown in the title of a pamphlet by Mr. Nash. It no longer had to try to explain what guaranteed prices were, but was able to point to *Guaranteed Prices—A Successful Reality*. In more than one pamphlet it drew a contrast with the 'bad old days'.[3] Its Social Security programme was so attractive that it was even able to print with impunity surely the most banal political strip cartoon ever reproduced: 'without the Government's generous scheme I might skimp and save all the time, and then after missing all the good things in life, my little nest egg might be gone in one stroke of bad luck.' In reply to this the National Party stated its opposition to socialism generally, and, more particularly, expressed its preference for private housing over state housing. In place of a guaranteed price, the Opposition proposed to reduce farmers' costs and/or to make compensatory payments to them. There was a certain degree of 'me-tooism' in their programme, except that Labour's Social Security proposals were utterly rejected, mainly on grounds of cost.[4]

At the 1938 election Labour actually increased its proportion of the vote; it did not, however, increase its proportion of seats,

[1] *Standard*, 22 Sept. 1928.
[2] *Press*, 17 Apr. 1937.
[3] e.g. *What New Zealand Labour means to you*; *The Prime Minister's Personal Message to You*; *The National Party's Policy means The People must Perish if Prices Fall*.
[4] *Speakers' Notes* (National Party, 1938); *Your Future is in Your Hand* (1938).

mainly because the anti-Labour vote was not split to the same extent as in 1935. Labour's vote actually fell in several North Island rural 'butter' seats, reflecting some dissatisfaction with the guaranteed price. The disappointing election result made the National Party look more critically at its Leader. In 1940 Hamilton was replaced by Mr. S. G. Holland, a dynamic Christchurch businessman, whose leadership of a party representing both city and rural interests was soon symbolized by his acquisition of a farm.

When war came in September 1939 it led to a tightening of the Government's grip on the economy. Even in wartime there was no real concerted 'planning', but at least some of the gaps in the system of control were plugged: for instance the free-exchange system which had existed side by side with import controls since 1938, was closed in July 1940.[1] And the limited size of the wartime 'cake' made its fair division of such pressing importance that an 'Economic Stabilization Commission, was set up to try to prevent too great economic inequities between contending groups.[2]

From the more immediately political angle, there were two major developments during the war. There was no 'orthodox' Coalition Government formed, mainly because the members of the existing Labour Cabinet were unwilling to give up their jobs. After much manœuvring a War Cabinet was set up in July 1940, consisting of three Labour and two National members (Coates and Hamilton).[3] But when there was a change of leadership in the National Party the new Leader, S. G. Holland, who replaced Hamilton, was outside the War Cabinet. Holland was one of six Opposition members who, along with seven from the Government, made up a new 'War Administration', formed in 1942, which was added to the existing 'domestic' Cabinet and the War Cabinet. The Opposition was represented on this administrative monstrosity for only three months. In September 1942 Holland and three other National Party members, who had already disagreed with their colleagues on several questions, withdrew from the War Administration on the issue of how to deal with a strike in the Huntly coal mines. Two others, Coates

[1] J. B. Condliffe, *The Economic Record*, p. 159.
[2] L. C. Webb in Parker (ed.), op. cit., pp. 11–32.
[3] Wood, *The New Zealand People at War*, pp. 134–44.

and Hamilton, stayed on as individuals, not as representatives of the party.[1]

The other major development took the form of an open split in the Labour Party. Mr. John A. Lee had a heroic record in the First World War, had published novels including *Children of the Poor* which had attracted favourable comment from Bernard Shaw, and was one of the Labour Party's ablest speakers and propagandists. He had been responsible for many of Labour's election pamphlets at the 1938 election, and in the same year published his *Socialism in New Zealand*. In the Labour Government Lee had been made an under-secretary with responsibility for housing. Unfortunately he differed from the leadership (Savage, Fraser, and Nash) on policy, mainly in his desire for cheaper credit and in his opposition to overseas borrowing. There were also differences of opinion on the organization of the party, as well as personality clashes. Lee was not an 'intellectual' in the accepted sense, but he had a quick mind, and felt frustrated by the domination of the 'old guard' over the party. 'If a man spits on his hands to think, nothing will stop him in the Labour Party.'[2] On the other hand, the party leaders regarded him as being somewhat overbearing and as a young man in too much of a hurry. These differences culminated in an attack on Savage by Lee when the latter was dying, although this was not public knowledge at the time. Lee was then expelled from the party by its 1940 Conference.[3] Lee, after his expulsion, founded a new party, the Democratic (Soldier) Labour Party. He was the only sitting Labour member to fight under its banner at the 1943 election. In contesting the election[4] the DLP programme advocated cheaper credit, and echoed the social credit aim of making financially possible whatever could be physically produced; in particular, it proposed increased family allowances and lower interest-rates for housing. Two minor parties, the right-wing People's Movement and the pro-Social-Credit Real Democracy Movement, also fought the election.

Labour fought the election under Fraser, a far abler wartime Minister than Savage. Labour election themes included the

[1] Wood, *The New Zealand People at War*, pp. 168–70, 231–9; Robinson, op. cit., pp. 136–8.
[2] John A. Lee, letter to the author, 22 June 1959.
[3] See p. 226, below.
[4] See Daniels, op. cit., pp. 118 ff.

party's successful conduct of the war, its expansion of industry and production, and its help to the farmers through planning and stabilization. It also pointed to the benefits of its rehabilitation legislation. Through the Trades Councils special anti-Lee propaganda was issued comparing Lee with Hitler under the slogan; 'This Man Apes the Fascists.' Only on food prices was Labour on the defensive. In *The Truth about Food Prices* it carefully explained the reasons for wartime shortages and how subsidies were being used to keep down the prices of essential foodstuffs. It was alleged that the Nationalists, if they gained power, would abolish these subsidies, and that food prices would soar.

The Nationalists had by 1943 worked out a well-reasoned programme, with some attempt at a 'philosophical' underpinning.[1] The electors, they said, possessed certain 'rights', for instance the right to employment, food, shelter, security, and so on. This approach would enable the Nationalists to find acceptable almost any Labour policies they wanted to, as coming within the scope of these rights. But duties corresponding to these rights, such as working for the common good, must also be performed. The National Party claimed that it stood for freedom in contrast to the Labour Party, which encouraged bureaucracy and officialdom and lacked freedom even in its own internal party machinery. At the election the Democratic Labour Party failed to win any seats, but took 4 per cent. of the vote, presumably mostly from Labour. National increased its proportion of the votes, and won ten more seats.

The 1946 election nearly resulted in a change of Government.[2] Shortages and rationing, cheerfully accepted during the war, were much less tolerable after it had ended. National Party propaganda, especially in its appeals to women, took account of this feeling. But the Nationalists had ceased to attack the social security system. 'With much that the present Government has done we do not quarrel, nor do we question the honesty of purpose of those who have formulated the Labour policy.' But there was a need for a different approach, less influenced by

[1] See S. G. Holland, *Passwords to Progress* (1943) and the party's 1943 *Election Manifesto*.
[2] For political comments on the period since 1946 see Robert Chapman, 'New Zealand since the War', *Landfall*, Sept. 1962.

'rigid theories and long-standing prejudices'. The National
Party proposal that the occupants of state houses should be
enabled to buy them was presumably an instance of this new
approach. The National Party was, in effect, accepting the
existence of the Welfare State, but offering itself as an alternative manager for it, more efficient and less doctrinaire. The
Labour Party recognized the dangers of this type of propaganda.
So, as well as standing on its record during 'The Ten Good
Years', it sounded a warning. 'In the hope of deluding the
electors, the Nationalists today are hiding their true intentions
behind lip-service to practically the whole of Labour's beneficial
legislation. This is nothing but a propaganda effort.'[1] Labour
won the election, but only by the narrowest of margins. It had
been clear from the 1943 election result that Labour had lost
many of its 1938 farming votes, and in 1945 it abolished the
country quota in the hope of cutting its losses (in seats) at the
next election. Consequently in 1946 Labour, with a few thousand
more votes than National, won the same number of European
seats, thirty-eight. For its majority in Parliament it was dependent on the four Maori M.P.s, who were now all Labour.

At first sight any comparison between Labour's post-war
problems and those which it had faced on taking up office in
1935 would seem to be quite inappropriate. Certainly there is no
similarity between the two periods in terms of human suffering
and despair. The post-1945 problems were largely problems of
plenty. But for members of the Government the second period
may have been the more trying one. The rise in the prices of
New Zealand exports, notably wool, 1946–9, considerably
increased the available purchasing power in New Zealand and
severely threatened 'stabilization'.[2] In 1948 inflation was somewhat checked when the New Zealand pound was revalued to
sterling parity. But prices still rose, and by the time of the 1949
election some trade unions, notably the watersiders, freezing-
workers, miners, and carpenters, had pressed their demands for
a larger share of 'the cake' to the point of striking. In the party
itself, while the glory of the early days remained, the *élan* had
departed. An unkind observer might have adapted Disraeli's

---

[1] *A Personal Message to the Electors from the Prime Minister* (1946).
[2] J. B. Condliffe, 'New Zealand's Experiment in Economic Planning', *The
American Economic Review*, vol. xlvii, no. 6 (1957), pp. 932 ff.

mot; some of the 'volcanoes' on the Government front bench were exhausted; others had never erupted. In 1936, when the Bill to nationalize the Reserve Bank was passed by the House of Representatives, the Labour members had joyfully sung 'The Red Flag'. Now the atmosphere was more sober and restrained. True, there was considerable legislative activity, resulting, for instance, in extensions of state ownership in civil aviation, the linen-flax-processing industry, and, in conjunction with private enterprise, the marketing of imported oil in New Zealand. Several industrial and social-security measures were also passed. But perhaps too much of the Labour Party's energy was spent in groping after extinguished visionary gleams rather than in bracing itself to meet new challenges. Opposition within the Labour Party (as well as from the National Party) prevented New Zealand from joining the International Monetary Fund. The root cause of the antagonism was the old wish for 'insulation', the belief that, by joining the IMF, New Zealand would surrender her 'sovereignty' over her currency, and would no longer be able to protect her economy by using import restrictions.[1] Neither was the nationalization of the Bank of New Zealand, following a resolution by the Labour Party Conference of 1944,[2] a response to any immediate difficulties of credit control. Even before the war there had been controversy and confusion on the nationalization of the bank, the nationalizers alleging that it was provided for in the party's platform, the anti-nationalizers contending in effect that the 'State Bank' in the platform corresponded to the already-nationalized Reserve Bank. In 1945[3] the Labour Party put up a reasoned case for nationalization, including the point that the bank, when nationalized, could be used by the Government to influence the interest-rates charged by the commercial banks.[4] But it is hard to believe that the main motive force was not largely symbolic— of past struggles against 'the money power' and of future determination to stick to the old objective of socialization.[5]

[1] Morgan Williams, *Tribune*, 31 Mar. 1945 and *N.Z.P.D.*, vol. cclxv, pp. 325–6 (10 Aug. 1944). [2] See p. 232, below.
[3] *Standard*, 15 Dec. 1939 and 21 Dec. 1939; *Dominion* and *Evening Post*, 5 Apr. 1940; Brown, op. cit., pp. 192 ff.
[4] *The People and the Bank of New Zealand, The Case for Public Ownership* (New Zealand Labour Party, 1945).
[5] C. G. F. Simkin, 'The Nationalization of the Bank of New Zealand', *Economic*

In general the party was content to follow policies of stabilization and import control.[1] Some of the intellectuals in the movement were sceptical about the compatibility of stabilization and
socialism,[2] and a lone non-New Zealand voice was raised in
favour of Labour's adopting a programme of 'Full Production'.[3]
Nevertheless, at the 1949 election Labour asked the electors to
support its established policies. The keynote of its Election
Manifesto was *security*; for the worker through full employment,
the forty-hour week, and the maintenance of his purchasing
power; for the farmer by Labour's marketing policy which
ensured stable prices; for the manufacturers by the continuation
of import control. But four years after the end of the war the
National Party had a receptive audience for its attacks on controls, especially those import controls which were most resented by consumers. The Government had also been seriously
weakened by industrial unrest, provoked by a group of militant
unionists, and by the challenge to the leadership's proposals for
compulsory military training in peacetime made at the 1949
Labour Party Conference. The Prime Minister, Fraser, was
forced to submit the conscription issue to a special referendum.
Even although the vote was in favour of compulsion, the political
consequences were still damaging. It was plain that the majority
for compulsory military training had been gained mainly
through the support of Nationalist voters. The confidence with
which the National Party fought the election was shown by the
title of its 'householder', *A National Party Victory and You*. It reaffirmed the party's faith in free enterprise, its opposition to
socialism and communism, and its guarantee that it would not
reduce wages, pensions, and social-security benefits. To the farmers it promised that the marketing of most items of primary
produce would be handed over to commissions or boards containing a majority of elected primary producers' representatives.
National's faith in victory was justified by the 1949 election

Record, Australia and New Zealand, vol. xxii, Dec. 1946. The objective was dropped
from the party's constitution in 1951.

[1] *Labour Plans for the Future* (report of a caucus committee of the Labour Party
(1946)). See also D. G. Sullivan (Minister of Industries and Commerce), *Stabilization in the Post-War Period* (broadcast address, printed by the Government Printer,
1946).

[2] *Stabilization or Socialization?* (by a Fabian Study Group, with comments by O.
Wilson and A. M. Finlay, 1947).

[3] Dudley Seers, *The Challenge to New Zealand Labour* (Christchurch, 1946).

result. Labour was defeated, after fourteen years in power, and won only 34 seats to National's 46.

The National Party Dominant?

The National Government's policies, 1949–57, were as moderate and as middle-of-the-road as the programmes it had put forward before gaining office. The most pessimistic Labour prophecies of what a National Government would do were not realized. Controls were not lifted all at once; industrial and social-security legislation was not repealed; nor did full employment suffer. Some diehard Nationalists now looked on Mr. Holland as a dangerous radical, who had drifted too far with the tide of social reform, but the rumblings on the party's right never grew to thunder. Under the new Government there was certainly a general tendency to relax state controls, but it did not amount to a wild 'dash to freedom'. The government shares in the mixed undertaking for the sale of oil were sold. However, the National Government actually set up a mixed undertaking for the manufacture of pulp and paper, and invested in one or two other companies. Attempts to sell the Government-owned National Airways Corporation came to nothing, because there were no satisfactory offers from private enterprise. The Reserve Bank and the Bank of New Zealand remained 'nationalized', although the Government attempted, not very effectively, to confer a certain degree of 'independence' on the Reserve Bank.[1] The party carried out its promise to set up agricultural boards, on which primary producers were strongly represented.

Controls on prices, on capital investment, and on the licensing of industry were eased, and later controls on land sales and on building were abolished. It is hard to judge, however, how much of the move away from controls was inspired by the party's ideology of 'freedom', and how much was simply part of a return to 'normal' peacetime conditions. In Britain, where the Labour Party remained in office until 1951, it had already enacted substantial measures of decontrol by that time. However, it was certainly National's declared policy 'to move away progressively *from direct and indirect controls wherever possible*'.[2] And when it did

[1] L. C. Webb, 'The Public Corporation in New Zealand' in W. Friedmann (ed.), *The Public Corporation; A Comparative Symposium* (London, 1954), p. 282.
[2] *Policy, General Election 1957* (New Zealand National Party), section 17, p. 3 (italics in the original).

undertake to regulate imports, the Government preferred to use tariffs and exchange controls rather than import selection. There was already industrial unrest when the National Party assumed office in 1949. This culminated in the five-month strike of 1951,[1] which Holland handled capably, after the fashion of Massey with the 1913 strike. Even before the strike right-wing National supporters had wanted to reverse some of the Labour's legislation on trade unions, in particular the law which made membership of a union compulsory for those working in certain industries. But when the strike was over Holland and his Minister for Labour, Mr. Sullivan, did not take undue advantage of their victory. Amendments were passed to the Industrial Conciliation and Arbitration Act, notably some providing for secret ballots on strike proposals and for the election of union officials. But the provisions for compulsory unionism were left untouched, with the minor exception that now exemption might be allowed on religious grounds.

The Nationalists had, somewhat rashly, promised that, once they were elected, they would stop prices from rising. But general inflationary tendencies all over the world were intensified by the outbreak of the Korean War. However, the electoral value of this issue for Labour was destroyed by the National Party's decision to go to the country at a snap election in 1951 to seek approval for the way in which it had dealt with the strike. This was a damaging issue for the Labour Party. The New Zealand Federation of Labour (corresponding to the British TUC) had condemned the strike and its leaders, Messrs. Barnes and Hill. But Mr. Nash, leader of the Parliamentary Labour Party since Fraser's death in 1950, was desirous of mediating between the hostile industrial groups, and was represented, in his own words, as being 'neither for nor against' the strikers. The National Party, on the other hand, held the initiative. It played down issues like the cost of living, and was able to present the conflict as one of *The People versus the Wreckers*,[2]

---

[1] Accounts of the strike from various angles are given in: Dick Scott, *151 Days* (Auckland, 1954); John Gordon *Crisis on the Waterfront* (Wellington, n.d.); *Waterfront Dispute Reflections* (reprinted from *The Clarion*, June 1951 by the New Zealand Federation of Labour, 1951).

[2] *The People versus the Wreckers* (1951 'householder'). The Labour Party complained (Labour Discussion Series, no. 62, 1951) that this pamphlet was 'anonymous', and did not state that it was published on behalf of the National Party.

while offering 'a fair go for moderate unionists'. In the face of this attack Labour failed to persuade the electors that the 'real' issues were bread-and-butter ones, and at the election National increased its majority to twenty seats.

At the 1954 election the cost-of-living issue came into its own.[1] The National Party blamed the Korean War for the failure of its 1949 plans 'to make the pound buy more', and was forced to argue that, although this had not happened, New Zealanders were buying more, and that this was what counted.[2] The Labour Party, as well as emphasizing the rise in the cost of living, promised increases in social-security benefits and upheld the merits of import control as opposed to exchange control. One of its main planks was, 'Labour will take immediate and effective steps to ensure that the State will become the sole authority for the issue of credit and currency. The public credit will be used to the fullest extent compatible with the public good.'[3] This pledge was reminiscent of Labour's platform at the 1935 election. The earlier proposals had been intended to attract those who shared the then prevailing sympathy with Social Credit ideas, the 1954 plank was meant to be a defence against a new, third, party, the Social Credit Political League.[4]

The newly formed League had the difficult task of conveying to the electors in a few months the whole intricate body of Social Credit Monetary Theory, to say nothing of the preliminary task of identifying 'the body' correctly. But, in addition to proposing that a 'National Monetary Authority' be set up, it made specific, easily comprehensible, promises to reduce taxation and increase expenditure at a total cost of £80–90 million.[5] It also campaigned on the plank that the policies of the major parties were indistinguishable from each other. In spite of having to work in a hurry, with only a skeleton organization, it managed to put up candidates in practically every electorate. The League won no seats, but obtained 11 per cent. of the votes, an astonishing proportion for a new party in a time of economic prosperity.

[1] On 1954 election issues generally see D. S. North, 'Political Campaign Tactics in New Zealand' (Victoria unpublished thesis, 1954).

[2] *The Challenge of the Future* (National Party 'householder', 1954).

[3] *Labour's 1954 Policy Means Progress, Security and Prosperity for All!* ('householder', 1954).

[4] See *Note: The Social Credit Political League*, below.

[5] *Social Credit's Solution* ('householder', 1954).

Labour and National divided the remainder of the vote almost equally between them, but National had a majority of ten seats, 45–35.

A few months before the 1957 election it did not seem that any particular issues would be outstanding. Presumably Labour would try to press home its attack on the rising cost of living; National would perhaps campaign on its record of having relaxed controls, especially import control, and contrast this with Labour 'regimentation'. But the Government's decision to introduce Pay-As-You-Earn income tax, previously approved in principle by both parties, altered the picture.[1] To bring the new legislation into operation the Government offered one year's remission of tax and also a 25 per cent. tax rebate. This was countered by a Labour offer of one year's remission of tax plus a rebate of £100 for one year,[2] which led to a later attempt by the National Party to reinterpret the 25 per cent. rebate as being for three years, not just one. This summary fails to convey the intricacies of the position, which was also complicated by changed provisions for payment of the social-security charge. But there was no intricacy or subtlety about what the parties were doing. They were conducting an auction for the electors' votes. The Labour Party's final bid was engagingly direct—'Do you want £100 or not'? Labour also put forward some interesting proposals on housing, including cheap housing loans, and it gave more publicity to a scheme, which it had already proposed at the 1954 election, by which future Family Benefit could be used in advance as a deposit for home ownership. With an eye on drawing support away from Social Credit, Labour promised that the net profit which the private trading banks obtained from the creation of credit should be returned to the State. During the campaign a new and menacing issue appeared, which was not deliberately 'created' by the parties, but arose from New Zealand's perpetual vulnerability to balance of payments crises. The President of the Federation of Labour,

[1] For the 1957 election campaign see Bruce Brown, 'The Labour Campaign', Alan Robinson 'The National Campaign', J. E. Colechin, 'The Social Credit Campaign', *Political Science*, vol. x, no. 1 (1958); R. S. Milne, 'Les Élections générales de 1957 en Nouvelle-Zélande', *Revue française de science politique*, vol. viii, no. 3 (1958).

[2] The Labour Party pointed out that the £100 offer was not new; it had been made in 1954. But see Robinson, art. cit., pp. 26–27.

Mr. Walsh, warned that such a crisis was imminent and that over-importing, especially of luxury goods, was leading to inflation.[1] Mr. K. J. Holyoake, who had become Prime Minister on Sir Sidney Holland's retirement a few months earlier, denied that such a crisis existed. Neither were the implications of Mr. Walsh's warning completely acceptable to the Labour Party; if there really was an inflationary situation, then this was not the proper time to promise lower taxes. Nor did the electors wish to be distracted from their choice between two attractive alternative offers. So it was not until *after* the election that the warning was taken seriously. Social Credit broadened its platform, compared with 1954, by making proposals on education, liquor licensing, and other topics. But, ironically in view of the major parties' tactics, it made fewer financial promises than in 1954; it quoted definite figures only in respect of payments for old-age pensioners and superannuitants. It was handicapped by the fact that its Leader, Mr. W. B. Owen, had not fully recovered from an illness by the time of the campaign.

The election result was one of the closest on record. With 4 per cent. more of the vote than National, Labour was returned to office with a majority of two seats, 41–39. Social Credit again failed to win a seat, and its share of the vote dropped to 7 per cent.

The Labour Government of 1957–60 introduced a few social-welfare measures, such as raising family benefit and universal superannuation. But its work was handicapped by its small majority and by the foreign-exchange crisis, on which Mr. Walsh had issued his warning, which became evident a few weeks after the party took office. A two-year period of austerity followed, and the 1958 budget made substantial increases in both direct and indirect taxation. Although taxation and controls were relaxed before the 1960 election, much of the campaign was concentrated on the Labour promises at the previous election, the responsibility for the foreign-exchange crisis and the 1958 budget. National Party policy, some of which was released several months before the 1960 election, included a proposal for a Monetary and Economic Commission to advise the Government on economic questions, for a written Bill of Rights (as advocated by the New Zealand Constitutional

[1] *Dominion*, 15 Nov. 1957.

Society) for an appeal authority, responsible to Parliament, to which appeals against administrative decisions of the Government could be made (Ombudsman), and for the abolition of compulsory unionism. Labour Party policy was less elaborate. The theme of industrial development was prominent, and was given more space in the Election Manifesto than any other item. It was also proposed to raise personal tax exemptions by a modest amount. The Social Credit Political League spelled out a number of tax proposals, to be made possible by the creation of a national credit authority. Its other proposals covered a broader field than at previous elections. The election results showed a swing to National of over 4 per cent. and a turnover of seven seats, giving National a majority of 46 to 34. Social Credit increased its vote by over 1 per cent.[1]

The 1963 election was a 'no change' election.[2] The campaign was gentlemanly, to the point of dullness. National had intended to fight the election mainly on the Government's successful handling of the negotiations resulting from Britain's joining the European Common Market. But when Britain's application to join was rejected there was a change of plan. Both major parties put the accent on development and incentives. National also stressed the satisfactory economic record of the last three years and the strength of its leadership. Labour's policy was designed to create a 'new look' under its new Leader, Mr. Nordmeyer, and specifically advocated incentives to exporters. Labour also proposed tax concessions on lower incomes together with tax increases on higher incomes, as well as medical, dental, and other social security benefits and three weeks' annual holiday for all workers. Tax reductions and provision for free fertilizer were features of a 'new look' in Labour farming policy. National replied by totalling the cost of these proposals, finding that it came to about £50 million, and reminding the voters of Labour's heavy taxation in the 1958 budget. Social Credit offered, among other policy items, the abolition of all direct tax on the first £520 of income. In addition to these parties, and the Communist Party, there was a new 'Liberal' Party. At one time it seemed to have two wings, one in Auckland and one in Christchurch, but

[1] The events leading up to the election, the campaign, and the issues are covered in Chapman, Jackson, and Mitchell, chs. iii and v.
[2] Robert Chapman, 'The "No Change" Election', *Comment*, Jan. 1964.

before polling day these were united under Mr. R. M. Hutton-Potts, a former editor of the *Southland Daily News*. Liberal Party policy was somewhat similar to that of the Constitutional Society, and included attacks on over-staffed government departments and proposals for a written constitution and for the restoration of an upper house. A feature of the election was that television was used for the first time at a New Zealand general election. Partly because of the conditions laid down by the New Zealand Broadcasting Corporation the programmes were not too exciting. Except for the final programmes the production, including lighting, was absolutely uniform. 'This meant that short persons with big noses got the same lighting as tall persons with small noses, with undesirable results in some cases.' Both parties selected the candidates to appear on television, not because of their position in the party hierarchy, but because of their effectiveness in the medium. Apart from the Labour Leader and Deputy-leader, the other seven Labour candidates who appeared included none of the former Labour Cabinet members who were seeking re-election. This was perhaps one aspect of Labour's 'new look'. The National speakers were better rehearsed than Labour.

When the results were announced there was a swing of about a half of 1 per cent. from National to Labour. In terms of seats there was a change of one; Labour lost a seat abolished in the South Island, but gained one existing seat and a new seat in the North Island. The Liberals, with over twenty candidates, collected only 1 per cent. of the vote, although they caused the National Party a little concern by drawing financial support from some farmers in Canterbury. The Social Credit vote dropped by an almost similar percentage, although it had the consolation of failing to win the Hobson seat by only a few votes. The result indicated that, in the absence of any foreign-exchange crisis, the political scene had become increasingly bare of controversial national issues.

III

THE DEVELOPMENT OF THE PARTY
SYSTEM: PATTERNS OF SUPPORT
FOR THE PARTIES

IN retracing the course of New Zealand's political history it
is tempting to stop at several points and imagine alternative
courses which events might have followed. Downie Stewart
thought that if Reeves had stayed in New Zealand the emergence of an independent Labour Party might have been postponed,[1] just as similar speculations have been made that, if they
had been more skilful, the British Liberals might have delayed
the formation of a Labour Party in that country.[2] But perhaps
the key word is 'postponed', and R. T. Shannon has argued
persuasively that by 1914 there was no longer sufficient identity
of interest between the New Zealand Liberal and Labour parties
to provide a firm basis for alliance, let alone amalgamation.[3]

Another line of thought concerns the relations between the
non-Labour parties, once the Labour Party had been firmly
established. For instance, after the First World War could the
Reform Party have quickly extended its appeal by being less
patently a farmers' party and so have killed off the Liberal
Party beyond any hope of revival?[4] Considering the amount of
trouble the Reform Party actually had from the farmers and
from the Country Party in the 1920's,[5] such a strategy could
hardly have been successful. On the other hand, the Reform
Party was not so *exclusively* a farmers' party that it corresponded
to the Australian Country Party. Apart from historical acci-
dents, the absence of a permanent sizable Country Party in
New Zealand, unlike Australia, must surely be attributed to the

[1] Introduction to Siegfried, op. cit., p. xiii.
[2] H. Pelling, *The Origins of the Labour Party, 1880–1900* (London, 1954), pp. 235–7;
Sir Ivor Jennings, *Party Politics; II: The Growth of the Parties* (Cambridge, 1961),
pp. 241–2.
[3] Op. cit., p. 230; Jennings, op. cit., pp. 250 and 286.
[4] L. C. Webb, 'Politics and Administration' in Belshaw, op. cit., p. 269.
[5] See pp. 41–42, above.

general lack of any sharp division between town and country. A further difference from Australia lies in the fact that the alternative vote was never used, as it was by the Australian Liberal and Country Parties, to enable two right-wing parties to survive without blighting each other's electoral prospects. In New Zealand Reform and Liberals did not go beyond *ad hoc* electoral pacts (as in the 1925 election) and intermittent talk about 'fusion' until eventually a form of fusion actually took place. Possibly Reform, which was the larger party during most of the 1920's, thought that the alternative vote would merely delay their expected 'inheritance' of the Liberal vote. Perhaps the alternative vote would also have been psychologically distasteful, because the essentially similar Second Ballot had been employed by the Liberals as a weapon *against Reform* as recently as 1908 and 1911.

The Labour Party's course of development might also have been different but for certain chance factors. Compared with its counterpart in Australia it was saved from several political misfortunes. Because it was founded later, it did not have the chance of holding office in the First World War, and so conveniently avoided the risk of being split on the issue of conscription. It had not even attained office by the time of the Great Depression of the 1930's; it was actually *helped* into office by the depression, and its good fortune continued when, shortly after it had formed a Government, economic conditions improved. Its experience was therefore totally different from the Labour Governments in Australia and in Britain. Instead of the top leadership, round Lyons and MacDonald, respectively, breaking away, with the result that the party lost office, New Zealand Labour sustained the lesser shock of losing a possible *future* leader, Lee, while remaining in power. Things might have been very different if, at the depth of the depression, Labour had been the Government in New Zealand. It is conceivable then, that if the Prime Minister and Finance Minister had clung to financial orthodoxy, the New Zealand split in the party might have followed the Australian and British pattern. Since the end of the last war New Zealand Labour has been fortunate again, compared with Australia. In both the party and the trade unions extreme left-wingers have been less influential. Partly because of this, and partly because the proportion of Catholics is smaller than in Australia, there has been no Catholic right-wing 'movement', and consequently no splinter party corresponding to the Democratic Labour Party. Of course, it would be wrong to argue that the avoidance of these 'misfortunes' was an unmixed blessing. Perhaps it is salutary for left-wing parties to be given an opportunity to shed their right-wing leaders on occasion, however painful the operation may be at the time. And maybe the relative security enjoyed by the New Zealand leadership has resulted in too high a degree of domination by the leaders.

These speculations are put forward only to suggest that there was nothing 'inevitable' about the precise course which political development assumed in New Zealand, although, in fact, the parties *did* develop that way. The rest of this chapter is concerned with three broad questions. First, it tries to supply some of the details of how a two-party system has evolved, how 'Independents' have declined in importance, and how issues have become less local and more 'national'. Second, it considers the (slender) evidence available on the extent to which the several parties draw votes from different sections of the population. Third, it is concerned with changes over time in the votes cast for the parties.

Development of a Two-party System

Broadly speaking, a system of two organized and disciplined parties has now become established in New Zealand. No Independent or member of a third party has been elected to the House of Representatives since 1943.[1] But it would be wrong to elaborate on this point without drawing attention to the amount of feeling which exists, or has existed until recently, against organized parties. This hostility has been expressed in several ways. One form, especially prominent in the 1890's, was to urge that the executive in New Zealand should be elected by the whole of the House of Representatives.[2] Such an 'elected executive', on the Swiss model, aimed at reducing the struggle of members for place and power, at making administrative ability the main quality for which ministers should be selected, at

[1] When Atmore (Independent, Nelson) was returned for the last time. He died before the election of 1946.

[2] This had been advocated in Australia by David Syme, editor and publisher of *The Age* (S. Encel, 'The Political Elite in Australia', *Political Studies*, vol. ix, no. 1, 1961, p. 18).

destroying the need for ministers to be unanimous (collective responsibility), and at preventing ministers from buying off opposition by spending public money. A reform of this kind was actually recommended by a Select Committee in 1891,[1] although it was never carried out. Several years later there was an additional motive for advocating an elected executive—a desire to curb Seddon's power as Prime Minister. 'Disraeli once said that the first duty of a Premier was loyalty to his Party. So far have we advanced since then, that a more correct political maxim for the present day would seem to be that the first duty of a party is loyalty to its chief—a maxim more immoral and certainly more deadly to liberty and good government than the older one.'[2] The movement for an elected executive fared no better when Reform was in power. Although Massey had previously voted for an elective executive bill, on attaining office in 1912 he chose his own Cabinet.[3] And later he sternly resisted Statham and his followers when they revived the proposal for an elected executive.[4]

Later on, less attention was given to the elected executive, and the attack on party was directed mainly against strict party discipline and against decisions being arrived at in confidential meetings of a parliamentary party (caucus). The Country Party attacked particularly strongly along these lines, holding that such caucus decisions were equivalent to a secret Parliament or to Star Chamber methods.[5] Mr. Sexton, a Country Party member, even introduced a motion in the House to give all members a free vote on matters affecting the safety, welfare, and honour of the Dominion.[6] He sat on the Labour Party benches and knew, from discussions, what the views of the Labour members were. But sometimes, because of party discipline, they voted against his amendments, even although these were in agreement with their own opinions. He also, incidentally, advocated an elective executive.[7]

[1] *Report of the Select Committee of the House of Representatives*, Session ii, 1891.

[2] *Parliamentary Reform* (1897), pp. 25–26, a pamphlet published anonymously by Edward Milland; an expanded version of a previous pamphlet, also published anonymously, *The Case against Parliamentary Government in New Zealand* (1891).

[3] W. J. Gardner, 2nd art. cit., p. 8.

[4] *Round Table*, vol. xi (1920–1), p. 213; Graham, op. cit., pp. 313–14.

[5] Rushworth, *Te Aroha News*, 20 June 1938.

[6] Rushworth, *Progress*, 27 Mar. 1939.

[7] Sexton, *Dominion*, 26 Sept. 1938.

Additional evidence of anti-party feeling is that organizations which, objectively, seem to have some of the characteristics of political parties, choose not to describe themselves as such. 'The People's Movement' denied in 1940 that it was 'just another party'.[1] And in 1954 Social Credit promised that, if it won any seats, it would not act like a political party except on financial questions. Like the French RPF, it originally claimed not to be a political party. This decision may have been partly influenced by misgivings about the propriety of forming a *party* to advance Social Credit instead of endeavouring to spread its influence by publicity and persuasion.[2] But also, conceivably, Social Credit 'was playing on the undercurrent of anti-party feeling in New Zealand'.[3]

One other manifestation of anti-party feeling takes the shape of wanting to reduce the initiative of the Member of Parliament so that he tends to become a mere delegate of the electors. An approach to this view, although not an extreme position, was adopted by W. J. Barnard when, after leaving the Labour Party, he fought the 1943 election as an Independent. In an election leaflet he promised that, as a member, he would be guided by a committee representative of all sections of the people, which he would consult from time to time. The nearest approximation to direct democracy, through almost entirely by-passing the member, was put forward by an Independent candidate in 1935. He asked the people to appoint him as their servant, and said he would obey their instructions. If elected he would issue a weekly paper, to cost not more than a penny. Each week there would be a coupon in the paper with space for name and address and the names of the measures being discussed in Parliament. The electors would instruct the member how to vote on each measure by filling in and returning the coupon. He would vote as the majority of the electors told him, provided that at least a quarter of them voted.[4] Less elaborately, in 1954 Social Credit said that on non-financial questions, any of their members who were elected would vote according to their own

[1] *A Lead for New Zealand: The Policy of the People's Movement* (Palmerston North, 1940), pp. 11–12. See p. 127, below. See also Daniels, op. cit., pp. 162 ff.
[2] See p. 63, above.
[3] North, op. cit., pp. 212–13.
[4] *Dominion*, 8 Nov. 1935.

convictions or would be instructed by citizens' advisory committees.[1]

Obviously, it is difficult to measure accurately the strength of anti-party feeling at any given time. On the other hand the general development of a 'two-party' system can be 'measured' by considering the decrease in the number of third-party and Independent candidates who contested elections, as well as the decrease in the number who *win* elections. The number of Independents contesting elections has declined during the last seventy years. From 1890 to 1914 major parties were often unable to prevent unofficial candidates from standing 'for' the party,[2] and complete Independents were also common. The early history of the New Zealand political Labour movement also provides many examples of Independent candidates.[3] The growth of party organization and the development of methods of candidate selection has almost eliminated 'unofficial' candidates. From 1918 onwards a very rough scheme might divide Independent candidates into the following main categories:

1. 'Anti-Labour Independents'. In the 1920's there were candidates, definitely opposed to Labour, who at some elections were unwilling to identify themselves completely with either one of the two parties. Included in this category were Statham, Bell, and Witty, also Wilkinson, originally Reform, who sat in Parliament as Independent member for Egmont from 1928 to 1943, with a brief spell in 1936 as a member of the National Party.

2. 'Anti-Fusion Independents'. These were candidates who belonged to one of the two non-Labour parties, but who opposed an official Coalition candidate in 1931. Some described themselves by using their original party label, but without the prefix, 'Coalition'. Others described themselves as 'Independents'. Black (Motueka), a previous United Party member, was elected as an Independent. Atmore, who had been Liberal and later Independent, had been a member of the United ministry, 1928–31. After 'fusion' he was dropped from the Cabinet, and he fought and won the 1931 election again as an Independent.

---

[1] North, op. cit., p. 213. Cf. Daniels, op. cit., p. 201, on the Real Democracy Movement, 1943.
[2] See pp. 249–50, below.   [3] Stevens, art. cit.

3. Members of a major party who were not nominated or renominated by the party, for reasons other than fusion, and who then ran as 'Independents'. Among them was Mr. Vallance, whose endorsement as National candidate for Marsden was withdrawn in 1954, and who then fought the seat as an Independent. A variation on this theme was provided by Mr. Sheat who failed in 1954 to win the nomination for a 'new' seat, Egmont (created by a change of electoral boundaries), which included portions of his existing seat (Patea). He resigned before the election, and at the by-election successfully contested his existing seat as an Independent against Labour, but not National, opposition. He did not fight the 1954 general election, although he fought, and won, as National candidate for Egmont in 1957.

4. Ex-major-party members who left their party on a difference of principle, and then stood as Independents. There is obviously some possible overlap with categories 2 and 3 here, depending on where the emphasis is laid. Among these were: McDougall, previously Coalition, who fought Mataura as an Independent in 1935 because of inadequate protection for Southland wheat;[1] Wright, who left the Coalition in 1933 when the exchange rate was altered and contested Wellington Suburbs as an Independent in 1935; Samuel, ex-Coalition, who fought Thames as an Independent in 1935;[2] Barnard, member for Napier, who, as previously mentioned, left the Labour Party after the Lee episode and fought as an Independent in 1943; Mr. Langstone, who fought his seat, Roskill, as 'Independent Labour' in 1949, after breaking with the Labour Party on conscription a few months before.

5. 'Simple Independents'. This group consists of Independents without any coherent or comprehensive ideology, who, in effect, have decided to 'have a bash' at getting into Parliament. One example was the single 'People's Party' candidate for Timaru in 1935 who advocated, among other things, a full 14 oz. pint of beer for 6d. instead of the existing 10 oz. Another was the *Dependent* (on the people's wishes) candidate for Petone in 1963. His only plank was 'No lies', and he literally took it around with him, a brightly painted yellow board with folding metal legs.

---

[1] *Mataura Ensign*, 21 Oct. 1935.
[2] See *Hauraki Plains Gazette*, 30 Oct. 1935.

6. 'Ideological Independents'. These included, for instance, those social crediters who ran as 'Independents' in the 1930's.

The examples given are illustrative, not exhaustive. Other, rarer, categories might be thought of, for instance that of 'Wrecking Independent', aiming specifically to secure the defeat of a particular major-party candidate. This category would contain Mr. C. G. Scrimgeour ('Scrim'), at one time a New Zealand 'radio personality', who dispensed a mixture of religion, radicalism, 'uplift', and sentimentality. Originally the tone of his programmes had been favourable to Labour, but after a quarrel with the party he was dismissed from his broadcasting job and then conscripted. He subsequently stood for Wellington Central in 1943 in an unsuccessful attempt to unseat Fraser, the Prime Minister. Still another possible category, 'Interest Group Independent', would include candidates who stood openly for a particular interest without going to the length of forming a party. A successful example was Polson, President of the Farmers' Union, who fought Stratford in 1928 in the interests of the farmers as an Independent candidate, and joined the National Party soon after the 1931 election.[1] T. C. Webb's candidature as 'Independent National' for Kaipara in 1943 defies easy classification. The previous National member, Coates, had been a Reform Prime Minister and 'strong man' of the 1931–5 Coalition Government. But he, and others in the National Party, including Kyle, differed from the leadership on the part which National should play in the War Administration.[2] Shortly before the 1943 election Coates stated his intention of standing as an Independent, and appeared to have the support of the local National Party organization.[3] When Coates died suddenly and T. C. Webb was adopted by the local organization, for tactical reasons he took the label of 'Independent National'.[4] Later he sat as a 'straight' National member. If a further category of Independents were contemplated, Webb might almost be classified as a 'tactical Independent'. Some temporary 'Independents' are also omitted from this analysis,

[1] The National Conference of the Farmers' Union had previously asked Polson to make the change (interview with Sir William Polson, Jan. 1959).
[2] See pp. 55–56, above.
[3] North Auckland Times, 3, 5, and 26 May 1943.
[4] Hokianga Herald, 22 July 1943. See also Daniels, op. cit., p. 224.

because, although they left a major party and sat as Independents in the House, they did not contest an election as Independents. In this group come Downie Stewart, who left the Coalition at the same time as Wright (1933) on the exchange question, and sat as an Independent until 1935, and Kyle, who broke with National in 1942 and remained in the House as an Independent member until 1943.

Above all the thing to note about the successful Independents is that they owed what success they had, in a double sense, to the 'support' of one of the major parties. Since 1935 all Independents who have sat in Parliament have previously belonged to a major party. More important, all those elected as Independents owed their election to the fact that they were not opposed by one of the major parties. Thus, taking the four Independents returned in 1935, the National Party did not oppose Wright (Wellington Suburbs) in 1935 or 1938, or Wilkinson (Egmont) in 1935 or 1938; Labour did not oppose Atmore (Nelson) in 1935, 1938, or 1943, or McDougall (Mataura) in 1935. Voting records in the House show that, in return, Wright and Wilkinson voted habitually for National, while Atmore and McDougall generally voted with Labour. One way of 'sealing the compact' between an Independent who is in general sympathy with a party and the party is for him to agree to support the party (or, alternatively, not to vote against it) on a vote of no confidence. At the 1954 election the National Party did not put up a candidate of its own for Westland, a hopeless seat. But it supported an Independent, who in turn agreed not to vote against National on a no-confidence motion, if he were elected.[1] A further illustration of the trend towards a two-party system is provided by the fate of the Country Party. In 1935 the two successful Country Party candidates, Rushworth (Bay of Islands) and Sexton (Franklin), were not opposed by Labour, and in the House, 1935–8, they generally voted for the Government. But in 1938 Labour decided to contest both seats. Sexton was defeated in a three-cornered fight, and Rushworth's decision to retire was caused partly by his knowledge that Labour would intervene at the 1938 election.

Summing up, the confused situation in the 1920's and early 1930's made it still possible for some Independents and minor-

[1] North, op. cit., p. 32. T. C. Webb had made a similar pledge in 1943.

party candidates to be elected. But their only chance of being elected lay in their not being opposed by one of the parties, and they would be exempted from such opposition only if they 'toed the line' almost as closely as a major-party member. After the death of Atmore in 1946 the trend has arrived at its obvious destination, and no Independents have since been elected to the House of Representatives.

Turning from Independents to minor parties, the most important of these, the Country Party, the Democrats, Lee's Democratic Labour Party, the Real Democracy Movement, the Social Credit Political League and the 1963 Liberals, have been mentioned in the last chapter. Paradoxically, the party which fought on the narrowest front, the Country Party, was most successful in winning seats. The greatest number of seats it ever contested (6) was in 1931. Yet it held Bay of Islands from 1929 to 1938 and Franklin from 1935 to 1938. On the other hand, other parties have fought on a much wider front, and have seemed to approximate more to being 'national' parties, and yet have failed to win a seat.

TABLE I

Minor Parties, Candidates, and Votes[1]
1935–63

Party	Year	No. of candidates	Proportion of total vote
Democrats	1935	51	8%
Democratic Labour	1943	43[2]	4%
Social Credit	1954	79	11%
Social Credit	1957	80	7%
Social Credit	1960	80	9%
Social Credit	1963	76	8%

Indeed one reason for their failure was precisely because, lacking a strong supporting 'base', they *did* fight on a wide front, both in terms of programme and in the number of seats contested. The Country Party, on the other hand, was really

[1] Only the more important minor parties are included. The Communist Party regularly contests several seats, but with little success. For instance in 1963 it fought just over a quarter of the seats but secured only about 1 per cent. of the vote for each.

[2] Estimates differ; some say there were over 50 DLP candidates, but an authority who ought to know (Lee, *Simple on a Soapbox*, op. cit., p. 242) says there were 43. But he seems to be wrong in claiming 5 per cent. of the vote.

an interest group with strong support in a particular locality, which had decided, temporarily, to act as a political party. *Potentially*, therefore, the Democrats, Democratic Labour, and Social Credit were 'national' parties, capable of appealing to electors on a nation-wide scale. Without radically altering its programme, and so possibly losing its hard core of North Island farming support, the Country Party was *not* capable of becoming a national party. But, just because its support *was* geographically concentrated, it succeeded in returning two members to the House. Even then, once the depression was over, it was unable to maintain this slender representation when opposed simultaneously by both the major parties.

Other minor parties, and rumours of parties, are still heard of from time to time. Small paragraphs appear in the newspapers saying that it has been decided to found a 'Socialist Party' or a 'Liberal Party' in a certain town. Less tangible, but potentially of greater interest, are the reports which have occasionally circulated in recent years that groups of businessmen have become dissatisfied with the National Party, because it is 'not conservative enough', and have contemplated raising funds to be used to finance a new right-wing party.

Of course, distinct groups may still exist *within* a superficially 'monolithic' party. The existence of such groups in the past can be easily documented. The Liberal Party in the 1880's contained 'inside' it a 'Young New Zealand Reform Party', which met in caucus, and even had its own 'constitution and rules', chairman, secretary, and whip.[1] In 1905 apparently there was a 'Country Party' within the ministry, which even had a Leader, Roderick Mackenzie, and a whip; its *raison d'être* was objection to further legislation on behalf of city interests.[2] More remarkable still, in 1900 the Auckland Members of Parliament, including members for farming districts in South Auckland, met weekly *without distinction of party*, to co-ordinate their efforts to obtain public works for the area.[3] More recently, after 'fusion' in 1931, the former United Party members in the Coalition used to hold informal meetings from which ex-Reform members were excluded.[4]

[1] Foster, op. cit., pp. 56–60. The party's minute book is in the General Assembly Library, Wellington.
[2] Foster, op. cit., p. 135, quoting *Evening Post*, 8 July 1905.
[3] Graham, op. cit., pp. 46–47.
[4] Interview, Sir Walter Broadfoot, Mar. 1959.

Ex-Reform members of the Coalition also held at least one separate caucus.[1] Not so much publicity is given to the activities of similar groups in the parties at the present day. But in the middle 1950's there was an identifiable group in the Labour Party which favoured a closer approach to neutrality in foreign policy and expressed dissatisfaction with the degree of influence which the Federation of Labour exercised on the party. Messrs. Freer (Mount Albert), Anderton (Auckland Central), and Connolly (Dunedin Central) apparently belonged to this group.[2] None of these groups, however, went to the lengths of the British Bevanites whose M.P.s not only met regularly, but also toured the country publicly attacking the official Labour leaders. However, the fact remains that not only has there been a movement towards a two-party system, there has also been a tightening of organization and discipline within each party.[3] In this sense there has been a tendency towards streamlining the party system—towards uniformity.

Swing, Candidates, and Local Issues

In another respect there has also been an approach towards 'uniformity'. Between one election and another changes in the votes received by the major-party candidates for the various constituencies are remarkably uniform throughout New Zealand. Calculations of these changes are made difficult by alterations of boundaries and also by movements of population from one place to another. For instance, it is generally believed that the Tamaki seat, which had a National majority of nearly 2,000 in 1954 and a Labour majority of over 700 in 1957, was lost largely because of population shifts. A similar reason may have contributed to Labour's winning Manukau and the new seat of Manurewa in 1963. But the 'swing'[4] in most constituencies has been remarkably uniform at recent elections. Between 1946 and 1949, 1949 and 1951, and 1957 and 1960,

[1] On the issue of whether Reform should end the Coalition and fight the next election as a separate party (interview with Sir William Polson, Jan. 1959).
[2] Milburn, art. cit. (p. 37 above), p. 180.
[3] See Ch. V., below.
[4] Defined as the average of one major party's loss plus the other party's gain, expressed as a percentage of the total votes cast for the two major parties (see H. G. Nicholas, *The British General Election of 1950* (London, 1950), Appendix by D. E. Butler, p. 315).

there were no boundary changes. However, at the elections in the first two periods some seats were contested by third parties, and in 1957 and 1960 all seats were contested by Social Credit. Table II shows the swing for over three-quarters of the seventy-six European seats for each period.

TABLE II

Non-Maori Seats Fought only by the Major[1] Parties, or where Minor Parties Obtained Less than 1 per cent. of the Vote

Swing between Labour and National Parties		Number of seats		
		1946–9	*1949–51*	*1957–60*
In favour of Labour		2	5	2
In favour of National	0–0·9%	2	6	4
,, ,,	1–1·9%	1	14	1
,, ,,	2–2·9%	8	21	10
,, ,,	3–3·9%	19	8	7
,, ,,	4–4·9%	14	3	14
,, ,,	5–5·9%	6	1	7
,, ,,	6–6·9%	5	0	12
,, ,,	7% or over	0	0	10
Total		57	58	67

Thus in 1946–9 72 per cent. of the seats in the table had swings of between 2 and 4·9 per cent., and in 1949–51 74 per cent. had swings of between 1 and 3·9 per cent. But in 1957–60 the swing was rather less uniform. Only just under half the comparable seats fell into a similar range of between 4 and 6·9 per cent. The swing *inside each Island* was rather more uniform. In the table above, 6 out of the 7 swings below 2 per cent. were in the South Island; 9 out of the 10 swings of 7 per cent. and above were in the North Island.[2] The uniformity of swing seems to have been about the same as in Britain.[3] Because of boundary

---

[1] For this table Social Credit is counted as a 'major' party in 1957 and 1960. Its existence, of course, affects the swing between the major parties. But its greatest impact was at the 1954 election, which does not feature in this table.

[2] Cf. Chapman, Jackson, and Mitchell, op. cit., p. 221.

[3] Thus in Britain, 1950–1, in three-quarters of the seats there was a swing of between 0 and 3 per cent. to the Conservatives (D. E. Butler, *The British General Election of 1951* (London, 1952), p. 242). The spread was rather greater in 1955 (Butler, *The British General Election of 1955*, p. 202), and was greater still in 1959 (Butler and Rose, *The British General Election of 1959*, pp. 236–7). It should be remembered that the calculations for New Zealand made above are for selected seats where the conditions at successive elections were closely comparable.

changes it would be hard to calculate uniformity of swing in 1960–3 without elaborate investigation. But there seems to have been considerable *lack* of uniformity, which was reflected in sitting members doing better than others. Although the total swing to Labour was small, it was appreciably higher in the South Island.

To show that swing is *relatively* uniform throughout the country is not to prove that there are no local variations in voting. But it suggests that the personality of the candidates and local issues are less powerful than they are sometimes believed to be. The old belief that a good candidate can attract a sizable personal vote dies hard. Although this was probably true in the past, it has almost certainly ceased to be true nowadays. The advent of the Labour Party and its use of 'class themes' took away the personal vote which established non-Labour members enjoyed. In Westland the Liberal member lost his seat partly because, according to him, in the 1920's Labour organizers persuaded mill-hands to vote the party ticket and not to cast a personal vote for him.[1] There was still some scope for 'personal votes' as between Reform and Liberal, but by 1935 this possibility had also disappeared. There is no reason to believe that normally New Zealand is substantially different from Britain on this question, and it has been said that only the truly exceptional British candidate has a personal advantage of more than 500 votes; this would correspond to about 150 votes in New Zealand. Of course, in a *very* marginal electorate, this could be decisive. It is not possible to quote lengthy instances to support this view, but the case of Mr. Kitts, a former Labour Member of Parliament, may be mentioned. Mr. Kitts was regarded as a popular figure in Wellington, and had been elected mayor in 1956. But in 1957, when he defended the Parliamentary seat, Wellington Central, which he held at the same time, there was little evidence of a large personal vote.[2] In 1960 he actually lost

[1] Interview, Mr. T. E. Y. Seddon, Dec. 1958.

[2] Either from the actual election figures or from an election survey (see Milne, *Political Science*, art. cit., p. 58). Fewer than 1 per cent. of the voters in the survey said that they had changed to Labour because of the candidate. Nor was there evidence of a large personal vote in Dunedin Central in 1960 (Austin Mitchell, 'Dunedin Central', *Political Science*, vol. xiv, no. 2 (1962), p. 66). Another version of Mitchell is given in Chapman, Jackson, and Mitchell, op. cit. N. M. Donald, 'The General Election of 1949', *Political Science*, vol. iii, no. 1 (1951), says that in one electorate in 1949 6 per cent. gave preference for the candidate

Wellington Central with a swing against Labour which was greater than the average, which may have been partly attributable to movements of population.

At the 1960 election there was no evidence of a personal vote, although there was one possible instance of an *anti*-personal vote.[1] In 1963, however, the situation was quite otherwise. In the absence of any marked uniform swing to either party, certain sitting members seem to have benefited, in some instances to the tune of about 5 per cent. Thus Mr. Lapwood (National, Rotorua) and, in two almost adjoining electorates, Messrs. Kirk (Labour, Lyttelton) and Walker (National, St. Albans) did outstandingly better than the party averages. Conceivably, in the absence of any deep division of the parties on national issues, voters were more influenced by the personalities of the candidates than in previous elections. Perhaps, unless subsequent elections produce more controversial issues, personalities may continue to be important in the future.

The relative uniformity of the swing in different constituencies, at least until 1963, also suggests that the electors are not greatly affected by local issues. 'Local issues' in this sense should perhaps be distinguished from major local claims, arising from deep-seated dissatisfaction with economic conditions. An instance of the latter is the claim of the Hobson electorate for general economic development. Another instance might be Buller, as shown by the by-election in 1962. Formerly it was widely thought that votes could be gained by use of the 'pork barrel', mainly by the allocation of particular public works projects to selected areas. Indeed it was even possible at one time to gain votes in the *House*, not only among the electorate, by this method. The classic instance of this concerns the four 'Auckland rats' who went over to the Hall Government in 1879 to obtain 'justice for Auckland'.[2] Some twenty years later Reeves wrote that members would sometimes support a Government for what they could get for their districts.[3] Later the emphasis altered. Members no longer changed parties so readily. 'Pork' was now a party weapon, wielded by the Government to

personally as their reason for voting. But the account does not say how many *changed* because of preference for a candidate.

[1] Chapman, Jackson, and Mitchell, op. cit., pp. 222–7 (Mount Albert).
[2] T. G. Wilson, *The Grey Government, 1877–9*, pp. 52–53.
[3] *The Long White Cloud*, p. 256.

increase support for government candidates. Seddon in 1905 'impressed the country districts with the notion that a district which did not favour the Government need not expect the Government to favour it . . .'.[1] The result was to divert the attention of members to 'the needs of the district' and away from national issues. 'With the development of politics into a contest between the various districts for votes from the Treasury, the member for Cow Flat is content to let others make the laws if he can but obtain a large enough share of the public funds to enable him to go back to his district with the reputation of being the best man who can be sent to Parliament.'[2] In 1935 Mr. Clinkard, standing for Rotorua against Mr. Doidge, claimed credit for his successful manipulation of the pork barrel. 'Although he gave all credit for the creation of the main baths to Sir Joseph Ward, Mr. Clinkard said that he rightly claimed the credit for the creation of the Blue Baths. Could Mr. Doidge have done as well, queried the speaker? This bath building had been built, not in times of prosperity, but in the years of depression, yet it had been finally accomplished by the "party hack", as Mr. Doidge had seen fit to call the speaker.'[3]

As late as the 1928 election the argument was widely used that it would pay electors to vote for the winning party, because they would receive more benefits through having a government member.[4] However, by this time some non-governmental candidates were maintaining that the merits of the projects and the assiduity of the local member were more important than pork.[5] Indeed there is a flaw in the argument that members who belong to the government party are in a unique position to solicit votes successfully by promising 'pork'. Governmental appeals in areas which do *not* have a government member, or appeals in any area by an Opposition which has a good chance of winning, would seem to be, prima facie, at least equally persuasive.[6]

[1] 'Back to Democracy', *Evening Post*, 5 July 1906.
[2] M. C. Keane, 'Political Sketches III—The Late Parliament', *Current Thought*, 2 Nov. 1908, pp. 94–95.
[3] *Rotorua Post*, 27 Nov. 1935.
[4] Interviews with Messrs. T. E. Y. Seddon, and A. A. McLachlan, Dec. 1958.
[5] W. A. Veitch (Wanganui), *Wanganui Herald*, 26 Nov. 1935; interview with Mr. A. C. A. Sexton, Nov. 1958.
[6] On pork, see P. Campbell, art. cit. (1955), pp. 201–3.

The present situation seems to be that, although members are most attentive to the needs of their districts and devote much (probably too much)[1] time to them, the influence of local issues in votes is small. One recent instance to the contrary may be quoted. At the 1957 election the Labour Party promised to connect the town of Nelson with the South Island railway system. This seems to have been responsible for the fact that the swing to Labour in Nelson was above the national average, and the drop in the National vote was the biggest for any seat.[2]

However, cynics could say that the pork-barrel still existed, but in a different form. In the 1940's a right-wing pamphlet said that, while in the Liberal era votes had been traded for material things, 'to-day it is by the unashamed flogging of humanitarianism and the conferring of legalised loafing at the expense of the tax-payer that these precious votes are secured in the name of Democracy and in the name of Progress'.[3] Particular offers to individual districts have been replaced by offers applying to the whole country, in the form of promised tax rebates, for instance. To use the previous terminology for indicating the growing uniformity of politics, pork has not disappeared; it has merely been 'nationalized'.

Sources of the Parties' Votes

The popular belief in New Zealand is that the National Party draws electoral support from the farmers and from the better-off people in the towns, while the Labour Party secures the votes of the industrial workers. This view is broadly correct, but it is not quantitative, nor does it account for *changes* in voting on the part of individuals. Nor are the categories exhaustive enough. There are various kinds of 'farmers', and there are many people such as clerks, civil servants, and small shopkeepers, who do not fit into any of these groups.

Of course, it is possible to make inferences from a party's programme about the groups from which it draws, and hopes to draw, support, even although parties which aspire to be 'national' in scope tend to offer 'something for everyone'. Thus Siegfried pointed to the Liberal policy of a graduated land tax

[1] P. Campbell, art. cit. (1955), pp. 201–3; Kelson, op. cit., ch. 11.
[2] Chapman, Jackson, and Mitchell, op. cit., p. 213.
[3] Iconoclast, *Politics is Paramount* (Wanganui, 1946), p. 7.

and a graduated income tax as having successfully secured the support of the small landowner and the working man.[1] And the sources from which parties obtain their funds are often suggestive of the policies they follow and of which sections in the electorate support them. The fact that Labour is financed mainly by trade unions, and the less open financing of the National Party by business and farming groups provides suggestive information. But the political process does not work in a strictly mechanistic way. Even if the sources of a party's finances are known and its propaganda to various groups is analysed, the effects on the electors can still not be calculated by using crude indexes of material benefits. Thus, the movement for freehold and the growth of the Reform Party are regarded as mainly North Island phenomena. And yet in the opening years of this century the Opposition (Reform Party) gained about the same increase in votes, varying to some extent with the exact dates chosen, in the South Island as in the North Island. In 1935 the Democrats, with an essentially 'town' programme and financed largely by city money, nevertheless secured as big a vote in the countryside as in the towns.

One form of electoral research in New Zealand has been to compare maps or tables, showing how the representation of particular constituencies has altered through time. This type of research has thrown light on differences in voting behaviour between the two islands; for instance it has indicated the advance of Reform in the South Island in the 1920s after it had ceased to make headway in the North Island, and, in the 1930s, the resistance to Labour Party penetration in Otago (South Island), an area with a static population and declining electoral representation.[2] Electoral maps have also illustrated vividly Chapman's hypothesis of the persistence of 'humanitarianism' by suggesting a close correspondence between the areas won by the Liberals in 1908 and those won by Labour in 1935.[3]

A development of this kind of research has taken the form of the investigation of electoral statistics, which in New Zealand are available down to polling-booth level. The most assiduous

[1] Op. cit., p. 189.
[2] Chapman, op. cit., pp. 153–7, and 143–4. This is reminiscent of the survival of Liberal loyalties in the 'Celtic fringe' in Britain.
[3] Ibid., pp. 120–1.

and ingenious exponent of this art is Professor Robert Chapman.[1] The findings are highly suggestive, but not conclusive. There is a limit to what can be learned about voting behaviour by studying electoral statistics. By themselves they cannot give a true picture of the pressures and cross-pressures affecting an individual voter, which come from parents, husband or wife, friends, co-religionists, fellow trade unionists, and so on. At worst this kind of study sinks into the sands of statistical aridity.[2] At best it does violence to the evidence by assuming, without proof, the existence of certain personal feelings and attitudes on the part of the voters—a statistical version of the pathetic fallacy.[3]

Information on voting behaviour in New Zealand has not yet been greatly amplified by opinion polls and sample surveys. The results of some polls, mainly on the popularity of the Government or on vote intentions, have appeared in the *Auckland Star*. The results of others conducted by political parties, for instance those taken for the National Party since before the 1957 election, have not been published. Some surveys did not cover the occupations or social class of the electors. The only surveys which have been published and which do contain information on these questions are for two constituencies, Wellington Central in 1957 and Dunedin Central in 1960.[4] Some of the results were much as expected; for instance people in the highest-ranked occupations tended to vote National, those in the lowest-ranked ones to vote Labour. Similar, expected, results were found for education and (in Wellington Central) when the voter's own estimate of his social class was compared with his

[1] Notably in Chapman, Jackson, and Mitchell, op. cit., chs. xi and xii, and Chapman, 'The Response to Labour and the Question of Parallelism of Opinion, 1928–1960', Chapman and Sinclair (eds.), op. cit.

[2] e.g. M. L. Prichard and J. B. Tabb, *The New Zealand General Election of 1960* (Auckland, 1961).

[3] See the review of Chapman's ch. xii, Chapman, Jackson, and Mitchell, by A. D. Robinson, 'Why Did Labour Lose?', *Political Science*, vol. xv, no. 1 (1963). Two main criticisms are of Chapman's assumptions on the nature of non-voters and of his neglect to take account of the possibility that electoral statistics 'hide a complex process of shifts among parties and in and out of voting' (p. 51). See also Austin Ranney, 'The Utility and Limitations of Aggregate Data in the Study of Electoral Behavior', in Ranney (ed.), *Essays on the Behavioral Study of Politics* (Urbana, 1962).

[4] Milne, *Political Science*, art. cit.; Mitchell, *Political Science*, vol. xiv, no. 2. The School of Political Science, Victoria University of Wellington, conducted a large-scale survey on the 1963 election, which will be published shortly.

vote. There may be a tendency for Roman Catholics, irrespective of social class, to vote Labour, but it is apparently not as strong as in Australia. The main value of such surveys is not to tell us what we know already, for instance, that most manual workers vote Labour, but to give quantitative information on *how many* of them vote Labour. About 15 or 20 per cent. of the manual workers vote National. Unless this and similar findings are kept in mind, it is only too easy to slide from correct, though not quantitative, statements, such as 'most manual workers vote Labour', to the incorrect, '(all) manual workers vote Labour'.

In practice the parties do not make an appeal on a purely class or group basis. They do not, in cold blood, look for a winning combination of classes or groups and then go all out to obtain their support, irrespective of the interests of other classes or groups of electors. This may be illustrated by considering the Labour Party's policy towards the farmer. It has been mentioned that in the 1920's Labour altered its land policy to make a greater appeal to farmers. But it was not until 1935 that it won any rural seats,[1] apart from seats which were only apparently 'rural', such as Westland and Waimarino (later Rotorua), which contained a substantial group of industrial workers.[2] In 1935 Labour contested most of the constituencies which were clearly rural, the majority of them for the first time, substantially increased its total rural vote, and won eighteen rural seats. At the 1938 election it again increased its total rural vote, although almost all the increase was the result of its having contested additional seats. But it lost more rural seats than it gained, including several dairy seats in the centre of the North Island. Various reasons were put forward for the loss of these 'butter seats'. Some small dairy farmers may have thought that Labour had broken its promise to bring in Social Credit legislation; recovery had followed depression and the farmers were no longer 'desperate' enough to vote Labour; they now considered that the guaranteed price offered them in 1938 was insufficient to meet rising costs of production. At any rate, in

[1] One source of Labour votes in rural areas has been the railway and construction workers who have been resident long enough in the area to acquire the right to vote there (Sharp, op. cit., p. 72). The Labour Government was accused of deploying these workers with an eye to their electoral effect at the 1938 election (Lipson, op. cit., p. 331).

[2] Lipson, op. cit., pp. 176 ff.

1938 the farmers were 'let off with a warning'. Mr. James Thorn, M.P., quoted in the Labour Party newspaper *Standard*, wrote,

> Two facts stand out strikingly in these election results. One is that New Zealand has come politically under the dominance of the cities and towns, and the other is that the farming vote is declining in importance as a factor that determines the complexion of Governments in New Zealand.
>
> As it is certain that the political structure of the towns will grow in future, and that what are now rural seats will tend to lose their purely rural character, the stability of the Labour Government is assured.
>
> For farmers . . . the elections have this lesson: that their welfare lies not in following ill-natured leaders or the moneyed daily press, but in a sympathetic co-operation with the Government. It is to be hoped they will appreciate this, because in the bitterness political conflict engenders any blindly prejudiced attitude on their part may easily react to their disadvantage.[1]

In spite of this warning the trend continued, and more rural seats were lost in 1943. The implied threat behind the warning was carried out in 1945, when the country quota was abolished. Abolition had been in Labour's programme before 1935, but so long as there were prospects that Labour could win majorities in the country as well as in the towns the quota was left undisturbed. But when it was clear that the quota was a permanent electoral liability it was removed.

The abolition of the quota was strenuously opposed by farmers' organizations and by the National Party.[2] But Labour was content to reap the electoral advantages of the change. Abolition was not a prelude to liquidation of the kulaks or even to anti-farmer legislation. Labour could obtain (and has obtained in 1946 and 1957) a majority in Parliament without winning any rural seats, although, in spite of Mr. Thorn's argument, this did not imply that the party could remain in power indefinitely. But for several reasons it cannot afford to neglect the interests of the farmers. New Zealand's survival depends upon her exports, and they depend on the farmers. Also the number of actual 'farmers' is much smaller than the number of persons

---

[1] *Standard*, 28 Oct. 1938.
[2] D. G. Harper, 'The Doctrine of the Mandate' (Victoria unpublished thesis, 1955), pp. 22–23.

identified with farming as a way of life.[1] As has been said already, New Zealand is not sharply divided into 'town' and 'country'. Many who are not actually farmers were born on a farm, have relatives who are farmers, make their living buying from or selling to farmers, or hope to buy a farm later on in life. Those who do business in a country town are speedily made aware of a drop in agricultural prices when they find that the farmers are spending less money. Indeed, when classifying the occupations of Members of Parliament, the difficulty of separating 'farmers' from 'non-farmers' has already been encountered. In passing, it may be mentioned that the man who was most often regarded as the personal embodiment of the industrial power of the trade unions, Mr. F. P. Walsh, worked as a shepherd when he was a boy, and owned before his death a highly mechanized, efficient, and lucrative farm. Lastly, the New Zealand sense of fair play would be offended by a Labour Government which seemed to be unreasonably 'tough' with the farmers.

Trends in Voting

The decline in the proportion of farmers in the population may be looked at from a different point of view: how does the decline affect the National Party's prospects? The pertinent question might no longer be 'Can the Labour Party gain a majority in the House of Representatives without winning any rural seats?' It might be rather, with the declining number of rural seats, 'How can the National Party ever win majorities in the future?' Fifty years ago the Reform Party was able to win its majorities only with the aid of the country quota, which the National Party has now lost. On this view the prospects of the National Party could be gloomy, because, with the passage of time, its 'core' of rural support will become less and less important electorally. On the other hand it could be argued that any National losses from a decline in the number of rural seats will probably be gradual, and that most electors do not change their votes after the age of thirty or so.[2] It would seem, however, that

[1] Cf. the tendency to overestimate the size of the British 'farming vote', J. Roland Pennock, 'The Political Power of British Agriculture', *Political Studies*, vol. vii, no. 3 (1959).
[2] On stability of voting in Wellington Central see Milne, *Political Science*, art. cit., p. 59. For more detailed information on the U.S.A. and Britain, respectively, see B. R. Berelson, P. F. Lazarsfeld, and W. N. McPhee, *Voting* (Chicago, 1954),

National Party fears could be unnecessarily pessimistic. When 'urban growth' occurs 'within the countryside', National Party supporters, even although they may change their occupation or their place of work or both may, so to speak, take their attitudes with them.[1]

A related point, which could favour National, is that the party seems to be strongest in those parts of the country which are growing fastest. One illustration of this is that the party is relatively stronger in the North Island, which is developing quicker. One of the surprising features of the 1963 election was the high National vote in the fast-growing constituency of Rotorua and the fact that National won the new Taupo seat. Again, inside the South Island, there is a clear difference in the rate of development of Invercargill (held by National) and Timaru (held by Labour).[2] This argument is not substantially altered by the fact that in some growing city areas (for instance, in the Manukau and Manurewa seats) the support for Labour has increased. The increasing Labour vote could be attributed to an increase in housing for particular income groups. Labour, on the other hand, 'is strongest now in the South Island, the home of dying parties'.[3] Apart from the influence of the relative rates of development in the two islands, some part of National's relative non-success in the South Island might be attributable to its comparative lack of enthusiasm for some Southern sectional claims, the Nelson railway and cotton mill, a cardiac unit for Dunedin, and encouragement of sugar-beet growing.[4] But such imperviousness to Southern local pressures might be to National's advantage in growing areas in the North. The correlation between rate of growth and voting National is worth attention in the future. But this is only one of many factors which need to be taken into account in guessing what the trend of party politics will be in New Zealand. The future composition of the electorate will be influenced by immigration; by differential

chs. 6 and 7 and pp. 302–3; R. S. Milne and H. C. McKenzie, *Marginal Seat, 1955* (London, 1958), chs. 5 and 6.

[1] Cf. Chapman, Jackson, and Mitchell, op. cit., p. 237.

[2] Cf. Mr. Holyoake's remarks *Otago Daily Times*, 9 Nov. 1963.

[3] Chapman, Jackson, and Mitchell, op. cit., p. 295.

[4] But in Westport, at the Buller by-election of 1962, National argued that the electors had returned Labour members for years who had done nothing to bring prosperity to the area. They should try National for a change.

birth-rates among different social classes and religions, which might be expected to favour Labour; by differential death-rates among different social classes, which might be expected to favour National; by the changing age-composition of the electorate, which will soon contain an increasing proportion of younger electors.[1] The attitudes of electors who have just reached voting age are of particular importance. The holding of a four-and-a-half day youth forum in May 1964, although in no way connected with party politics, showed the National Government's awareness of this point. One temporary influence, clearly favourable to National, is that those regular Labour voters, who are implacably opposed to any right-wing party because of their sufferings in the depression, are now dying off increasingly rapidly. All of these factors are relevant, although it may be hard to estimate them quantitatively.

Some recent speculations about the future of British parties may be looked at with reference to New Zealand. For instance, it has been observed that in Britain the number of workers in tertiary occupations (such as clerks, salesmen, and other white-collar workers) is increasing, compared with the number in jobs such as mining and manufacturing. This would seem to point to potential long-term gains for the Conservative Party.[2] In New Zealand, although the proportion of the population engaged in mining is decreasing, the existing emphasis on building up local industry may mean that future increases in the number of manufacturing workers may approximate to increases in the numbers engaged in tertiary occupations.[3] However, manufacturing in New Zealand is not conducted in large-scale dark Satanic mills, and workers engaged in manufacturing are unlikely to have similar attitudes to their 'counterparts' in nineteenth-century Britain. In Britain a bleak outlook has also been predicted for Labour, because the electors see the party as closely identified with the working class, while fewer and fewer

[1] Frank G. Dickinson, *The Younging of Electorates* (Bulletin 105, The American Medical Association, Chicago, 1958).

[2] H. A. Turner, *Guardian*, 20 Oct. 1959. But this increase was not reflected in a comparable increase in the Conservative vote, 1955–9 (Richard Rose, 'How the Party System Works', Mark Abrams *et al.*, *Must Labour Lose?* (London, 1960), p. 77.

[3] Cf. Colin R. Larsen, 'New Zealand's Future Development', *New Zealand Economist and Taxpayer*, 26 Apr. 1953, quoted in J. B. Condliffe, *The Welfare State in New Zealand*, pp. 166–7.

electors actually regard themselves as being working-class.[1] The evidence in New Zealand is not so conclusive. A survey, based on a single constituency, suggests that many electors identify the party with the working class and that few electors think of themselves as being working-class.[2] One handicap which afflicts the New Zealand Labour Party, probably to a greater degree than the British Labour Party, is its loss of *élan* and deeply held convictions. Here it is enough to say, with proper academic caution, that so many considerations may affect support for the New Zealand parties in the future, that no single one seems to be of outstanding importance. However, in view of Labour's short tenure of office after being returned to power in 1957 the National Party is now almost assuming the character of a 'dominant party'; there has been only one three-year interruption in its rule since 1949.

However, Labour is undeniably the 'dominant' party in the four Maori seats. National's vote has recovered a little since its lowest point in 1957, but Labour can still collect 70 per cent. of the major-party vote. Further National gains may result from the energy of the Minister of Maori Affairs and from National Party legislation, for instance on the Maori Educational Foundation, which provides for a capital fund for the promotion of Maori education. In the long run the National Party may gain from the spread of education and prosperity and the diminution of depression memories among the Maoris, which may reduce economic and 'class' reasons for voting Labour. National has also been putting more effort into Maori organization through its Maori Advisory and Organization Committee. It may take a long time, however, for the image of Labour as 'the party which helps the Maoris' to fade. Abolition of the four Maori seats has often been considered in a speculative way. But Labour is as unwilling to lose four certain seats as National is to take the chance that it might suffer a net loss from the spread of so many Labour votes among the European electorates.[3]

[1] Abrams, *Must Labour Lose?* pp. 20–23.
[2] Milne, *Political Science*, art. cit., tabs. i and x. From a preliminary look at the findings of the 1963 election study by the School of Political Science, Victoria University of Wellington, it seems that few people in the sample (even those in trade unions) identify themselves with trade unionists.
[3] W. K. Jackson and G. A. Wood, 'The New Zealand Parliament and Maori Representation', *Historical Studies, Australia and New Zealand*, vol. xi, no. 43 (1964).

The study of recent election results throws some light on the *changes* in support for the parties between one election and another. One point to notice is that the seats gained by a New Zealand party are not always proportionate to the percentage of the vote which it wins. This is partly the consequence of the fact that, in what is substantially a two-party system, a major party with more votes than its nearest opponent tends to win a disproportionately large share of the seats.[1] In previous years there was also the distorting feature of the country quota, which gave a 'bonus' to parties, such as Reform and, later, National, which polled strongly in rural areas. The National Party still draws a minor 'bonus' from two different sources. First, there is a tendency, also found in Britain, for the biggest Labour majorities to exceed the biggest anti-Labour ones. This means, so to speak, that a number of 'spare' Labour votes are piled up in safe Labour seats, without benefit to the party. Second, although the country quota has gone, the Representation Commission is allowed a certain 'tolerance' in drawing boundaries, and this has the effect of reducing the size of those constituencies which are largest in area, namely the rural seats. Furthermore, by the 1956 Electoral Act, representation is based on total, not adult, population;[2] therefore the higher birth-rates in the rural areas, and the tendency of adults to migrate from them to the towns, tend to raise their representation. Consequently the National Party has recently had an advantage at elections. As an extreme instance, it won only a fraction more of the votes than Labour in 1954, about one-third of 1 per cent. more, but gained ten more seats.[3]

In studying 'swings' between one election and another two broad considerations must be borne in mind. There is 'massive stability' in voting behaviour. 'Neither the National nor the Labour Party has fallen below 40 per cent. of the total vote since

[1] See the 'Nuffield' series of accounts of the British general elections since 1945, particularly Butler, *The British General Election of 1951*, pp. 275-7.

[2] Total population was used up to 1945, when it was changed to adult population at the same time that the country quota was ended. In 1950 total population was again made the basis. On the 1956 Electoral Act, see Scott, op. cit., pp. 6-10.

[3] See R. H. Brookes, 'Seats and Votes in New Zealand', *The Australian Journal of Politics and History*, vol. v, no. 2 (1959) and 'The Analysis of Distorted Representation in Two-Party Single-Member Elections', *Political Science*, vol. xii, no. 2 (1960); K. J. Scott, 'Gerrymandering for Democracy', *Political Science*, vol. vii, no. 2 (1955); Chapman, Jackson, and Mitchell, op. cit., pp. 294-5.

the present party system was established in 1936.'[1] It may also
be guessed, although election survey data are far from complete,
that most individual electors vote the same way at successive
elections. This stability is also seen in parliamentary seats. About
three-quarters of the seats are unlikely to change parties at most
elections.[2] National has a firm hold on the rural seats and some
'blue ribbon' city seats, such as Remuera (Auckland), Karori
(Wellington), and Fendalton (Christchurch). Labour has most
of the other city seats, apart from the marginals, and the 'mining'
seats, Buller and Westland. But the 'massive stability' is concealed by the fact that a comparatively small change in votes
produces a disproportionately greater change in seats. As the
parties are fairly evenly divided, this means that a swing of 2
or 3 per cent. of the vote away from the Government will be
almost certainly sufficient to defeat it. There are also a number
of strategic or marginal seats. Most come into the category of
city-marginal, for instance Manukau (Auckland), Miramar
(Wellington), or large-town, such as New Plymouth and
Palmerston North. There is a third category (the new Taupo
seat is an example) which, although partly rural, contains a
substantial proportion of industrial workers. One consequence
of the 1963 election, in which some sitting members in marginal
seats seemed to do better than average, is that in 1964 there were
apparently fewer 'marginal' seats, vulnerable to a very small
unfavourable swing, than there used to be.

The Floating Vote

When influences on voting are analysed, much obviously depends on the identity and the behaviour of those electors who *do*
change their votes, the floating voters. There is no satisfactory
evidence that the floating vote consists mainly of lower-middle-
class electors (however defined), or that it consists of persons
with 'no economic interest to distort their moral judgement'.[3]

[1] Alan Robinson, 'Class-Voting in New Zealand', S. M. Lipset and Stein
Rokkan (eds.), *Party Systems and Voter Alignments: An approach to Comparative Politics*
(Glencoe, Illinois, to be published).
[2] Chapman, Jackson, and Mitchell, op. cit., p. 251.
[3] K. J. Scott, 'The Floating Vote in New Zealand', *Landfall*, Mar. 1950, and
letter in *Landfall*, Sept. 1950; D. H. Monro, 'Some Thoughts on the General
Election', *Landfall*, Mar. 1950; Cf. R. S. Milne, ' "Lower Middle Class" et "Vote
Flottant" en Grande-Bretagne', F. Goguel (ed.), *Nouvelles études de sociologie
électorale* (Paris, 1954).

The argument that the floating vote consists largely of the lower-middle class, because most marginal seats have been in the large towns (such as Palmerston North, Nelson, and so on) or the suburbs of the four main centres where the lower-middle class is strongly represented, is not convincing. Even if the strong representation of the 'lower-middle class' (satisfactorily defined) were granted, these seats are not marginal because their electors float or 'swing' more than others. Figures over a period suggest that they do not. They are 'marginal' only in the sense that they are on the margin—that the votes for Labour and National are almost evenly divided, with the consequence that a swing which is no higher than the New Zealand average may result in a change in the winning party.[1] Nor does the Wellington Central survey provide any reason for identifying floaters with the lower-middle class.[2] As it stands, the view that lower-middle-class people have 'no economic interest' is implausible, although it might be guessed that their economic interests were more conflicting, or that they were more subject to economic cross-pressures than other voters. Evidence is completely lacking about the way they have used their 'moral judgement', if they possess any.

Changes of Government: Erosion

Until recently it was generally agreed that 'swings of the pendulum'[3] were slow in New Zealand, and, once in power, parties such as the Liberals (1890–1912), Reform (1912–28), or Labour (1935–49) stayed in office for a long time. They gave the impression of being 'dominant' parties,[4] although the Reform Party's hold on power was probably too precarious to qualify for this description. Indeed commentators seem to have felt that it was not the slowness of the swing, but rather the infrequent *changes* of Government, which required explanation. Attempts to account for these changes have usually taken the form of maintaining that new classes or groups had become prominent in the electorate (1890, 1911–12) or that economic

[1] Chapman, Jackson, and Mitchell, op. cit., pp. 250–4.
[2] Milne, *Political Science*, art. cit., pp. 55–58.
[3] The arguments of Scott, art. cit., pp. 61–62 and Shannon, *The Decline and Fall of the Liberal Government*, p. 253, against using this term to apply during particular periods, are not convincing.
[4] Duverger, op. cit., pp. 410 and 417–18.

depression had driven some electors to vote for a change of government (1890, 1928, 1935).[1] Long periods in office have been explained by references to 'pork' and the personality of Seddon (for the Liberals) and later by the argument that the State was the largest employer in New Zealand and possessed important economic regulatory powers, enabling it to exercise enormous patronage and influence.[2] Another reason which has been offered for the longevity of Governments is their intelligent, and unscrupulous, timing of certain measures to take account of the normal three-year electoral cycle. Seddon's Old Age Pensions Bill was proposed in 1896, but was not passed into law until 1898 (election year), and was to be valid for only three years, thus ensuring that it would come up again in 1901 (election year). Similarly the Labour Government's Social Security Act was not passed until election year, 1938.[3] The familiar tactic of offering tax reductions in election year may also be followed.

But of recent years the tempo of the swing of the pendulum in New Zealand has quickened. This is most easily seen by a comparison with Britain. True, the term of Parliament there is longer, five years (before 1911, seven years), although it is the practice for dissolution to take place earlier. In the period 1891–1935 (if coalitions and changes of Prime Minister as opposed to changes in the governing party are not counted) there were eight different Governments in Britain and only four in New Zealand. But from 1935 to 1964 there have been four in Britain, compared with four in New Zealand.

The most likely basis for any explanation of changes of Government is the 'erosion' theory; after a Government has been in office for some time enough electors believe it is 'time for a change' for the Government to be turned out. More precisely, '. . . the party division of the vote is most likely to be *changed* by a negative public reaction to the record of the party in power. . . . A majority party, once it is in office, will not continue to accrue electoral strength; it may preserve for a time its electoral majority, but the next marked *change* in the party vote will issue from a negative response of the electorate to some

[1] Lipson, op. cit., p. 197.
[2] L. C. Webb, Belshaw (ed.), op. cit., p. 265.
[3] Lipson, op. cit., p. 253.

aspect of the party's conduct in office, a response that tends to return the minority party to power.'[1] If this hypothesis is applied to New Zealand, it fits reasonably well. There are, however, exceptions to the hypothesis that, once in power, a party will not 'accrue electoral strength', namely the 1938 and 1951 elections. The commonsense explanation would be that, for 1938, the 1935 election had been a *realigning* election, where popular feeling had been sufficiently intense to cause the basic partisan commitments of a portion of the electorate to change.[2] The shift was, presumably, sufficient to generate extra support in 1938, thus postponing the setting-in of erosion. In 1951 the pattern was disturbed by the National Party's tactic of an early dissolution, asking in effect for a 'vote of confidence' from the country on its capable handling of the waterside strike.

The 'erosion' theory also needs to be qualified. In 1963 there was indeed a swing from National to Labour. But why was it so small, compared, say, with the swing from Labour to National in 1960? One confusing factor is the existence of credit squeezes and stop–go import restrictions. Instead of the old-fashioned trade cycle there have recently been a series of short sharp credit squeezes and import cuts.[3] Parties may still offer tax reductions in election year, but they are liable to be 'caught', as Labour was after 1957, between unpopularity from a quickly imposed austerity programme and Opposition charges of having 'bribed' the electors.

As in Britain, by-election results do not bear much relation to general-election results. The numbers voting are lower and a higher proportion of the electors ventilate their grievances by voting against the Government.[4] It is not even possible to compare successive by-election results and try to detect a trend which may be used to forecast the result of the next general election; compared with Britain there are too few by-elections to do this successfully.[5]

[1] A. Campbell *et al.*, *The American Voter* (New York, 1960), pp. 554 ff.
[2] Ibid., p. 534.
[3] Chapman, *Landfall*, art. cit., pp. 263–6.
[4] The big exception was Buller, a depressed mining area, in 1962 (Martin Nestor, 'By-elections', *Political Science*, vol. xv, no. 2 (1963), p. 60).
[5] For a recent study in depth of a by-election see Austin Mitchell, *Waitaki Votes* (Dunedin, 1962).

IV

PARTIES AND INTEREST GROUPS

THE study of interest (pressure[1]) groups which began in Britain on any scale about 1955[2] has still hardly touched New Zealand. Apart from some research on trade unions, there is an almost complete lack of organized material on this subject.[3] This chapter does not seek to fill the gap. But, because of the gap, it attempts to make a general analysis of the relations between parties and interest groups in New Zealand.

The most recent view of interest groups is that, far from constituting excrescences on the body politic, they play a vital part in the democratic political process.[4] Through voting, the elector

---

[1] The term 'interest groups' is preferred to 'pressure groups', mainly because the latter has an unnecessarily nasty connotation and because 'pressure' does not adequately describe the techniques of such groups.

[2] See, particularly: W. J. M. Mackenzie, 'Pressure Groups in British Government, *British Journal of Sociology*, vol. vi, no. 2 (1955); Samuel H. Beer, 'Pressure Groups and Parties in Britain', *The American Political Science Review*, vol. l, no. 1 (1956); S. E. Finer, *Anonymous Empire* (London, 1958); 'Pressure Groups in Britain', Special Issue, *Political Quarterly*, vol. xxix, no. 1 (1958); J. D. Stewart, *British Pressure Groups: Their Role in Relation to the House of Commons* (Oxford, 1958); Allen Potter, *Organised Groups in British National Politics* (London, 1961). The study of interest groups began much earlier in the United States. Two outstanding classics are: Arthur F. Bentley, *The Process of Government: A Study of Social Pressures* (Chicago, 1908); David B. Truman, *The Governmental Process* (New York, 1951).

[3] On the trade unions consult Brown, op. cit.; F. M. J. Irvine, 'The Revolt of the Militant Unions' (Auckland unpublished thesis, 1936); R. C. J. Stone, 'A History of Trade Unionism in New Zealand, 1913–1937' (Auckland unpublished thesis, 1948); P. G. Morris, 'Unemployed Organisations in New Zealand, 1926–1939' (Victoria unpublished thesis, 1950); R. M. Martin, 'Contemporary Unionism in New Zealand' (Victoria unpublished thesis, 1954). For the agricultural boards see the annual reports of each board; also T. R. Smith, 'The Administration of Internal Marketing', *New Zealand Journal of Public Administration*, vol. vii, no. 2 (1944); M. J. Moriarty, 'The Marketing of Dairy Produce', *New Zealand Journal of Public Administration*, vol. x, no. 1 (1948); M. J. Moriarty, 'The Changing Structure of Marketing', *New Zealand Journal of Public Administration*, vol. xvi, no. 2 (1953); M. J. Moriarty (ed.), *New Zealand Farm Production and Marketing* (Wellington, 1963). On pressure groups generally see M. J. Moriarty, 'Pressure Groups', *New Zealand Journal of Public Administration*, vol. xiii, no. 1 (1951); Norman D. Stevens, *Organisation and Techniques of Pressure Groups in New Zealand* (Victoria University College, mimeo, 1954).

[4] Cf. Wilfrid Harrison. 'The New Pluralism' (unpublished paper read to the Political Studies Association of the United Kingdom Conference, Durham, 1958).

expresses a general desire to have one party in power rather than another, but more specific demands on government are made in other ways, notably through interest groups. The problem of government is to temper and co-ordinate the special interests which express these demands so as to produce policies which are in accordance with the elusive 'public interest'. But, although unbridled special interests are destructive of the public interest, the latter can be ascertained only if special interests are freely expressed.

New Zealanders are well accustomed to the existence of interest groups in their midst and to hearing the groups voice their demands. Some of these 'economic' groups, such as trade unions, business associations, and farmers' groups, correspond to what Professor Miller has called 'syndicates' in Australia.[1] 'Each section is quick, not only to defend its own privileges but also to attack any rival section which seems likely to gain too much. The New Zealand economy produces only a limited quantity of cake; each section is concerned to safeguard its own slice and prevent other sections from cutting off too much.'[2] Perhaps there are two reasons why such economic groups are especially prominent in Australia and New Zealand. For one thing, because of the prevailing materialistic atmosphere, cultural and intellectual groups play a less important role than in, say, Britain. Secondly, the prominent role of the State in economic life, and consequent concern with the economic benefits or losses from arbitration, import selection, tariffs, marketing schemes for farm products, price control, public works schemes, and so on, is a powerful incentive to activity on the part of economic groups. In some spheres, such as arbitration and marketing, groups may be strengthened by government activity and so may become 'implicated' in the governmental process. Indeed groups have actually been *created* by state intervention; the National Milk Scheme (1943) quickly resulted in the formation of the Town Milk Producers' Federation and the Milk Vendors' Association.[3] In view of the preponderant part played in New Zealand by economic interests it seems odd to read in a 1927 article on New Zealand politics that political life had become an

[1] J. D. B. Miller, *Australian Government and Politics* (London, 1959), pp. 65–67.
[2] Oliver, op. cit., p.277.
[3] Moriarty, 'Pressure Groups', p. 19.

open battle of sectional interests between manufacturers, farmers, and workers, and that a growing number of people viewed
the shameless battle of sectional interests with disgust.[1] There is
nothing unusual about this 'open battle' in New Zealand.
Indeed it is generally recognized that sectional interests are
least dangerous when their activities are open and publicized.
The only remarkable and reprehensible feature at this time was,
as mentioned in the same article, that the ministry seemed to be
quite incapable of asserting its power over and above these
sectional interests. It should perhaps be added that, as in
Australia, many conflicts between interests are resolved by
'institutionalized' adjudication. Therefore some interests seek
to further their cause through a bureaucratic or judicial process
rather than through the political process.[2]

The aim of this chapter is therefore a limited one; its purpose
is merely to indicate the relations between the parties and
certain interest groups, mostly economic. The relation between
the trade unions and the Labour Party is a special case, because
the two are linked formally and continuously. It will therefore
be considered at some length. The other groups discussed are
not linked to parties in this way, although at times they have
founded parties (as the Auckland Province of the Farmers'
Union founded the Country Party), have contributed to party
funds, or have in other ways aligned themselves with particular parties. Three headings will be used for the groups discussed here: trade unions, farming groups, business groups and
pro-business groups. The relative power of the groups and their
inter-relations are of interest. Reeves, when discussing the
Liberal Government's arbitration law, remarked that the most
powerful class in New Zealand politics was not the wage-
earners but the farmers.[3] But since then, although agricultural
exports are still vital to New Zealand's prosperity, the proportion of farmers in the population, and their voting power, has
declined. The proportion of industrial workers has risen, and so
has the power of the trade unions, aided by the first Labour
Government's pro-trade union legislation. Soon after the Second

---

[1] *Round Table*, vol. xviii (1927–8), p. 416.
[2] Cf. Colin A. Hughes, on Australia, in *Journal of Politics*, vol. xxv, no. 3 (1963),
issue on comparative party finance.
[3] In introduction to H. D. Lloyd, *A Country Without Strikes* (New York, 1900),
p. ix.

World War Leicester Webb could write that the balance of groups which was most important in New Zealand was that between the trade unions and the farm organizations. The economic stabilization policy announced in December 1942 was, in essence, an agreement by the unions to accept a 'wage freeze' in return for an agreement by the farm groups to accept the stabilization of farm incomes.[1] This is probably still the most important balance, and, in their campaigns for higher wages, trade-union leaders persistently call attention to the size of farm incomes compared with other wages and salaries.[2] But the balance between the farmers and the unions is a balance of power, not of numbers. The small number of farmers, compared with trade unionists, is compensated for by the importance of agricultural exports and by the sentimental regard for the farmer which continues to invest him with all the virtues of the hardy pioneer on the frontier. Neither the trade unions nor the farmers' organizations are 'monolithic', as will be evident from the account given below. But organizations of employers are even more divided because of the increasing importance of tariffs and import controls in New Zealand, which has tended to intensify the division between manufacturers and importers.

The Trade Unions and the Labour Party

The trade unions in New Zealand are 'fragmented'.[3] The scattered population and the absence of concentrations of heavy industry have given rise to a large number of small unions, just as they have resulted in a large number of small factories;[4] 325,000 trade unionists are spread over just under 400 unions.[5] The United Federation of Labour, set up in 1913, was soon supplanted, in 1920, by the Alliance of Labour. At first rather suspicious of the political Labour movement, the Alliance came to co-operate with it in the early 1930's. The depression and the 1932 amendment to the Industrial Conciliation and Arbitration

---

[1] Webb in Parker (ed.), op. cit., p. 18.
[2] e.g. F. P. Walsh, *Minutes and Report of the Eighteenth Annual Conference of the New Zealand Federation of Labour* (1955), p. 7, and *Statement*, quoted *Evening Post*, 24 Aug. 1957.
[3] Overacker, *Political Science*, vol. ix, no. 1, art. cit., p. 27; A. E. C. Hare, *Report on Industrial Relations in New Zealand* (Wellington, 1946), p. 173.
[4] J. B. Condliffe, *The Welfare State in New Zealand*, p. 150.
[5] *New Zealand Official Yearbook*, 1963, p. 1020.

Act (which removed the protection of compulsory arbitration until it was restored by the Labour Government in 1936) made the Alliance draw closer to the party. So did the rivalry of the Unemployed Workers' Union, which was linked with the Communist Party.[1] After the Labour Party became the Government in 1935 the industrial side reorganized, and the existing Federation of Labour was founded in 1937.

After the war, however, it became evident that there was a 'dual system' in the unions. On the one hand, there were some large aggressive unions whose members operated key sectors of the economy, the watersiders, seamen, miners, transport workers, and freezing workers, who used their strength and bargaining power to try and secure wage increases. Following in their wake were the smaller, more cautious, unions, who profited from the gains of the first group through the apparatus of industrial arbitration.[2] In the later 1940's the demands of the militants did not stop at wage increases. The militants wanted to scrap the arbitration system and rely on their striking power, and they desired workers' control in certain key industries and also extensions of public ownership.[3] In 1950, after some of the more militant unions had resorted to striking,[4] the watersiders were expelled from the Federation of Labour, and were followed by a number of other trade unions. A rival 'Trade Union Congress' was formed, which temporarily deprived the FOL of about a third of its members. The introduction of compulsory unionism in 1936 in conjunction with the 'de-registration' provisions of 1939 (cancellation of registration under the Industrial Conciliation and Arbitration Act, with the effect that a union's current award or agreement would also be cancelled) provided an effective weapon against strikes, which was employed against the Auckland Carpenters in 1949 and against the Watersiders and five other unions in 1951. In brief, a striking union could now be 'de-registered' and a new, more amenable, union (or unions) registered in its place. Strikers were then debarred from employment in the same trade unless they joined the new union.[5]

---

[1] Brown, *The Rise of New Zealand Labour*, especially pp. 173–5. On the Unemployed Workers' Union see P. G. Morris, op. cit.

[2] W. Rosenberg, *Compulsory Arbitration: Barrier to Progress* (Wellington, 1952).

[3] Oliver, op. cit., pp. 213–14.

[4] See p. 62, above.

[5] Martin, op. cit., pp. 111–13, and 'Twenty Years of Compulsory Unionism',

After the 1951 strike had failed the Trade Union Congress ceased to exist and the Federation of Labour was left without a rival. In 1963 it claimed that over 200 unions, with about 230,000 members, were affiliated to it.[1]

Compulsory unionism is not an issue which divides supporters and opponents into neatly separated camps—workers and the Labour Party for, employers and the National Party against. The Labour Party has supported it on principle, the principle that those who enjoy the benefits won by trade unionism should pay for their share of them. The National Party opposes it, also on principle, because, since it is compulsory, it deprives the individual of freedom of choice. But, looking a little more deeply, practical considerations must be considered as well as principles. In some unions, legal compulsion was superfluous before 1936. In the watersiders, for instance, someone would simply 'put the hard word on you to join'. The seamen, too, imposed their own 'compulsory unionism' by refusing to sail with non-unionists.[2] But in other unions, particularly 'middle-class' ones, membership was low before compulsion was introduced. It was in these unions that the new legislation produced a big jump in membership[3] and in subscriptions. Less enterprising trade-union secretaries could now sit back and watch the money roll in; they were no longer faced with the challenge of winning new members. But not all who were compulsorily drafted into trade unions became genuine 'trade unionists'. The increase in numbers represented, in effect, a dilution of the militants. The right-wing element in existing trade unions was strengthened and new right-wing unions were created.

These considerations were presumably of some weight in persuading the National Government not to abolish compulsory unionism during its term of office, 1949–57. The party's election programme pledged it to look into the matter of abolition. It actually brought in a Bill providing for abolition, but changed its mind on the question later, as did the Manufacturers' Association

Political Science, vol. viii, no. 2 (1956); L. C. Webb, *Australian Quarterly*, Dec. 1951, pp. 48–51; Woods, *Industrial Conciliation and Arbitration*, p. 147.

[1] *The New Zealand Federation of Labour Calls all Trade Unionists* (Wellington, 1963).

[2] *Dominion*, 26 Mar. 1938.

[3] Trade Union membership rose from 80,929 at the end of 1935 to 232,986 at the end of 1937 (*New Zealand Yearbook*, 1940, p. 849).

and the Employers' Federation.[1] One of the deciding factors may
well have been the value of compulsory unionism, previously
referred to, in helping to 'break' the militant unions in 1951.

In 1961 the National Party 'abolished' compulsory trade
unionism. During the 1960 election campaign the proposed
change had been attacked both by Mr. Walsh, President of the
FOL, and by Mr. P. J. Luxford, secretary to the Employers'
Federation.[2] When the legislation was before Parliament the
Labour Party determinedly opposed it. Part of the reason for
introducing new legislation was that it was in accord with the
party's principle of giving as much freedom as possible to the
individual.[3] However, in effect, the Bill provided for 'unqualified
preference' for trade unions, either with the agreement of the
employers, or if they could show by ballot that more than 50 per
cent. of the workers concerned desired it. And it had been
remarked that unqualified preference 'bears a considerable
resemblance to the present compulsory unionism'.[4] When the
Bill came into force unqualified preference was awarded in
every case, even, rather unexpectedly, to unions of clerical
workers.[5] Consequently there was no drop in trade-union
numbers. It appears that the FOL, even before the Bill became
law, had decided that there was no question of a serious blow
being aimed at trade unionism. It soon showed that its attitude
had undergone a radical change.[6] At its 1963 Conference a proposal to restore compulsory unionism was defeated by 207 votes
to 46.[7] It was said that when the Government brought in the
legislation they thought it would destroy the trade-union movement. But the movement had acted collectively 'in seeking an
unqualified preference clause for all awards and agreements, and
as a result there had been a new spirit within the trade-union
movement in the last two years.' He [Mr. F. P. Walsh] was of

[1] Martin, *Contemporary Unionism in New Zealand*, pp. 107–10.
[2] Chapman, Jackson, and Mitchell, op. cit., pp. 100–1. See also *Survey of the Development of the Trade Union Movement in New Zealand* (FOL, 1961); *Minutes and Report of Proceedings of the 24th Annual Conference of the New Zealand Federation of Labour* (1961, p. 23).
[3] Mr. J. R. Marshall, *N.Z.P.D.*, vol. cccxxviii, p. 2293 (14 Sept. 1961).
[4] Mr. T. P. Shand, ibid., p. 2285.   [5] *Evening Post*, 8 Sept. 1962.
[6] *Minutes and Report of Proceedings of the 25th Annual Conference of the New Zealand Federation of Labour*, 1962, pp. 9–14.
[7] *Minutes and Report of Proceedings of the 26th Annual Conference of the New Zealand Federation of Labour*, 1963, p. 38.

the opinion that 'it would be a retrograde step to reintroduce compulsory unionism, as its abolition had proved beneficial to the trade-union movement by virtue of the fact that workers were now realising the value of a trade-union organization and that their conditions could only be obtained and retained by their own efforts'.[1] As in the days before 1936, trade-union officials now had to work hard in order to keep up membership. The Leader of the PLP accepted this change in the attitude of the FOL and said the party would not propose to restore compulsory unionism.[2]

Related to compulsory unionism is the question of contributions by registered unions to (Labour) party funds. The Political Disabilities Removal Act of 1936 empowered trade unions to make grants to a political party, even if this were not provided for in their rules. By an amending act of the National Government in 1950 it was stipulated that such political expenditure could be sanctioned only by a majority vote of the total membership (not just of the votes cast).[3] In practice this provision was widely, and safely, ignored by the unions, a favourite device being to make a contribution to the Labour Party in the disguise of a 'loan', which was not repaid and was later written off. Unlike Britain, there is no provision by which individual members of unions can contract out of union contributions to party funds. Legislation by the Labour Government in 1960 substantially restored the 1936 provisions.

The links of the unions with the Labour Party are numerous and hard to disentangle. By its constitution the party makes provision for trade unions to be affiliated to it. The importance of this provision may be seen from the high degree of 'overlap'. The great majority of the unions in the Federation of Labour are affiliated to the party. On the other hand, approximately 80 per cent. of the Labour Party's membership consists of trade-union members. The alliance between the party and the unions is symbolized at the highest level by the existence of the Joint Council of Labour, consisting of the central executive of the party and the executive of the FOL, which corresponds to the British National Council of Labour. The Council has usually

[1] *Minutes and Report of Proceedings of the 26th Annual Conference of the New Zealand Federation of Labour*, 1963, p. 37.   [2] Ibid., p. 94.
[3] Martin, *Contemporary Unionism in New Zealand*, pp. 120–1.

met about four times a year. Some idea of the ground it covers
may be gained from the *Minutes and Report of Proceedings* of the
21st FOL Annual Conference (1958).[1] During the previous year
the Council considered the means test and a proposed increase
in weekly benefits under the Social Security Act; a case under
the Workers' Compensation Act; opposition to requests for
the repeal of the Economic Stabilisation Regulations; Pay As
You Earn Income Tax; the disfranchisement of seamen; financial support for the 1957 Labour Party campaign fund; correspondence between the FOL and a government department on
the revision of the Consumers' Price Index.

There are no formal provisions for meetings between the FOL
and the Parliamentary Labour Party. But even if there were no
special links betweens the trade unions and the party, the unions
would still be consulted on legislation affecting their interests,
as would any other organized group. Long before a separate
Labour Party was founded, the Liberal Governments after 1890
used to submit their proposed industrial legislation to the unions
for advice and amendments.[2] At one time, before 1935, there
was a National Labour Legislation Committee, consisting of
representatives of the party and the trade unions which 'met
regularly and had special meetings when necessary to discuss
and consider labour legislation and the different lines of action
necessary for the political and industrial movement to take'.[3]
From 1942 to 1946 McLagan was both President of the FOL
and also in the Cabinet, which improved liaison between the
two bodies. During the period when the Labour Government
was in power, 1935–49, officers of the FOL used to be called in
to sit with the members of the parliamentary party (caucus)
when industrial matters were being discussed.[4] However, these
meetings no longer occurred when the Labour Party held office
between 1957 and 1960. Informal meetings took place between

[1] p. 68. The Council apparently languished during the 'new look' dispute
1963–4. But at the 1964 FOL Conference Mr. Nordmeyer said it would meet
oftener in future (*New Zealand Herald*, 8 May 1964).

[2] J. D. Salmond, *New Zealand Labour's Pioneering Days* (Auckland, 1950), pp.
49 and 129.

[3] A. McLagan, *Minutes and Report of the Fifteenth Annual Conference of the New
Zealand Federation of Labour*, 1952, p. 21. See also Brown, op. cit., pp. 129–30, who
states that the Committee was set up in 1926.

[4] Overacker, *American Political Science Review*, art. cit., p. 729; interview with Mr.
K. McL. Baxter, Secretary FOL, Oct. 1958.

Cabinet members and FOL officials during both periods, 1935–49 and 1957–60.[1]

The chapters which follow will deal with the unions' role in the parliamentary party, on the national executive of the party, in the local party organs at the Labour Party Conference, and in the selection of parliamentary candidates. At this point, however, some general observations may be relevant on the relations between the party and the unions. A prominent feature, which dominates the whole relationship, is the financial dependence of the party on the unions. With regard to annual revenue, it is true that the individual subscription to the party is a minimum of 5s. a year (some branches set a higher figure), while the fee paid for each member of a union affiliated to the Labour Party is only 1s. 6d. But, since affiliated members outnumber individual members by about four to one, the regular income from the former is larger.[2] In raising funds for elections the unions also contribute a substantially higher proportion of the total campaign revenue. It is impossible to be quantitative about this, because large donations to the party from business and other non-trade-union groups are not made public. But a contribution of £1 per adult worker to the election campaign fund was the target set by H. E. Holland for 'insurance' against wage cuts as long ago as 1930.[3] After the first Labour Government won office and passed the legislation on compulsory unionism, some of the stronger unions came close to achieving Holland's target. The unions are particularly helpful in supplying money towards the end of a campaign when funds are short. At an election in the 1950's the campaign fund was £9,000 'in the red' two weeks before polling day, but a substantial part of the deficit was made good by a grant of £2,000 from the FOL and a similar amount from an individual union. In 1960 the FOL gave £2,500 and the Seamen's Union £2,000.[4]

Another general feature of the relationship concerns policy. Many years ago H. E. Holland believed that the political movement must always be the more revolutionary wing, because the industrial movement would necessarily be engaged in fighting

[1] *Minutes and Reports* of FOL Annual Conferences.
[2] For British figures see M. Harrison, *Trade Unions and the Labour Party since 1945* (London, 1960), ch. ii.
[3] H. E. Holland, *Political Non-Unionism* (Wellington, 1930), p. 7.
[4] Chapman, Jackson, and Mitchell, op. cit., p. 79.

for palliatives.[1] But this argument no longer applies. Industrial conditions are no longer so desperate that palliatives are required. On the other hand, militancy can be blunted by the attractions of comfortable living as well as by absorption in the struggle for existence. However, the political movement, after enjoying many years of office, is also obviously less revolutionary than it was.

A remarkable feature of the 1950's was the decrease in the number of proposals for further nationalization and of schemes for workers' control advanced at the Federation of Labour's Annual Conferences. In the 1940's there was an average of three or four resolutions on these topics at each FOL Conference. But after Labour lost office in 1949, and even during the Labour Government of 1957–60, there were hardly any similar resolutions put forward. Of course, further nationalization was supported by the FOL's rival, the Trade Union Congress founded in 1949. And in view of the approaching breakaway the attitude of the national executive of the FOL in 1949 to remits on nationalization is significant. At previous Conferences resolutions on these subjects had generally been endorsed in principle by the conference. But in 1949 the two resolutions were referred to the national executive which blasted them in a report. Too many remits like these were coming forward, said the report, which ignored the fact that nationalization would lead to socialism only through more efficient production. A union favouring nationalization should in future put forward a detailed plan for it. This 'will be of greater value and more lasting benefit than the mere affirmation of principles in resolutions which our minutes record as passed but in the main forgotten' [sic].[2] In short, until 1963, at any rate, the FOL had accepted the fact that the vast majority of the workers do not want to change 'the system'. 'At present the workers do not want the abolition of masters: they want kind masters, and we are obliged to accept the collective opinion of the trade-union movement which put a Labour Government in.'[3]

[1] R. J. Tizard, 'H. E. Holland's Blueprint for New Zealand and the World: its Inspiration and Influence' (Auckland unpublished thesis, 1949), p. 47, quoting Holland's *The Scandal of War Profits* (Wellington, 1917), p. 24.
[2] *Supplement to the Minutes of the Twelfth Annual Conference of the New Zealand Federation of Labour*, 1949, p. 8.
[3] Mr. K. McL. Baxter, *Minutes of the Extraordinary Conference of the Federation of*

On the whole the FOL and the Parliamentary Labour Party have worked in general agreement since the FOL was founded in 1937. From the beginning of the Cold War, until 1963 at least, both have been predominantly anti-Communist, anti-industrial-action, and opposed to further socialization. Criticisms and clashes have been rather in terms of 'right' and 'left', but these descriptions have not always applied to unionists and politicians, respectively. Some mutual distrust exists between some FOL officials and certain intellectuals in the political movement. The former sometimes regard the latter as 'visionary' and as 'without practical experience'; they, in turn, are seen as 'reactionary' and 'not receptive to ideas'. But there has also been conflict between left-wingers in the unions and the leaders of the parliamentary party. Thus Fraser at the 1947 Party Conference hit out at the 'wreckers' who threatened unofficial strikes, and this attack was pursued by Robert Semple, a Labour minister, in his pamphlet, *Why I Fight Communism*.[1] On the other hand, the Minister of Labour, McLagan, alleged that the leaders of the Watersiders Union had asked the Prime Minister and Cabinet to dismiss him.[2] And the Watersiders also passed a resolution asking that Semple should be 'disciplined and removed from the Cabinet'.[3]

A curious situation developed during the strike of 1951. The actions of the National Government in dealing with the strike were more in accordance with the wishes of the FOL leadership than was the relative *inaction* of the Labour Government before it lost office in 1949, or the pronouncements of the Labour leadership during the strike. According to one prominent unionist, the Labour Party missed an opportunity by not taking action against the left-wing unions while it was in office. It had, he claims, prepared all the necessary regulations[4] for taking a stand, which were later put into operation by the National Government. But in the event it was National, not Labour, which reaped the electoral credit of defeating the left-wingers. During and after the 1951 strike the wrath of the FOL was also

Labour, Jan. 1947, p. 23. These minutes (in the Trades Hall, Wellington) give the only verbatim account of any FOL Conference.
    [1] Wellington, 1948.   [2] *Evening Post*, 17 May 1947.
    [3] Ibid., 3 June 1947.
    [4] A possibility mentioned by Fraser in 1947, *Minutes of the Extraordinary Conference of the Federation of Labour*, p. 38.

directed at a few Labour Members of Parliament who had not supported the FOL vigorously enough or who had even favoured the strikers.

Relations between the FOL and the party in 1951 were also affected by the recent change in party leadership. Fraser, who died in 1950, had been a trade unionist and worked closely with the FOL leaders and in particular with Mr. Walsh, usually identified as the 'strong man' of the FOL and later its president.[1] Mr. Nash, Fraser's successor, had not been a trade unionist and was not so closely identified with the industrial side of the Labour movement. It is true that in 1954 Walsh supported Nash's claims to be re-elected Leader of the parliamentary party, but probably this arose more from the respect owed by one 'strong man' to another than from any great personal sympathy.

The events of 1963 and early 1964 revealed a difference of view between the new Leader, Mr. Nordmeyer, and a section of the PLP, on the one hand, and FOL leaders on the other. On assuming the leadership, Mr. Nordmeyer, perhaps with an eye on the forthcoming general election, restated his own position on the meaning of democratic socialism, which came to be known as the 'new look'. Harmony was important in the Labour movement and in the community generally. 'There is no place today for what used to be known as the class struggle.'[2] He amplified this point a month later in addressing the FOL Annual Conference. He did not deny that workers should fight for their rights to ensure that they received a fair share of the national dividend. 'But I believe anybody going on to a platform and advocating a class struggle would be sounding the death knell of the Labour Party.'[3] No immediate public controversy resulted, but the Secretary of the Federation of Labour, Mr. Baxter, immediately circulated a statement to the delegates who attended the Conference, affirming the existence of the class struggle. Marx, Kautsky, H. E. Holland, and the National Executive of the Federation of Labour had all been forced to accept the fact that there was a fundamental conflict between those who invested their money in industry to make a profit and those who

[1] L. C. Webb, 'Leadership in the Labour Party', *Political Science*, vol. v, no. 2 (1953).

[2] *Dominion*, 2 Apr. 1963.

[3] *Minutes and Report of Proceedings of the 26th Annual Conference of the New Zealand Federation of Labour*, 1963, pp. 98–99.

'invested' their lives in industry in order to live. In support of this view he referred to the address which the FOL President, Mr. Walsh, had made to the Conference and to the aim of the FOL constitution (Rule 3 (j)), 'To work for a more equitable share of the national income and ultimately production for social use and not for private profit.' Possible open controversy was temporarily avoided because Mr. Walsh died a few days later. During the election the Labour Party, apparently partly on the advice of a public relations consultant, strove to acquire a new image by emphasizing its 'new look' policy. This phrase was used repeatedly in its publicity. The stress was clearly on development and incentives rather than on the class struggle. During the campaign Mr. Edwards, M.P. for Napier and son-in-law of Mr. Nordmeyer, was quoted as having said that the 'new look' members were coming to dominance in the Labour Party, and they had chosen Mr. Nordmeyer as Leader. The older group harked back to past achievements.[1] Mr. Baxter waited until after the election, and then wrote to the Secretary of the Labour Party, attacking Mr. Edwards. Referring to the founders of the Labour Party in New Zealand, he pointed out that they had their roots deep in the trade-union movement. The new lookers were more concerned with the electorate, with soliciting the voters. If there were a few more new lookers like Mr. Edwards, the Labour Party in office would become merely the executive committee of the capitalist class. The choice of Mr. Edwards as a target, instead of Mr. Nordmeyer, was some-what reminiscent of the Russian Communist Party's choice, a few years since, of the Albanian Communist Party to attack rather than the Chinese. The controversy then came into the open through statements by the President of the FOL, Mr. T. E. Skinner, and the deputy leader of the PLP, Mr. Watt.[2] Some of Mr. Skinner's phrasing seemed to indicate that he was moderating the FOL line somewhat.[3] But the 1963-4 Annual Report of the FOL, presented at the 1964 Conference by the national executive, reaffirmed the class struggle as explained by H. E. Holland and deplored the dropping of socialization as the objective of the Labour Party in 1951.[4]

To some extent the dispute is a necessary reflection of the

[1] *Evening Post*, 7 Nov. 1963.   [2] *Dominion*, 15 Apr. 1964.
[3] *Evening Post*, 20 Apr. 1964.   [4] Ibid., 23 Mar. 1964.

different stands taken by a party and by an interest group, even one as closely allied with a party as the FOL. 'It is true that the Labour Party is a political party which stands for the best interests of the New Zealand people as a whole, while the Federation of Labour stands specifically for employees' interests, and this must at times lead to a difference of approach or emphasis.'[1] Part of the FOL reactions to the new look are no doubt based on personalities and express opposition principally to 'new lookers' who have no roots in the industrial movement. Of course, with today's greater educational opportunities, it is less and less likely that able younger people in the Labour movement will have come into it through the unions, as, for instance, Peter Fraser did. It also perhaps reflects the reactions of old-guard sentimental socialists, who do not wish to see the class struggle become too institutionalized and too much overlaid by talk of growth and development. To them any explicit statement of the new look is a heresy, bringing the Labour Party too close to the Nationalist position, and (with the restraining hand of Mr. Walsh absent) must be resisted. To some degree also, the reactions of the FOL leadership may be explained by a desire to attract left-wing support in the fluid power situation following Walsh's death. At the 1964 FOL Conference, the national executive's support of the class struggle and repudiation of the new look was unanimously endorsed.[2] But two days later the Conference also expressed confidence in Mr. Nordmeyer when he said that the new look did not depart from the fundamental principles of socialism, but that there were too few socialists in New Zealand to be able to implement a policy of full socialism.[3] It is doubtful whether the revival of the class struggle motifs is taken seriously, except by some older members. It may be noted that, at the 1964 FOL Conference, there were only two remits on nationalization compared with six on annual holidays. Affluence is the enemy of the class struggle.

Some 'external' views of the Labour Party and the trade unions are much too simplified—for instance, the statement

[1] George Broad, 'No split in Labour ranks . . . Unions and party united for social progress', *New Zealand Statesman*, Apr. 1964.
[2] *Dominion*, 6 May 1964.
[3] Ibid. 8 May 1964. He made a substantially similar speech which received a long ovation at the Labour Party Conference a few days later (*Auckland Star*, 12 May 1964).

that the Labour Party 'was simply the tool of the trade unions which controlled its activity, directed its policy and gave orders to it'.[1] Trade-union money, organization, and votes mean a substantial voice in the Labour Party, but they do not necessarily add up to domination or control. An interesting instance, which at first sight seems to suggest trade-union control, occurred at the Extraordinary Conference of the FOL in 1947, when Fraser said that, if the Conference considered his policy wrong, it would be his duty to resign as Prime Minister before the Labour caucus.[2] But, on reflection, the constitutional dubiety of this offer is overshadowed by its tactical astuteness. With the Labour Party's narrow majority in Parliament (mentioned by Fraser in his speech a few moments later) his resignation might quickly have resulted in the formation of a National Party Government. As Michels has suggested,[3] such an 'offer' to resign from a leader is not a capitulation but rather an offensive weapon.

The militants in the trade-union movement have also oversimplified the issue by pointing out the dangers of Labour Party control over the unions: '. . . never will the trade union movement be a trade union movement if all its actions are going to be determined by how it [sic] affects a Government. If it means that, you might as well close all your offices now and pay your money in to the Parliamentary secretary of the Labour Party.'[4] Labour Party domination over the unions was denied by Fraser at the 1950 Conference.[5] In effect these charges and countercharges were, once more, really based on policy differences rather than on evidence of domination by one wing over the other.

A more accurate picture is that the unions are not a conspiracy but a 'club'.

The Party and the Labour movement as a whole still has its 'establishment' and the surest entry to it is still via the union rather than the branch—or even Parliament. . . . There is little of ideology or politics in this. It is a matter of social and personal attitudes. It is

---

[1] C. A. Wilkinson, *Taranaki Herald*, 12 Oct. 1938.
[2] *Minutes of the Extraordinary Conference*, 1947, p. 26.
[3] R. Michels, *Political Parties* (Glencoe, Illinois, 1958), pp. 50 ff.
[4] Mr. T. Hill, *Minutes of the Extraordinary Conference*, 1947, p. 129.
[5] *Minutes and Report of the Thirteenth Annual Conference of the New Zealand Federation of Labour*, 1950, p. 27.

not that unionists fear that a professional man aspiring to some party
office may be too left in his thinking; it is that he is simply not their
man: he is not one of them. Whatever his ability, whatever the
strength of his convictions, the outlook lingers in some quarters that
he is an intruder. He may win acceptance but unless he has fortunate
connections it may be a long time in coming.[1]

This analysis explains a good deal about the FOL resistance to
Labour's 'new look' in 1963 and 1964.

If simple explanations in terms of 'domination' are unsatis-
fying, so are metaphors and similes. To view those at the top of
the party and the unions as an interlocking directorate[2] is
indeed, correctly, to *avoid* simple explanations, but perhaps it
has the drawback of *appearing* to explain more than it actually
does. Mr. Nash, at the 1958 Labour Party Conference compared
the two wings of the movement, the political and the trade-
union, to the wings of a bird, and said that both were necessary
for flight. But his simile is more hortatory than explanatory.
The dynamics of the model are not evident. It is open to the
same objection as Montesquieu's account of how the 'separated'
powers of government can contrive to move together; 'as there
is a necessity for movement in the course of human affairs, they
are forced to move, but still in concert'.[3] However, there is no
guarantee that the powers will move quickly enough, or move
at all, just as there can be no certainty that Mr. Nash's bird will
fly. Perhaps, on the relation between the political party and the
trade unions, we should simply accept the sober, non-meta-
phorical conclusion that it may indeed be 'illusory to seek one
focus of power' in the party.[4]

The Farmers' Organizations

The farmers' organizations are not constitutionally linked
with any party. They are 'political', but not 'party political'.[5]

[1] Brown, *The Rise of New Zealand Labour*, pp. 219–20.
[2] Overacker, *Political Science*, vol. ix, no. 2, art. cit., p. 27.
[3] *The Spirit of the Laws*, book xi, 6.
[4] Saul Rose, 'Policy Decision in Opposition', *Political Studies*, vol. iv, no. 2 (1956),
p. 138, referring specifically to intra-party democracy and the role of Conference
in the British Labour Party.
[5] Interview, Sir William Polson, Jan. 1959. See also *Dominion*, 1 July 1937, for
the 1937 Dominion Conference's decision to go on record as opposing State ownership, except for certain public services.

Nevertheless, the organizations are usually 'aligned' with the National Party, most of the rural seats are held by National, and National has the higher proportion of farmers in the House. But little detailed information is available about contributions from farmers to party funds, not even the rumours which are sometimes current about big-business contributions to these funds.[1] Nor do farmers constitute a single solid separate interest group. Like the various trade unions, individual farming organizations for sheep farmers, dairy farmers, wheat farmers, and so on, may not be in agreement. However, the Farmers' Union and since 1944 Federated Farmers (an amalgamation of the Farmers' Union and the Sheep Owners' Federation) have attempted to speak for the farmers with one voice, as the Federation of Labour tries to do for the unions.

As is evident from Chapter II, the Reform Party was originally closely linked with the Farmers' Union. Indeed, throughout its history the Reform Party was, in its own words, 'the one party in New Zealand which consistently worked for the welfare of the primary producers and endeavoured to safeguard their interests'.[2] Even during the Coalition the alteration of the exchange rate expressed the Government's view that its priority was to restore to health primary industry, the basis of the country's prosperity.[3] Farmers distrusted the Labour Party, not only because it was identified as 'socialist', but also because it has few, if any, farmer members in Parliament. Editorials in the country Press went further: 'Most of the Labour representatives in this country as elsewhere have never done a hard day's work in their lives except as talkers and even if they wished to do so, could not understand the problems of the farmers.'[4]

So at times 'non-party political' may in effect mean 'anti-Labour Party'. It was possible for two newspapers, published on the same day in 1935, to report two statements by Mr. W. J. Polson, President of the Farmers' Union, and also, at that time, an Independent member of the House. In one he said that,

[1] However, it was stated after a meeting of the Dominion Executive of the Farmers' Union that a fund of £250,000 was being established by the farmers to help to fight the abolition of the country quota, *Evening Post*, 8 Nov. 1945.
[2] *Reform Party's Record*, 1931, no. 1, p. 3.
[3] Coates, *N.Z.P.D.*, vol. ccxxxvii, p. 456 (21 Nov. 1933).
[4] *Taranaki Herald*, 23 Nov. 1935. A similar editorial appeared in the *Rangitikei Advocate* three days later.

although he had given the Coalition Government general support, there were times 'on a matter affecting the interests of the primary producer [when] he had had to vote against the Government and he had done so fearlessly'.[1] But in the other speech he was pro-National (Coalition) in the sense that he was determinedly anti-Labour. He reminded the farmers that, although the Farmers' Union belonged to no party, it still had a set of definite principles, which were threatened by Labour's opposition to the freehold and to the country quota, and by the fact that it was committed to restoring compulsory arbitration.[2]

But the Reform Party was in a more difficult situation than Mr. Polson. As a party seeking nation-wide support, it had to consider interests other than the farmers'. It was also faced with the Country Party,[3] whose base was in the north and north-central portion of the North Island. Indeed this area coincided substantially with the area of the Auckland Province of the Farmers' Union, whose leading members launched the Country Party. The Farmers' Union in the rest of New Zealand stood aloof, and regarded the Auckland Province members as eccentric and extremist. The reasons why this area gave birth to the Country Party in the 1920's, and why it was also the centre of the Social Credit movement in New Zealand in the 1930's and later, have never been fully explained. In some areas, for instance the extreme north, it has been said by a very prominent New Zealand farmer that the farmers' discontent arose partly from the poorness of the soil, which resulted from a cobalt deficiency. More generally the predominant primary industry was dairying, which is largely an export industry, and which, unlike sheep farming, is subject to fluctuations in prices all the year round. It has also been suggested that sheep farmers were for the most part longer established and operating on a larger scale than dairy farmers, and were also more likely to have interests which were wider than farming, often in the form of industrial investments. So, the argument runs, it was the dairy farmers who were least protected and cushioned against unfavourable movements of prices. In any case Country Party strength was confined almost entirely to this area. Its status, on the borderline

---

[1] *Stratford Post*, 18 Nov. 1935.   [2] *Timaru Herald*, 18 Nov. 1935.
[3] See B. D. Graham, 'The Country Party Idea in New Zealand Politics, 1901–1935', in R. Chapman and K. Sinclair (eds.), op. cit.

between an interest group and a party, is shown by its agreement to withdraw its parliamentary candidates in 1922 on certain conditions, including the promise of a satisfactory agricultural banking system.[1] This status was reaffirmed in 1928 when its promoters said that it would be easy to get rid of the Country Party 'as a disturbing element at election time' by removing 'entirely the need for its existence'.[2]

The Country Party, and other expressions of unrest among the farmers, were founded on a number of specific grievances. But they were also symptomatic of a more deep-seated resentment and distrust of 'townies', whose wives did not have to work without pay, and who were really being supported by the farmers. The farmers welcomed reassurance of their superiority from the party: 'farmers seem to suffer from an inferiority complex. They wilt and bend at the knees whenever they see a businessman. For some obscure reason they screw a halo and wings on them [sic]. Actually there is no more inefficient person in the Dominion than the average business man ... the natural aristocrat of New Zealand is the farmer, not the retired draper or publican.'[3] They also believed that 'some unfair power must be operating against the interests of the primary producer'.[4] The argument, when developed, pointed to two main enemies. The first was the banks and the vested interests, 'the Finance Houses that are bleeding you, the Shipping Companies that overcharge you, the Banks which carry on legalised usury, the merchants who seek to deprive you of your most elementary rights'.[5] The other was the party system, organized from the top, which was 'dominated by the Party Caucus, which in turn was dominated by the financial and vested interests'.[6] The farmers' more specific

[1] Farming First, 10 Nov. 1928, p. 15.
[2] Ibid., 10 Feb. 1928, p. 6.
[3] Rushworth, Waikato Times, 3 Mar. 1939.
[4] B. M. O'Dowd, 'The Postwar Years of Massey's Ministry' (Auckland unpublished thesis, 1948), p. 58, quoting W. Miller Smith, The Marketing of Australian and New Zealand Primary Products (London, 1936), p. 51. Explaining the relative weakness of the Country Party in New Zealand compared with Australia he says that in New Zealand anti-urbanism was less pronounced and the farmers were never as 'politically isolated' as were the Australian wheat farmers (p. 198).
[5] Farming First, 10 Apr. 1931, p. 23.
[6] Rushworth, Waikato Times, 1 Oct. 1928; cf. the Albertans who left the Progressive Party in 1924 partly as a protest against a party system organized from the top which enabled economic and financial interests to retain power (W. L. Morton, The Progressive Party in Canada (Toronto, 1950), pp. 194–5).

grievances were the shortage of credit and the relation between prices and costs. Those who had bought land at high prices soon after the end of the war, found that when prices fell they could not meet the annual charges in respect of the land. In the Auckland Province there was an almost perpetual demand for more credit, which in the 1920's took the form of agitation for agricultural banks and in the 1930's supported Social Credit. In 1933 the Executive of the Auckland Farmers' Union and the Parliamentary Labour Party held a joint meeting which found common ground in the view that Parliament should assume absolute control of the nation's credit and currency.[1] Secondly, there were protests against rising costs, partly labour costs kept high by arbitration, and also those arising from the tariff on the cost of farm implements and consumer goods.[2]

But one sophisticated appreciation of the situation held out little hope of lowering costs. Once the Labour Government was in power, it was unthinkable that labour costs could be reduced. But, equally, there was little prospect of reducing tariffs. Quite apart from the opposition of manufacturers and trade unions, the wheat growers and tobacco farmers could not agree to this, because they themselves depended on protection; therefore any radical attack on the tariff would break up the unity of the farmers. Possibly some reduction in taxation might be expected. But the best prospect of restoring the balance between costs and prices was to concentrate on trying to raise the latter.[3] The strategy favoured by Colonel Closey, the author of the foregoing analysis was a 'compensated price', 'designed to close the gap between the level at which a farmer is compelled to sell his produce and the over-weighted prices that he has to meet, directly or indirectly, through tariff and other charges for everything for which he has to pay'.[4] This really amounted to offering a 'deal' by which the farmers would accept tariff protection for manufacturers, provided that they themselves were

[1] Letter from Colonel Closey to the writer, Jan. 1959. The meeting also agreed, *inter alia*, to raise and maintain the returns available to farmers for their exports (according to Colonel Closey, the foundation for the Guaranteed Price).

[2] In 1929 the tariff was said to be the most serious item in the primary producer's costs; see W. J. Polson, *President's Address, Annual Conference, 1929* (New Zealand Farmers' Union, 1929, p. 6). See also J. B. Condliffe, *The Welfare State in New Zealand*, pp. 265–6.

[3] Closey, *Progress*, 1 Mar. 1938.

[4] Ibid. 6 Oct. 1937.

also 'protected'.[1] The compensated price was not really so very different from the notion behind the Labour policy for the farmer who was producing for export.[2] But in practice the Labour Party's 'guaranteed price' was based on farm costs rather than on differences between internal and external price levels.[3] Of course, a further possibility, advocated by a special committee of the Farmers' Union and Sheep-owners' Federation in 1939, was to allow the exchange rate to rise still higher than £125 N.Z. to £100 sterling, and so give the farmers a better return without a corresponding increase in their costs.[4]

In the depression of the 1930's the Reform Party (as a member of the Coalition) lost farming support to the Labour Party. When the National Party was formed in 1936 it was faced with a task similar to the Reform Party's. It had to be 'pro-farmer', but it also had to unite all anti-Labour forces. The Leader of the party, Adam Hamilton, exposed the problem when, speaking on the choice of a policy, he said 'we must have one that the Farmers' Union and the Chamber of Commerce may equally support.'[5] Later in 1937 he was still making public speeches on the problem of finding a policy, although he no longer mentioned these two organizations by name, but referred to the 'farming' and 'business' communities, and also, belatedly, included the 'working community'.

Eventually the National Party did produce a policy, even though much of it consisted merely of opposition to 'socialism'. Even before the 1938 election, two groups with partly conflicting interests, the Farmers' Union and the New Zealand Manufacturers' Federation, issued a joint statement, drawing attention to the high costs of production in New Zealand and the fact that lower-priced manufactured imports were driving local manufactured products off the local market.[6] The presidential address at the 1943 Dominion Conference of the National Party continued to play down differences between potentially

[1] Cf., on the Australian Country Party, F. W. Eggleston, *Reflections of an Australian Liberal* (Melbourne, 1953), p. 121; J. P. Abbott, in A. Campbell Garnett (ed.), *Freedom and Planning in Australia* (Univ. of Wisconsin, 1949), p. 302.
[2] Closey, *Progress*, 6 Oct. 1937.
[3] Letter from Colonel Closey to the writer, Mar. 1959.
[4] *Press*, 24 Apr. 1939.
[5] *Southland Daily News*, 29 Jan. 1937.
[6] *Taranaki Herald*, 7 Oct. 1938.

antagonistic groups. The party had held meetings and discussion with the Farmers' Union and the Manufacturers' Federation.[1] 'The difficulties and differences that appear, superficially at any rate, to separate these two organizations are not really so very great. The reasonable men in both groups would have no difficulty in securing agreement on a common policy, fair to both when considered from a national and not a sectional view-point, and we are fortunate in having a Leader [S. G. Holland], who claims membership of both organizations and can do something towards harmonizing and reconciling the apparent cleavage between them.'[2] But the process of obtaining agreement was not completely smooth. For instance the Compensated Price proposals were reputedly accepted by the National Party, but were later dropped, allegedly because of the domination of city interests.[3] There was also a remarkable outburst by the President of the Farmers' Union at the Annual Conference of 1939, and the Conference passed a resolution in favour, ultimately, of political action through a rural party. The president hit out at extreme conservative elements, particularly 'important people in the financial world', who had exercised disproportionate influence on previous governments. These elements were not opposed to controls, provided it was control of *their competitors*, and some manufacturers supported exchange control. Big business interests had tried to kill farmer co-operative movements.[4] He also referred to 'auxiliaries' promoted by these elements. This may have been a reference to the 'Freedom Association', which was in existence at this time. Certainly the National Party was well aware that any formal amalgamation with the Freedom Association, which, at least in the minds of the farmers, was too closely linked with Auckland big business, would be strongly opposed by its rural supporters. When the parliamentary party discussed a change in the leadership in 1940 it was used as an argument against Mr. Holland that to

[1] Apparently the discussions took place before both the 1938 and 1943 elections (A. D. Robinson, *Oligarchy and Democracy: the Distribution of Power in the New Zealand National Party, 1936–1949* (The Hague, 1959 (mimeo.), p. 39)). See also pp. 176–7 below, on representation of interests on the policy committee of the Dominion Council.

[2] Dominion Council, *Report*, 1943.

[3] Daniels, op. cit., p. 231; Closey, *Manawatu Evening Standard*, 16 Sept. 1943; letter from Colonel Closey to the writer, 15 Feb. 1959.

[4] *Evening Post*, 11 July, 1939.

choose him would drive the farmers into forming a Country Party.

The abolition of the country quota in 1945 was a blow to the National Party, but it had two compensating advantages. It made the Labour Party more unpopular among the farmers, and it also helped to underline the fact that no party could ever hold power on the basis of country support alone, and so tended to moderate rural demands. Since 1949 relations between the farmers and the National Party have been good, compared with the 1930's, although in 1952 Federated Farmers of New Zealand (Inc.), which replaced the Farmers' Union in 1944, protested against National Party policy in the name of the party's own cry of 'free enterprise'—when they opposed the Land Settlement Promotion Bill in 1952.[1] In Federated Farmers there are tensions between different elements in the organization: between dairy farmers and sheep farmers; between members in different provinces; between the leaders and the rank and file. Also the organization's financial position is weak, compared to that of the statutory agricultural producer boards.[2] These boards are in some ways better placed to be 'articulators' of agricultural interests than Federated Farmers itself. The organization strives to be non-partisan, but many of its members also belong to the National Party. Farming organizations and the party are so close together that one division of the party could, proprietorially, state that 'our [sic] Young Farmers' Clubs are performing excellent work, and with a membership approximately 80 per cent. National.'[3]

The farmers have no longer a party which is predominantly their own, but they hold a position of very special influence in the country, especially those farmers who produce for export. 'In New Zealand there are only about 33,000 dairy farmers but they constitute probably the strongest pressure group the country has known and have been able to get things practically all their own way.'[4] This description, by the late Mr. Walsh, exaggerated the power of the dairy farmers just as *their* public pronouncements over-emphasized Mr. Walsh's own position in

[1] e.g. *Evening Post*, 4 Sept. 1952.   [2] *Dominion*, 15 July, 1964.
[3] National Party, *20th Annual Conference, Agenda and Conference Arrangements* (1957), p. 40.
[4] *Evening Post*, 24 Aug. 1957.

the trade unions. Nevertheless, because of the importance of exports, the dairy farmers and other farmers who produce for export will continue to exercise influence quite out of proportion to their numbers.

Business Groups

Business organizations in New Zealand, like the farmers' ones, are not 'party political'. They are not affiliated to a party, nor do they, as organizations, contribute to party funds. However, Professor S. E. Finer's analysis of the situation in Britain could also be applied, with some qualifications, to New Zealand. 'In practice . . . it would be mere pedantry not to affirm the existence of a positive link between the business lobby and the Conservative Party. But this link is not organic; it is *not* affiliation. A better word is "alignment". The associations making up the business lobby are "aligned" with the Conservative Party. And they are aligned, not as associations, but through personalities—through persons who belong jointly to the association in question, and the Conservative Party.'[1] But, although the position in New Zealand is broadly similar, if 'National' is substituted for 'Conservative', two qualifications are necessary. First, because of the special roles of the manufacturers in New Zealand, they are probably not so closely aligned with the National Party as their British counterparts are with the Conservative Party. Second, if alignment is to be inferred from the behaviour of 'personalities', the New Zealand data are not so conclusive as the British. For instance, too little information exists on occupation and voting in New Zealand for any firm figures to be given on the percentage of businessmen voting for the National Party. Nor has any statistical research been done on the degree of overlapping in New Zealand between the executive committee-men of business associations and the committee-men of local units of the National Party. One would *expect* that, with the possible exception of the manufacturers, the New Zealand picture would be similar to the British, but the actual evidence is not very firm. As regards representation of businessmen in Parliament, there is a striking difference between the two countries, mainly because of the preponderance

[1] Finer, *Anonymous Empire*, pp. 47 ff.

of farmers among National Party members. The proportion of businessmen among Labour members in the New Zealand House is as high as the proportion in the National ranks.[1]

The other argument for believing in the Business–Conservative 'alignment' mentioned by Finer, is the financial contributions given by businessmen to the Conservative Party. The New Zealand data for the National Party and its predecessors are scanty. Certainly, in the earlier right-wing parties, there seems to have been some approach to what Eggleston described as the 'dual organization' which operated in Australia; behind the public party organization there was a shadow organization in the background, which collected the funds and exercised some influence on the financial policy of the party.[2] Most of the Reform Party's money apparently came from wealthy supporters and not from the grass roots.[3] From more than one account the Dominion Executive of the Reform Party when appealing for funds in the 1920's, used, rather casually, to ring up a few key people, some of whom would give as much as £1,000 each. It was also rumoured that the Reform Party was supported in 1925 by a business group in Auckland, popularly known as 'the Kelly gang'. A. E. Davy, the political organizer, was reputed to be particularly adept at securing large 'business' contributions on behalf of Reform in 1925, United in 1928, and the Democrats in 1935. Even after the formation of the National Party, Labour taunted Hamilton as representing in Parliament 'the hidden powers outside Parliament'.[4] The National Party now collects contributions from business through its regular party machinery. It does not publish accounts, but there is nothing particularly underhand or secretive about its proceedings. It also aims to collect as much money as possible in the form of individual subscriptions.

The licensed trade, and in particular the brewers, have often been mentioned as contributors to campaign funds. In 1914 Reform alleged that the Liberals received £3,600 from this source to finance their paper, the *New Zealand Liberal*.[5] In 1928 Reform was denying a statement that 'the trade' was subsidizing

[1] Mitchell, op. cit., and pp. 21–22, above.
[2] Eggleston, op. cit., p. 132.
[3] Gardner, 1st art. cit., pp. 23–24.
[4] *Standard*, 22 Sept. 1938.
[5] *Light and Liberty* (Journal of the Reform Movement), 23 May 1914, p. 29.

the party to the extent of £45,000 for the coming election.[1] This denial was probably made with some feeling, because it appears that Reform lost popularity with the brewers, 1925–8,[2] and that the contributions it formerly received from this quarter were mostly switched to United in 1928. If this is true, it may only have been a sign of the general disgust felt by business groups for the Reform Party's 'socialism'. On the other hand, a United candidate said later that A. E. Davy had told him that the liquor interests had promised United £40,000 but had not kept their promise.[3] A recent researcher believes that the liquor interests give substantial support to both the major parties, the National Party having received the larger share since 1946.[4] The brewers, incidentally, also seek to influence voters directly, as well as via the parties and via individual candidates, by conducting propaganda in favour of 'continuance' at the times when licensing referenda are held. They have also conducted registration drives and provided cars to take voters to the polls in the belief that a high turnout will favour their cause. The (pro-temperance) New Zealand Alliance confines itself to publicity aimed at the voter at referenda. It does not subscribe to party funds.[5]

In 1935 the banks intervened in the election, in effect against the Labour Party. Large advertisements appeared in the newspapers,[6] sponsored by the Associated Banks of New Zealand, giving warning against currency reformers and experiments with savings.

A formidable problem which faces business interest groups is the difficulty of achieving 'solidarity'. In certain organizations, such as the Employers' Federation and the Associated Chambers of Commerce, the emphasis is naturally laid on those topics on which it is relatively easy to find agreement. For instance, in 1945, when the Labour Government was about to nationalize the Bank of New Zealand, the Associated Chambers of Commerce presumably had not much difficulty in identifying this as

[1] *Newsletter*, 27 Oct. 1928, p. 8.
[2] Lipson, op. cit., pp. 222 and 225.
[3] McDonald (candidate for Mataura), *Otago Daily Times*, 11 Nov. 1935.
[4] Because of Labour's support of the Invercargill trust (North, op. cit., *Supplementary Statement* (in Librarian's Room, Victoria University of Wellington)).
[5] Ibid., pp. 176–7.
[6] e.g. *Dominion*, 23 Nov. 1935; *New Zealand Herald*, 25 Nov. 1935.

a threat to private enterprise, and they consequently decided to fight nationalization by raising a fund of £25,000.[1] And, later, the General Secretary of the Associated Chambers of Commerce appeared before a Price Tribunal hearing as spokesman, not only for his own organization, but for six others as well, one of which was the Manufacturers' Federation.[2] Another example of co-operation is the Joint Tax Vigilance Committee, which includes representatives of the Associated Chambers of Commerce, the Manufacturers' Federation, the Retailers' Federation and also Federated Farmers.[2] But the façade of 'solidarity', prominent in the pages of *New Zealand Commerce* (organ of the Associated Chambers of Commerce), is easily penetrated by turning to, say, *The New Zealand Manufacturer* (organ of the Manufacturers' Federation) and noting the emphasis on the manufacturing, as opposed to the importing, interest. In the late 1930's, when the manufacturers were securing extra protection through higher tariffs and import licensing, the protests of importers were particularly vocal,[3] and the rifts in the façade of business 'solidarity' were blatantly obvious.

The 'manufacturing interest' has gained steadily in strength in recent years, particularly since the introduction of import licensing in 1938. Just before that date it was said that the Manufacturers' Federation was 'almost apologetic' when it claimed government assistance.[4] If this were ever so, it is now no longer true. By 1957 an economist in government employment could say that 'for the sake of employing our rising numbers and of maximizing our living standards, the development of our manufacturing will have to be recognized as one of the central elements of public policy'.[5] This theme was repeated at the Industrial Development Conference in 1960.[6] On a more popular level, the well-known fact that the tariff and the

---

[1] C. G. F. Simkin, 'The Nationalization of the Bank of New Zealand', *Economic Record, Australia and New Zealand*, vol. xxii, Dec. 1946.

[2] Stevens, *Organization and Techniques of Pressure Groups in New Zealand*, op. cit., p. 3.

[3] e.g. *New Zealand Herald*, 26 Nov. 1937; *Dominion*, 2 Mar. 1938; *Dominion*, 25 July 1938.

[4] *Contemporary New Zealand* (New Zealand Institute of International Affairs, Auckland, 1938), p. 64.

[5] Dr. W. B. Sutch, *Evening Post*, 17 Jan. 1957.

[6] Chapman, Jackson, and Mitchell, op. cit., pp. 56–57.

Arbitration system were complementary,[1] has been brought
up to date, and full employment and the forty-hour week have
been represented as depending on the growth of New Zealand
manufacturing.[2] The Labour Party attacked the National
Government in 1951 (and at the same time defended New
Zealand manufacturers) by saying that the new policy of
admitting more imports aimed 'to destroy full employment
and produce a pool of surplus labour'.[3] The parties are keenly
aware of the importance of support from the manufacturers. In
1949 the National Party thought it necessary to issue a special
leaflet, '*We Support N.Z. Manufacturing Industries*', Mr. S. G.
Holland's Pledge. There is reason to believe that at the 1957
election the Labour Party was supported financially by a substantial body of manufacturers, because it was thought likely
to give them greater protection. In 1960, apparently, manufacturers gave the party several thousand pounds, more than
ever before.[4] A Labour view, which may be typical, is that
relations with manufacturers are cordial while those with importers have always been difficult.

The manufacturers themselves are subject to cross-pressures.
Businessmen are opposed to control in general; but manufacturers obviously favour one type of controls, namely those over
imports of 'their' product, while, at the same time, they resist
other controls, such as price control. The situation may be even
more complicated than this. For example, a manufacturer,
while welcoming controls over competing imports, will normally
be opposed to import controls on the raw materials which he
uses. Diversification of interests can lead to a rapid *volte face*. In
1950, to quote a National Party official, one businessman was
perpetually 'squealing' about the slowness with which import
controls were being removed. But, upon becoming a director
of a firm protected by import control, he smartly changed
course and began to squeal, just as loudly, in the other direction.

Another feature which affects the political activity of business
groups is the relatively small number of businessmen in New
Zealand. Even on a wide definition, there are not enough

---

[1] Siegfried, op. cit., p. 158; *Round Table*, vol. xviii (1927–8), p. 422.
[2] Mr. A. R. Dellow, general secretary of the New Zealand Manufacturers'
Association, *Evening Post*, 6 June 1957.
[3] *Labour Discussion Series*, no. 51 (1951).
[4] Chapman, Jackson, and Mitchell, op. cit., p. 79.

'businessmen' to provide voting strength for a business party which would be comparable with a 'labour', or workers' party. Business can provide the money for such a movement, but not the votes. So parties (or groups) which are in essence 'pro-business' seek a wider appeal, which will attract other sections of the population, and tend to present themselves as being 'for freedom', 'anti-socialist', 'against bureaucracy', and so on. The number of movements of this kind is so great that it is impossible to mention more than a few. For convenience they may be placed under three heads. Some actually became political parties, like the United Party (erected on the residue of the previous Liberal Party) and the Democrat Party. The People's Movement, which in 1940–1 agitated against controls, too many government employees, too much government expenditure, and high taxation,[1] threatened to enter the 'political arena', saying that there was a need for a safe and sane 'middle party'.[2] These threats, and the fact that the movement was organized by the redoubtable A. E. Davy, apparently persuaded the Nationalists to handle the movement very carefully. Some of its members amalgamated with the National Party in 1941,[3] but others remained outside, and fought a few seats at the 1943 elections. The Liberal Party of 1963 was a free-enterprise party, but had too little money from business behind it to be considered a 'business party'. Those under the second head seem to have been on the verge of becoming a party, but did not actually do so. For instance in 1923 Mr. J. H. Gunson, Mayor of Auckland, and others were said to have founded a businessmen's party, because of dissatisfaction with the Government's high taxation of companies and its creation of the 'socialist' Meat and Dairy Boards. But this report was denied, and the body seems to have been an interest group rather than a party.[4] There have been later rumours of new right-wing parties, financed by businessmen dissatisfied with the National Party.

A third heading would include 'pro-business' groups which have not shown signs of wanting to contest elections. One was the '1928 Committee', founded in Auckland to resist encroachments

[1] *Dominion*, 1 May 1940; *The Policy of the People's Movement* (Palmerston North, 1940); Daniels, op. cit., pp. 162 ff.
[2] *Dominion*, 1 May 1940.
[3] Ibid., 19 Feb. 1941.
[4] *Round Table*, vol. xiv (1923–4), p. 413.

by the Government.[1] It seems to have been in lineal
descent from the 1923 movement, and included Mr. Gunson
among its members. Another was the Freedom Association,
founded in Auckland at the end of 1937. The Association opposed 'socialism and extravagant and costly bureaucratic
government', because both involved a denial of personal
liberty.[2] The Association supported the National Party at the
1938 election in preference to founding a third party, but it was
'free from, and . . . independent of, all party ties and allegiances'.[3]
The Association appealed neither to the extreme right nor to the
extreme left but to 'the average New Zealander'.[4] Regardless of
the maxim *qui s'excuse s'accuse* the Association denied that it was
'a grouping together of city businessmen for the purpose of pro-
tecting their own interests at the expense of those who live and
work in the country'.[5] After the 1938 election the Association
faded away. A proposal that it should fuse with the National
Party was not carried out. But its organizer, Professor Algie,
fought and won Remuera as a National in 1943, and proved to
be a valuable acquisition to National's debating strength in the
House, and later to the strength of the National Cabinet.

The 'Constitutional Society for the Promotion of Economic
Freedom and Justice in New Zealand' was founded in February
1957. Its more general aims and objects included conservation
of the liberty of the individual, for instance by opposition to
too-long-retained emergency powers, and by supporting the
claims of persons unfairly affected by the decisions of an
authority acting under delegated powers, who lacked the
right of appeal to the courts. It also aimed at promoting 'an
economy based on freedom and private ownership and management', and wished steps to be taken to produce 'stability in the
buying power of all earnings, savings, and pensions'.[6] The first
few issues of the Constitutional Society's Journal, *Liberator*,
developed, among other themes, the case for a written constitution, civil servants' abuse of their powers, the dangers of the
welfare state, and the disinclination of the National Government to halt the 'dangerous trends towards socialism'. The

[1] *Evening Post*, 21 Feb. 1929; *Round Table*, vol. xix (1928–9), p. 666.
[2] *Auckland Provincial Freedom Association: Aims and Objects* (n.d.).
[3] *Democracy Re-Discovers its Backbone* (n.d.), p. 4.   [4] Ibid., p. 5.
[5] *Auckland Provincial Freedom Association: Aims and Objects.*
[6] *Evening Post*, 7 Feb. 1957.

Constitutional Society is no exception to the general tendency of these pro-business movements to be based on Auckland. Its head office is in Auckland, one of its original Vice-Presidents was Sir James Gunson, and when it applied for registration to the New Zealand Registrar of Incorporated Societies, thirteen out of the twenty-three signatories were from Auckland.[1] The activities of the Constitutional Society (and the ultimate threat of a competing new party) were probably instrumental in persuading the National Party to include proposals for a bill of rights and for considering the provision of a written constitution in the 1960 election policy. It has been emphasized that most of these organizations were based on Auckland. Just as depressed areas throw up movements of political protest, so the booming Auckland area produces men who have made money and then feel the urge to save New Zealand for free enterprise.

In 1959 a body was set up, the National Research Association, which represents business, and, to a lesser extent, farming groups. Its aim is apparently to encourage the Government to circulate its proposals affecting business for comment by the Association. It has no formal links with any party, but in practice the National Government has made use of it, while the Labour Government did not. Presumably this organization could serve a valuable function for the National Party by 'institutionalizing' pressures and cushioning their impact on the Leader.

The Parties and the Groups

Although business interest groups are generally 'aligned' with the National Party, nevertheless 'all pressure groups try their best to maintain good relations with both parties; they have to deal with the Government regardless of which party is in power and they therefore cannot afford to become too closely tied to either Party'.[2] This is true not only of business and farming groups; it even applies to the Federation of Labour, as has been shown by the FOL's relations with the National Government, notably during the 1951 strike.

On the other hand the major parties usually do more than simply 'articulate'[3] the interests of groups which are aligned

[1] *Evening Post*, 7 Feb. 1957.
[2] Stevens, op. cit. p. 7.
[3] On articulation and aggregation of interests, see G. A. Almond and J. S. Coleman (eds.), *The Politics of the Developing Areas* (Princeton, 1960), especially pp. 33 ff.

with them. Even assuming that 'classes' were more distinct than they are, and that the parties acted solely from self-interest, under capitalism the Labour Party must pay some attention to the needs and advice of employers, or the workers will suffer, and, although the farming vote is not so important as it was, Labour cannot ignore the farmers without endangering exports. Nor can the National Party disregard the working class. Some of them vote National, and the party needs all the votes it can get. Moreover, if the claims of 'moderate' unionists are not given consideration, the position of 'militants' will be strengthened, strikes will spread, and productivity will suffer.

However, New Zealand parties do not act purely from self-interest. Each of them has the task of aggregating conflicting demands, whether they come from groups aligned with it, from groups aligned with the other party, from non-aligned groups, or from sections of the community which are not even organized into groups, such as consumers. It would not be helpful to try and use Eggleston's terminology and to divide parties into those which represent major interests (such as the Australian Labour and Country Parties) and into 'residual parties' (such as the Australian Liberal Party), which represent less important interests and also 'the common good'[1] (public interest). Both the major parties in New Zealand 'represent', or 'are aligned with' interests.[2] At the same time both also attempt, in a groping and pragmatic way, to aggregate demands and aim at realizing the common good.[3]

In principle, the whole New Zealand way of life, which expresses itself in the wish to see fair play and in the acknowledgement that all should be given a 'fair go', is in sympathy with the concept of the aggregation of interests. In practice, interest aggregation may be imperfect for two main reasons. Non-material interests, for instance claims for cultural enjoyment or for the protection of civil liberties, may be given insufficient

[1] Eggleston, op. cit., ch. 6; Henry Mayer, 'Some Conceptions of the Australian Party System, 1910–1950', *Historical Studies, Australia and New Zealand*, vol. vii, no. 27 (1956).

[2] Cf. Sidgwick's view that parties are not 'naturally' united, but that the system of parliamentary government imposes some unity on different interests (*The Elements of Politics* (London, 1891), pp. 563–9. See also Meyer, op. cit., p. 262).

[3] Cf. the statement by a National Party minister that some party supporters were raising prices and so alienating 'the neutrals' or 'floating voters' (*N.Z.P.D.*, vol. ccciii, p. 30 (24 June 1954)).

weight by governments, because of the New Zealand bias towards material things. Also, because of the New Zealander's pragmatic approach to politics, 'compartmental' solutions may be attempted in certain sectors without reference to possible repercussions in other sectors. Perhaps the present management of various forms of transport, for which several different government departments are responsible, is a case in point.

V

THE PARTIES IN PARLIAMENT

MEETINGS of members of the New Zealand parliamentary groups have been traced back to 1956; the first use of the word 'caucus' to describe such meetings occurred, apparently, in 1876. Like some other parliamentary terms it was first used in a derogatory sense. But by the period 1879–89 there were many references to 'caucus' without explanation or apology.[1] Today the word is almost completely accepted, although there are still a few members of the New Zealand House of Representatives who would apply the term to meetings of the *other* party, but not to meetings of their own. 'Caucus' has a meaning in New Zealand quite different from that it had in Britain. It was used by Ostrogorski[2] and others to refer to British party organizations only outside Parliament, which perhaps gives some support to Lipson's view that the word probably came direct to New Zealand from the United States.

The Role of Caucus

Many of the early caucuses, according to Lipson,[3] were convened while a ministry was being constructed; few were held during the lifetime of a ministry. It was only gradually that the decisions of caucus took on a binding quality. Not until the 1890's, in the Liberal and Labour Federation, was a parliamentary party committed to support a number of common objects written down in a constitution.[4] The coming of the Labour Party also strengthened the disciplinary aspects of caucus. As in Australia,[5] caucus and the pledge were in existence

[1] 'The Origins of Caucus in New Zealand', *Historical Studies, Australia and New Zealand*, vol. ii, no. 5 (1942). See also Dean E. McHenry, 'Origins of Caucus Selection of Cabinet', ibid., vol. vii, no. 25 (1955).

[2] *Democracy and the Organization of Political Parties* (New York, 1902), vol. i, pp. 120, 182. In referring to the United States, however, he gives early examples of congressional and 'mixed' caucuses (vol. ii, pp. 13 and 34–38).

[3] *Historical Studies, Australia and New Zealand*, vol. ii, art. cit., pp. 9–10.

[4] B. J. Foster, 'Development of Unity and Organization in the New Zealand Political Parties of the Liberal Era' (Victoria University thesis, 1956), p. 126.

[5] J. D. B. Miller, 'Party Discipline in Australia', *Political Science*, vol. v, nos. 1 and 2 (1953), no. 1, p. 7.

before Labour came on the scene, but Labour made them more effective instruments of party discipline than previously. In all parties through discussions in caucus 'any differences of opinion between the cabinet and the back-benches or between rival wings of the party might be adjusted *in camera*. The speeches and the voting in Parliament itself normally presented an appearance of party unity which could not be attained without preliminary discussions'.[1]

From 1939 until the abolition of the upper house Labour members of the Legislative Council attended caucus meetings.[2] But there is no evidence that in other parliamentary parties Legislative Councillors ever attended caucus regularly. The *New Zealand Labour Party Constitution and Rules* also provides that the National President and National Secretary, or their deputies, shall have 'the right to attend caucus, but without voting power'.[3] Other persons, such as officials of the Federation of Labour,[4] may also attend by invitation. Membership of caucus need not be restricted to the members of the parliamentary party concerned. Members of minor parties or Independents may sometimes be invited, as were Labour Members of Parliament to Liberal caucus meetings in 1912.[5]

Procedure in caucus does not appear to be very elaborate. Nowadays short minutes are taken at each of the major party caucuses, and are read out at the start of the next meeting. In each party caucus has an agenda, but it is not circulated beforehand. Apparently motions are not circulated beforehand. In the words of a former National Party minister, 'people just stood up, and you didn't know what was coming until it came'. Votes are not taken very often, only about once per caucus meeting on the average. In the National Party a show of

---

[1] Lipson, *The Politics of Equality*, p. 335.

[2] This amendment to the *Constitution with LRC Branch Rules and Standing Orders* (*1937*), 21 (3) was passed at the Twenty-third Annual Conference, 1939; cf. H. Morrison, *Government and Parliament* (London, 1954), p. 128, on British Labour Party practice.

[3] *Constitution and Rules (1955)*, 22 (C).

[4] See p. 106, above. At the Labour Party Conference, 1964, Mr. Nordmeyer announced that in future the FOL would be represented at caucus meetings when industrial affairs were to be discussed (*New Zealand Herald*, 8 May 1964).

[5] Foster, op. cit., p. 254; Shannon, op. cit., p. 163. After Massey died in 1925 invitations to the caucus to select his successor were sent to the three non-Reform members who were pledged to vote for the party on a no-confidence motion (*Round Table*, vol. xv (1924–5), p. 844).

hands is sometimes used to obtain some idea of what caucus thinks on a particular issue, but only a rough indication is required, and often the hands are not even counted. Both parties have now evolved a system of caucus committees. In the National Party this dates from early in 1944.[1] In 1958 there were sixteen 'regular' committees, each specializing in a particular field.[2] The committees are formed roughly along the same lines as the Select Committees of the House. In 1963 each committee consisted of those members of the corresponding Select Committee of the House plus others experienced in the particular field or problem. According to one member, 'as a public accountant I am often called into a financial discussion group, or, as a former staff member of an agricultural college, I am often directed to take part in various discussions on various types of agricultural problems.'[3] Caucus committee chairmen are appointed by the Leader. When the party is in office they are usually ministers. When it is in opposition, the chairmen of the committees roughly correspond to a 'shadow cabinet'. But there is no guarantee that the chairmen will actually be included in the next National Party Cabinet. They may have left Parliament by the time a Cabinet is formed, or there may be a 'reshuffle'. These regular committees provide a means of dividing up the party's work in the House and of making sure that members are well prepared before they speak. The chairmen have the duty of reporting to the Leader in caucus which individuals in a committee are prepared to speak on a Bill and at what stage.[4] They also help to inform and 'educate' members, and, more specifically, they may collect facts and formulate policy recommendations for caucus and Cabinet.[5] The party Leader allocates members to committees according to previous experience, occupation, and interest. Individuals may request to be switched from one committee to another, but in the last resort the Leader is able to overcome a member's reluctance to go on a particular committee by using such arguments as, 'If you don't know much about it, now's the time

[1] Robinson, *The Rise of the New Zealand National Party*, pp. 162–3.
[2] *Evening Post*, 21 Mar. 1958.
[3] H. J. Walker, 'A Government Back-bencher', *Political Science*, vol. xv, no. 2 (1963), p. 45.   [4] Interview, Mr. K. J. Holyoake, Oct. 1958.
[5] R. J. Polaschek, *Government Administration in New Zealand* (Wellington, 1958), p. 229.

to learn.' Apart from these regular caucus committees, special committees may also be set up, for instance in order to consider particular Bills. When the party is in office sometimes public servants have given evidence before caucus committees, and on occasions public meetings were even held at which interest groups made submission.[1]

Labour has both regular and *ad hoc* caucus committees. The regular committees are the less important, and seem to be fairly recent in origin. Apparently they did not exist during the early days at least of the Labour Government 1935–49.[2] One estimate is that they did not start until the mid 1950's. In 1962 there were twenty-four Labour Party caucus committees, each with from four to six members.[3] But the number of committees was reduced to four in 1963 and later altered to six, one of which was on Maori Affairs. The reason was apparently the difficulty of arranging meetings for all the committees at times which did not clash.[4] Each M.P. is on only one committee, although he may be invited to attend others. In May 1964 three of the committee chairmen were ex-ministers; three were not. The latter are recommended by the Leader to caucus. Probably when Labour is next in power the previous practice of having only back-benchers as chairmen will be resumed.

In the early years of the first Labour Government *ad hoc* committees were set up on finance, the guaranteed price,[5] social security, and other items. Later there were others on the nationalization of the Bank of New Zealand and on price stabilization.[6] More recent *ad hoc* committees have included one with the function of co-ordinating discipline and tactics in the House (1956)[7] and another, in operation in 1958 and 1959, on Pay-As-You-Earn income tax. The former is used only when the party is in opposition; it was discontinued 1957–60 and then revived. The latter seems to have been concerned largely with

[1] R. J. Polaschek, op. cit., p. 229.
[2] At that time the need for them may have been reduced because members helped ministers under the 'salary pooling' scheme (pp. 156–7, below).
[3] H. J. L. May, 'The Rôle of the Whips', *Political Science*, vol. xv, no. 2 (1963), pp. 49–50.
[4] Interview, Mr. H. J. L. May, Apr. 1964.
[5] John A. Lee, *I Fight for New Zealand* (Auckland, n.d.), pp. 8–10.
[6] Interview, Mr. F. H. Langstone, Nov. 1958.
[7] *Evening Post*, 27 Oct. 1956.

Public Relations aspects, and was responsible for issuing pamphlets on the working of PAYE.[1]

In general the Labour caucus committee system seems to have been, at least originally, more *ad hoc* than the National one in almost every sense. At least some of the committees do not seem to have been taken too seriously by their members. It is said that a few years ago, when a caucus committee on a financial subject was called together eighteen months after it had been set up, two of the five members replied by telegram denying that they had ever been put on the committee. Nevertheless, in spite of the rough-and-ready organization of the groups, their status and importance is higher than that of their opposite numbers, the 'subject-matter' groups of the British Parliamentary Labour Party. In Britain, apparently, Labour ministers have resisted giving these groups advance information about government policy on the ground that it would be constitutionally improper; they have also 'felt that the groups tended to be composed of militants and extremists . . .'.[2] The first of these considerations would not be taken as seriously in New Zealand as in Britain. Nor is the number of 'militants and extremists' in the New Zealand parliamentary party sufficient to make ministers afraid to take caucus into their confidence in advance.

Caucus and Party Discipline

Caucus is now a familiar feature of Government in New Zealand. It has also become a target for those who distrust the discipline and secrecy of organized political parties.[3] Rule by caucus is by definition 'less oligarchical' than rule by Cabinet, but attacks on caucus stress the loss of freedom to the individual member which is entailed by discipline. The emphasis on discipline by such critics is perhaps overdone. Members are naturally closely aligned with their party's policy, otherwise they would not have taken the step of putting themselves forward as candidates and committing themselves to it. And, once they are in Parliament, the two-party system, with its resemblance to a team game, cements the solidarity of 'us' as opposed to 'them'. Military analogies may also be invoked. It was pointed out many

---

[1] Interview, Mr. A. H. Nordmeyer, Dec. 1958.
[2] McKenzie, op. cit., p. 448.
[3] See p. 71, above.

years ago in New Zealand that it was not enough for a member to give the Government 'discriminating support'; who had ever heard of a soldier giving his general discriminating support?[1] In addition there are 'rewards' for good behaviour, such as the favourable opinion of one's fellow members in the party, ministerial office, government appointments on retirement, honours, trips abroad, and so on.

Labour Party practice is laid down as follows. 'The Policy of the Party shall be binding on all Members, but on matters other than Policy Members shall vote in accordance with decisions of a majority of Members at a duly constituted caucus.'[2] 'But if it is a subject that is felt to be one of individual conviction (as the licensing matter was for some years) then the decision of the caucus is that members should have the right to vote as they will, on a subject where permission is given in that way. In certain cases a given member may say, "Well, that's not the way I see things; I hope that I won't be compelled to vote in accordance with that rule." Then either the Parliamentary Leader or the caucus can give the member concerned permission to vote as he will.'[3] The tightness of Labour discipline is explainable in historical and sociological terms. It derives partly from trade-union traditions of 'solidarity' and partly from the need of a Labour group in Parliament to guard its 'independence' in its dealings with longer-established parties. As was said of Labor members in Australia, the 'idea of the solidarity of the working class, the condemnation of those who would not obey the party mandate as a "scab", the victimization of the scab by any means however cruel, the implicit obedience to party leaders, the submission of the rank and file', all followed from Labour members' conviction that their class had been oppressed and from their determination to relieve that oppression.[4]

Significantly, the Parliamentary Labour Party has not in practice made extensive provision for allowing its members a free vote on matters of conscience. Indeed, when this issue was raised at a recent Party Conference, a comment from the platform was that the question of independent voting on matters of

---

[1] *N.Z.P.D.*, vol. lxix, p. 45 (15 Aug. 1890).

[2] *Constitution and Rules (1955)*, 23 (D).

[3] Walter Nash, 'The Leader of the Opposition', *Political Science*, vol. xv, no. 2 (1963), p. 33.

[4] Eggleston, op. cit., pp. 63–64.

conscience did not arise because Labour was an 'important political party'. This is reminiscent of Attlee's remark: 'I always recall Tom Shaw saying to me once: "When I was young I was always talking about my conscience till one day I realised that what I called conscience was just my own blooming conceit".'[1] When Mr. Freer, M.P., said that, although the National Party might be the only one with a free vote, yet he was proud to belong to a party that had a conscience,[2] he was presumably referring to some 'collective conscience' of the party and not to the consciences of individual members.

In contrast, the National Party has laid great emphasis on the individual member's conscience. The fullest, although perhaps the most confusing, exposition of this is probably to be found in S. G. Holland's *Passwords to Progress* (1943).[3] 'Time was when every member had to dance to the Leader's tune, but the National Party of today has changed all that and every one of its members is absolutely free and unfettered to vote on every question according to his or her own conscience and judgement. The only occasion on which members are under any pledge to vote with the Party is on a motion of no confidence in the Government and such a motion can be introduced only after opportunities have been provided for full discussion and a majority decision arrived at.' The sharp contrast which Holland drew with previous practice does not appear to be justified. Discipline in the Reform Party was probably no stricter than in the National Party. In the Liberal Party up to 1928, and even in the United Party 1928–31, it was decidedly slacker. There seems to have been little difference between the Coalition and the early days of the National Party, on the one hand, and the National Party after Holland became Leader, on the other. The rest of Holland's argument would seem to commit a member of the party in Parliament to giving it only the same degree of support as an Independent who has promised to vote with the party on a vote of No Confidence. But such a conclusion is hard to believe. Some of the difficulty may lie in the use of the phrase 'conscience and judgement' instead of simply 'conscience'. In fact, over the last few years, National Party members seem to

[1] Earl Attlee, 'The Attitudes of M.P.s and Active Peers', *Political Quarterly*, vol. xxx, no. 1 (1959), p. 32.
[2] *N.Z.P.D.*, vol. ccxciii, p. 4339 (17 Nov. 1950).   [3] p. 19.

have been allowed a free vote on matters which on a broad definition would come under 'conscience', such as capital punishment, liquor licensing, gambling, and (less obviously matters of conscience) on New Zealand's participation in the General Agreement on Tariffs and Trade (GATT),[1] and on the residential clause of the Land Settlement Promotion Amendment Bill (1959).[2] There is also the possibility of a free vote where caucus has not made a decision and the matter appears to be not of major political significance. The instance, quoted by Kelson, of five National members voting against their party on New Zealand expenditure on UNESCO in 1947, seems to fall into this category.[3] But to say that a National Party member was free to use his 'judgement' in voting would be to ignore his obligation to abide by caucus decisions and by the party's platform on matters outside the scope of 'conscience'. No doubt when Holland made his statement in 1943 he was greatly influenced by the approaching general election and by the desire to stress the party's theme of 'freedom' in every aspect.

Even in the same year, at the 1943 Party Conference, Holland gave a somewhat different account of the conscience provision. 'This is not an invitation or a licence to Members of the Parliamentary Party to run away whenever it gets a bit difficult. We have our plans prepared. It is going to take tough men to stay with us. All our candidates will be given an opportunity of saying whether they agree with our policy or not. The time to disagree with policy plans is now.'[4] Holland's last reference was to the candidates' conference. Because, since 1943, the candidates have been asked to approve the policy by resolution, it does give them an opportunity to raise problems of conscience. And the need for obtaining complete approval may result 'in the policy being so *framed* that all candidates could wholeheartedly accept it. For example, in 1949 the policy of the party on capital punishment was that it would introduce legislation with a free vote in Parliament on the restoration of capital and

---

[1] R. N. Kelson, 'Voting in the New Zealand House of Representatives, 1947–1954', *Political Science*, vol. vii, no. 2 (1955). Another general reference is the same author's, *The Private Member of Parliament and the Formation of Public Policy* (Toronto, 1964). See also Therese May, 'Parliamentary Discipline in New Zealand since 1954', *Political Science*, vol. xvii, no. 1 (1965).

[2] *Freedom*, 13 Oct. 1959.   [3] Kelson, *Political Science*, art. cit., p. 106.

[4] Robinson, *Oligarchy and Democracy*, p. 70.

corporal punishment. All candidates could thus agree with the policy as framed.'[1] And in 1957 Roman Catholic candidates were released from any obligation to support party policy on the issue of state aid to private schools; they could therefore speak and, if elected, vote according to their conscience.[2] Apparently this procedure was also followed in 1960 and 1963.[3]

Some indication of the extent of party discipline may be gathered from the answers to two questions. What recent instances are there of members voting against their party when they had not been allowed a free vote? What sanctions have been applied against members who voted against their party in the House? Admittedly, voting in the House is only one of several possible indications of party discipline. Speaking against one's party in the House but voting for it, is a sign that discipline is being applied. And voting in caucus compared with subsequent voting in the House would, if enough data were available, also be a valuable indication. But, apart from the information given by Lee and Barnard about voting in the Labour caucus, 1936–40, there is just not enough material available. The data on voting in the House are much more complete and much easier to analyse.

Before 1936 there were many instances of members voting against their party in the House without permission.[4] But the only clear instance since then occurred in 1942. In two votes of No Confidence moved against the Government for its leniency with the striking Huntly coal-miners, three National Party members, Coates, Hamilton, and Massey, voted with the Government. Kyle, who had left the party very recently, also voted with the Government. The situation was peculiar, because Holland, who moved the vote of No Confidence, had just resigned from the War Cabinet, while Coates and Hamilton, with the approval of caucus, remained in it. Therefore considerations of how best to win the war were relevant; it was not a straight 'party' issue. A further complicating factor was that Coates had been a former Prime Minister and Hamilton a former Leader of the Opposition.[5] This seems to be the only

---

[1] Robinson, *Oligarchy and Democracy*, pp. 41–42. For a further account of National Party methods of 'countering opposition within the ranks' see Therese May, art. cit., p. 51.   [2] Robinson, *Political Science*, art. cit., p. 30.
[3] On the candidates' conferences see pp. 269–70, below.
[4] Lipson, *The Politics of Equality*, pp. 340–4.   [5] Robinson, op. cit., pp. 63–66.

example of its kind, although it is possible for members to 'abstain' from supporting their party by intentionally disappearing from the House before a vote is taken. Messrs. Carr and Langstone, both Labour members, apparently did this on the vote on GATT in 1948.[1]

Considering the small number of votes cast in defiance of party in the House of Representatives, it is not remarkable that formal sanctions have also been rare. A few days before the 1942 'revolt' against the National Party, the Dominion Council of the Party endorsed Holland's 'right to expel disloyal members should that course become necessary'.[2] This right was exercised when Holland said, after the revolt, that Coates and Hamilton had severed their connexion with the party.[3] But it seems that the right was withdrawn at the next Dominion Council meeting.[4]

Kyle had previously explained his resignation thus: 'The National Party organization has built up a watertight compartment that makes one become a "yes man" with expulsion as an alternative.' Kyle thought it 'better to retire from the party than to place on it the onus of expulsion, a point which the gentleman [presumably Holland] who moved the resolution was expounding when I left the caucus meeting'.[5] Kyle remained an Independent until 1943, but did not contest the election in that year. Coates prepared to fight the election as an Independent, but died before the election took place.[6] Hamilton and Massey started attending caucus meetings again in June 1943,[7] and stood, successfully, as National Party candidates at the 1943 election. But this has been the nearest approach to expulsion on the National side.

To turn to the Labour Party, Mr. J. A. Lee was expelled in 1940, but not because he voted against the party in the House. His expulsion was followed by the resignation of Mr. W. J.

---

[1] Kelson, *Political Science*, art. cit., pp. 107–8.

[2] Robinson, *The Rise of the National Party*, p. 214, quoting Dominion Council *Minutes*, 29 Sept. 1942. Earlier Kyle had stated that Coates, Hamilton, Massey, and he were leading members of a new 'win the war' group (*Evening Post*, 7 Apr. 1942).

[3] *Star Sun*, 6 Oct. 1942; cf. the expulsion of Spender from the United Australia Party, 1944 (Overacker, *The Australian Party System*, p. 218).

[4] Robinson, op. cit., p. 214.   [5] *Dominion*, 5 Oct. 1942.

[6] His successor, Webb, fought as 'Independent National'.

[7] Daniels, op. cit., p. 78.

Barnard. Two independent-minded Labour M.P.s, Mr. Langstone and Mr. Kearins, also left Parliament, although neither
was expelled from the party. Mr. Langstone resigned in 1949
on the issue of conscription, although he had had several differences with the party previously.[1] He fought his old seat as an
Independent Labour candidate, and later on behalf of Social
Credit, each time without success. Mr. Kearins neither resigned, nor was he expelled, but when electoral boundaries were
altered for the 1945 election, he was not re-selected as Labour
candidate for the new seat which corresponded closely to his
old one. It has been alleged that there was some link between
Mr. Kearins's exercise of a free vote on liquor licensing in the
'King Country' (an area containing a large proportion of
Maoris, situated in his constituency) in 1953 and his subsequent failure to be re-selected. However, Mr. Nash maintains
that Mr. Kearins was specifically given permission to vote the
way he did.[2]

   Bearing in mind that the attitudes of the parties to free voting
are different, it is still possible to see three different types of
situation. One is on questions which are obviously recognized
to be moral or conscience questions, such as liquor or capital
punishment. Another is on questions devoid both of political or
moral significance, questions of taste. Thus in 1962 both parties,
by agreement, had a free vote on whether the new parliamentary
official to hear complaints on administration should be called
the 'Ombudsman' or the 'Parliamentary Commissioner'. No
party pattern was discernible in the voting.[3] A third type occurs
when a party does not intend to have a free vote, but a member
(or members) requests to be allowed to abstain or to vote against
his party. This might arise from a wish not to displease constituents, for instance Mr. Kearins on licensing in the King

   [1] Kelson, *Political Science*, art. cit. He had previously wanted to leave the party
on the issue of the abolition of the Second Chamber, but had been persuaded to
stay (interview with Mr. Langstone, Feb. 1958). In 1942 Langstone had resigned
from the Cabinet after Nash, not he, had been appointed Minister to the United
States (Wood, *The New Zealand People at War*, p. 196).
   [2] Kelson, art. cit., pp. 110–12; *N.Z.P.D.*, vol. cccxix, pp. 281–2 (8 July 1959);
Walter Nash, *Political Science*, art. cit., p. 33.
   [3] *N.Z.P.D.*, vol. cccxxxvi, p. 1859 (5 Sept. 1962). Neither has there been a
distinct party pattern in the voting on licensing. In 1950 only one National member
voted against capital punishment. By 1961 the number had increased to nine
(*N.Z.P.D.*, vol. cccxxviii, p. 2990 (12 Oct. 1961)).

Country in 1953 or Messrs. Harker, Roy, and Cooksley on the residential clause of the Land Settlement Promotion Amendment Bill in 1959.[1] In these cases the members concerned were apparently given a dispensation from having to follow the party line. However, the third type might also arise if a member (or members) invoked 'conscience' when the party had not thought of the issue concerned in terms of conscience. This apparently happened in the National Party over the Indecent Publications Bill in 1963. One National member voted against the Bill; another, who was a minister, abstained. Two Opposition members voted for it. In both varieties of this third case one Labour view is that a decisive consideration in inducing a Government to allow a free vote would be the calculation that it could permit it and still have a majority.

There have been instances of free votes on several issues between 1961 and 1963, on liquor licensing, indecent publications, capital punishment, and the title of the Ombudsman. But this frequency seems to have been largely a consequence of the *kind* of issues concerned rather than any broadening of the area in which free voting is permitted. Some other observations on free voting may be in order. In a free vote members have no guidance from the party whips; one member's enthusiasm for freedom in the dispensing of liquor is said to have been once so great that, paradoxically, he found himself voting against it by mistake. Untidy legislation may result from free voting, as in the recently passed legislation on serving liquor to minors. Also party discipline is so ingrained that some M.P.s may not take advantage of a free vote. One member, in order to avoid voting for his convictions, but 'against' the party, on a free vote is said to have absented himself from Parliament for a not very pressing engagement.

To sum up: the respective traditions and 'philosophies' of the parties, taken together with the record of 'cross-voting' in the House since 1935, indicate that Labour discipline is stricter than National. But the difference is not great, not nearly so great as Mr. Holland claimed it was in 1943. A few years ago a person in a very high position in the National Parliamentary Party gave it as his opinion that Labour discipline was 'only slightly

[1] *Freedom*, 13 Oct. 1959; Therese May, art. cit., pp. 38–42.
[2] *N.Z.P.D.*, vol. cccxxxvii, p. 2468 (15 Oct. 1963).

stricter'. But, to discuss party discipline properly, we need to look not only at the relations between caucus and the individual, but also at the relations between caucus, on the one hand, and the party Leader and Cabinet (if the party is in office), on the other.

Party Leadership

The Labour Party in Parliament has shown remarkable continuity of leadership. In over forty years it has had only five Leaders[1]—H. E. Holland, Savage, Fraser, Mr. Nash, and Mr. Nordmeyer. The first three died while Leader.

The practice until 1964 was for caucus to elect the Leader on the death or resignation of the previous Leader or at the start of the parliamentary session which precedes a general election, that is normally every three years. The election, like all caucus elections in the Labour Party, is by 'exhaustive ballot', by which successive polls are taken, bottom candidates being eliminated until a winner is left who has an absolute majority. It has been suggested that the Leader should be chosen *after* each general election. But this would be unrealistic. Many electors are interested in knowing who will be Prime Minister if Labour becomes the Government. If the choice of Leader after the election were to be more than purely formal, they might be unwilling to vote for a party whose future Prime Minister would be 'unknown'. However, a change of a different kind was agreed on at the 1964 Labour Conference. It was decided that the election should take place at the last caucus of the year *preceding* a general election year. The direct effect of this would be to give a new choice a longer time in which to 'dig himself in'. An indirect effect might be that the chances of re-election of an incumbent Leader were slightly reduced, because it could no longer be said that a successor would lack sufficient time as Leader to learn the job properly before the election.

On most occasions the elections for Leader have not resulted in a close fight. But at the very first election (1918) the result was a tie between H. E. Holland and McCombs, Holland winning when the two drew lots.[2] On Holland's death, Savage,

---

[1] More correctly, chairmen of the Parliamentary Labour Party. Before Holland, Hindmarsh had been 'unofficial leader' (Bruce Brown, *The Rise of New Zealand Labour* (Wellington, 1962), p. 35).   [2] Paul, op. cit., p. 70.

the Deputy-leader, was elected unanimously.[1] He was re-elected, again unanimously, in October three years later, just before the general election.[2] It is of course unthinkable that at such a time and as the first Labour Prime Minister, he should have been seriously opposed. For all the violence of his attacks on Savage, Mr. Lee found it impossible to shift him from the leadership a year later. 'Democracy', wrote Mr. Lee, 'is the best of systems, not because it inevitably produces the best leader (history demonstrates freakish exceptions) but because it offers a means, short of bloodshed, of getting rid of a discredited leader.'[3] But what Mr. Lee was unable to do was to 'discredit' a Leader as immensely popular as Savage.

On Savage's death Fraser, the Deputy-leader, was elected, but not without friction. Fraser seems to have had a large majority over McMillan and Carr.[4] But the voting was preceded by a dispute over 'democratic control' in the party,[5] and Fraser, in the chair, refused to allow the Leader to be elected by secret ballot and preferential voting, and insisted that it be done simply on a show of hands.[6] Six months later, before a Cabinet reconstruction, Fraser was re-elected unanimously.[7] In 1943 Fraser was re-elected unanimously,[8] and again in 1946.[9] But 'unanimous' re-election may sometimes conceal the fact that there has been a contest, but that the selection of the winner has then been unanimously endorsed. It has been reported that in 1946 Fraser's re-election was contested unsuccessfully by McLagan before he was re-elected 'unanimously'. There was no contest in 1949.

When Fraser died in 1950, once again the Deputy-leader, this time Mr. Nash, was re-elected to succeed him. Somewhat surprisingly in view of the lack of co-ordinated action between Mr. Nash and the FOL leadership during the 1951 waterside strike, the FOL threw its weight behind Mr. Nash as Leader in 1952.[10] Apparently the FOL saw the issue in terms of 'solidarity', and

[1] James Thorn, *Peter Fraser* (London, 1952), p. 104; *Dominion*, 12 Oct. 1938.
[2] *Dominion*, 12 Oct. 1938.
[3] 'Psychopathology in Politics', *Tomorrow*, 6 Dec. 1939.
[4] *Evening Post*, 5 Apr. and 8 Apr. 1940.
[5] See pp. 160 ff., below.
[6] W. E. Barnard, *The Speech of a New Zealander* (Napier, 1940), p. 6.
[7] *Dominion*, 30 Nov. 1940.   [8] *Evening Post*, 27 Oct. 1943.
[9] *Southern Cross*, 6 Sept. 1946.
[10] *Dominion*, 'Lobby Letter', 22 Feb. 1954.

believed that Mr. Nash was the best potential Prime Minister
the party had. In 1954, only two months before the three-
yearly election of the Leader at a caucus meeting, Mr. Nash,
who was being opposed by Mr. Nordmeyer, was again helped
by an expression of confidence from the quarterly meeting of the
National Executive of the Labour Party and also from the
National Council of the FOL.[1] Mr. Nordmeyer's chance came
in 1963 when, on Mr. Nash's retirement, he was elected unanimously. 'He was nominated by Stan Whitehead, and there was
no argument, no nothing.'[2] The slow turnover in Labour's
leaders has had its disadvantages. It seems that H. E. Holland
had lost most of his drive by about 1930 and that he was apparently content to let the party 'carry' him until his death. It
was fortunate for New Zealand that Savage's fatal illness was not
even longer and more drawn-out. The reluctance of the party
to replace him might have led to disasters which even Mr. Lee's
pen would have found almost too horrible to describe.

Before 1936 non-Labour parties generally kept their Leaders
when they were victorious, or had good prospects of victory, and
changed them in defeat. There is a striking contrast between the
Liberals, 1890–1911, and Reform after Massey became Leader,
on the one hand, and 'the Opposition' in the 1890's and the
Liberals after 1911, on the other. After the defeat of 1935 the
National Political Federation had apparently agreed on the
need for a change in the leadership. But there was 'obstruction'
from caucus, which thought that a change during the parliamentary session would convey an impression of weakness to the
public. The extra-parliamentary organization was unable to
press the matter immediately, because it had merely provisional
status, and was therefore not competent to choose the party's
Leader.[3] Forbes, as retiring Prime Minister, continued as
Leader, though Coates had not conceded that Forbes had any
automatic claim to the post, because in his view a coalition was
still in existence.[4] Two possible Leaders came into prominence,
Wilkinson and Hamilton. Wilkinson, originally a Reform member but an Independent for many years, had the appeal of a

[1] Dominion., 19 Feb. 1954.
[2] Mr. Nash, as quoted in Evening Post, 26 Feb. 1963.
[3] Robinson, Oligarchy and Democracy, pp. 42–45.
[4] Sir George Wilson, Dominion, 18 Nov. 1936.

'new face', not having been associated with the 'depression' Coalition Government. He had considerable support in the North Island, particularly in Auckland and the Waikato, and also from some former United Party followers who may have thought that too many positions in the 'new' party were being filled by ex-Reform Party members. He joined the party in October 1936, presumably in order to have the chance of contesting the election for Leader. Hamilton had the advantages and disadvantages of having been a member of the Coalition Government. He had the backing of Coates, who may have thought that Hamilton would keep the Leader's seat warm for him to occupy later, and also of 'certain influential and wealthy supporters of the Party in the South Island',[1] who did not regard Wilkinson favourably. The new extra-parliamentary Dominion Council discussed the question of the leadership at great length at its first meeting, on 31 October 1936, but did not come to any decision. The choice was therefore left to caucus, where Hamilton won by one vote, Polson having switched sides at the last moment.[2] The vote was then endorsed by the Dominion Council, which elected Hamilton as Leader of the party.

But National's lack of success at the 1938 election revealed that Hamilton had failed to shake off the impression that the party was still run by 'the old gang'. When Hamilton, along with Coates, joined the War Cabinet in July 1940, a good opportunity occurred to raise effectively the question whether the party ought not to have another Leader who would not be distracted from the task of leadership by being at the same time a member of the War Cabinet.[3] In the party organization discussions on a change of leadership had been going on for 'eighteen months' before the matter was brought into the open.[4] By 1940 it was also fairly clear who the successor might be. Two possible contenders were absent from the scene; Mr. K. J. Holyoake was out of the House, having lost his seat in 1938, and J. Hargest was overseas on war service. This strengthened the claims of S. G. Holland, who had in effect, though not in name, been acting as Hamilton's deputy. The way in which the

[1] Auckland Division Committee of the National Party, *Minutes*, 12 Nov. 1936.
[2] Broadfoot, op. cit., pp. 10–11; *Standard*, 21 July 1938.
[3] *Press*, 19 July 1940; *Evening Post*, 6 Nov. 1940.
[4] Holland, *Evening Post*, 28 Dec. 1940.

machinery for a change was set in motion was described in some
detail by Mr. Beaven of Canterbury.

[Beaven] became deputy-divisional chairman when the country,
from one end to the other, was working for a change of leadership.
The electoral committees did not like to discuss it and the divisional
committees also discussed the question with bated breath. On making
a trip to Wellington, he gained an insight into the feelings of the
other divisional committees, and he was definitely satisfied that the
question should be tackled with the gloves off. 'The divisional committee of Canterbury discussed it very freely and frankly and, with
Mr. H. G. Livingstone and Mr. Gilbert Grigg, I [Beaven] went to
Wellington for an urgent meeting of the dominion executive. We
went with the feeling that we had the backing of every electoral
committee in Canterbury. The dominion executive is composed of
the four divisional chairmen, three co-opted members, and two
members of Parliament, making ten with the chairman. We discussed
this most difficult question of leadership. What I have to tell you is
that the decision of the executive was unanimous. . . .' Further, said
Mr. Beaven, they knew that Mr. Holland was the right man for the
job. The change of leadership was very awkward for the executive
and the council, whose diffidence in a delicate situation could be
appreciated. Mr. Holland was the man for the job, but the appointment had to come from outside Canterbury.[1]

In accordance with the view that the initial move should come
from outside Canterbury, Mr. Holland's home territory, each
of the five divisional committees from North to South, starting
with Auckland, resolved in turn that Hamilton should be replaced by Holland.[2] The Dominion Executive also passed a
resolution that Hamilton should be succeeded by Holland,[3] and
this information was conveyed to Hamilton by the President of
the party.[4] Caucus selected Holland as Leader on 26 November
1940. No nominations were made, but members were asked to
write down the name of the person they wanted as Leader on a
piece of paper.[5] The vote seems to have been 13 for Holland,

[1] *Evening Post*, 28 Dec. 1940. The term 'divisional executive' in the report has
been corrected to 'dominion executive'.
[2] Mr. Alex. Gordon (at that time chairman of the National Party), interview,
Oct. 1958.
[3] Robinson, *The Rise of the New Zealand National Party*, p. 207, quoting *Minutes*
of the Dominion Executive, 1 Nov. 1940.
[4] Gordon interview, Oct. 1958.
[5] *Press*, 27 Nov. 1940.

8 for Hamilton.[1] Holland's selection was then confirmed by the Dominion Council.[2] Hamilton's supporters probably included Coates and Kyle.[3] In a sense, therefore, the 1942 'revolt' was a continuation by other means of the 1940 struggle over the leadership.

Since 1940 the National Party has had few problems of leadership, at least on the surface. There seems to have been a tradition, derived from the Reform Party, that a Leader, once elected, did not have to face re-election. Massey, it is said, was elected only once, and his 'election' in 1912 was 'merely an endorsement'.[4] Nor does there seem to have been any subsequent provision for regular re-election in either the Reform or National parties. Special procedures, including activity on the part of the extra-parliamentary party, were required to remove Forbes from the leadership in 1936 and Hamilton in 1940.

When the Dominion Executive resolved that Holland should succeed Hamilton, it also decided that after the next election he must be prepared to submit his name to caucus for re-election. The notion behind this was the hope and belief that there would be a big increase in the number of National members after the next election. When Holland was elected caucus included only twenty-five persons, under a third of the total membership of the House. So it was only fair that the new members should be given a say on the leadership.[5] Holland did submit himself for re-election in 1943 and 1946,[6] but the practice was not continued, either by Holland or his successor, Mr. Holyoake.

It should be added that there are no 'complications' about the choice of Prime Minister, similar to those which occurred in Britain after Mr. Eden's resignation in 1957, or after Mr. Macmillan's resignation in 1963. When a British Conservative Prime Minister dies or resigns (personally, not as part of the resignation of the whole ministry), the monarch designates a new Prime Minister before the party makes a formal choice of a new

[1] *Standard*, 30 Jan. 1941.
[2] Robinson, *Oligarchy and Democracy*, p. 106.
[3] *Press*, 22 Nov. 1940. The eight votes for Hamilton probably came from the eight ex-Reform Party men in caucus.
[4] Gardner, *Political Science* (Sept. 1961), art. cit., p. 18.
[5] Robinson, *The Rise of the New Zealand National Party*, p. 106.
[6] Ibid., p. 208.

Leader.[1] But in New Zealand in such a case the convention is presumably that the Governor-General designates as Prime Minister the man *previously* chosen as Leader by the larger party. This is certainly the Labour Party practice, and the only relevant National Party example (the succession of Mr. Holyoake) followed the same pattern. Conceivably there might still be 'stop-gap' Prime Ministers, such as Bell in 1925, or such as Seddon was until he was endorsed by caucus.[2] But this has been made less probable by the increased weight carried by the designation of Deputy-leader/Deputy Prime Minister, and by the fact that air travel now makes it possible for an absent Deputy to return quickly to New Zealand if the Prime Minister dies or becomes incapable. Complications would arise only if the two-party system ceased to exist, and no single party had a majority.

The number of party Leaders in New Zealand has been too small to support elaborate generalizations on the subject. What has been said previously about the necessary qualities for New Zealand politicians generally, also applies to Leaders in particular. Tenacity and robustness are all. It was only by exercising such qualities that Seddon prevailed over Stout,[3] and that Massey emerged from the ranks of numerous, apparently better-qualified, rivals. More recently, these characteristics enabled Holland for seventeen years to lead a party successfully, which, to begin with, contained three former party Leaders, two of whom had been Prime Minister.

To turn from personality traits to the 'mechanics' of rising to be Leader, it may be worth mentioning that the position of Minister of Finance, unlike the Chancellorship of the Exchequer in Britain, is a position which aspirants to the leadership might do well to avoid. 'Tough' budgets make a Finance Minister unpopular with the people, just as 'toughness' in scrutinizing departmental estimates makes him unpopular with his colleagues. Perhaps the 'intimacy' of New Zealand politics makes the minister's role a more personal and a more invidious one than would be the case in a larger country. There is also less

[1] Presumably the situation has changed as a result of the new method for selecting a Conservative Leader which was first used in 1965.

[2] Lipson, *The Politics of Equality*, p. 288.

[3] R. T. Shannon, 'The Liberal Succession Crisis in New Zealand, 1893', *Historical Studies, Australia and New Zealand*, vol. viii, no. 30 (1958).

rotation of the post of Finance Minister than there is of the Exchequer in Britain, so that a minister who is once given the job tends to 'get stuck' with it. Whether these explanations are adequate or not, the fact remains that in the last fifty years only three ex-Finance Ministers have become Leader of a major party for any length of time, Ward, Mr. Nash, and in 1963 Mr. Nordmeyer. More recently it has been said that tenure of this office contributed to Mr. Watts' failure to become Deputy-leader of the National Party (1957) and damaged Mr. Nord-meyer's prospects of one day becoming Leader of the Labour Party. In spite of his outstanding qualifications, Mr. Nordmeyer's election to the leadership in 1963 was possible only because of a chance combination of events—the death of Mr. Skinner, the illness and death of the next Deputy-leader, Mr. Hackett, and perhaps also the 'non-availability' of another prominent contender. A later development, under Mr. Holyoake, has been to make the Finance Minister's job less invidious, but also less important, major decisions on economic policy being taken by the Prime Minister.

The position of Deputy-leader is obviously of paramount importance as a stepping stone to the leadership. The Labour Party has always had a Deputy-leader; in 1918 the election of its first Leader, H. E. Holland, was immediately followed by the election of the first Deputy-leader, McCombs. McCombs resigned in 1923 and Savage was elected in his place. Holland, Savage, and Fraser were all succeded, on their deaths, by the current Deputy-leader. However, Skinner and Hackett, Deputies under Mr. Nash, died before he resigned as Leader.

It is only recently that a Deputy-leader has existed in the National Party. In previous right-wing parties, when the party was in power and the Prime Minister went abroad, the minister acting for him subsequently became recognized informally as the Prime Minister's deputy, with a strong claim to succeed him on death or retirement.[1] If a party were out of power, there would not be even this degree of informal recognition. Massey, for instance, was never regarded in any sense as a Deputy-leader. Holland was never officially Deputy-leader, although the Labour paper, *Standard*,[2] in speaking of his ambitions to succeed Hamilton, said he had become recognized as

---

[1] Lipson, *The Politics of Equality*, p. 287.   [2] 16 June 1938.

'an unofficial deputy leader'. More poetically, the mayor of
Masterton once referred to him as Hamilton's 'trusty lieu-
tenant'.[1] After Holland became Leader, Forbes,[2] and later
Polson, acted as his Deputy when he was out of the country.
Holland's choice of Polson has been commented on from various
angles. One speculation was that this 'protected' Holland,
because another possible choice, Mr. W. Sullivan, was potentially too dangerous a rival to leave in charge in his absence.
Another opinion was that Polson, who was approaching retiring
age, was nominated in order that a vacancy should exist later
for Mr. Holyoake, who was temporarily out of Parliament,
1938–43.

Polson retired from the House in 1946. In 1947[3] Holland
consulted caucus on the appointment of a Deputy-leader, and
asked members to write down their preference on a piece of
paper. The voting was not announced, but afterwards Holland
appointed Holyoake as Deputy-leader. Presumably Holland
regarded this vote as purely advisory, because of his later statement that he 'picked him [Holyoake] out'.[4] Although this was
the party's first regular Deputy-leader, on Holland's resignation
there was apparently no doubt about Holyoake's claim to succeed. His succession was announced by Holland at the 1957
Annual Conference of the party before he had been formally
chosen by caucus.[5] Subsequently Mr. Marshall was chosen
Deputy Prime Minister and Deputy-leader.

The Choice of Ministers

In the National Party, and in previous right-wing parties,
ministers have been appointed by the Prime Minister (party
Leader).[6] Sometimes it has been the practice, when a ministerial
vacancy occurs, for the Prime Minister to invite the views of
individual members of caucus in writing. But he is not compelled
to accept them. But, almost from the beginning, Labour ministers
have been appointed by caucus, although the allocation of

[1] *Wairarapa News*, 24 Mar. 1938.   [2] Daniels, op. cit., p. 92.
[3] Mr. Holyoake's own impression is that the date was 1947 (interview Oct.
1958), and when Mr. Holland retired in 1957 he said he 'picked him out ten years
ago' (*Evening Post*, 12 Aug. 1957).
[4] *Evening Post*, 12 Aug. 1957.   [5] Ibid.
[6] K. J. Holyoake, 'The Task of the Prime Minister', *Political Science*, vol. xv,
no. 2 (1963), pp. 20–21.

individuals to particular ministerial posts has always been made by the Prime Minister. The practice may have recommended itself as being 'democratic', or as being in accordance with trade-union tradition. There may have been some influence from Australia, and also from previous publicizing of the notion of an 'elected executive',[1] although the latter was to have been elected, on the Swiss model, by the whole House and not just by members of one party.[2] Selection by caucus has recently been criticized severely by Earl Attlee, apparently on the ground that 'someone with particular technical qualifications may get left out because he doesn't happen to be the popular man.'[3] Possibly this criticism loses some of its force when the Parliamentary party is as small as it is in New Zealand. In a compact parliamentary group every member has the chance to gain a pretty accurate impression of the capabilities of every other member. There is, of course, the danger that some able members may be too aloof and 'superior' to overcome caucus's New Zealand trait of distrusting uncommon men. But it may be doubted whether such men, if appointed by a Prime Minister, would be very successful. After all, they would have to do their work as ministers in an atmosphere equally suspicious of their superiority. Arguments about favouritism seem largely to cancel out. Downie Stewart thought that choice by caucus would make for intrigue and log-rolling, because of the desire to be popular with one's fellows.[4] On the other hand, it may be argued that selection by the Leader may result in favouritism being shown by him and may also have a tendency to inhibit healthy criticism of him.[5] In New Zealand the consensus of opinion among Cabinet and ex-Cabinet ministers of both major parties is that selection by caucus usually does not have very different results from choice by the Leader. In a Cabinet of, say, fifteen, on the average only two or three of the men chosen would be different under the other system.

[1] See pp. 70–71, above.
[2] Miller, *Australian Government and Politics*, p. 112, and *Political Science*, vol. v, no. 2, art. cit., pp. 21–22; S. Encel, op. cit., pp. 18 ff.
[3] Francis Williams, *A Prime Minister Remembers* (London, 1961), p. 85. See also R. T. McKenzie, *British Political Parties* (London, 1955), pp. 297–334 *passim*.
[4] *Dominion*, 13 Dec. 1940.
[5] L. F. Crisp, *The Parliamentary Government of the Commonwealth of Australia* (London, 1949), p. 198.

When Labour came to power in 1935 a joint meeting of caucus and the national executive gave the new Prime Minister, Savage, authority to select the Cabinet,[1] although, years before, Labour's previous Leader, H. E. Holland, had declared in the House that he favoured the Australian system of selection by caucus through preferential voting.[2] The exact reason why Savage was allowed to choose the Cabinet is not known. But the fact that over half the Labour caucus had only just been elected for the first time and consequently had no experience of Parliament, may have been considered important. But after the 1938 election, although a majority of caucus voted for selection of the Cabinet by caucus, Savage did not accept this decision.[3] The question was referred to a committee drawn from the national executive and from caucus, and its recommendations were discussed at the 1939 Annual Conference of the Labour Party, where it was decided that Cabinet vacancies should be filled by the Leader's submitting names for the endorsement of caucus. If any were rejected, caucus would submit names to the Leader, and from this list the Leader would nominate to caucus for its approval members to make up a full Cabinet. In effect, this would give caucus a veto on appointments by the Prime Minister.[4] But Savage, in reviewing the Conference's decision, said, 'It might be necessary to make a change or two, but it was for him to say whether that should be done or not.' If there was a deadlock he could ask the national executive for assistance, but, after hearing them, he would make the decision. This principle would apply for all major issues. He would discuss with caucus, if necessary with Conference or a special Conference, and the executive and then make the decision.[5] What happened afterwards, apparently, was that Savage proposed in caucus an addition to the Cabinet, for which he made one nomination and would accept no others, as well as the appointment of four under-secretaries. Caucus rejected the latter appointments, but, after several members had abstained

[1] Lee, *Simple on a Soapbox*, pp. 39–40.
[2] Lipson, *The Politics of Equality*, p. 337.
[3] Barnard, op. cit., p. 4, says there was a majority of five. Lee, *I Fight for New Zealand*, p. 25, and *Simple on a Soapbox*, p. 127, says the voting was 26–22.
[4] Lee, *I Fight for New Zealand*, op. cit., p. 27; *Evening Post*, 3 Apr. 1940; *Standard*, 2 May 1940; Brown, op. cit., pp. 197–200.
[5] *Dominion*, 13 and 21 Apr. 1939.

or walked out, approved the new Cabinet member by a very narrow majority.[1]

On Savage's death, after Fraser became Prime Minister, the choice of Cabinet passed entirely to caucus. But in 1940 there was no wholesale reconstruction of the Cabinet. Existing members were confirmed *en bloc*, and only those vacancies which occurred were filled in by caucus selection.[2] So, although there was a small infusion of new blood, through D. G. MacMillan and afterwards through A. H. Nordmeyer, the rate of turnover of the original members was rather slow. After the 1943 and 1946 elections there was a fresh choice of Cabinet, and all the members had to submit themselves for re-election by caucus. However, few changes seem to have resulted, and it would not have made very much difference if the existing members had been confirmed *en bloc*.

Not much information is available about the methods of election in 1943 and 1946, but from several verbal accounts the procedure in 1957, when Labour returned to power, seems to have been somewhat as follows. The six newly elected members and one or two others without much seniority declared that they did not wish to stand. The Prime Minister then pointed out the importance of obtaining a good geographical 'spread' in the Cabinet. In fact, out of the fifteen eventually selected, five came from Auckland and the North of the North Island, five from Wellington and the remainder of the North Island, and the other five were from the South Island. Possibly geographical considerations influenced the selection of two or three persons chosen at the 'tail' of the fifteen. Preferential voting was used, and in the first ballot thirteen of the candidates obtained an absolute majority of the votes, 21 or over out of 41. Only about half a dozen members contested the second ballot, and the two who received over 21 votes were elected. After the election the Prime Minister alone was responsible for the allocation of portfolios. In Australia Leaders of the Labor Party have been known to indicate their preferences, before caucus chooses Cabinet, by means of an 'official ticket'.[3] But this did not happen in New

[1] Lee, *I Fight for New Zealand*, pp. 30–31; *Simple on a Soapbox*, p. 160.
[2] *Southland Times*, 14 Dec. 1940; *Star*, 11 Nov. 1940.
[3] Don Whitington, *The House Will Divide* (Melbourne, 1957), pp. 93 and 121; Crisp, op. cit., p. 198.

Zealand in 1957. The PLP elects its whips. The National Party now elects its whips; in 1964 the Leader nominated which one of the two elected was to be senior whip and which junior whip.[1]

No member of a New Zealand Labour Cabinet has ever been dismissed, although Mr. Lee, an under-secretary who was not in the Cabinet, was dismissed in 1939. Indeed this might seem to be an unwelcome consequence of the Cabinet's selection by caucus, that Labour Prime Ministers are inhibited from getting rid of incompetents except by devious means such as 'kicking them upstairs' into other jobs.[2] But reluctance to dismiss is not just the result of caucus selection. There have been no outright dismissals of ministers in the National Party, which does not choose the Cabinet in this way. Such a dismissal, in the words of a National Party Leader, would be 'unheard of'. It would conflict with strongly held New Zealand views on the security of job-tenure.

It is reported that in either 1943 or 1946 the Prime Minister, Fraser, 'saved' a Cabinet member who had not been re-elected by caucus. He was retained 'temporarily' on the plea that he was soon to be considered for an outside appointment and that a bad impression would be created if he had just been 'demoted' previously. In fact he was not given the appointment, but stayed on in the Cabinet instead.

A remarkable feature of the first Labour Government was the 'pooling' of ministerial salaries. The plan had been agreed to in principle at the 1935 Labour Party Annual Conference.[3] A similar project had been discussed by the Federal Conference of the Australian Labor Party as far back as 1919, but had been rejected.[4] As carried out in New Zealand, 'pooling' meant that members who were prepared to give all their time to parliamentary and government duties were to co-operate with various ministers and help them with administration and research work. In exchange there was a partial pooling of salaries by which the £400 p.a. of the backbenchers who participated was raised by nearly £100, while ministerial salaries were

[1] Interview, Mr. R. G. Gerard, May, 1964.
[2] It has been suggested that in Australia Labour Prime Ministers cannot dismiss Cabinet members (Crisp, op. cit., p. 199).
[3] *Truth*, 1 May 1935.
[4] Miller, *Political Science*, vol. v, no. 2, op. cit., p. 24.

correspondingly reduced.[1] There seem to have been several impulses behind the scheme. One of the motives was to secure participation from back-benchers in the work of government. To some extent the arrangement served a rather similar purpose to the system of caucus committees which grew up later. Another reason may have been to ease the heart-burnings of those who were not appointed to the Cabinet, by reducing the difference in financial rewards. It was certainly a way of raising Labour back-benchers' salaries, which were low, at a time when there would have been great public opposition to any 'straight' increase. The 'pooling' of salaries does not seem to have produced any spectacular results in improving administration or research. It was apparently discontinued in 1944 at the same time that an increase occurred in parliamentary salaries.

Cabinet and Caucus

In considering the relations between Cabinet and caucus it is well to bear in mind the New Zealand tendency to egalitarianism and distrust of hierarchy, and the relatively high proportion of caucus members who are also in the Cabinet—at least a quarter, sometimes almost two-fifths. At first sight this second circumstance might seem to make it easier for the Cabinet to gain a majority in caucus, and so increase its relative power. But perhaps the main effect is in the opposite direction. In Britain it is clear that a parliamentary party of 300 or 400 members is too unwieldy to make any attempt at governing. Intermediate bodies, between the leaders and the parliamentary party exist—the Conservative '1922 Committee' and the Labour 'Parliamentary Committee'.[2] But in New Zealand caucus, numbering from thirty to fifty, is small enough for some of its members at least to *believe* that they can govern. It is not possible to make exact comparisons, but there is a strong impression that the parliamentary party is of more account, *vis-à-vis* the Cabinet, than in Britain. R. T. MacKenzie has this to say of the British Parliamentary Labour Party, 1945–51: '. . . as in 1924 and 1929, there was no question of the Government revealing in detail its parliamentary proposals or seeking formal approval for them in advance of their presentation to Parliament. The broad outlines

[1] D. Wilson, *History in the Making* (Wellington, 1937), pp. 9–10.
[2] McKenzie, op. cit., pp. 57–61 and 412 ff.

of policy were of course discussed at the PLP meeting and back-benchers were given an opportunity to ventilate their views.'[1] It is perhaps significant that these meetings were less frequent when the party was in power than they had been in opposition, and that ministers, when their duties permitted, attended only 'usually'. Caucus meetings in New Zealand are as frequent when the party is in office as they are in opposition, and attendance by ministers is more regular than in Britain. If important topics arise while Parliament is in recess a special meeting of caucus is convened. The only occasions on which it would not be consulted would be if highly confidential decisions were being made, for instance on changes in taxation, alterations in the exchange rate, or external affairs. To be sure, the first Labour Government, in its public pronouncements, was possibly inclined to over-emphasize the degree to which it consulted caucus, compared with previous Cabinets.[2] But descriptions such as one of Thorn's, '. . . at meetings of the Parliamentary Labour Party on 20th February and 24th March, 1936, the principles in the Bills prepared by the Government were explained and approved'.[3] seem to indicate that consultation of caucus in New Zealand is carried further than in Britain.

It should not be thought that the important role of caucus is confined to the Labour Party. Before the National Government decided to go to the country in 1951, earlier than the end of the normal three-year term, caucus was consulted and approved of the decision; this followed the Labour precedent of consulting caucus on the postponement of the election in 1941. During the 'Suez' crisis in 1956, not only did the National caucus pass a resolution endorsing 'its own' Government's handling of the crisis; the endorsement was also given publicity by the Press.[4] In the National Party it has not been unknown for the Leader to use caucus as a counterweight to Cabinet on some issues.

Within this broad framework caucus can play a number of possible roles. In the United Party, under Ward, the prevailing atmosphere seems to have been one of apathy tempered by anarchy. On other occasions caucus's power can be reduced by its being consulted by Cabinet only in the later stages of a project when outside commitments have been made and when

---

[1] McKenzie, op. cit., p. 447.
[2] e.g. Savage, *Dominion*, 25 May 1938.
[3] Thorn, op. cit., p. 126.
[4] *Evening Post*, 11 Dec. 1956.

it may be impossible for Cabinet's proposals to be substantially altered. Alternatively, proposals, which would otherwise be treated as contentious, may be approved with little discussion if they are put to caucus just before the meeting ends—that is just before lunch begins. Obviously a great deal depends on the personality of the Prime Minister. To a great extent the United Party's difficulties arose from the fact that Ward was either absent from caucus meetings, or, if he attended, was not well enough to manage them properly. According to one source, Fraser ruled caucus absolutely, aided by his mastery of detail and of the rules of procedure. 'If he had said that black was white they would have agreed.'[1] S. G. Holland was also reputed to have been very strict in caucus and even to have 'dominated' it, according to a minister who had served under him. So potent was Holland's influence that, reportedly, one minister, starting to develop an argument but catching sight of disapproval in Holland's face, would change his line accordingly and end by saying the opposite from what he had intended. Nevertheless, even during Holland's period as Prime Minister, 1949–57, Cabinet was apparently cautious in putting forward proposals to caucus when any appreciable opposition was expected.

The threat of dissolution was formerly regarded as an important factor in enforcing party discipline in Britain. But it has never been used for such a purpose in New Zealand. As noticed earlier, the only recent instance of a 'premature' dissolution (1951) was directed against the Opposition, not against members of the Government caucus. In spite of Lipson's arguments,[2] dissolution is an extremely unselective threat which may imperil the seats of loyal supporters without causing anxiety to rebels with large majorities. It is significant that in the caucus disputes which centred round Savage and Lee there does not seem to be any record of a proposal for dissolution to be used in order to enforce party discipline. The weapon employed against Mr. Lee, with his huge majority in Grey Lynn, was expulsion, not dissolution.

Other factors may be important too. *A priori*, since caucus meets less frequently when the House is not in session, its influence is presumably less at such times. On the other hand,

[1] Interview, Mr. F. H. Langstone, Feb. 1958.
[2] Op. cit., p. 249.

as an election approaches, the influence of members who hold marginal seats may increase, at least on questions which may be thought to affect the vote they receive. In the National Party, if a question of conscience is concerned, opposition by quite a small group of members may be decisive. In the period 1955–7 the Government proposed to relax the regulations governing the hours during which liquor could be served with meals. But about half a dozen members determinedly opposed this in caucus, and the matter was dropped. The decisive factor probably was that the vote of the half-dozen, which they would have been entitled to cast freely on grounds of conscience, plus a solid Labour vote, would have been enough to defeat such a measure in the House.

Critics who allege that the influence of caucus is too great should ask themselves if they would be happy to see it reduced to the British level. Criticisms of the impotence of back-benchers in Britain would seem logically to amount to a claim that caucus should be accorded a *more prominent* role.

The most extensive information on caucus refers to the Labour Party between 1936 and 1940. The party had just come into power for the first time, and there was a conflict between the enthusiasm of caucus, increased by the magnitude of the Labour victory (and the consequently large number of back-benchers), and the sobering effects of office and responsibility on the Cabinet. The newly elected Labour members were younger than the previously elected members and tended to have more formal education and less trade-union background.[1] A number of sources of conflict arose, mainly of policy (monetary reform and borrowing), 'democracy' (the extent to which caucus should determine Cabinet and other appointments and decide policy), personalities (Lee versus Savage, Fraser, and Nash). Because of Lee's brilliance and ambition and the god-like 'image' of Savage, personality clashes reinforced differences on issues. When some members of caucus expressed the wish that the Bank of New Zealand should be nationalized Savage either 'stalled' or questioned the competence of caucus to decide.[2] He initially refused to accept caucus motions for additional increases in old

[1] Daniels, op. cit., pp. 42 and 54.
[2] Lee, *Simple on a Soapbox*, pp. 87–88; and *A Letter every New Zealander should Read* (Auckland, n.d.) ('the Lee Letter'), pp. 11 ff.

age pensions, but eventually yielded—and received the gratitude of the public for the increase.[1] Such disputes led the Prime
Minister's supporters into attacks on caucus. One member
wanted to know what right a 'hole and corner business like
caucus' had to force Savage's hand on the nationalization of
the Bank of New Zealand. And David Wilson, the National
Secretary, said that, if caucus tried to press Savage, he would
use a 'veto' and would probably be backed by the national
executive.[2] Lee also became more intransigent, and challenged
the leadership more openly. In 1938 the 'Lee Letter', which
denounced Mr. Nash's financial orthodoxy and which obtained
a wider circulation than Lee apparently intended, led to his
being censured by the national executive and the 1939 Annual
Conference.[3] In 1939 he attacked Savage's leadership in an
article at a time when (as it turned out) the Prime Minister was
fatally ill.[4] Shortly afterwards, at the 1940 Annual Conference,
he was expelled from the party.[5]

During the fight the contending forces became quite clearly
defined. On the one side was the vast majority of the Cabinet and
about a third of the back-benchers, along with the leaders of the
Federation of Labour and the national executive of the party.
On the other side were the remainder of the back-benchers,
who generally had the support of one minister, Langstone,
and occasionally the support of other ministers, for example
Armstrong.[6] Much of Lee's support was not principally for
himself, or even for his policies, but because he upheld caucus
powers as against Cabinet powers. As the struggle came to its
climax the role of the trade-union leaders and the extra-
parliamentary organization became more evident. At the 1940
Annual Conference (at which Lee was expelled) the chairman,
Mr. James Roberts, said 'If your Parliamentary representatives do not do what is wanted, we will soon find men who
will. . . . If our Parliamentary representatives do not conduct
their business better, Conference will itself elect the Cabinet.'[7]

[1] Lee, *Simple on a Soapbox*, pp. 97–106.
[2] *The Lee Letter*, p. 16; p. 154, above.
[3] See p. 226, below.   [4] *Tomorrow*, art. cit., 6 Dec. 1939.
[5] See p. 226, below.
[6] See Miller's analysis of the cabinet-caucus relation, *Political Science*, vol. v,
no. 2, art. cit., p. 25.
[7] Barnard, op. cit., p. 2.

It is natural to compare Mr. Lee's 'rebellion' with that of Bevan in the British Labour Party a dozen years later.[1] Both of them were men of eloquence and ideas, although neither had much formal education. Even the physical resemblance between the two is striking. Each had to fight a party leadership which had the support of the industrial chiefs of the movement. Lee had a higher proportion of Labour back-benchers in favour of his policies than Bevan. Both drew strength mainly, though not exclusively, from constituency parties, although, from his own constituency party, Bevan probably had relatively greater loyalty than Lee. Also, partly because of the different methods of election of the national executive in the two countries, Bevan had relatively more support than Lee on this body.[2] The circumstances of the time and the nature of the rebels' opponents were also quite different. Savage had been a pioneer Labour Leader and was head of a wartime government with a huge majority. The attack on him was a personal one, and he had become sensitive after four years' adulation and also partly because of a serious illness. Attlee was a bourgeois in the second generation of Labour Leaders who, at the height of the Bevan 'rebellion', was at first Prime Minister with a precarious majority and then in opposition. He was not provoked by a direct personal attack, nor could he use the uncritical hero-worship of his supporters to crush a formidable opponent. All these considerations would seem to be relevant in explaining why Lee was expelled from his party and Bevan was not.

Even when Savage and Lee left the Government (for different destinations) in March 1940, the dispute did not end at once. At the start of his Premiership Fraser refused to allow a motion in caucus which stipulated that there should be democratic control in the party. His ruling was challenged, but he was upheld by 26 votes to 18.[3] Barnard resigned from the party immediately afterwards, complaining, *inter alia*, of the infringements of the rights of caucus and of 'the growing political domination of some five or six industrial chiefs'.[4]

Gradually the struggle subsided, but it left its marks on the

[1] Marcel Merle, 'Le Bevanisme ou la crise du parti travailliste en Grande Bretagne', *Revue française de science politique*, vol. iii, no. 4 (1953) and vol. iv, no. 1 (1954); Ralph Miliband, *Parliamentary Socialism* (London, 1961), ch. x.
[2] On the degree of support for Lee, see Lee, *Simple on a Soapbox*, p. 174.
[3] Barnard, op. cit., p. 6.   [4] *Standard*, 11 Apr. 1940.

party. The 'monetary reformers' in caucus did not forgive the party leadership for having resisted their efforts by 'undemocratic' methods. Towards the end of the war they returned to the attack. A caucus committee on the nationalization of the Bank of New Zealand was set up (while Fraser and Nash were out of the country). It reported in favour of nationalization, and caucus accepted its report. The question of nationalizing the bank then came up at the 1944 Annual Conference of the party, where after some manœuvring it was passed.[1] Another 'victory' on the part of the monetary reformers occurred when, after Bretton Woods, Mr. Nash suggested that New Zealand should join the International Monetary Fund. Several members objected, no vote was taken, and the proposal was dropped.[2] A contributory reason was probably the amount of feeling against joining the IMF which existed *outside* the Labour Party, including inside the National Party.

A further consequence of the 1936–40 dispute was that, by dying at the time he did, Savage acquired a martyr's crown, and thereafter disloyalty to the leadership was reckoned as blasphemy, as well as treason. Under his successor there was an increase in the formal powers of caucus, for instance as regards the election of ministers. But the overwhelming tendency, strengthened by the need for even more 'solidarity' in order to wage the war, was to augment the authority of the leaders and to diminish the resilience and liveliness of the led.

[1] See p. 232, below.
[2] Interview, Mr. F. H. Langstone, Nov. 1958.

VI

THE PARTIES OUTSIDE PARLIAMENT—
CENTRAL ORGANIZATION

BOTH existing major parties now have an extra-parliamentary organization, although, in each, this organization
dates from a different stage of the party's development.
The predecessors of the National Party, the Liberal and Reform
Parties, began by being mainly parliamentary parties with only
a rudimentary organization outside. But, with the coming of
universal suffrage and the parties' wish to mobilize votes,
organization over the country as a whole was stimulated, at
first in the Liberals and then in the Reform Party. The crushing
defeat of the National (Coalition) Government in 1935 led to
the creation of a new, National, Party and to an extreme concern with organization in order to make sure of capturing the
entire anti-Labour vote. The Reform and Liberal Parties,
which, in spite of their skeleton organization in the country,
remained largely 'cadre' parties, have thus been replaced by
a 'mass' party. Indeed, as far as membership is concerned, the
National Party has claims to be one of the most outstandingly
'mass' parties in the world. Nearly half of those who vote for the
party at elections are also members of the party.

The Labour Party's evolution has followed different lines from
National's, but the pattern is similar to that of its counterparts
in Britain or Australia. Extra-parliamentary organization, in
the sense of trade-union organization, preceded parliamentary
representation. But after a foothold was gained in Parliament
a new extra-parliamentary organization was set up, in which
the unions held a special position. As a result, membership in
the New Zealand Labour Party could be acquired in one of
two ways—'directly' as a member of a branch of the Labour
Party organization, or 'indirectly' as a member of a trade union
affiliated to the organization.

The relation of the extra-parliamentary organization to the parliamentary party is not a simple one. Obviously there is interaction between them, but it is possible to conceive of two widely different extreme types. In the one, the party outside Parliament expresses its wishes on the policies, and perhaps the leadership, of the parliamentary party, and these wishes are in the main obeyed. In the other, the extra-parliamentary party is a mere 'transmission belt' through which the parliamentarians organize resources for winning elections: caucus treats the wishes of the organization with about as much respect as the management in paternalistic business firms accords to workers' suggestions; ideas for minor improvements are in order, but advice on how to run the business would be regarded as an impertinence. In countries whose citizens are accustomed to democratic procedures, the second type of relationship will not easily be accepted. Why should the men and women in the organization outside Parliament work for a party which uses them only as a transmission belt? For a time some may be driven to action by fear of 'socialism' or hatred of 'capitalism', while a few key workers may remain active because they aspire to become parliamentarians themselves or to win honours or decorations. But such motives will not keep the organization in good shape and in good heart for long. The parliamentarians may wish to organize external support 'without sacrificing their own freedom of action within Parliament'.[1] But, in return, the mass organizations 'can and do exact a certain price for their labour; they expect to be listened to by their leaders'.[2] The price may even be higher; they may wish the leaders not merely to listen, but to listen and obey.

The kind of conflict just outlined has been liable to arise mainly in non-Labour parties. Labour Party problems have been different, and have corresponded roughly to those of the first 'extreme type'. In such an organization it has been assumed that there should be 'democracy' within the extra-parliamentary party. As L. F. Crisp, writing on Australia, has put it, all members have a moral, and should have a constitutional, right to a basic equality of voice in the determination of the aims and purposes of the party.[3] In any large organization, of course,

---

[1] McKenzie, *Political Parties*, p. 6.   [2] Ibid., p. 636.
[3] *The Australian Federal Labor Party, 1901–1951* (London, 1955), pp. 3–4.

'equality of voice' may be distorted, because of the existence of 'oligarchy', and in effect R. T. McKenzie contends that this has been true of the British Labour Party. Formally the wishes of the Annual Conference are supreme, but in fact up to the late 1950's, either Conference said what the party leaders wanted it to say, or else its wishes were ignored.[1] In practice 'democracy' may also be affected by the special position of the trade unions in the Labour Party. In deciding on 'equality of voice' what weight is to be given to the unions, and how much allowance should be made for the fact that many union members, although members of the Labour Party through affiliation, are politically inactive and apathetic?[2] A further consideration is that, if 'democracy' *is* achieved within the party, this may lead to a potential conflict when the party becomes the Government. In such a situation, how is responsibility to the wishes of the mass party to be reconciled with the Government's constitutional responsibility to the legislature and the electors? McKenzie[3] thinks that such a conflict would be serious, but holds that fortunately, during the period studied in his book, it did not arise in Britain, because of the *lack* of intra-party democracy in the British Labour Party.

The next four chapters are concerned with the extra-parliamentary organization of the parties: central organization; regional and local organization; party conferences; the selection of candidates.[4] As far as organization is concerned, there are many similarities of structure between the parties, but two outstanding differences. First, as already mentioned, membership of the Labour Party may be either 'direct' or 'indirect' (through membership of a trade union), while the National Party has only 'direct' members. Second, it will be seen that the National Party has quite an elaborate regional organization, which has hardly any counterpart in the Labour Party.

[1] Op. cit., pp. 485–517; Saul Rose, 'Policy Decision in Opposition', *Political Studies*, art. cit.
[2] Ivan Yates, 'Power in the Labour Party', *Political Quarterly*, vol. xxxi, no. 3 (1960), pp. 304–5.
[3] 'Policy Decision in Opposition: A Rejoinder', *Political Studies*, vol. v, no. 2 (1957). See also Ralph Miliband, 'Party Democracy and Parliamentary Government', *Political Studies*, vol. vi, no. 2 (1958).
[4] On party organization see Kent M. Weeks, 'Political Party Personnel in New Zealand' (Victoria unpublished thesis, 1961). In some instances, however, the value judgements seem to be over-simple.

The Organization of the Earlier Parties

It is not possible to describe the central organization of the National Party's predecessors in detail. But, while the provisions in their constitutions are quite extensive on paper, their working seems to have been spasmodic, and to have been dependent more on personalities than on rules. It is significant that the first permanent central organization, the Liberal and Labour Federation, was founded in 1899, soon after a resolution for a separate Labour Party had been carried at the annual Trades and Labour Conference.[1] This timing suggests that the federation may have owed its existence partly to the desire to avoid a Labour breakaway from the Liberals. In the constitution the Parliamentary Leader (Seddon) headed the Executive,[2] and apparently had every intention of controlling it.[3] The meeting of the Council of the Federation offered the delegates, elected from the branches, the opportunity of co-operating with the parliamentary party in drawing up the party's platform.[4] The delegates also chose the elected members of the Executive. In practice the Executive tended to be chosen from those who lived in and near Wellington, 'the reason being that they were always handy, and could be called together without expense and inconvenience'.[5] Undoubtedly all this helped to make it possible for members of the party to play an intelligent part in its direction and control. But Dr. Findlay, when a charter was presented to the Wellington branch of the Federation, perhaps waxed a little too lyrical: '. . . this organization was not local or transient, to keep certain men in power, but it was the inevitable product of matured democracy. Below the creation of this Federation lay one of the profoundest changes which had marked modern society for the last century—the creation of political organizations having for their object the transference of political power from the classes to the mass of the people.'[6] The Federation was too obviously the creature of Seddon for this description to apply. And, even after his death, there is no evidence that the

[1] R. M. Burdon, *King Dick*, p. 259.
[2] *Constitution of the Liberal and Labour Federation of New Zealand* (as amended at the 1903 Conference), reproduced in Foster, op. cit., Appendix IV (J)).
[3] Burdon, op. cit., p. 260. [4] Foster, op. cit., pp. 120–1.
[5] *Report of Proceedings of the Conference of Delegates of the Liberal and Labour Federation of New Zealand*, 1903, p. 12.
[6] *New Zealand Times*, 8 Sept. 1903.

extra-parliamentary Liberal organization exercised much appreciable influence on the parliamentary party.

Reform Party central organization was in large part stimulated by the desire to emulate Liberal organization. Before then any Opposition arrangements seem to have been improvised, for instance before the Reform Party proper was started the former 'Opposition' formed a 'Central Executive Committee' for corresponding with friends and arranging for speakers in order to fight the 1899 election.[1] But the first issue of *The Reformer*, published by the newly founded Political Reform League, called for Mr. Massey's supporters to devote their energy to working within the 'nucleus of organization' provided by the League. 'We, the Opposition, must learn from the enemy.'[2] More than a year later, E. E. Vaile, the Reform Party organizer, among his many proposals for organization, suggested that there should be a 'Colonial Executive', elected by provincial executives, which, in turn, should be elected by subordinate bodies.[3] In 1912 the Political Reform League held its first Dominion Conference, which drew up a constitution for the League. Massey was President of the League and also of its Colonial Executive of thirteen, which contained two other members of Parliament.[4] But the new organization fell into decline during the First World War, and was not re-established during Massey's lifetime. 'Indeed, from 1919 to his death, the Reform organization was provisional and largely unco-ordinated. Paper schemes were discussed and even set on foot, but the practical direction of the Party in parliament and elsewhere remained with Massey or committees which he set up.[5] It was only after Massey had been succeeded by Coates that another Dominion Conference was held (1926). Three years later the constitution was revised. But the Leader of the Reform Party in the House still played a dominant role. By the constitution he was President of the League and also of the Dominion Executive. Moreover, although the majority of the members of that Executive were to be elected by the Divisional Executives, five

---

[1] Brand, op. cit., p. 42, quoting *Evening Post*, 24 Jan. 1899.
[2] *The Reformer*, no. 1, Sept. 1905.
[3] 'Suggestions by E. E. Vaile' (MS., Auckland Public Library, 23 Jan. 1907).
[4] Gardner, art. cit., vol. xiii, no. 2, pp. 19–21; *Reform Party Year Book* (Christchurch, 1913), p. 4.
[5] Gardner, art. cit., p. 22. See also *Newsletter*, 31 July 1926.

of them were to be nominated by the Leader-President.[1] The revived organization was hardly given time to get into operation. After the Reform–United coalition and the 1931 election each of the coalescing parties seems to have let its organization run down, perhaps through relief at not having to fight the other, suggesting that neither feared any immediate threat from the Labour Party.[2]

The Reform Party's central extra-parliamentary organization, like that of the Liberal and Labour Federation before it, is best seen as an ornament on the top of the party structure. The main effects of party organization were evident at the local level, in reducing multiple candidatures and in helping to get out the vote. But nationally the party was run by the party Leader with the assistance of the party secretary and latterly, apparently, the Dominion Executive. This is illustrated by the fact that the party had no regular system of finance. There was no attempt to collect small amounts of money regularly from a large number of members. Instead, when the need arose, someone from the party headquarters or from the Dominion Executive would ring up a few key people and ask for substantial sums. Some of those approached in this way would give as much as £1,000 each. The funds so collected seem to have been partly controlled by the Dominion Executive, but were mainly at the disposal of the Leader.[3] The flavour of these arrangements is indeed reminiscent of a small-scale version of the 'dual organization' concept which Eggleston used in describing the early Australian Liberal Party.[4] The Reform Party's central organization seems to have done little more than act as a link between the Leader and the groups and interests supporting the party. Judged by any appropriate test of a 'mass' party—large membership, number of active members, widespread sources of finance, consultation of members on policy—the Reform Party fails to qualify.

[1] *Constitution and Rules of the Political Reform League*, as revised and adopted at the 1929 Conference.

[2] Robinson, *The Rise of the New Zealand National Party*, p. 12. But in *The Sun*, 13 May 1935, it was claimed that the Reform organization had remained almost intact throughout the Coalition, while the United Party organization was a mere skeleton. This claim apparently comes from a Reform Party source, however.

[3] Gardner, art. cit., vol. xiii, no. 2, pp. 23–24; interview, Theo Hills, Oct. 1958; interview, Mr. C. A. L. Treadwell, Mar. 1959.

[4] Eggleston, op. cit., p. 132; p. 123, above.

National Party Central Organization

Although the Reform and United Parties formed a Coalition in 1931, they did not amalgamate. Even when they fought the 1935 election they had only gone as far as forming a National, Political *Federation*. But under the spur of defeat in 1935 the Dominion Executive of the Federation decided to convene a conference for the formation of a new party. This was done in May 1936, when such a conference adopted a new constitution for the 'New Zealand National Party'.[1] At the first meeting of the Dominion Council provided for in that constitution Adam Hamilton was chosen first Leader of the party.

The Coalition (National Party) had thus reacted to the loss of office in 1935 by a change of Leader. Its second consecutive defeat in 1938 was followed by another change in the leadership and, later, by a change in policy which amounted to accepting Labour's version of the 'Welfare State'. But a more immediate and instinctive reaction to the 1935 defeat was to blame 'faulty organization'.[2] This was perhaps a natural reaction. Right-wing parties in defeat tend to blame weak organization rather than weaknesses in policy. There was also a tendency, shared by Reform in the early years of the century and the National Party in 1936, to exaggerate the perfection of the rival party organization and also to magnify the electoral importance of 'organization', in the narrow sense. To some extent poor organization may have contributed to the result of the 1935 election. The Democrats' intervention perhaps lost the Government a dozen seats, and it is arguable that, if the Coalition had allowed more effective discussion of policy by the extra-parliamentary organization and more 'democratic' selection of candidates, this loss would have been prevented or reduced. But, on any intelligent calculation, the Democrats' intervention was not decisive. Even if their votes and the National Party's are added together, the figure falls far short of the votes cast for Labour.

However, the reaction against the previous organization (or the lack of it) was not based merely on considerations of efficiency, narrowly defined, or on a desire to excuse the election defeat. As early as March 1937, Holland, later to become the

---

[1] *National Party Handbook* (Wellington, 1960), pp. 76–77.
[2] e.g. T. G. Wilkes, National Party organizer, *Southland Times*, 20 Mar. 1937; *Waiuku News*, 18 Feb. 1938.

party Leader, mentioned three important differences between the new National Party and its predecessors. First, it could give the public the nucleus of a new parliamentary team, co-operating with the older members. Second, it could provide a new and progressive policy. Third, although Holland is not reported as having used the term, it would allow more intra-party democracy. The new party's constitution would make provision for supporters outside Parliament 'to formulate its policy', instead of its being written inside Parliament. Holland admitted that, under the old régime, there had been 'small simmerings of discontent' over this and over the method of candidate selection.[1] To some extent the provisions of the new party's constitution (outlined below) represented a reaction against caucus dictation and, in particular, against the Leader's power over funds, policy, and organization.[2] Hargest, a National Party M.P. who might have risen to high office in a National Government had he not been killed in the War, went even further. 'It was felt that in the past the parliamentary members ran the party and they decided to alter that. "We wanted our supporters to feel that we were only their instruments in Parliament." '[3] Indeed on one occasion it was plainly stated that organization would be useful as a *means of achieving* intra-party democracy. In the past the party leaders had issued a 'take it or leave it' policy. But now 'policy was to come from the party members themselves, and for this they must have good organization and a large membership'.[4] So 'better organization' was held to be desirable for a number of reasons. Sometimes it arose from a wish to have more 'democracy' in the National Party than in its predecessors. On other occasions it was perhaps a rather vague way of calling attention to the party's need for a new image, without being too precise about specifying what changes in policy or leadership were desirable.

The constitution of the new National Party, adopted in 1936, was based on 'the principle of division of control between the party organization and the Members of Parliament'.[5] This principle was believed to be similar to the British Conservative

[1] *Manawatu Standard*, 5 Mar. 1937.
[2] Robinson, *The Rise of the New Zealand National Party*, pp. 27–30.
[3] *Southland Times*, 27 May 1938.
[4] Wilkes, ibid., 20 Mar. 1937.
[5] A. D. Robinson, *Oligarchy and Democracy*, p. 22.

Party arrangement by which the 'business side was run by the party organization and the political side by the Leader'.[1] Division of control made it necessary that the President of the extra-parliamentary organization should not only be a different person from the Leader (unlike the Reform Party), but also that he should be elected by the organization, not chosen by the Leader. At the 1939 party Conference a proposal that the chairman (President) should be appointed by the Leader, was opposed by one of the 'architects' of the party's constitution. The arguments he used were shaky; he quoted Massey to support the view that the organization should be free of caucus dictation, and attribute the 1935 defeat directly to a breach of this principle. However, his main point was clear. He objected to Reform and Coalition Leaders' having appointed 'substitutes' to take their places in the organization and exercise secret control over party funds.[2]

It has now become accepted that the President of the party is chosen by the organization outside Parliament, and, by the constitution, he is elected each year by the Annual Dominion Conference.[3] Nothing has been made public about the informal aspects of the President's election. Until 1962 only one candidate was put forward for election at the Dominion Conference, but in that year there was a ballot. Previous experience on the Dominion Council now seems to be a necessary qualification. The first President, Sir George Wilson, an Auckland businessman, remained in office only from May to November 1936. He was a victim of the aftermath of the Hamilton–Wilkinson duel for the leadership and the reluctance of the National Party in Auckland to accept the choice of Hamilton.[4] Subsequent Presidents have lasted longer; there have been only five, including the current President but not counting one acting chairman of the Dominion Council. The tendency has been for the period in office to lengthen; Sir Alex. McKenzie held the post from 1951 until 1962. After Sir George Wilson, the occupations of the Presidents were: lawyer, retail merchant, sharebroker. Mr. J. S. Meadowcroft, who became President in 1962 represents,

[1] A. D. Robinson, *Oligarchy and Democracy*, p. 22.
[2] Ibid., p. 23, quoting *Minutes* of Dominion Conference, 12–13 July 1939.
[3] *Constitution and Rules of the New Zealand National Party (1963)*, rule 22a.
[4] *Minutes* of Quarterly Meeting of the Auckland Divisional Committee, 12 Nov. 1936; *Dominion*, 18 Nov. 1936.

in his person, a wonderful combination of 'aligned' interests. He might be briefly described as a businessman, but, at greater length, 'is chairman of directors of ten companies, covering the fields of export, finance, insurance, primary production, manufacturing, importing and wholesaling'.[1] No President, except the first, has died while holding office.

The President's job is a time-consuming one. Apart from the task of ensuring that the organization is properly run, when the party is in office he is liable to be approached by all kinds of party 'supporters' who want favours or advice. It would be difficult, and impolitic, to turn them away abruptly, and it takes time to put them in touch with the correct people to deal with their applications or grievances. The President must also keep in contact, through the Leader, with the parliamentary party. If the President is close to the Leader, he may also be consulted by him on a wide range of problems. Holland said,[2] before his retirement, that Sir Alex. McKenzie had been his most intimate friend, 'which must have made informal consultation easier'.

The Dominion Council is a large body, and the details of its composition have altered from time to time.[3] Its present membership, in addition to the President and the Leader, falls into several sections. By far the largest section, numbering thirty-five persons in 1956–7, consists of members elected by the Conference: vice-presidents (by divisions plus one for the Maori race); women vice-presidents (one for each island); divisional representatives (numbers in proportion to the number of electorates (constituencies) in each division, one of the representatives to be a woman). The divisional chairmen are members *ex officio*. So is the Dominion Treasurer (appointed by the Council). The Council also includes five parliamentary representatives, chosen by the parliamentary party. There are also up to six co-opted members and possibly one co-opted past President. The proportion of parliamentarians on the Council is smaller than the proportion on the corresponding body in the Reform Party.[4]

A minor adjustment in organization after the party lost the

---

[1] *Dominion*, 23 July 1962.   [2] At the 1957 Party Conference.

[3] Robinson, *Oligarchy and Democracy*, p. 31. However, there is no large body corresponding to the Conservative 'Central Council', which includes, among others, all M.P.s and four representatives of each constituency association.

[4] Ibid., p. 23.

1957 election was to change the membership of the five parliamentary representatives so that three of them represented marginal seats, Mr. Hanan (Invercargill), Mr. Aderman (New Plymouth), and Mr. Gotz (Manukau). One report attributed the change to expressions of discontent in caucus by members holding marginal seats, who claimed that they had been 'inadequately consulted on policy matters.'[1] The change ensured that these three would be especially useful as representatives on the Council because of their being in close touch with public opinion.[2] Apparently it was believed that the prospect of electoral defeat must concentrate a member's mind wonderfully on finding out what the public wanted.

The powers of the Dominion Council are extensive; to 'deal with all matters in regard to which no express provision is made in these Rules', and to 'do such things and issue such directions, consistent with the said Rules, as it may think necessary or expedient for the well-being of the Party, and its decisions on all questions shall be binding unless and until set aside by a Dominion Conference . . .'.[3] It also appoints, and may dismiss, the General Director (formerly Secretary). But the Council is so unwieldy a body, and the cost of bringing it together is so heavy, that it usually meets only twice a year, for two days each time, as well as meeting during the party's Annual Conference. In practice much of its power has now passed to the smaller Dominion Executive Committee. Copies of the minutes of Executive Committee meetings do not even have to be forwarded to individual members of Council.[4] It has been maintained that this shift of power has arisen largely because in 1941 the divisional chairmen were put on the Executive as of right, thus increasing its importance as a link with the organization all over the country.[5] The composition of the Executive is not fixed precisely (except that it must include the President, Leader, Treasurer, the divisional chairmen, and one other representative from each division).[6] In 1962 it comprised nineteen persons, three of whom were members of the House of Representatives.[7]

[1] *Dominion*, 'Lobby Letter', 31 Mar. 1958.
[2] Interview, Mr. K. J. Holyoake, Oct. 1958.
[3] *Constitution and Rules* (*1963*), rule 40.
[4] Kelson, op. cit. (1954), p. 21, n. 25.
[5] Robinson, *The Rise of the New Zealand National Party*, p. 219.
[6] *Constitution and Rules* (*1963*), rule 49.   [7] *Dominion*, 1 Sept. 1962.

The obvious power of the Executive and the fact that it meets about six times a year or more, compared with twice or thrice for the Council, has led to some complaints by members of the Council who are not also members of the Executive.[1] As might have been expected, these murmurs grew louder after the election defeat of 1957. But, in the opinion of a former National Party official, this discontent did not arise mainly from concern that lack of consultation of the Council had reduced efficiency, but rather from feelings of slighted self-importance and regret at having missed trips to Wellington. However, if an important enough matter arises at short notice, the Dominion Council will be called together, not the Dominion Executive. In 1942 when the Government's handling of the Huntly coal strike raised the question of the party's continued representation in the War Cabinet, it was the Council, not the Executive, which was convened.[2] And if at any time a possible change in the leadership were being seriously canvassed, this would be sufficiently important to warrant a meeting of the Council. There is a feeling in some quarters in the party that even the Dominion Executive is not a small enough body for some purposes, such as keeping in close touch with the parliamentary party and discussing questions in an intimate rather than an oratorical way. It has been suggested that a smaller group, consisting perhaps of the President, Leader, and divisional chairmen, should meet from time to time.

When the National Party is the Government, members of the Dominion Executive, just like the President of the party, are frequently approached by the people with grievances or seeking help in their dealings with Government departments. Discussion of particular cases often leads to consideration of general issues and to suggestions on policy. Occasionally the Dominion Executive has held a joint meeting with the Cabinet, but this is not a regular practice.

The Dominion Council also has small standing committees on Finance, Rules, Publicity and Information, and Research. On the finance committee all five divisions are represented. It is laid down that the President and the Treasurer shall be members of the finance committee.[3] Very little has been published on

[1] *Dominion*, 'Lobby Letter', 31 Mar. 1958.
[2] Robinson, *The Rise of the New Zealand National Party*, p. 222.
[3] *Constitution and Rules (1963)*, rule 46.

finance, but the information available indicates that the position is radically different from what it was in the days of the Reform Party. The 'organizational revolution' of 1936 was in part a protest against financial secrecy at the centre. Nowadays finance has been systematized and, within the party, to a great extent publicized. For instance, each one of the divisions pays a 'levy', a certain proportion of its income, to Dominion Headquarters.[1] A special routine is also followed in collecting contributions from businesses which operate in all four of the main New Zealand cities. To prevent a firm being approached more than once, the division in which the firm's headquarters is located is made responsible for collecting the contribution. The whole sum is then sent to Dominion Headquarters, which retains its percentage and then distributes the remainder among the five divisions in the same proportions as those used for collecting the 'levy'.[2]

The most important standing committee of the Dominion Council is the policy committee, which has an equal number of representatives from the parliamentary and non-parliamentary parts of the organization. It consists of the Leader (who has a casting vote) and three other parliamentary members appointed by him, and three persons (*not* from the parliamentary party), to be appointed by the Dominion Council. The President and the Deputy-leader are usually members. But the practice of having the Wellington divisional chairman on the committee[3] appears to have been discontinued.[4] In the selection of this committee 'there is an attempt to gain representation for the major occupational lines of thought in the Party, the current membership (1954) including spokesmen for farming, manufacturing, and financial interests.'[5] According to another source, the attempt to represent these different interests used to take place through consultations between President and Leader, the President's selections being confirmed by the Council in the early years of the period 1936 to 1949, and later by the

[1] The basis of this levy, different for each division, is neither the number of votes cast for the party in the division nor the number of seats held by it. According to a former General Secretary of the party no one can now remember how the proportions were originally worked out (interview, Theo Hills, Oct. 1958).

[2] Inferentially a 'possible estimate' of total party income in 1960 might be something approaching £300,000 (Chapman, Jackson, and Mitchell, op. cit., p. 78).

[3] Kelson, *Political Science*, vol. vi, no. 2, art. cit., p. 21.

[4] Robinson, *Political Science*, art. cit., p. 29.

[5] Kelson, *Political Science*, vol. vi, no. 2, art. cit., p. 23.

Executive.[1] The party constitution gives extensive powers to the policy committee.[2] It receives and considers recommendations on policy from the parliamentary party, the annual Dominion Conference, the Council, and the Divisional Committees of the party, as well as from its own sub-committees. But it is not bound to *accept* any of these recommendations. It is the duty of the committee alone to 'draft and finalise the general policy of the Party'. Nor is there any mention of the committee's submitting recommendations to the Council for its approval. It need only 'report' to the Council all alterations made to the 'general policy' of the party. According to A. D. Robinson, a distinct trend has been noticeable in the machinery of approval for policy, as produced by the policy committee, in election years. In 1938 policy was submitted to the Council for confirmation. In 1941 (for the 'election' which was postponed) and 1943 there was official confirmation by the Dominion Executive. In 1946 and 1949 there was only *informal* confirmation by the Executive.[3] Before the party policy is actually submitted to the electors it is explained to the candidates, and possibly altered by them, at the candidates' conference.[4]

Some confusion might arise in interpreting the provision that the Leader of the party shall 'from time to time, after consultation with the policy committee, announce outstanding features of the policy'.[5] This might suggest that the policy committee's concern was with general, long-range policy, while the Leader was responsible for short-term 'fighting policy', the equivalent of what the British Maxwell Fyfe Report called the 'programme', or 'the specific plans for the application of policy'.[6] But in fact the policy committee has assumed responsibility for fighting policy also.[7] Indeed one might go further and say that its *main* concern was with fighting policy. Between 1937 and 1959 there was no public statement of the party's policy.[8] As in the Labour

[1] Robinson, *Oligarchy and Democracy*, p. 39.
[2] *Constitution and Rules (1963)*, rule 134.   [3] Robinson, op. cit., pp. 38–39.
[4] See pp. 139–40 above and pp. 269–270 below.
[5] *Constitution and Rules (1963)*, rule 136; cf., on the Australian Liberal Party, Overacker, *The Australian Party System*, p. 245.
[6] McKenzie, *Political Parties*, p. 64; *Final Report of the Committee on Party Organisation* (London, 1949), usually referred to as the *Maxwell Fyfe Report*.
[7] Robinson, op. cit., p. 36, quoting Holland, *Minutes* of Dominion Conference, 5–6 July 1948.
[8] Robinson, *The Rise of the New Zealand National Party*, p. 194.

Party nowadays, the party's 'policy' has usually consisted simply of the policy put forward at the previous election. Long-range policy is comparatively neglected by New Zealand parties. There is little 'middle-range' policy lying in the desert area between fighting policy and general statements, such as that the National Party's policy is 'the private ownership of the means of production, distribution and exchange'.[1]

However, the influence of the Leader on policy remains considerable, even though the policy committee may represent 'interests' and may be in a position to tell the parliamentarians what the organization in the country will not stand. The Leader is chairman and has a casting vote, and parliamentary members, who, along with the Leader, make up 50 per cent. of the members of the policy committee, are accustomed to deferring to him in caucus. Nor is the fact that the Leader announces the fighting policy of the party (even though he may not make it as an individual) completely without significance. In announcing it he may be able to convey particular interpretations of his own. And, in arguing against the adoption of any particular policy in the policy committee, he could take the line that, if the policy were adopted, he would find it difficult to be convincing when putting the issue before the electors. He is leader of the 'front-line troops', the parliamentarians, who have to face the electors on the platform and at the polls. The non-parliamentarians are the equivalent of the supporting arms.

As provided for in the constitution, the policy committee makes use of sub-committees, composed partly of co-opted persons, often professionally expert in the subject-matter. Sub-committees are used mainly for issues which are both politically contentious and technically difficult, such as changes in the Tenancy Act or the consideration of import anomalies. One development, started in 1954,[2] was to set up an advisory committee on policy in election years, with both parliamentary and non-parliamentary members,[3] in order to go through remits passed by party Conferences since the last election, and pick

---

[1] Robinson, *Oligarchy and Democracy*, p. 36.

[2] Interview, Sir Alex. McKenzie, Feb. 1958. However, in preparation for the 1941 'election' a rather similar special advisory body seems to have existed (Robinson, *The Rise of the New Zealand National Party*, p. 117).

[3] In 1954 the divisional chairmen were included in this body (*Freedom*, 7 July 1954).

out a number of them for the consideration of the policy committee. In 1957 members of this body were also asked to produce
ideas of their own on policy for the policy committee. In 1960
and 1963 much of the work of the policy advisory committee
seems to have been carried out by the divisional chairmen. The
Dominion Council may also set up *ad hoc*, as opposed to standing,
committees. Thus in 1949 it constituted a 'key electorates committee', which was made responsible for taking special steps to
improve the party's organization in marginal seats.[1]

The 'organizational revolution' of 1936 also had the result of
changing the nature of the party headquarters. In the Reform
Party in essence the Party Secretary, apart from typists, *was* the
headquarters, and the Secretary was the Leader's 'man'. Now
he is appointed, and may be dismissed, by Dominion Council.
And changes in the direction of 'democracy' in the branches,
electorates, and divisions, have increased the scope of the
Secretary's duties, and given him an important liaison role
between caucus and the Leader, on the one hand, and the extra-
parliamentary organization on the other. At the start of the
party's history there was a quick turn-over of Secretaries; three,
and one acting Secretary, served for a total of only five years.
There was then a long 'partnership' between T. G. Wilkes, who
took over as Secretary in 1941, and Holland, who had become
Leader in the previous year. After Wilkes's retirement in 1955,
the turnover has again been rapid, and there were two secretaries between Wilkes and the present one. Wilkes and the two
secretaries after him were both already in the organization as
divisional secretaries when they were appointed, and it appeared
that a convention might be growing up by which the appointment would always be made from 'the field'. The practice was
criticized by some who thought that this resulted in Secretaries
having acquired too 'parochial' an outlook by the time they
were appointed. The present Secretary, Mr. Ralph Wilson,
appointed in 1959 with the title 'General Director' of the party,
was not drawn from the organization but had previously been
a public servant and secretary of the New Zealand Retailers'

[1] Robinson, *The Rise of the New Zealand National Party*, p. 173. This committee
is now inactive, although Dominion headquarters pays special attention to marginal seats, for instance by giving them priority for the services of visiting speakers
and by requiring special reports from them.

Federation.[1] Mr. Wilson is a trained economist and has given special attention to policy. Before his appointment, in spite of the existence of the policy committee, the process of policy-framing for an election sometimes tended to be short and casual. The 'policy' presented at the election also included long lists of individual works projects completed by National Governments. Now the process is more thorough. For instance, the 1963 section on 'Taxation and Finance' was re-drafted four times, after Mr. Wilson's preliminary draft, by the policy committee. From November 1962 until October 1963 the policy committee met for about forty hours. Ministers in 1963 (in 1960 former ministers and members of caucus committees) were brought into the process, by helping both in the production of the original draft and in the revisions. Presentation of policy for the election was also more streamlined in 1960 and 1963. The 'election policy' for each year was divided, under each main subject heading, into 'Basic Policy' and 'Details'.[2]

The Secretarial and Organizing Department of party head-quarters includes the General Director, an Assistant Secretary and clerical staff. There is also a Publicity Department, a Department which publishes *Freedom*, the official organ of the party, as well as several series of informational bulletins for circulation inside the party, and a Research Department, consisting of a Director of Research and an assistant. This last department has proved useful in providing material for members' speeches and also in supplying relevant information to those in the organization who wish to make suggestions on policy.[3] The total headquarters staff in May 1964 was fourteen.

From this account of the central organization of the party, as in the New Zealand Labour Party and most other political parties in democracies, it is impossible to point to any one locus of power. Even if it is assumed that the policy committee is the citadel of power within the party, the riddle is still unsolved, because representatives of the parliamentary party, of the

---

[1] On Mr. Wilson and his functions see Weeks, op. cit., pp. 43–57.

[2] Interview, Mr. Ralph Wilson, May 1964. The corresponding meetings of the Policy Committee, 1959–60, lasted for ten full days and some evenings between November and May (*23rd Annual Conference, Annual Report and Remits* (1960), p. 11).

[3] See p. 198, below. For the Research Director's account of his functions see Martin Nestor, 'The Role of Research in New Zealand Politics', *Political Science*, vol. xv, no. 2 (1963).

organization outside Parliament, and even of 'interests' are all found on the committee. To explain the situation one is driven to invoke terms, such as 'interlocking directorate', without being able to say precisely who or what directs the directors themselves. Nevertheless, three observations may be pertinent. First, since the 'organizational revolution' of 1936 the whole party structure has been systematized and institutionalized into a great complex of committees. Second, the extra-parliamentary organization has been given a more important role in the formal structure, and apparently a more effective voice in the making of policy. The new emphasis on the role of the extra-parliamentary party was very marked at first, although it is reasonable to suppose that the parliamentary party gained in strength after a National Government was formed in 1949. Third, the 'organizational revolution' was aimed at securing 'results', namely at getting the party back in office. The 'revolution', and the replacement of Forbes by Hamilton, occurred under the stimulus of a heavy electoral defeat. After an equally severe defeat in 1938, the extra-parliamentary organization intervened and the 'new' Leader was deposed in favour of Holland. In 1942 it backed Holland against the former Leaders, Hamilton and Coates, by passing a motion for submission to caucus that it approved of his stand against the Government's handling of the Waikato strike.[1] When the party is in office the organization, which represents a range of varied interests, may not be too sure of its exact wishes on some aspects of policy. But, when the party is out of office, the organization is united to a much greater extent, in expecting results—and in pressing the Leader and the parliamentary party to achieve them.

Labour Party Central Organization

In appearance Labour's central organization is more complex than National's, because of the provisions for 'indirect' membership and for the representation of trade unions in the party structure. Yet, in a way, this makes the organization *simpler* to describe. To be sure, there is no single 'trade-union interest' represented in the party; nevertheless, relatively, there is more *approximation* to a homogeneous interest than there is in any part of the National Party's structure.

[1] Robinson, *Oligarchy and Democracy*, pp. 64–65.

The references to the links between the Parliamentary Labour
Party and the unions, made in the last two chapters, provide
some relevant information about the party's extra-parliamentary organization. As a consequence of the role played by the
trade unions in the formation of the Labour Party, the extra-
parliamentary organization has always been strong, and so
there has been no equivalent of the 'organizational revolution'.
Indeed, in the early days of the movement, it was the parliamentary wing of the party that was on the defensive. At the
1920 Annual Conference a resolution was carried that no
Member of Parliament should hold an executive position in the
Labour Party. It was only on the motion of the Leader, H. E.
Holland, that the matter was recommitted, put to the affiliations
in a plebiscite, and defeated by a small majority.[1]

Apart from the Annual Conference, the party's central organs
are the national executive and the head office. In the national
executive there is no distinction made between the method for
representation of unions and that for the representation of
constituency parties, as there is in Britain. But there is a distinction according to *geography*. The President, Vice-President,
and Secretary-Treasurer and five members (resident in the
Wellington area) are elected annually by Conference as a
whole, and constitute a 'central executive'. The whole Conference also elects a Women's Representative and a Maori
Representative. The remaining members of the national executive are elected according to geographical areas, at present
twelve, by postal ballot of the branches and affiliations in each
area. Two members representing the PLP (one of whom is, by
convention, the Leader and the other the Secretary of the PLP)
also attend executive meetings, but without the power to vote.
In accordance with Labour notions of 'democracy' in party
organization,[2] there are no co-opted members, as there are
in the National Party Dominion Council. The existence of a
central executive, in addition to the executive as a whole, dates
from 1921.[3] Considerations of time and expense and the fact
that some meetings may have to be called at short notice, have
made some such arrangements necessary in other New Zealand

[1] Brown, *The Rise of New Zealand Labour*, p. 69.
[2] Crisp, *Australian Federal Labor Party*, pp. 3 ff.
[3] Brown, op. cit., pp. 76–77.

political parties. The National Party has its Dominion Executive as well as its Dominion Council. Even the skeletal Liberal and Labour Federation faced the problem that its executive tended to be drawn from Wellington or nearby. And the provisional Dominion Executive of the National Party in 1936 consisted of the Wellington members of the Dominion Executive of the National Political Federation.[1] But the Labour Party arrangement has been subject to special criticism because of the degree to which it strengthens the influence of 'Wellington'. In addition to the five Wellington members on the central executive, the Secretary-Treasurer also comes from the head office in Wellington and either the President or the Vice-President often comes from Wellington too. The full executive meets only quarterly, while the central executive meets about once a month, slightly more often when an election is approaching. If particular members of the 'outer' executive are in Wellington when the central executive meets, they may attend, provided that they know that a meeting is taking place. The Divisional Area Representative for the area which includes Wellington does, in fact, usually attend nearly all the central executive meetings. On the other hand, a non-Wellington member may be specially invited to attend a particular meeting. Otherwise, these members keep in touch with the doings of the central executive by its minutes being circulated to them. It is not possible to give any quantitative analysis of the decisions made by the central executive compared with those made by the whole executive. One informed opinion is that the central executive seldom makes a decision which the whole national executive cannot override if it wants to. On the other hand, the larger body does not often make changes in the smaller body's recommendations.[2] This situation could be interpreted equally well to indicate 'oligarchy' on the part of the smaller body, or to illustrate its responsiveness to the wishes of the larger. It is the opinion of a former member of the central executive that this body likes to keep power in its own hands, rather than in the executive as a whole. The central executive had four committees in 1958,[3] but no

---

[1] Robinson, *Oligarchy and Democracy*, p. 43.
[2] Interview, Dr. A. M. Finlay, Feb. 1958. This would also apply to the relation between the National Party's Dominion Council and Dominion Executive.
[3] President of the Labour Party, 1958 Annual Conference.

details of them were made public. In July 1961 the following committees were set up: Finance; Organization and Branch activities; Publicity; Administration; Conference Affairs.[1]

There is as yet no consistent pattern for the election of the party's President. In the early 1930's it seemed that a practice was growing up by which a different Member of Parliament was elected to the office each year.[2] But the sequence was broken by the 'reign' of Mr. James Roberts of the Watersiders' Union, often referred to as the 'uncrowned king of New Zealand', who was President from 1936 until 1950. Since then the Presidency has been held by two parliamentarians (Messrs. Nordmeyer and Moohan) for five years each, from 1960 to 1964 by Dr. A. M. Finlay, a previous M.P. who regained his seat at the 1963 general election, and from 1964 by an M.P., Mr. N. E. Kirk. A convention seems to have grown up that a President is succeeded by the previous Vice-President. Messrs. Nordmeyer, Moohan, Finlay, and Kirk all came to Presidential office in this way.

The composition of the rest of the national executive is completely different from that of the British Labour Party's national executive. M.P.s have constituted a majority on the latter body, which, at various times, helped to ensure that the NEC's views conformed with those of the parliamentary leaders (1937–51),[3] or, in the years immediately after 1951, produced a sizeable Bevanite opposition group.[4] But neither of these situations is at all likely in the Labour Party in New Zealand. True, one of the five Wellington representatives in 1963–4 was an M.P. and one a former M.P. But of the twelve 'Divisional Area Representatives' none was an M.P. More important, since there is no separate election by the constituency parties (as in Britain), and as the trade unions on the whole work closely with the parliamentary leadership, it is harder for parliamentary 'rebels' to obtain representatives on the executive than it is in Britain.

Trade-unionists, or ex-unionists who have gone into politics

---

[1] As stated at the Forty-Sixth Annual Conference, 1962. The national executive is also represented on two 'joint committees', the Joint Council of Labour and the policy committee (see below). The Maori Policy Committee is not a national executive committee, but appoints its chairman to be its representative on the national executive.

[2] Paul, op. cit., Appendix G.

[3] McKenzie, *Political Parties*, pp. 420 ff. and *Political Studies*, p. 178.

[4] Rose, op. cit., p. 136.

are strongly represented on the national executive, but there are also a few members of constituency parties, who are not trade-unionists. In the voting for the national executive there is no evidence that a 'ticket' exists[1] giving directions on who the 'official' candidates are. It is true, however, that, once elected, a member of the executive is likely to go on being re-elected. The Chairman and Secretary, or two other members, of the PLP may attend national executive meetings, but without voting power.[2]

The powers of the national executive are wide. When Conference is not in session the national executive interprets the party's rules and may make policy pronouncements. Among the decisions made by the national executive in recent years have been: to print and distribute pamphlets on certain topics; to make a recommendation to Conference on establishing a Women's Advisory Council; a ruling on the representation of the party at a Commonwealth Labour Conference in London; to apply for a magisterial recount in electorates where the National Party had a very small majority over Labour; to rule that a member belonging both to a junior and a senior branch was entitled to full privileges in both branches. The executive has the power to expel a member subject to appeal to Conference, although the most publicized expulsion, that of Mr. Lee in 1940, was made by Conference itself. The national executive controls the party's funds. It decides which bodies are Communist 'front' organizations, whose members may not also be members of the Labour Party.[3] It is also responsible for the organization of the Annual Conference of the party, and has a considerable say in the selection of parliamentary candidates.[4]

The national executive also provides half of the representatives for a committee on policy, the other half coming from the parliamentary party. This committee has operated at election times, beginning with the 1938 election.[5] Its size has varied from

---

[1] As in Australia (Miller, *Political Science*, vol. v, no. 2, art. cit., p. 28).
[2] *Constitution and Rules (1955)*, 11 (F).
[3] Overacker, *American Political Science Review*, art. cit., p. 723.
[4] See Chs. VIII and IX, below.
[5] A reference is made to it in the national executive *Minutes* in 1936. As early as the minutes of 1917 there is reference to a subcommittee of three from the executive to draft the election manifesto. Brown, *The Rise of New Zealand Labour*, mentions a 'policy committee' set up by the 1933 Annual Conference (p. 160). But its terms of reference were restricted.

time to time; it had ten members in 1962. The policy committee is now a continuing body which meets regularly, not just a piece of pre-election machinery. Perhaps, under the influence of defeat at the 1960 election, this was an attempt to produce better liaison between the national executive and the PLP. At the 1961 Conference stress was laid on the need for more regular meetings of the national and central executives and of the Joint Council of Labour. The policy committee goes through the remits passed by the last three conferences of the party, and then produces an Election Manifesto. It uses the remits only as a guide; it is not compelled to take account of all of them, and it is free to include proposals from other sources. Remits, even when included, are not reproduced verbatim, but are 'toned down' and made more general. Usually figures are avoided.[2] On some past occasions, apparently, sections of what later become the manifesto have been drafted by a single member of the committee, although later submitted to the whole committee for approval.

In 1916, 'They gave Mr. J. Glover a lead pencil and a postage stamp and appointed him secretary'.[3] But Labour's 'head office' dates only from 1922, when it was set up on the initiative of Mr. Nash, the then Secretary. By comparison with the National Party, Labour's headquarters staff is small. Apart from typists it consists of the Secretary,[4] an Assistant Secretary, and one organizer, who may in fact spend some of his time away from the office, for instance helping the party organization at a by-election. It used to be the convention that the Secretary later entered Parliament. Mr. Nash did so, even retaining the secretaryship for some years after he became an M.P. James Thorn, the next Secretary, also entered Parliament. For the next four years the job was held by David Wilson who was at the same time a member of the upper house, the Legislative Council. His successor, Mr. Moohan, also stood successfully for Parliament while serving as Secretary. There appears to have been some criticism of this practice, and when 'the present Secretary [Mr. Alan McDonald] was chosen his lack of political

---

[1] This arrangement was approved by the Forty-fifth Annual Conference (1961) by amending Clause 12(d) 3 of the *Constitution and Rules*.

[2] Interview, Mr. A. J. McDonald, July 1957.

[3] Overacker, *American Political Science Review*, art. cit., p. 715.

[4] The full title is 'Secretary-Treasurer'.

ambitions was cited by some as an asset'.[1] Possibly, now that routine has established its sway over the party organization, the nature of the Secretary's job has changed. Earlier there was perhaps a greater need for Secretaries to travel round and inspire organization in the field. This kind of work would attract a prospective politician to the job. But now the Secretary's functions have become more 'secretarial'.[2] It may be noted that the present Secretary was trained as an accountant, and was therefore interested, and qualified, in the 'secretarial' aspects of the job.

Until 1958 the Secretary had to face annual re-election at Conference. But he was not always unopposed, and was quite seriously challenged by a rival at the 1958 Annual Conference. It was decided at that Conference that in future the Secretary, once elected by Conference, should hold office at the pleasure of the national executive. Annual election was clearly a carry-over from the early days of the Labour Movement, when the Secretary's duties were part-time, and when there was no obvious conflict between 'democracy' and the organization's requirements of continuity and efficiency. But by 1958 the problem was viewed in different terms; as one speaker at the Conference remarked in this context, 'let's get away from this claptrap about democracy!' Unfortunately another modern requirement for the Secretary's job has not been recognized. The salary is not in keeping with the importance of the Secretary's duties. He is paid at the level of a Member of Parliament (without a member's allowances and perquisites) instead of at the level of a Cabinet minister.

There is no permanent separate research section at Labour headquarters. The Secretary and, in particular, the Assistant Secretary have had to be mainly responsible for providing research and information, for instance by pamphlets to the public, particularly at election times, as well as for producing election 'notes' (with a good index) for the use of election speakers.[3] The lack of a separate and adequate research staff has been criticized from within the party. It has been alleged

---

[1] Ibid., p. 716, n. 24.
[2] Interview, Mr. M. Moohan, Oct. 1958.
[3] For the 1954 election some research work was done for the party by a member of the staff of the Leader of the Opposition (North, op. cit., p. 54).

that there is a lack of 'attractive, challenging material on controversial issues',[1] and sometimes a failure to link a current
issue (for instance, a shortage of some particular commodity
when a National Government is in office) with Labour's general
philosophy. Perhaps this latter defect arises from the lack of a
'middle-range policy'[2] in the party. Two Labour back-bench
members, both of whom had previously been organizers, complained of a lack of research material in 1960. There have also
been complaints by young Labour intellectuals that when they
offered their services for the production of pamphlets, interest
was expressed by top men in the party but that nothing actually
came of it.

Although the job of Secretary at Labour Party headquarters
has ceased to be a stepping-stone to Parliament, a new avenue
of entry was opened up in the 1950's.[3] The 'organizers' employed
by the party tended to become candidates and later M.P.s.
Some of the organizers, before they were appointed, had already
tried unsuccessfully to enter Parliament, and may even have
consciously calculated that an organizer's job might open up
an easier route to success. Not only is a member's job more
glamorous; his pay is also better than the very low salaries which
the party is able to give its organizers. With a few exceptions
the organizers were assigned areas to organize both between
elections and during election campaigns. One was even put in
charge of a 'provincial office', covering roughly the Auckland
and South Auckland region (Areas 1, 2, 3, and 4) between
the 1954 and 1957 elections, a device which raised problems of
'dual control'.[4] This arrangement was repeated, with a different
organizer, from 1960 to 1963. Both these organizers became
M.P.s in the Auckland area. Organizers often picked a likely
seat, and entered their names for selection as a candidate at the
next election. Because they were above the average in knowledge
and ability, and because of the strategic advantages of their job,
they had a very good chance of being selected. Among the
organizers who became members during the last dozen years

[1] Overacker, *Political Science*, vol. ix, no. 2, art. cit., p. 22.
[2] Weeks, op. cit., p. 147.
[3] The *Report* of the Thirty-seventh Annual Conference (1953) stated that two
full-time organizers had been appointed and that two more were about to be
appointed.
[4] Weeks, op. cit., pp. 102 ff.

are Messrs. Holloway, Keeling, Pickering, Faulkner, and Moyle. Mr. Boord, who had been Assistant Secretary to the party, also became an M.P.

This development attracted some criticism, particularly from Labour Party members, themselves interested in becoming candidates, who think that the organizers have an unfair advantage. Other critics pointed out that the organizer's attention naturally became concentrated more on his own prospects of selection and election than on organizing the entire area for which he was responsible. Certainly, the system of organizers was never put into operation fully. The 'establishment' for organizers in 1957 was eight.[1] But funds have never been sufficient to employ all these, and, for the last ten years, the actual number employed has varied between one and four. Another criticism is that there is not enough local control over the organizers, and that they are too much tied to party headquarters. To put this right a substantial increase in the number of organizers (and in the money available to pay for them) would have been necessary. It might then have been possible to allocate one organizer to each of the twelve divisional areas, or perhaps in some cases for two adjacent areas to share an organizer. As it is, *ad hoc* measures have had to be employed. For instance, at by-elections all available organizers have had to be switched to the electorate concerned. To organize the Hamilton by-election in 1959 the party had to make use of its single organizer plus a number of M.P.s, most of whom had previously been organizers for the party. For organizational, and other, reasons the by-election campaign was so ineptly fought that a National Member of Parliament taunted his opponents with the assertion that after the by-election the Prime Minister (Mr. Nash) 'paid a tribute to the National Party organization but was discreetly silent about the Labour Party organization . . .'.[2]

A useful, though unplanned, by-product of the tendency of organizers to enter Parliament might have been the infusion of new, and capable, blood into the Parliamentary Party. In 1954 and 1957 this seemed to be the trend; organizers who became members were probably above the average in ability. But this windfall gain to the party was arrested at the 1960 election.

---

[1] Interview, Mr. A. J. McDonald, July 1957.
[2] *N.Z.P.D.*, vol. cccxix, p. 176 (3 July 1959).

Mr. Holloway, who had quickly become a Minister, did not stand for re-election. Messrs. Keeling and Pickering, previous organizers, lost their seats. So did Mr. Boord, previously Assistant Secretary, who had become a Minister. A further break in the pattern occurred when Mr. Shamy, who had been an organizer since 1956 and had contested the 1957 election, left his job towards the end of 1959 to take up a business appointment. Since Mr. Moyle, the only organizer, became an M.P. in 1963 no more organizers have been appointed. Instead existing M.P.s were given an organizing job to do.[1]

This brief account of Labour's central organization reveals both its strength and its weakness. There has been an absence of violent disagreement between the various sections of the party represented on the national executive, and between the national executive and caucus, and only an undercurrent of feeling against 'domination by Wellington'. Only once, during the Lee episode, was it necessary to bring into operation the machinery for settling a national executive–caucus dispute, namely a joint conference of the members of the two bodies.[2] Compared with both the British and Australian Labour Parties, the internal politics of the New Zealand Labour Party have been remarkably free from friction and controversy. At the same time it is impossible to avoid the feeling that this absence of friction is not completely healthy; that, at the top of the party, it may have resulted less from a *consensus* of ideas than from a relative *absence* of ideas.

Organizationally the party is in bad shape. Several suggestions for improvement were made at the 1959 Annual Conference, after the defeat at the Hamilton by-election, but none was adopted which involved the hiring of new staff, although later attempts were made to tighten up the organization, particularly the policy committee. A symptom of the party's difficulties is a shortage of money, which makes it impossible to pay enough to attract good staff for long (as shown by the rush of organizers to become M.P.s), or to employ sufficient numbers of staff. The figures quoted by Overacker[3] for the party's receipts might be misleading, if taken as an indication of what money is available

[1] See pp. 216–17, below.
[2] Overacker, *American Political Science Review*, art. cit., p. 728.
[3] Ibid., p. 718.

to run the headquarters organization. For instance, the last figures given by her are £23,000 for 1950–1 and £36,000 for 1951–2, an election year. These amounts have increased since, along with the general rise in costs. But they include some 'double counting' (e.g. on refunds of affiliation fees, and on receipts from sales of literature which are largely balanced by the cost of producing the literature). Moreover, particularly in election years, some of the receipts are spent on grants to organizations and on other expenditure in the field. Consequently, even today, the total amount available for running the headquarters organization cannot be more than £15,000 or £20,000 a year.[1] Yet, some years back, at the 1958 Annual Conference, Mr. Nash said that to run 'the organization' (presumably, the headquarters organization) properly, between £25,000 and £50,000 a year was needed. Compared with the National Party, Labour's organization is run on a shoestring. The difference in scale is striking, even if allowance is made for the fact that the structure of the Labour Party is more centralized, and less loaded with committees and regional bodies, which means that fewer staff may be necessary.

Labour parties in Britain and Australia have also suffered from a feeling in the party that most work should be voluntary, and that something is wrong if the party is too obviously organized according to concepts of 'business' and 'efficiency'.[2] But the New Zealand party is under a double disadvantage. In New Zealand, a new and small country, there is a *general* prejudice, outside the actual world of business, in favour of voluntary action and against setting up an efficient large-scale organization and paying employees at market rates. The existence of this double burden in New Zealand largely explains the stunted growth of Labour's organization.[3] It is one thing for Labour to attribute election defeats partly to National's superior organization. It is another, apparently, for it to set about improving its own organization. Not until it tackles this task can it hope to reap the electoral benefit.

---

[1] Cf. Chapman, Jackson, and Mitchell, op. cit., p. 78.
[2] Cf. Morgan Phillips, *Labour in the Sixties* (London, 1960), p. 23.
[3] Cf. Weeks, op. cit., p. 1, who argues that the main obstacle to improving Labour's organization is not lack of money but a lack of conviction that the organization needs improvement, resulting in a lack of the *will* to raise money.

VII

PARTY ORGANIZATION, REGIONAL AND LOCAL

EACH of the major parties has a hierarchical organization, through which the centre is linked with the smallest geographical unit, the branch. But only the National Party has a permanent *regional unit*, the division. In the Labour Party there are as yet no permanent country-wide units at any level between the national executive and the 'Labour Representation Committees' (LRCs), of which there are over fifty in the whole country. To some extent the 'divisions'[1] of the National Party may be regarded as the successors of the provincial executives of the Reform Party. Initially there were three of these;[2] later there were as many as eleven.[3] But the Reform Party's provincial executives were not very active. As will be observed later, even the 'grass roots' organization of the party was intermittent, and came to life only at elections. Indeed many surviving active members of the party are quite unaware that the provincial executives ever existed.

National Party Regional Organization

There are now five divisions in the National Party.[4] They are largely autonomous, for instance they appoint and pay their own staff, although salary scales are laid down at Dominion level. To be sure, there are certain broad similarities of organization and procedure in the divisions, which are laid down specifically in the party's constitution. Each has a Divisional Committee, composed of representatives elected by the Electorate Committee. Where Junior Sections exist in an electorate,

---

[1] Much of the information which follows was obtained from interviews with the five divisional secretaries and with the secretary-organizer for the Southland Sub-Division.

[2] *Reform Party Year Book*, 1913, p. 5.

[3] *Constitution and Rules of the Political Reform League*, p. 12.

[4] Auckland, Waikato, Wellington, Canterbury, and Otago-Southland.

each has the right to be represented on the Committee. Additional persons may be co-opted, and National Party Members of Parliament in the area are entitled to be invited to attend all Committee meetings and are eligible for election to the Committee. Each Committee must appoint an executive committee to act for it between meetings, also a policy sub-committee to make recommendations on policy. The duties of the Committee—such as carrying out the decisions of Dominion Council, controlling and co-ordinating Electorate Committees, collecting contributions and membership subscriptions, assisting in candidate selection and so on—are also listed.[1] But in practice this leaves a good deal of scope for variation between divisions; for instance, the committee structure differs in all five, and although there is the equivalent of a 'sub-executive' in each division, the exact form varies.[2] There is also considerable variation between divisions in the way they work, as distinct from their structure. Usually, each divisional secretary is happily convinced that his particular 'scheme' on any subject is superior to the others. Certainly, differences are apparent between divisions in the energy and expertise devoted to concentrating resources on marginal seats, and to holding 'National Party Weeks', when M.P.s come and address various groups in an electorate, social and fund-raising activities take place, and mass canvassing is organized.

The secretaries, unlike the divisional chairmen, are full-time and so perhaps have more opportunity to gain first-hand knowledge of the division and its organization than have the chairmen. They also receive reports and returns from electorates and branches. Their own Divisional Committee, members of Dominion Council, M.P.s, and (if the party is in power) ministers will expect them to be knowledgeable on a multitude of topics: how a particular policy will 'go down' in the division; what are the areas of greatest Social Credit support; what will be the effect of a redistribution of seats, and so on. Although the salaries of the divisional secretaries are modest in comparison with the earnings of divisional chairmen in their private occupations and of the National Party members likely to be on a 'sub-executive', in the egalitarian atmosphere of New Zealand

[1] *Constitution and Rules of the New Zealand National Party (1963)*, rules 50–61.
[2] More than is indicated in Kelson, *Political Science*, vol. vi, no. 2, art. cit., p. 12.

the secretaries are not obviously at a social disadvantage.[1] A few years ago, for instance, the Auckland divisional secretary was on Christian-name terms with the President of the party. So there is no 'social' barrier against acceptance of the secretary's ideas and proposals. The divisional secretaries meet twice a year in Wellington.

There is no standard pattern for the divisional sub-committees. The most usual subjects covered are policy, finance, publicity, and organization. But in some divisions these subjects are combined, and a single committee deals with more than one.

Apart from the divisional secretary the staff at divisional headquarters usually includes an assistant secretary-organizer and two or three typists or clerks. Beyond this there are once again wide differences among the various divisions. In one division in 1957 there were nearly thirty staff at divisional headquarters, half of whom had been temporarily engaged for the 1957 general election. The remainder consisted partly of the catering and domestic-service staff of the National Club, which was situated on the same premises, and partly of organizers (canvassers). There is more than one school of thought about the employment of permanent organizers. In one division they are hardly used at all. The reasoning behind this is that, as the division is 'compact', it is comparatively easy to obtain the bulk of the necessary finance through a 'personal approach' to businesses by supporters, supplemented by voluntary canvassing of electors in their homes. The only exceptions are in two non-urban electorates, where permanent canvassers are used in the metropolitan centre towards election time. The divisional secretary has calculated that in the urban areas a full-time canvasser would have to work very hard to show any substantial return over the cost of employing him. In a neighbouring division, which has no metropolitan centre, all the electorate organizations but one have an organizer, a pattern which was established about twenty years ago. The other three divisions seem to lie between these two extremes. They have organizers for all, or nearly all, the 'country' electorates, but for only

---

[1] Salaries were given as £1,200 p.a. in 1954 (ibid., p. 11). The rate was not completely uniform for all five. On the status of agents, cf. A. M. Potter, 'The English Conservative Constituency Association', *Western Political Quarterly*, vol. ix, no. 2 (1956), p. 374.

some of the city ones. Sometimes one organizer is given the task of looking after two adjacent electorates. Alternatively, in one division the 'weak' (i.e. pro-Labour) city electorate organizations are told to do as much as they can through their own efforts, and when these have been exhausted organizers from divisional headquarters are put in to do the rest of the canvassing.

Apart from the question of whether organizers should be employed or not, there is the further problem of *who* should employ them—the division or the electorate? Both arrangements exist, even inside the same division. One divisional secretary, in conversation, expressed himself as strongly in favour of their being employed by the division, although subject to day-to-day direction by the electorate officials. His argument ran along the following lines: if an organizer stays too long in one electorate, say as long as ten years, he may become 'stale' or make too many enemies; it is easy to move him earlier than this only if he is employed by division. Again, an individual organizer may come up against prejudice in a particular electorate if he shows eccentricity, for instance if he is in the habit of wearing a bow tie. In that case, if he is employed by division he can be switched to a slightly more broad-minded electorate where he may be quite acceptable. Also, it is quite usual for the organizer to get to know the electorate chairman rather well and be on Christian-name terms with him, which may make it hard for the chairman to reprimand him, if the necessity arises. But, if the organizer is employed by division, the chairman can inform the divisional secretary when he goes round the electorates, and *he* is in a position to deliver a 'rocket'. A further advantage in employment by division is that differential salaries can be paid for the various electorates according to the difficulty of the job. This makes it possible to have a career ladder for organizers.

Information on divisional finance is scanty. However, just as Dominion headquarters imposes a 'levy' on the divisions, these, in turn, 'levy' the electorates. Sometimes the amount has been calculated according to the concept of 'ability to pay', based, for instance, on the number of party members, sometimes according to the proportion of votes cast for National candidates at a previous election. In one division the metropolitan electorate organizations are lumped together and treated as a unit for the purpose of this calculation. In collecting money the divisions are responsible for the collection of subscriptions from the head-quarters of businesses with branches in all four metropolitan centres and for forwarding the money to Dominion headquarters, where it is split up and distributed to divisions in the same pro-portions as for the headquarters 'levy'.[1]

In addition to the constitutional provisions regarding women and juniors, some divisions have organized extra activities. In at least one division there have been regular monthly meetings, attended by representatives of the women's sections in the division, for 'co-ordination of the work of the different electorates'.[2] In another, each meeting of the Divisional Com-mittee (four times a year) is preceded, the evening before, by a meeting of the five women representatives from each electorate. Sometimes women's 'rallies' have been held, at which prominent politicians and their wives have been present. As a divisional secretary has remarked, it is important that these meetings should not be too 'heavy'. For instance, for one typical rally the programme's longest item was a thirty-five-minute speech by the party Leader. A woman Dominion Councillor's talk and two summing-up speeches, one by the Dominion Secretary, were allocated only twenty minutes each. Speeches from the floor by 'city, suburban and country women', on 'What I expect of Good Government', were limited to five minutes each, and contributions to an 'open forum' were also strictly limited in time. In some divisions there are provisions for regular 'mass' meetings of women. In one, these meetings have been held for about the last twenty years, and nowadays have an average attendance of three or four hundred. Such meetings have the advantage, one divisional secretary believes, of en-couraging women to speak in public for the first time, who would be too shy to speak in front of a 'mixed' meeting. In effect these meetings approximate to a 'women's divisional conference', because they discuss selected remits from a women's angle, for instance the use of flogging as a punishment for interfering with children.

The party emphasizes the importance of junior sections, which may be formed under the auspices of divisions, electorates, or

[1] See p. 176, above.
[2] National Party, 20th Annual Conference, *Agenda and Conference Arrangements*, 'Chairman's Reports, Auckland' (1957), p. 30.

branches.[1] In one large division in 1964 there was a total of about 3,000 juniors. But in practice there are many difficulties in the way of running the sections successfully: the rapid turnover in members; the need for supervision by seniors especially on the financial side; the difficulty of obtaining suitable organizers who are interested in juniors without becoming *too* interested romantically in particular juniors. Enthusiasm, as well as apathy, has its pitfalls. In one city a hastily constructed junior section held a premature 'Victory Dance' at the 1957 election, and then dissolved, leaving only a deficit behind. Several approaches have been tried, including the appointment of an Advisory Committee of seniors, a yearly debating competition for a cup presented by an M.P., rallies, and even a rally of 'old juniors', a social gathering designed to renew contact with previous members and perhaps, in time, persuade them to work for the party. An interesting development occurred in 1957. A group of juniors made some criticisms of party policy to one divisional secretary. He asked them if they would be willing to meet regularly and see if they could make their criticism constructive by themselves formulating resolutions on policy. He would supply the necessary information if they would make the effort. In the end these juniors produced six policy suggestions, three of which were 'retained by the Policy Advisory Committee for further consideration'.[2] To some extent the work put in on junior sections is a calculated risk. A high proportion of junior activities are 'social' rather than 'political'. One divisional secretary said in 1964 that only about 3 per cent. of his junior membership were really interested in politics. But it may be reasonably expected that the juniors' early association with the party may pay dividends, because they will be more likely to join, and work for, the party later in life. The social advantages from junior sections are similar to those derived from the 'National Clubs', which exist in several towns.

The divisions also carry out a 'screening' process for remits (resolutions), most of which originate at branch level and come up through electorates, to determine which shall be sent forward from divisions. Some of the remits are 'administrative' and

---

[1] *Constitution and Rules of the New Zealand National Party (1963),* rules 83–86 and Appendix A.
[2] 20th Annual Conference, 'Chairman's Reports, Wellington', p. 36.

concern particular problems or grievances; they tend to be more numerous when the party is in office. This type is screened at divisional level, usually by the policy sub-committee or its equivalent. Those approved are then sent to the appropriate minister, if the party is in power; if it is in opposition, they are sent to the parliamentary party. Remits dealing with policy have to be screened from two points of view. Those that are obviously impracticable, incoherent, or redundant are rejected, often after the Research Department at party headquarters has been consulted by the policy sub-committee. Sometimes the screening process produces 'quite a slaughter'. For instance, in one division a remit to introduce compulsory voting and pre-ferential voting was turned down on the ground that it was against party policy, while a proposal that pilots engaged on aerial top-dressing should be compulsorily insured was rejected, because this was felt to be a matter for private enterprise. Generally, however, divisions are sorry to see remits blocked, because they wish to encourage them as signs of interest and vitality in the electorates and branches. The remainder of the remits, even if they are sensible, have to be arranged in order of priority. Each division, according to size, is given a quota for remits to go before Dominion Conference. Non-priority remits go to Dominion Council. The proportion of policy remits sent forward from division therefore depends, not only on their intrinsic worth, but also on the existence of the quota. In some divisions there is real competition between remits to be included in these quotas. In others sometimes it might be quite a job to scrape together enough sensible remits to fill the quota. In a division where there has been a special 'drive' for remits only a quarter or a fifth may be sent on. Where there has not been such a drive, as many as 75 per cent. may survive.

In most divisions the selection of remits to go before Dominion Conference is made, formally at least, at a full divisional meeting. Branch, electorate, and divisional annual meetings and Do-minion Conference are therefore timed so as to follow each other in sequence each year, so that remits, if successful, may progress from the 'bottom' to the 'top'. It is clear, therefore, that there is a fair measure of control over remits at divisional level before they ever reach Dominion Conference or Dominion Coun-cil. A particular instance of 'control', combined with some 'reconnaissance', occurred at a divisional Annual Meeting a few years ago. The research secretary attached to the Prime Minister's office attended the meeting and commented on some of the remits, for instance by pointing out that some were impracticable, and why. But, in addition, he also tried to gauge the reactions of the meeting to particular remits as a guide to likely reactions at the Dominion Conference, which was due to be held a few weeks afterwards.

Provision is made in the party constitution for subdivisions, under the control of a division.[1] So far only one of these exists, the Southland subdivision containing the Invercargill, Wallace, and Awarua electorates, which was set up just after the last war. There is a subdivisional committee (containing three representatives from each electorate) which meets every three months or so, with a secretary-organizer and a woman clerk (as well as part-time canvassers) for staff. The scheme has worked well. If each electorate had been allotted a separate organizer, it could not have afforded to hire anyone of the same calibre as the present secretary-organizer. In addition all three seats are held by the National Party, and are a considerable distance from Wellington. The secretary-organizer is therefore able to interview constituents and hear their queries and grievances, thus taking some of the load off the shoulders of the three M.P.s for the area.

Labour Party Regional Organization

There is no corresponding regular regional or divisional structure in the Labour Party. At one time divisional councils, consisting of representatives from the LRCs in the area, could be set up 'for the purpose of more efficiently conducting the propaganda and organising work of the party'.[2] But when the constitution was amended in 1951 they were no longer included.[3] It seems that some of the councils were claiming too much power for themselves. From time to time proposals are heard that divisional conferences should be held, mainly on the ground that the time for discussion of remits at the Annual Conference

---

[1] *Constitution and Rules of the New Zealand National Party (1963)*, rule 62.

[2] *Constitution and Platform (1925)*, 9.

[3] A proposal to retain them, made at the Thirty-fifth Annual Conference, 1951, was lost.

is too short. Such a demand was recently rejected, at a Dominion Conference, partly because it might hinder direct access by a branch to Conference. The central Labour organization watches very carefully for any signs that intermediate bodies might weaken the links between itself and branches and LRCs. An ex-President of the party was of the opinion that divisional conferences might actually contribute to 'Wellington' domination; if some sections of the movement outside Wellington came to feel that attendance at these conferences was a *substitute* for attendance at the Annual Conference they might cease to attend it. Another drawback would be that the proceedings of such Conferences would not be properly informed, unless members of the national executive attended and explained things to them.[1]

In 1961 an experimental, extra-constitutional 'Auckland Regional Advisory Council' was set up,[2] covering originally seventeen electorates. Delegates from LRCs and Inter-Branch Councils (IBCs)[3] the three divisional area representatives, and the organizer who then worked in Auckland were members of the executive. The Council was meant to co-ordinate the major activities of the party in the greater Auckland area. It attempted to hold education classes in public speaking and debating, social activities, fund-raising, publicity and propaganda, policy suggestions. If successful the scheme may be extended to other parts of New Zealand. An obvious difficulty is that, because it is 'voluntary' and 'advisory' only, the bodies represented on it sometimes may not regard themselves as bound by its decisions. The central organization feels that the RAC has sometimes been trying to go beyond its powers and has acted as if it were an intermediate governing body in the party. An example of this attitude was that, for the 1963 election, the RAC sent suggestions on policy direct to the policy committee.[4]

The Regional Advisory Council is a *continuing* body, although it is on an experimental basis. But 'area conferences' are also held from time to time, for one or several of the twelve areas.[5]

---

[1] Interview, Mr. A. H. Nordmeyer, Dec. 1958.
[2] Interview, Mr. A. J. McDonald, Apr. 1964. The Council is referred to in the *Report of the Forty-fifth Annual Conference* (1961). [3] See p. 215, below.
[4] Interview, Mr. A. J. McDonald, May 1964.
[5] The constitutional basis for these Conferences is that provisions exist permitting joint meetings of representatives of two or more LRCs, *Constitution with LRC and Branch Rules (1951)*, p. 22.

These do not have any formal remit system, which might tend to bypass the functions of Dominion Conference.

The absence of a regular regional or divisional unit in the Labour Party reflects the distribution of the party's strength and weakness. Where support for Labour is strongest, in the four big centres, the large metropolitan LRCs constitute an intermediate level below party headquarters. Where support is weaker, in the rest of the country, it has not proved so difficult to co-ordinate electorates direct from the centre. Nevertheless, if Labour is to advance its strength in rural areas, it would surely be to its advantage to develop a divisional or regional organization—provided that it can raise the necessary funds.

Local Organization: Historical

Turning to organization at local level, one or two general observations may be made before considering the National and Labour parties specifically. It was said earlier that the belief that there was a 'golden age' of New Zealand politicians is probably not borne out by fact. It is perhaps equally fallacious to imagine that there was ever a 'golden age of electors', when interest in politics was intense and when only ignorance of modern methods of organization prevented this interest from transforming itself into large-scale political activity. This conception is surely false on two counts. There is no reason to believe that interest in politics was ever much more intense than it is now (with the exception of particular elections, such as 1890 and 1935). It is true that in 1935 a writer expressed nostalgia for 'the days of our youth when full-bearded candidates bedecked in bell-toppers and moleskin trousers, enjoyed—totally irrespective of Party allegiances—triumphal tours through the country districts, where they dispensed beer and epigrams with equal nonchalance and largesse'.[1] Epigrams may not have been typical. More representative, perhaps, was the experience of an ex-Cabinet minister, who in the early years of the century received more bruises from being chaired shoulder-high after an election than he would have sustained in a rugger game, and who, decades later, still carried a bump on his head which had been made by an 'election' brick. But a potent source of 'interest' in politics, both fifty years ago and today, has often been simply the

[1] 'Notes from the Hustings', *Waikato Times*, 24 Aug. 1935.

202 PARTY ORGANIZATION, REGIONAL AND LOCAL

desire to see who will win; politics is viewed as a sport. This was evident in Westland in the early years of the century when, soon after one election, bets were deposited with local tradesmen on the result of the next election.[1] And it should be remembered that the competing attractions of the cinema, radio, and television were not available fifty years ago. Moreover, what interest existed may have seemed to be greater because it was more full-bloodedly expressed; manners were generally rougher, and the sweetening influence of women in public life had only just started to be evident.[2]

Also, theories of political and electoral organization in the early years of this century were just about as advanced as they are today, provided that the necessary allowances are made for changes resulting from speedier means of travel, the use of the radio, and so on. The main difference was that, in the early years of the century, although a blueprint of a party consisting of a hierarchy of permanent representative bodies existed, it had not yet been put into effect. As early as 1903 a temperance organization, the New Zealand Alliance, had issued its *Hints on Organisation*.[3] Some of the phraseology in this publication may seem a little old-fashioned. Pairs of Women's Christian Temperance Union members were allocated blocks of twenty houses where the tenants' allegiance was not known. 'These ladies were able to pay several visits to each doubtful house, and without doubt good was done. . . . In other parts of the electorate diligent promiscuous canvassing at all hours and places was pursued by men and women eager to win.'[4] But the techniques were more modern than the language. *Hints on Organisation* gives sound advice on the deployment of canvassers, making out electoral rolls, distribution of 'How to Vote' cards, the use of chalked signs on pavements, employment of personal friends to win over 'doubtfuls', preparation of special lists of the sick and aged so that transport may be provided to take them to the poll, and on other electoral techniques.

The Liberals, at the beginning of the century, were concerned not only with making conversions and getting out the vote at

[1] Interview, Mr. T. E. Y. Seddon, Dec. 1958.
[2] On interest in New Zealand politics see R. S. Milne, 'Citizen Participation in Political Life, New Zealand', *International Social Science Journal*, vol. xii, no. 1 (1960).
[3] *Hints on Organisation* (Wellington, 1903).
[4] Ibid., p. 9.

elections but also with building up a healthy local organization which would operate between elections. The main evil to be fought was 'branches' which came to life only when a candidate was being chosen, and which consisted of transient 'members' interested only in having their particular choice of candidate approved.[1] To be sure, the organization of the Liberal and Labour Federation, on paper, was sufficiently elaborate and explicit in its provision for meetings, the election of office-holders, and the selection of candidates.[2] But it was acutely remarked that the branches were not sufficiently representative of the party. The allegiance of the people was due, not to the local influence of the branches, but to 'the popularity of the Liberal leaders and the beneficent legislation they have promoted'.[3] The problems of infusing vitality in the branches were analysed with insight two years later.[4] Branches, and their government, must be based on the representative principle. 'Each member ought to have, and should recognise that he or she has, a voice in the conduct of the affairs and policy of the Federation.' The writer was in favour of small compulsory subscriptions in order to produce 'more vitality'. He was aware that 'vitality' might take the form of a wish to express an opinion on 'leading political questions'.[5] But the branches should bear in mind 'that in the first place they must not act hastily or on imperfect information, otherwise their opinion will be of little worth; secondly the more rarely they give their opinion, and the more firmly and measuredly they express that opinion, the more likely it is to be valued'.

At about the same time E. E. Vaile, of the Reform Party, showed himself to be equally knowledgeable on political organization. One of his main concerns was that the bodies at various

[1] *Report of Proceedings of the Conference of Delegates of the Liberal and Labour Federation of New Zealand*, Culver (secretary), p. 10.

[2] *Constitution of the Liberal and Labour Federation of New Zealand* (as amended at the 1903 Conference).

[3] *Report of Proceedings of the Conference of Delegates of the Liberal and Labour Federation of New Zealand*, Findlay, p. 19.

[4] *The Liberal Herald*, July 1905, 'The Organisation and Work of Liberal Associations', pp. 36 ff.

[5] Cf. Findlay's view that the Liberal organisation had two purposes, to fight elections and to be a means of ascertaining the will of the whole, or a majority, of the party (*Report of Proceedings of the Conference of Delegates of the Liberal and Labour Federation of New Zealand, 1903*, p. 18).

levels in the party should all be elected by the units immediately below them, and that candidates should be selected by a representative body at electorate level, 'in conjunction with the Provincial Executive and the Leader of the Party'.[1] Vaile clearly saw the need to have permanent bodies functioning regularly at all levels of the party hierarchy. However, apart from the introduction of elections at all levels and more 'democratic' selection of candidates, he did not explain what incentives might be used in order to keep the branches, and other units, functioning regularly.

Practice lagged behind precept: in both the Liberal and Reform parties the branches and other units functioned only intermittently. Just before the First World War there were over 130 branches of the Reform Party in New Zealand. There was a 'practical dissolution' of the branches during the war, and by the 1922 elections there were not more than twenty branches still in existence. Even in 1925 there were no branches in some electorates.[2] Candidates were *not* selected 'democratically', nor was there any regular system for collecting subscriptions or for the employment of paid organizers.[3]

National Party Local Organization

In contrast to this the National Party from its inception has gone all out for a large membership, and the regular collection of the minimum annual membership fee of 2s. 6d. Early in 1938 a party spokesman said that in one electorate organization there were almost 2,500 subscribing members, compared with twenty in past years (that is, presumably, for the Reform Party).[4] More recently the National Party's membership has fluctuated from 250,000 in an election year to 143,000 in an 'off year'.[5] This means that in 1954 National Party membership reached the astonishing proportion of about half[6] the total vote cast for the

[1] 'Suggestions by E. E. Vaile' (MS., Auckland Public Library, 23 Jan. 1907).
[2] *Newsletter*, 31 July 1926.
[3] Robinson, *The Rise of the New Zealand National Party*, pp. 25 and 43; interview, Theo Hills, Oct. 1958; interview, Mr. C. A. L. Treadwell, Mar. 1959.
[4] *Clutha Leader*, 21 Mar. 1938, referring to the Waitaki electorate.
[5] *President's Address* to Nineteenth Annual Conference, 1956.
[6] Note, however, that according to North (op. cit., p. 40) before the 1954 election Labour built up party membership in the marginal St. Kilda seat to more than two-thirds of the Labour vote.

party. The reason for the decline in non-election years is said to be that voluntary collectors naturally felt they were then entitled to 'take it easier'.[1] This squares with the answer given when party officials in various parts of New Zealand are asked what percentage of members fail to renew their membership when approached by a canvasser. For recent years the figure seems to be about only 2 per cent. In other words the fluctuations in membership, apart from this 2 per cent., and any drop arising from failure to recruit new members to take the place of those who emigrate or die, arises mainly from the amount of activity shown by canvassers rather than from fluctuations in the enthusiasm shown by electors. However, as an indication of enthusiasm or interest membership figures are misleading. When a canvasser calls to enrol members for the party he will very often be given more than the minimum subscription of 2s. 6d. for one member.[2] Indeed, depending on the area, the wealth of the subscriber, and whether it is election year or not, he may receive 10s., £1, or even more. But, in return, he may be asked to 'sign up the whole family'. It is therefore quite possible for many members of the National Party to be unaware of the fact of their membership.[3]

Even allowing for the three-year cycle in membership figures, changes in membership are not a very good indication of changes in *votes*. One divisional secretary, interviewed shortly before the 1957 general election, was understandably optimistic, because whereas previously in off years membership had fallen to about 70 per cent. of the peak figure, in 1956 it was over 90 per cent. of the 1954 'peak'. Yet in his division, as in the rest of New Zealand, there was almost as big a swing against National in 1957 as there had been in 1954.

[1] *President's Address*, 1956.

[2] Kelson, *Political Science*, vol. vi, no. 2, art. cit., p. 9, says that in one division 2s. 6d. per member would produce less than 5 per cent. of the money spent by the party in the division.

[3] In one (Labour) city seat, where the National Party polled about 6,000 votes in 1957, its membership after the election was about 2,300 (including members who had been 'signed up' without their knowledge). The average amount subscribed per member (apart from collection from business) was about 7s. 6d. There was a tendency, in at least one division, for the average amount subscribed to fall steadily after the party came into power in 1949. The impression of the rank and file seemed to be that, since the party had become the Government, there was not the same need for the organization to run in top gear (*New Zealand National Party, 18th Annual Dominion Conference, 1955, Report*, p. 35).

In the first years of the National Party there seem to have been several motives behind the drive for membership. One was undoubtedly the desire to get all anti-Labour voters, and also all potential non-Labour candidates, 'under one roof',[1] and so avoid a repetition of the 1935 'split vote'. A large membership was also closely linked with the new procedure for selecting candidates.[2] The existence of a large membership, plus democratic methods of selection, made the choice of candidate so demonstrably fair that the risk of rival candidatures was almost eliminated. At the same time the requirement that an electorate organization must normally have 2,000 members in order to be allowed to choose its own candidate stimulated the drive to obtain more members.

The basic unit in the party is the branch, of which there are some 1,300 in existence. The regulations governing branches are laid down in the party constitution.[3] They may include sections for juniors or women. The most important posts at branch level are those of chairman and secretary; indeed, according to Kelson, they 'often hold the fate of a branch in their hands'.[4] The turnover of branch chairmen and secretaries appears to be small, although no figures are available on this. Their long tenure may be a consequence either of their competence or of the difficulty of shifting them even if they are incompetent. The latter task may be a difficult one except, perhaps, in small 'homogeneous' branches. The writer was present at one branch meeting attended by about a dozen members, practically all farmers, where the party organizer told the branch chairman, in a matter-of-fact way, that he had fallen down on his job. The chairman admitted this, but tentatively suggested that maybe there were people who were better fitted to do the job. The organizer replied, 'Yes, but not anyone who's willing', and the chairman was unanimously re-elected. If a better man had been available there would have been no difficulty, and no hard feelings, about electing him.

The branch annual meeting, in addition to hearing the annual report and the annual financial statement, elects its officers, its committee, and its representatives to the Electorate Committee.

---

[1] Robinson, *The Rise of the New Zealand National Party*, pp. 22–23.
[2] See pp. 252–3, below.
[3] *Constitution and Rules (1963)*, rules 75–81. [4] Art. cit., p. 7.

It also initiates remits, the great majority of which are approved and are sent forward to electorate level, and discusses methods of retaining and increasing branch membership. Most branches meet only once a year; the branch committee meets, on the average, every two or three months.[1]

On the next level above the branches, the Electorate Committee consists of representatives elected by the branches in the proportion of one for every twenty branch members.[2] Not more than six members may be co-opted by these representatives. There are one or two exceptions to this rule. In very rare instances an electorate may have only one branch.[3] It is also provided that, with the consent of the Divisional Committee, a city Electorate Committee may be composed, not of branch representatives, but of not fewer than twenty representatives elected at a general meeting of party members in the city.[4] The Electorate Committee holds an annual meeting. Apart from hearing and discussing the annual report and the annual financial statement, remits forwarded by branches are considered and, if approved, sent forward to division; remits originating at electorate level may also be sent on. The meeting may also be addressed by visiting speakers. But perhaps its most important function is electoral—to elect representatives to the Divisional Committee, to choose delegates to the annual Dominion Conference and to consider nominations for officers to be elected at the annual divisional meeting. The meeting also chooses its own executive, sometimes consisting of all branch chairmen, sometimes chairmen and secretaries, sometimes chairmen, secretaries, and representatives from women's and junior sections. There may even be a 'sub-executive', especially in widely scattered electorates, of about half a dozen members to deal with urgent matters between meetings of the executive. It also elects its own officers: chairman, vice-chairman, secretary, and treasurer.

There is more competition for office at electorate level than at branch level, in the opinion of a divisional secretary. As in the branches, there is the problem of moving those who have become undesirable 'fixtures' in office. In 1959 one electorate

[1] Kelson, *Political Science*, vol. vi, no. 2, art. cit., pp. 6 and 7.

[2] *Constitution and Rules (1963)*, rule 63.

[3] For instance, at different times, Timaru, Remuera, and Wellington Central.

[4] *Constitution and Rules (1963)*, rule 64.

secretary had been obviously too infirm for the job for the past five years, but he had been a 'foundation member' of the party, and it was 'almost socially impossible' to get him out. On occasion, given time, an office-holder can be replaced by going through the process of obviously grooming a younger man as his successor.

It would be wrong to imagine that electorate organizations were strictly controlled by division. They have their own methods and idiosyncrasies in such spheres as canvassing and publicity. Perhaps one divisional secretary exaggerated slightly when he said that the role of division was limited to making suggestions and giving financial help to the weaker electorates. For instance, he himself attends all the meetings of electorate executives and is obviously in a strong position for giving authoritative advice. But divisional secretaries cannot go beyond this. Changes in the 1956 Electoral Act made it possible to improve the method of deploying party workers outside polling booths on election day. But in one division the secretary was quite unable to wean some electorates away from the old and 'tried' methods. A divisional secretary drew a sharp contrast with the early 1930's when he was secretary to an electorate committee of the Reform Party. In these days officials from higher formations in the party hardly ever came round the electorates at all. When they did, they gave *orders* to the local people. Nowadays, according to another secretary, any suggestion of dictation would result in divisional officials being told to 'go and jump in the lake'.

Remits, forwarded from branches, are considered at the annual meeting of the Electorate Committee. Not many are held back, except perhaps those that are redundant because their recommendations have already been accepted as part of party policy. In some divisions the divisional secretary, who attends the annual meeting, makes frequent suggestions for improvements in the wording of remits in order to increase their chances of survival at divisional level.

As mentioned above, there are broad differences between divisions in the use of organizers. The pattern is still more intricate when variations between particular electorates are taken into account. The 'ideal' system would be for an electorate to have so many volunteers available for canvassing for membership subscriptions that no paid canvassing would be necessary.

The only payment needed would be to a voluntary part-time secretary, who would be paid up to several hundred pounds a year for doing paper-work that, if costed, might be worth up to five times as much. But, as has been seen, this can be achieved only in compact urban areas and, even there, voluntary canvassing usually has to be supplemented by paid canvassing in the most pro-Labour electorates. So most electorates either have a full-time organizer, or the voluntary system exists 'in principle', but in fact alternates with the employment of paid canvassers. Admittedly it is expensive to employ canvassers, either full-time or on commission. A few years ago it was estimated that in an urban area the cost of a canvasser for a year might be £800 plus £100 in expenses. In some cases a canvasser was appointed who raised only about enough to pay for his own keep. In rural areas expenses are naturally greater. For instance in the middle 1950's one canvasser was paid $33\frac{1}{3}$ per cent. commission, and in ten months earned £1,000 gross. But the distances he had to cover were so great that his expenses for transport and hotels cost him roughly £600 out of the £1,000. Nevertheless, if voluntary efforts cannot be mobilized effectively, paid canvassing, though expensive, is justified. Apart from the actual monetary profit, mass membership is important for the party, and the contacts made while collecting subscriptions serve to show that the party is active and may help to keep a certain amount of interest alive. After all, this was the distinctive approach adopted by the National Party from the beginning of its life. The importance of maintaining frequent contacts with members is relevant when considering the merits of a scheme which has been used for some country electorates. Time spent in collecting subscriptions has been cut by adopting the system, employed by the Farmers' Union, of calling on members only once every three years and receiving, not a single payment, but a money order valid for three years. However, this system has been described as 'pernicious' by other officials in the party, who believe that it is bad public relations not to keep in touch with members every year. This view looks beyond the immediate 'profitability' of canvassing to its role in building up morale and interest inside the party.

Some of the existing full-time organizers are retired men. But there is a tendency towards 'professionalization', and younger

men are being appointed as organizers.[1] Organizers do not
usually seem to exercise great power in their electorate organizations, although their power might increase as a consequence
of professionalization. A possible exception was the organizer for
Egmont (Willis) whose antipathy to the member (Mr. Sheat) is
reputed to have cost the latter the nomination for Patea in 1954.[2]
In some cases they perform the duties of secretary as well. This is
another example of 'professionalization'; the existing voluntary
secretaries are paid only small honoraria, and, because they
have other jobs as well, they cannot be expected to attend to
business promptly. So far, however, no formal professional
training scheme has been put into operation for recently trained
organizers, for instance along the lines of the courses given for
'new agents' in the British Conservative Party. A new organizer
is trained on the ground, under the supervision of an experienced
organizer. However, in the early 1960's one division introduced
a scheme for examining its organizers twice a year in election
law and procedure and in the National Party's constitution and
rules. These examinations are used solely as a training device
and not for grading or promotion purposes.

Maori organization has been weak, but since 1960 there has
been a drive to improve it, especially in Eastern and Northern
Maori, which has met with some success.[3] It has been very hard,
however, except in Eastern, and more recently in Northern,
Maori, to enrol members who actually pay their subscriptions.

Labour Party Local Organization

The Labour Party, like the National Party, has branches, but
to be a member of a branch is not the only way of belonging to
the party. It is also possible to be a member through membership
of an affiliation, which in practice means a trade union. Of
course, as individuals, trade-unionists may be branch members.
The party, unlike the British Labour Party, has no societies
comparable to the Fabian Society affiliated to it.[4] A Fabian

[1] For an analysis of age, length of service, pay, &c. of organizers, based on answers
to a 1960 questionnaire, see Weeks, op. cit., pp. 120–32.
[2] North, op. cit., p. 45.
[3] *New Zealand National Party, 26th Annual Dominion Conference, 1963, Report*, pp. 17
and 19–20.
[4] See Overacker, *Political Science*, vol. ix, no. 2, art. cit., p. 15.

group has existed intermittently in New Zealand,[1] but it has not been a constituent unit of the party. The stimulating effect of Fabian research on party policy has therefore been largely absent in New Zealand.[2] Above branch level are 'Labour Representation Committees' (LRCs), which are made up of delegates from branches and affiliations.[3]

Membership figures for the party as a whole have sometimes been given in the reports of the Annual Conferences. The most recent figure quoted by Overacker, for 1947–8, is 201,765.[4] A peak was reached of 236,605 in 1939–40, a result of the introduction of compulsory unionism a few years earlier, but, because of members' service in the armed forces, this figure fell by more than a third during the war. In 1960 membership was about 180,000.[5] The party has said that it does not keep records of the numbers who are members through branches and through affiliations, respectively.[6] However, it may be estimated that affiliated members make up about 80 per cent. of the total. Some party officials have confirmed that membership fluctuates in the same way as in the National Party, going up in election years and down between elections, but no actual figures are available for this.

Most of the six hundred or so branches in existence are 'ordinary' branches. But there are four other types, Women's, Junior, Maori, and Headquarters. It is possible to be a member of a Women's, Junior, or Maori branch and also to be a member of an ordinary branch. The Labour Party has been less successful with Women's and Junior organizations than the National Party. Organization of Women's branches is

---

[1] In the late 1890's and early 1900's there were several groups which called themselves 'Fabians'. In 1946–9 there was a revival of the Wellington Fabian Society. Two M.P.s, Wilson and Finlay, were active in the group. These two published the study by a Fabian Study Group, *Stabilisation or Socialisation?* (1947), with their comments. Other publications included *Martial Plan* (1948), *The Price of Full Employment* (1949), both by G. Fraser, and, edited by Fraser, *Programme for Socialism: Twenty-four Urgent Steps towards a better New Zealand* (1949).

[2] See *Fabian Journal*, Apr. 1954, 70th Anniversary Number, 'Fabian Research' by Austen Albu; and 'The Fabian Society and the Labour Party', by Arthur Skeffington.

[3] On the development of LRCs, see Brown, *The Rise of New Zealand Labour*, pp. 16–17 and 23–25; and Hunt, art. cit., pp. 24–25.

[4] *American Political Science Review*, art. cit., p. 718.

[5] Chapman, Jackson, and Mitchell, op. cit., p. 17.

[6] North, op. cit., pp. 42–43.

particularly difficult in the country districts, where women supporters are spread rather thin on the ground. Labour's Junior
branches seem to be fewer, and their activity more intermittent
than National's. Certainly Labour stresses the social side less
than its rival, or, as one Labour official put it, 'the snob appeal
is lacking'. Maori branch organization is strongest in Southern
Maori and weakest in Eastern and Western Maori. Membership
of Headquarters branch is by application to the National Executive. The purpose is to cover persons living in areas where
there is no Labour Party branch, those who wish to keep their
membership of the party secret, or those who are not acceptable
to the nearest branch.[1] The first two of these purposes now
seem rather out of date, while it is unlikely that many intending
members would be acceptable to the National Executive but
unacceptable to a branch.

An 'ordinary' branch must contain at least ten members who
are over eighteen and who have paid the necessary membership
dues. Membership is denied to persons who already belong to
any of a number of 'proscribed' organizations which are believed
to be Communist 'front' organizations.[2] An odd point about
membership is that, although the branches are based on a particular area, members need not be residents of any specified area.

By the constitution, branch meetings must be held at least
monthly. Every branch must elect an executive, made up of a
chairman, vice-chairman, secretary-treasurer (or secretary *and*
treasurer), and five others. But there are no rules laid down
about the powers of the executive or the frequency with which
it shall meet. So, in practice, it may be possible for the chairman
and the secretary to 'run' a branch, as they sometimes do in the
National Party. In practice most branches have a very long 'tail',
activity being confined to the executive and a few others. Some
office-holders in the party would also draw a distinction between
various types of 'activity'. Some of the branch members who
are most vocal at meetings between elections, for instance in
proposing remits, are least active as election workers, and vice
versa. Eagerness to give voluntary help at elections, on which
the Labour Party with its small number of paid organizers
largely depends, seems to have decreased compared with the

[1] Penfold, op. cit., p. 5.
[2] Overacker, *American Political Science Review*, art. cit., p. 723.

1930's. One LRC secretary says that a common excuse heard nowadays to explain away a job badly done, 'I'm only a voluntary worker', would never have been given before the war.

The Labour Party seems to have the same problem as the National Party in obtaining the resignation of some of its long-term office-holders. One particular version of this occurs in cities when an office-holder moves out of the branch area, but hangs on to office and tries to do the job from a distance. This seldom works well, but the persons concerned are reluctant to resign. Not many LRCs are as ruthless as the one whose secretary claimed that he 'chucked out' branch chairmen who were too inefficient or 'independent' after having reminded them that, after all, they were 'only hewers of wood and drawers of water'. Amusingly enough, this LRC secretary also complained of 'dictation' from party headquarters in Wellington.

Labour Representation Committees (LRCs) are fifty-four in number (1964). Except in the four main centres the area of an LRC generally corresponds to that of a parliamentary electorate. But in these centres it covers the bulk of the electorates in the city, in Auckland, for instance, eight electorates and over fifty branches. The number of branches per electorate varies greatly; for example, in Christchurch between one and eight. The number seems to depend on geography, tradition, and also on current developments such as the building of a new industrial estate. As has also been found in the National Party, it is a bad arrangement to have only one branch in an electorate, because this fails to 'spread' the organization sufficiently at the grass roots. But the short-term answer to criticism on this score may be that in a solid Labour seat such as Sydenham (Christchurch), which has only one branch, the organization does not *have* to be superb in order to win crushing victories at every election.

Representation of branches and affiliations on an LRC is on a scale, somewhat less than proportionate to membership, which slightly 'overweights' smaller branches and affiliations.[1] This tends to under-represent the unions which, for New Zealand as a whole, have a larger total membership than the branches.

[1] Representation on the LRC is: 1 delegate for 10–50 members; 2 delegates for 51–125 members; 3 delegates for 126–200 members; 4 delegates for 201–300 members; 1 additional delegate for each 100 additional members, up to a maximum of 7.

Consequently, although the unions have a majority on practically all LRCs, this majority is not as large as it would be if
representation were completely proportional. The number of
delegates on an LRC may vary from approximately 300 down
to 25.[1] Before taking part in LRC proceedings, delegates must
sign a pledge, saying *inter alia* that they accept the constitution
and policy of the party. Elections for the LRC executive, consisting of a president, vice-president, secretary-treasurer, and
five other members, are also more formal than those for the
branch executive.[2] Indeed formality is the keynote of, as well as
the key to, much of what occurs in an LRC. A large slice of the
time at meetings is taken up with reading correspondence and
with the reports of Labour members on local bodies. And any
matters coming before an LRC have to be submitted in writing
by a branch or affiliation, and are first discussed by the executive
committee. Often when they reach the LRC they are accompanied by a recommendation from the executive.[3]

LRCs are required by the constitution to meet monthly. But
at the Annual Conference of the party a few years ago it was
stated that the national executive had sent round a letter to find
out whether they actually did meet monthly. This was not necessarily to *force* them all to meet monthly, but, in order to get
the facts about how many were meeting less often, for example
because the LRCs branches and affiliations were very scattered
and the expense of holding monthly meetings was proving to be
a heavy burden. LRCs have important functions in enforcing
discipline, in contesting, and nominating candidates for, local
elections, and, together with the national executive, in selecting
candidates for parliamentary elections.[4] It seems to be the practice for LRCs to 'look at' remits from branches, but apparently
it is very rare for an LRC to prevent a branch remit from going
forward. LRCs also originate their own remits.

Because of the preponderance of trade-unionists on LRCs,
to say nothing of the importance of trade-union financial contributions, it might be thought that perhaps LRCs were 'dominated' by trade unions. Certainly, in some, although not all,
LRCs the trade-union representatives attend less often than the

---

[1] Penfold, op. cit., p. 7.   [2] Ibid., p. 8.
[3] Overacker, *American Political Science Review*, art. cit., p. 726.
[4] See Ch. IX, below.

others on 'normal' occasions, but turn up in strength when
something which they feel is really important is at stake. For
instance, just after the war in one of the four metropolitan LRCs
a very large number of trade-unionists came along to one meeting in order to elect a particular unionist as LRC secretary. But
it would seem equally logical to blame the trade-unionists for
their *apathy* in not turning up at most LRC meetings rather than
to denounce their 'dominance' when they do. In some LRCs it
has been said that this variation in trade-unionists' attendance
'results in a continual tug-of-war between the officers, who
represent the union viewpoint, and branch delegates, who tend
to be more "left" in their views'.[1] As might be expected, prominent trade-unionists on LRCs deny that there is any trade-union
dominance. One has pointed out that on the executive of his
metropolitan LRC there is a 'non-industrial' majority. Another
metropolitan LRC secretary, himself a trade-unionist, referred
to his toughness as a member of the city council in dealing with
members of a transport drivers' union. He claimed that the
existence of union dominance was disproved by his not having
favoured the union in an industrial dispute with which he was
concerned in his capacity as a councillor, and by the fact that,
soon afterwards, he was re-elected secretary by a large majority.
Several trade-unionists on LRCs have denied, in conversation,
that there was any clear line-up of unionists and non-unionists
on these bodies. A prevailing impression is that the influence of
trade-unionists on LRCs is not so strong as it was ten or fifteen
years ago.

In 1955 it was decided to set up a new unit of party organization, the Inter-Branch Council (IBC). This development may
be regarded as in the nature of a limited concession to those who
were opposed to LRCs covering more than one electorate.
Before 1955 the LRCs in the four main centres included several
electorates, and there was no formal provision for any permanent organization at electorate level. For each election a special
committee was formed, with some such title as 'Election Campaign Committee' or 'Combined Branch Committee'. In some
cases these seem to have persisted between elections; at the
1958 Annual Conference of the party a speaker claimed that
Wellington had had the equivalent of permanent inter-branch

[1] Overacker, *American Political Science Review*, art. cit., p. 726.

committees since about 1950. IBCs do not have any voice in policy; they may not originate remits, for example. One IBC has even been refused permission to join the National Film Institute in order to rent, and show, films for educational purposes. Their whole aim is to organize for the next election and to co-ordinate party activities within the electorate with that end in view, for instance by raising finance and, where necessary, by forming new branches.[1] IBCs need not have an executive, but, if they do have one, it must consist of not fewer than five persons, including the chairman and the secretary. Some concern has been expressed lest IBCs, in spite of their limited functions and the fact that they are subject to the general supervision and control of the LRC, should invade the spheres of LRCs or branches, and one delegate at a recent party conference said that in his area the existence of a new IBC had led to a loss of interest in the functions of branches.

Labour's local organization is much less elaborate than National's, and is much less expensive to run. The only paid permanent officials at local level, apart from clerks and typists, are the secretaries of the four metropolitan LRCs. Even these, although permanent, are not full-time, because each is a trade-union secretary as well. One of them, interviewed in 1958, represented as many as four trade unions, although the job of LRC secretary took up most of his time. Otherwise most of the salaried officials have been organizers appointed in some electorates for the duration of the campaign (although a few have been employed for a longer time), and paid approximately £15 a week, or organizers detached from the small group of organizers at party headquarters in Wellington[2] and sent out to 'the field' for a period. Sometimes the organizer appointed for the duration of the campaign (or seconded from party headquarters) has also been the candidate for a seat in the area. The job of secretary at LRC level is not paid, not even at the modest level of payment for constituency secretaries in the National Party.

A scheme for strengthening weak electorates was adopted early in 1964.[3] Practically all Labour M.P.s will become responsible for helping with the organization of either one or two

[1] *Constitution and Rules (1955)*, 9 (2).   [2] See pp. 188–90, above.
[3] Interview, Mr. A. J. McDonald, Apr. 1964. A similar adoption scheme had been approved by the national executive after the 1951 election defeat.

Labour seats. They would be expected to spend time visiting these seats. Because of the geographical distribution of Labour members, it will not be possible for the seats to be contiguous. So an M.P. from Wellington might find himself allocated to a seat or seats in Taranaki. A more intensive supplementary scheme which may be put into force would provide for twenty M.P.s to be assigned to looking after twenty selected 'key' electorates. Until 1964 several Labour organizers 'organized themselves' into Parliament. Under this scheme M.P.s were to be organized into becoming organizers.

Local finance is less thoroughly regulated in the Labour Party than in the National Party. A fixed proportion of branch subscriptions, and also of affiliation fees, goes to the national executive in capitation fees. The executive hands back a sixth of what it receives in this way to the LRCs in the area in which the branches and affiliations are situated.[1] The branches also collect money by canvassing, jumble sales, and so on, and make contributions to the LRC, to the Inter-branch Council (if any), and possibly also direct to head office.[2] The LRCs also receive contributions from affiliations and from businesses, although these may contribute at national level. Particularly urgent appeals for money are sent out from headquarters at election time, 'but there exists among the lower echelons of the party an understandable but sometimes embarrassing reluctance to disgorge their hard-won funds. Constituency finance is something of an unknown quantity during the course of a campaign since it is a matter for the local LRC to raise money and expend it.'[3] Ideally, the stronger electorates should show a surplus and should send it to head office for the National Campaign Fund. Some in fact do this. 'For example, one strong Labour electorate spent a little under £200 [at the 1957 election] and sent more than they spent to head office.'[3] But others, often the majority, do not. The wide variations in effort which exist between branches and between electorates are obvious to party officials. In 1959 the national executive went some way to remedying the situation by deciding that, before each election, a quota should be allotted to each LRC which would be a target for the funds it should raise for the requirements of head office.

[1] Penfold, op. cit., p. 15.   [2] Brown, *Political Science*, art. cit., pp. 20–21.
[3] Ibid., p. 21.

Branch Activities and Branch Apathy

In spite of the Labour Party's dedication to 'democracy' within the party and the National Party's attempts to build up a 'grass roots' organization, there is a prevailing impression of apathy in the branches in both parties, and to a lesser extent in LRCs and electorate committees. There does not seem to be any great difference between the parties in this respect. Duverger's hypothesis that the branch system corresponds primarily to working-class mentality, and is therefore commoner and more successful in Labour parties, does not apply to New Zealand. He argues that the middle classes are not fond of collective action, think that their political education is adequate and have other distractions and enjoy other opportunities of affirming their social importance.[1] But this dichotomy between middle-class and working-class *mores* does not exist in any sharply defined form in New Zealand. There is no large section of clearly working-class people, except perhaps in mining areas, whose social life is conducted largely apart from the social life of the other groups around them. On the other hand, in New Zealand country areas farmers, who live some distance away from the main centres of population but who own cars, may be attracted by the social features of National Party branches.

In the National Party Kelson sees most branches as 'little more than dummy arms of the Electorate Committee', and believes that political apathy 'effectively cuts down the active participants to a handful . . .'.[2] This view is confirmed by a divisional secretary who has said that it is very hard to get up any enthusiasm in the branches. 'Most people feel they've done their bit once they've given money to the party.' Indeed one former secretary of the party is credited with the view that the branches simply would not stand for attempts to keep them permanently 'whipped up' and excited. This could safely be tried only in election years. In the Labour Party Overacker writes of the 'atrophy of the branches', which she attributes partly to 'tight control from the center'.[3] Certainly, correspondence, reports, and points of procedure seem to take up an inordinate amount of time at Labour branch meetings. In one branch

[1] Duverger, op. cit., p. 26.
[2] Kelson, *Political Science*, vol. vi, no. 2, op. cit., p. 8.
[3] Overacker, *American Political Science Review*, op. cit., p. 731.

attempts to discuss capital punishment completely failed to arouse any interest. In another branch efforts to initiate a discussion on whether or not New Zealand should join the International Monetary Fund had to compete, at first unsuccessfully, with the desire of a member to show his collection of slides. A typical response to any proposal on policy which is put forward is to say that if it had really been a good idea the leadership would have done it already. Failure to discuss policy adequately may have a cumulative effect. The few members who are anxious to discuss, and who alone are capable of introducing and debating serious subjects, may cease to attend meetings because they are repelled by the dreariness of the proceedings. The picture should not be overdrawn. In a branch (Labour or National) where the office-holders are determined enough, and knowledgeable enough, to hold discussions on policy, it is possible to cut down the amount of time spent on formal business and to exchange views on issues such as old-age pensions or import control. But such branches are rare exceptions.

Almost sixty years ago it was said that a (Liberal) branch had three functions: practical political work; the work of political education; and the social function of bringing people together.[1] The author tentatively added a fourth function—the expression of opinion on leading political questions. But in this context the word, 'function' is ambiguous. From the point of view of the party leadership, 'practical political work' is an important function. Less immediately, so is political education. The expression of opinion is, constitutionally, given more weight by the leadership in the Labour Party than in the National Party. A former secretary of the Labour Party wrote that all Labour's decisions 'whether made by the National Executive of the Party or by the Party's representatives in Parliament are but the will of the rank and file members expressed in pronouncements, decisions and legislation'. He added, 'in matters of policy the power rests with the individual member as expressed first in his Branch or his Union and then through the LRC to Annual Conference, where the final decisions are made by the representatives of the branches and affiliations.'[2] The National Party has never made

[1] *The Liberal Herald,* July 1905, 'The Organisation and Work of Liberal Associations', p. 38.
[2] David Wilson, *Constitutional Democracy* (Wellington, 1938).

any such claim. In fact it may be doubted whether *either* party's leadership is highly receptive to policy suggestions from below. But from the view-point of the party members the situation is different. Only small proportions are interested in practical political work, in being politically educated, or in expressing their opinions on political questions. To be sure, those who *are* interested in any of these aspects of the party's work should be catered for, because such active members have an importance out of all proportion to their numbers. For instance, it is essential that keen members should be able to see clearly what happens to a branch's remits when they are sent on to higher levels. But, in order to persuade the great mass of branch members to have anything to do with politics, the 'social side' must be given prominence. It may be combined with some 'improvement', for instance a film show may be followed by a semi-serious discussion. Alternatively, attendance at branch meetings may be stimulated if the local M.P. comes along, because members may wish to meet him socially. But he will probably also be 'politically educative', for instance by commenting on remits, and his presence may induce some members to volunteer for canvassing duties. Other local party functions are almost purely 'social', at least on the surface. The National Party has been particularly active on the social side, through 'National Clubs' in the larger towns and by arranging functions for women and juniors.

Some satisfactions obtained by members do not fall under any of these headings. There are those who are attracted by the prospect of holding any party office, even the humblest. Others seem to enjoy dealing in personalities, even if this is pushed to the point of creating 'personal vendettas', or find a means of self-expression at meetings in initiating procedural tangles and wrangles. Some other members are cranks with an *idée fixe*, not concerned with expressing their opinions on 'leading political questions' but intent rather on voicing their ideas on *one* peripheral question, such as (in the National Party) the eradication of wallabies or a written constitution for New Zealand.

Perhaps there is more surprise and heart-burning about apathy in Labour branches than in National branches. Labour has always laid stress on the role of branches (and LRCs) in helping to formulate policy, while the National Party has not done so to the same extent. The New Zealand Labour Party, as well as the

British Labour Party, has branches which do not 'put policy on the agenda'.[1] For a party which has in the past held the 'initiative' in making policy proposals, apathy in the branches could be a significant symptom of future decline.

[1] See 'Put Policy on the Agenda', *Fabian Journal*, Feb. 1952; D. V. Donnison and D. E. C. Plowman, 'The Functions of Local Labour Parties: Experiments in Research Methods', *Political Studies*, vol. ii, no. 2 (1954).

VIII

PARTY CONFERENCES

THE business done at the two parties' Conferences is, in form, broadly similar. Both elect party officers; both hear addresses and reports and consider remits (resolutions); both are empowered to alter the party's constitution. But in the conception of the role of Conference within each party, as opposed to mechanics and procedures, a radical difference is apparent. The Labour Conference is 'the supreme governing body of the party',[1] while no such claim has ever been made for the National Party Conference.

The Labour Party Conference

The position of the Labour Conference has been stated by a former Secretary of the party. 'In matters of policy the power rests with the individual member as expressed first in his Branch or his Union and then through the LRC to Annual Conference where the final decisions are made by the representatives of the branches and affiliations.'[2] This view is a logical consequence of the extra-parliamentary origins of the Labour Party,[3] which have tended to concentrate power in a body representative of the mass membership.

Such a conception of the role of Conference did not raise any difficulties in the early days of the party. But when Labour became the Government 'direct' policy-making by Conference would have had the unwelcome effect of tying the hands of the Cabinet. At the 1936 Conference Savage, the Prime Minister, said, 'There will be no attempt on the part of the conference to interfere with the policy. The Government alone is charged with the development of Labour's policy along the best possible

---

[1] 'The Annual Conference shall be the supreme governing body of the Party' (*Constitution and Rules* (*1955*), 13A).

[2] David Wilson, *Constitutional Democracy*.

[3] See pp. 36–40, above, also H. Pelling, *The Origins of the Labour Party*, p. 232, on the British Labour Party's 'inheritance' of 'a supreme annual conference' from the trade unions, via the ILP.

lines, and there can be no interference from outside either in matters of policy or of administration.'[1] Fraser, as Acting Prime Minister, went even further at the 1937 Conference, and informed it that its resolutions were not binding but were merely expressions of opinion. 'The final word lay with the Cabinet, after consultation with caucus and the party's national executive. The Labour Party, as Government, was now responsible for the welfare of the whole community.' This claim was accepted by the Conference.[2] Of course, Fraser's statement raises directly the question of a possible conflict of responsibility—between a Labour Government's responsibility to party members (through Conference) and its responsibility to the electors (through Parliament).[3] A reconciliation of the two responsibilities was attempted by Mr. Nash, when he implied that policy resolutions could be passed at any Conference, but that they would take effect only after the next general election. He is quoted as having said, 'The policy of the party will not be altered until the next election comes; and sometime between now and the election there will be three conferences of the party. At these conferences any alterations considered necessary by the delegates to be in the interests of the Dominion will be written into the policy of the party to be submitted to the electors in 1938 when the next general election takes place.'[4] In the early years of the 1957–60 Labour Government, the leadership was also unwilling for too specific policy resolutions to be passed, presumably in case some delegates or other party members would expect policy changes to be put into effect before the 1960 election.

At the 1940 Conference, however, Fraser elevated the status of Conference, and of the national executive, as a counterweight against dissident sections of caucus: '. . . the democracy of the Labour Party is the rank and file of the Party, which is represented at this Conference, and in the periods between Conferences, by the National Executive.' At the same Conference James Roberts of the Watersiders' Union, the President of the Party, strongly affirmed the parliamentary party's responsibility

[1] *Round Table*, vol. xxvi (1935–6), p. 866.
[2] Ibid., vol. xxvii (1936–7), p. 876, quoting *Standard*, 8 Apr. 1937.
[3] See pp. 244–6, below.
[4] *Dannevirke Evening Press*, 6 Sept. 1937.

to the 'Parliament of Labour', and said that if the parliamentarians did not give satisfaction Conference would itself elect the Cabinet.[1]

The Labour Conference meets in May of each year, usually in Wellington. It is immediately preceded by two smaller meetings, one of women delegates and one of farmer delegates. The composition of Conference and the provisions for voting are complex. It would be possible to devise many other schemes, just as logical, and other systems have actually been used in the past.[2] Apart from representatives of the national executive and the parliamentary party, the organizations represented are LRCs, branches and trade unions. All LRCs are entitled to two delegates, and a total of two votes, but branches and unions have representation and voting power according to membership, though not proportionately. Those with fewer than 201 members are entitled to one delegate with one vote; those with 201–500 have two delegates and two votes; those with 501–1,000, three delegates and three votes; those with 1,001–1,500, four delegates and four votes. Larger bodies are allowed an extra delegate and vote for every 500 members. Although each body is entitled to the same number of delegates as votes, one vote need not be cast by each delegate. A body might empower only one delegate to cast several votes, either sending him alone or along with non-voting delegates. The only restriction is that a body casting more than twelve votes must be represented by at least four delegates.[3] A further complication is that a single person may represent more than one body, a scheme which, under certain conditions, may make that person's voting power less than if the bodies had been represented separately.[4]

These intricate arrangements make it difficult to relate the number of delegates attending Conference to the number of organizations represented, or to estimate the comparative voting power of union delegates compared with that of other delegates. The number of delegates attending rose rapidly soon after Labour became the Government in 1935, mainly because of the increase in the number of trade-unionists produced by

[1] Barnard, op. cit., p. 11.
[2] Brown, *The Rise of New Zealand Labour*, pp. 33–34, 174, 210–11.
[3] Penfold, op. cit., p. 11.
[4] The votes which such a delegate can cast are limited to three (*Constitution and Rules* (1955), 14A).

compulsory unionism. In 1937, for instance, there were said to be about 500 delegates, whereas in the previous year, which had been a record, there were only 220.[1] In 1939 there were 543 delegates representing more than 600 organizations.[2] A new peak was reached for the 1940 Conference, at which John A. Lee was expelled, which approximately 750 delegates attended.[3] During the war attendance fell. For the second half of the 1950's the pattern seemed to be that about 50 LRCs were represented, 70 out of over 200 unions, and about 250 out of over 600 branches. In addition there is usually a handful of Maori representatives. But, although the big organizations send more than one delegate, because of the provision that a delegate may represent more than one organization the total number of delegates is less than the number of organizations. Normally nowadays some 350–400 organizations are represented by a slightly smaller number of delegates. The total voting strength, on the average, would be rather over 600 votes. According to Overacker, considerations of expense are important in keeping away branch delegates. 'The larger unions pay the expenses of their delegates, and union secretaries incur no loss of income if they are sent as delegates. For this reason branches are often represented by union delegates. Area representatives on the national executive have their expenses paid by the head office and sometimes represent their respective branches.'[4]

The respective voting power of branches and LRCs on the on hand, and unions on the other, has not been made public. At one Conference in the late 1950's an estimate was that the voting power of these two groups was roughly equal. This calculation is rather misleading, because trade unions, and the trade-union point of view, are strongly represented on LRCs. However, the balance is quite different from the Labour Party Conference in Britain, where the trade unions cast about five-sixths of the votes.

Numerically, this does not quite square with the view that the delegates are 'a regiment, easily controlled by a handful of industrial drill-sergeants'.[5] Allowance should be made, however, for the fact that the delegates from the big unions are more likely

[1] *Tomorrow*, 27 Mar. 1937.
[2] *Dominion*, 11 Apr. 1939.
[3] *Evening Post*, 26 Mar. 1940.
[4] Overacker, *American Political Science Review*, art. cit., pp. 725–6.
[5] Barnard, op. cit., p. 3.

to attend and are more 'cohesive' than the delegates from the branches, and may be exercising some 'branch' votes. What is even more important is that most of the large unions work in conjunction with 'the platform', on which the national executive and the Leader of the parliamentary party are represented.

Conference's range of functions is very wide. Some of its time is taken up with various reports and addresses, principally the President's Address, the Report of the national executive and the Parliamentary Report given by the Leader of the PLP, and with short debates on these. Other 'standard' items are the election of officers and the consideration of remits. At particular Conferences other items hold the centre of the stage. For instance, the dispute about whether the selection of Cabinet should be by Savage, the Prime Minister, or by caucus was put to the 1939 Conference.[1] In 1939 there was another 'special feature', a debate on Mr. Lee's letter attacking Mr. Nash's financial policy, which ended in a vote censuring Lee. The 1940 Conference again discussed Lee, and voted that he should be expelled from the party.[2]

Usually most of the time of Conference is taken up with the consideration of remits. In different years there is specialization in various types. Conferences held in the year after a general election usually concentrate on remits dealing with constitutional changes, while the Conference held six months or so before an election is devoted mainly to policy questions. Branches, LRCs, and affiliations must send in their remits to head office at least three months before the Conference. The national executive then sets up a sub-committee to screen and consolidate them. Some are rejected, often on the ground that they have been considered at the previous year's Conference. A few remits may be sent on elsewhere. Thus remits on workers' compensation and other items which are clearly 'industrial' in nature may be sent to the Federation of Labour Conference. Or, if remits are

[1] *Dominion*, 10 May 1939, giving a summarized report of the Conference Proceedings, released by David Wilson, the national Secretary.

[2] The procedures used were allegedly doubtful constitutionally. See Barnard, op. cit., p. 7; Lee, *Simple on a Soapbox*, pp. 178–96; Overacker, *American Political Science Review*, art. cit., pp. 721–2. Among other things, Lee claimed that, in order to ensure his expulsion at the Conference, the voting rules were changed to enable large unions to cast all their votes through as few as four delegates (*John A. Lee's Weekly*, 15 Jan. 1941).

on questions of administration, they may be sent direct to ministers, if the party is the Government party; if the party is not in
office they go to the policy committee or national executive. The
rest are consolidated and arranged under a number of different
subject-matter headings; for instance Finance, Education,
Justice, Land and Agriculture, and so on. Under each heading
will be found one or more numbered remits, each with a number
of sections indicated by letters. In this way hundreds of remits
sent in, sometimes over a thousand, are reduced to fewer than a
hundred, each with several lettered sections. There is no attempt
to weed out remits on the grounds of inanity or impracticability
at this stage. Indeed the reduction in the *number* of remits is more
apparent than real, and results mainly from the device of having
up to ten or so lettered sections 'inside' each numbered remit.
The *Remit Paper* at Conference shows, after each numbered
remit, the source of the *original* remits which have been used to
make up the new one. An analysis of the *Remit Paper* a few years
ago shows that few remits originate with the unions. In this
particular year 70 per cent. of the remits came from branches,
20 per cent. from LRCs, and only 10 per cent. from unions.
These percentages correspond very closely to Overacker's figures
for 1952, for the numbers of *organizations* which submitted remits.[1]

Two months before Conference the *Remit Paper* is circulated
to LRCs, branches, and affiliations. This is done in order to allow
discussion of the items, so that branches may instruct their delegates on how to vote. But in some branches the remits are never
even considered. In others the branch members start going down
the order paper, but fail to get through all the remits, so that the
delegates remain uninstructed on some of them.

Conference lasts for only four days or so, and has other business to deal with besides remits. In view of the short time available and the fact that the number of remits originally sent in
has, in reality, been reduced only very slightly, some way has to
be found to enable Conference to dispose of them all. This is
effected by setting up a number of committees, usually between
six and ten, to examine and report on the remits before they
come before the whole Conference.[2] Each of these committees

---

[1] Overacker, *American Political Science Review*, art. cit., p. 725.
[2] This system was first put into practice in 1936 (Brown, *The Rise of New Zealand
Labour*, p. 171).

is given a range of subjects wider than that under which remits are grouped in the *Remit Paper*. For example, a 'Social Security, Health and Education' Committee would concern itself with the items under these three individual headings on the Paper.

There are usually between twenty and twenty-five people on each committee. Before the Conference organizations write in to headquarters suggesting names for committees. Not all of these can be selected or can be placed on the particular committee requested, but in choosing them the national executive takes some account of geography, for instance a delegate from a remote area would be given preference over one from a main centre. For assignments to a particular committee the field of interest of the person concerned would also be taken into consideration. On the other hand a delegate who had already served on one committee several times in succession might be moved to another in order to widen his experience. Even at Conference itself there may be some last-minute changes, for instance some persons who have been placed on a committee may decide that they do not wish to sit on it after all, and may propose substitutes.

The chairman (or 'convenor') of each committee is chosen by the national executive, and is almost invariably a member of the national executive or, failing this, an M.P. It is he who has the task of reporting to the full Conference what the committee's recommendations are on each section of each remit which was referred to the committee, and, briefly, the reasons for its recommendations. One or two of the committees need to do their work quickly in order that the committee reports shall not all be crowded together towards the end of the Conference. So it is essential that at least one or two of the chairmen must be businesslike, even ruthless, in their methods. Sometimes the committee will slightly alter the wording of a remit, for instance if a remit is phrased in terms of 'women's and children's shoes' the committee may reword it to apply to 'footwear' generally. A chairman may admit to Conference that the committee does not know exactly what a remit is about or what its purpose is. Sometimes it has been suggested that each remit should be accompanied by an account of the *reasons* why it is being moved. A contrary view is that most of the remits are self-explanatory, and that the example of the proposers of one single-page remit who accompanied it by seven pages of 'explanation' is not one to be imitated. Occasionally a chairman will confess that the subject is so difficult technically (for instance a resolution to colour motor spirit on which tax exemption is claimed) that the committee itself hesitates to make a definite recommendation. Other chairmen, with a definite manner of stating their committee's views, are sometimes caught out by questions from the floor, and are obliged to take refuge in saying that various proposals are 'impracticable', without being able to say exactly why. From time to time a chairman may mention that the committee's views were unanimous, or nearly so; occasionally a chairman may even state that his own personal opinion differs from the committee's.

Committee recommendations assume an almost infinite variety of forms. Even complete approval may take the shape of saying that the remit be 'approved', 'adopted', 'supported', 'agreed to', 'endorsed'. It may also be 'approved' &c. in a slightly amended form. It may be 'approved in principle', and referred to some other body, such as the national executive or the policy committee. A remit that 2 January should be a public holiday was recently agreed to in principle, subject to the approval of the Federation of Labour. The next possibility is reference to another body, for instance to the Parliamentary Labour Party, 'for favourable consideration'. Again, the recommendation may be completely neutral in form, for instance that the proposal simply be 'referred' to the Parliamentary Labour Party, the policy committee, the Joint Council of Labour, or to some other body. Such references may indicate that the subject is too complex for a snap decision, or may arise from a desire to 'shelve' it. A remit may be rejected outright, in so many words, or by using the slightly more refined phrasing that 'no action be be taken' or that 'no recommendation be made'. More remits are rejected than are adopted, especially if 'shelvings' are included in rejections. Detailed or quantitative remits are more likely to be rejected than others.

When each chairman has read out the committee's recommendations and proposed their adoption, amendments may be moved from the floor. There is a three-minute limit on speeches with extensions of time if approved by Conference. Perhaps an average of one or two amendments will be moved to each numbered remit, amounting to up to about a hundred amendments altogether. Very few of these are passed, perhaps ten or a dozen out of all those that have been moved. Most of the successful ones are concerned only with small changes in wording. Ordinarily the voting on these is by voice. But about six or ten times in the course of a Conference a 'card vote' is called for, which means that the voting strength of the larger unions is brought into play. It is very seldom that a committee's recommendation is defeated on a card vote. This is not to say that there is any exact New Zealand equivalent of the 'block vote' of the trade unions in the British Labour Party Conference.[1] There is no counterpart in New Zealand of the almost astronomical total of votes which can be cast by a few delegates in the British Conference. Even a union with a membership of 5,000, very large by New Zealand standards, would have only 11 votes at Conference, less than 2 per cent. of the usual total voting strength represented there. Nor would it be correct to regard 'the unions' as a monolithic force at Conference. There are some left-wing unions, such as the New Zealand Amalgamated Society of Railway Servants (NZASRS), which do not vote along with the majority of the unions on any topic which is even faintly 'ideological'. And there are unions which may be moved to oppose or support a measure simply because a rival union is supporting or opposing it.

The strength of the 'Platform', that is, the national executive and the PLP leadership, is obvious in Conference. But it does not rest exclusively, or even predominantly, on union support, or any other single factor, but rather on a series of 'prepared positions'. It is, so to speak, an example of defence in depth.[2] First, the choice of persons to serve on the committees on remits, and their chairmen, is made by the national executive. Second, the acceptance of the committees' recommendations is helped by the fact that the chairmen, in presenting their report, are not under any time limit, while speakers from the floor are strictly timed. Third, if a committee's recommendations are defeated, a card vote may be called for. This increases the ratio of the 'industrial' vote (which, on the whole, is more likely to favour the Platform) to the 'non-industrial' vote, as well as constituting

---

[1] See Martin Harrison, *Trade Unions and the Labour Party since 1945*, ch. v.
[2] For 'defences' at the British Labour Party Conference see McKenzie, *British Political Parties*, pp. 485–516.

a signal that the vote is to be treated as a 'question of confidence'.

But these are not the only lines of defence. The President of the party, as chairman of the Conference, is in a position to guide the Conference, if he desires to do so. Indeed, to judge from reports, the term, 'guidance' quite fails to convey the influence which Mr. James Roberts exercised over the Conference during his long Presidency, 1937–50. Since then chairmen have been much less 'positive' in their methods. The Party Leader may also be used to sway the Conference if necessary. For instance, if a 'sensitive' subject were up for discussion, such as whether or not the security police should be retained under a Labour Government, it would be an intelligent tactic to have the Party Leader speak on this, and give the proper assurances to Conference before a vote were taken.

The parliamentary party, through its Leader, has also insisted on a curtailment of Conference's powers over policy when Labour is the Government. At a recent Conference the Leader, who was then also Prime Minister, said that the Government had gone before the electors pledged to a certain policy for the next three years. The Government was responsible for carrying out that pledge, which meant, in effect, that the Conference was not empowered to recommend any changes which would go into effect during the three-year period.[1] This view was accepted by Conference, although not without dissent, expressed in the complaint from the floor, 'What's the use of coming to Conference, unless resolutions can be carried on policy?' This limitation of Conference's powers has been said to derive from Fraser's view of Conference's limited role, quoted above.

There is one further, 'last ditch', defence at Conference—recommittal. A question which has already been decided may be reopened, if Conference decides to do so, by a simple majority, and voted on again. Ideally, recommittal should seldom be necessary; the 'awkward' questions should be spotted before they arise and the other defences used against them. In particular, the technical problems which might make it difficult to give effect to a remit can be pointed out to Conference, also the danger that, if the party is in power, the Government might be embarrassed by a resolution which might seem to be mandatory.

[1] See p. 223, above.

However, recommittal has been used once or twice in recent
years, once when Conference expressed its wishes for a change in
social security payments in too quantitative a way. When the
recommittal took place, the argument just outlined, that when
Labour was the Government Conference could not recommend
changes within the three-year period, was employed. Then the
item was voted on again, and the Platform succeeded in having
the original decision reversed. But proposals to recommit are
not invariably successful, especially if the 'big guns' of the party
are not wheeled up in their support.[1]

Two instances are often quoted of the defeat of the Platform
by Conference—the votes on the nationalization of the Bank of
New Zealand in 1944 and the introduction of Compulsory
Military Training in 1949. But these occurrences were atypical.
In each case Conference won, not because it was thought to be
changing policy, but because it was believed to be reaffirming the
accepted ideals and policy of the movement. It is doubtful
whether nationalization of the Bank of New Zealand (as opposed to the creation of a Reserve Bank which would control
all currency and credit) was ever specifically included in the
party platform.[2] But many members of the party *thought* that it
was, and it had previously been accepted by caucus.[3] At the
1944 Conference it came up as a remit, and was referred to a
committee with a friendly convenor (chairman), Mr. H. E.
Combs, M.P. It is significant that, at previous conferences, when
similar remits had been referred to committees of which Mr.
Nash was convenor, they had progressed no further. The committee endorsed it and sent it back to Conference. Conference
then recommitted it, and it was again recommended by the
committee. By this time the opposition had been worn down,
and, in full Conference, Mr. Nash, who had been an inveterate
opponent of the proposal, actually seconded the motion to endorse the remit for nationalizing the bank.[4]

In 1949 the Prime Minister secured the support of caucus,

[1] Other 'defences' beyond the Conference exist, e.g., the policy committee's
power to reword or consolidate remits when drawing up the election manifesto.
[2] See p. 59, above.
[3] Some months before the Conference, when both Fraser and Nash were out of
the country, it was approved by a caucus committee and afterwards by caucus
(interview, Mr. Langstone, Nov. 1958). See also pp. 160–1, above.
[4] Interview, Mr. F. H. Langstone, Nov. 1958.

with only one dissentient, for his proposal to enact Compulsory Military Training. But subsequently Conference was unreceptive. When the Labour Party was formed in 1916 its unity had been achieved partly on the basis of opposition to conscription. And even during the Second World War a special Conference had been convened, in June 1940, to explain the need for conscription and obtain support for it.[1] But in 1949, in peacetime, although Fraser had been convinced of the necessity for conscription, Conference was not. It upheld the traditions of the party by refusing to accept it, and would go only so far as to agree to the holding of a referendum on the question.

From time to time delegates express curiosity, and sometimes frustration, about the fate of remits which have been approved by Conference or have been referred by it to some other body for consideration. Perhaps some delegates may subscribe to an over-simplified view of the role of Conference, similar to that expressed in a small Labour pamphlet published in 1957. Describing the discussions which take place in 'local groups' of the party, the pamphlet said, 'The results of these discussions are generally considered as remits submitted to the Annual Conference of the Labour Party and, if adopted, will become part of the policy of the second Labour Government.'[2] At a recent Conference a remit proposed exactly this—that any policy remit, if adopted, should automatically be included in the next election manifesto of the party. Of course, this suggestion would be hard to put into operation. It ignores the need to reword resolutions to form part of a coherent election manifesto. It takes no account of the changes which may be necessary because of altered circumstances, whether in the party, in the rival party, in New Zealand or in the world. That is why the policy committee, in drawing up the manifesto, is given discretion in choosing, amending, or rejecting the various policy resolutions which have been approved by Conference. Generally this system seems to have been accepted. 'In 1952 Conference rejected the suggested "That where decisions on policy prove to be inoperative, the reason be explained to Conference". That is, Conference imposed on itself a self-denying ordinance.'[3]

[1] Wood, *The New Zealand People at War*, pp. 138–9.
[2] *Land of Ideas* (Wellington, 1957).
[3] Penfold, op. cit., p. 14.

A related problem concerns the fate of remits which have been passed on to some other body. Usually at each Conference a cyclostyled report is circulated giving the comments of the Parliamentary Labour Party on the remits referred to it by the previous Conference. The comments are short and are expressed in rather general terms, although they draw attention to any specific action which has already been taken by the party. For instance a PLP comment on a remit recommending the encouragement of saving for home ownership drew attention to a Labour Government scheme already in operation through the Post Office Savings Bank. However, there is no provision for a special session of Conference at which the PLP comments on remits can be debated, although it is possible for some relevant points to be raised in the discussion which takes place every year after the Leader's presentation of the Parliamentary Report to Conference.

The Annual Report of Conference sometimes contains a list of the resolutions of the Federation of Labour Conference on those industrial remits which have been referred to it by a previous Labour Party Conference. However, there is no procedure for debating these. There is no regular system of reporting to Conference on remits which have been referred to the national executive or to the policy committee.

Particular Conferences may give special attention to constitutional or policy matters. Thus the 1951 Conference adopted a revised constitution, although the existence of the waterfront dispute seems to have prevented wholehearted concentration on constitutional issues.[1] In 1952 the national executive put forward a number of 'policy resolutions' on reports which it had drafted on *Principles of Labour, Labour versus Communism, Industrial Relations,* and *Peace and War*.[1] These were based on a tour of New Zealand, during which the President and Secretary had sounded out opinion in the LRCs. Unlike remits, these resolutions were not circulated to organizations beforehand. Some delegates objected to this on the ground that, because the resolutions concerned policy, they required more time to think about, not less, than some remits which concerned details of party organization. However, the then President believes that the experiment was

---

[1] Overacker, *American Political Science Review*, art. cit., p. 725.

successful in that it stimulated discussion on the subjects of greatest importance from the policy point of view.[1]

The Labour Conference was originally not open to the Press or to those who were not members of the party. This may have been the consequence partly of the party's distrust of the 'capitalist' Press and of fear that newspaper accounts would distort the proceedings. A previous President of the party used to say, jokingly, to those journalists who asked him for more information about Conference than was contained in the 'handouts' for the Press, 'I have to sit there all the time. Aren't you lucky to get the information without having to be there? During the meetings you can go out and have a spot.' However, from 1963 onwards the Press was allowed to hear discussions on those committee reports to which Conference decided to admit it. At the 1963 Conference it was admitted to all of them except that on Finance. The proceedings of Labour Conferences are published, in a condensed form which gives no summaries of individual speeches from the floor.

The National Party Conference

The National Party Conference is held rather later in the year than the Labour Party Conference, usually in July. It meets in various places, but more often in Wellington than anywhere else. Organizationally its regular meetings mark it off from its predecessor, the Reform Party, which did not hold Conferences in the years between 1914 and 1926.[2] But the role of Conference in the power-structure of the National Party is in contrast to the role of Conference in the Labour Party, and is similar to Conference's role in previous non-Labour parties. It is not the supreme policy-maker, nor has anyone ever claimed that it is or that it should be. In Chapter VI mention was made of the verbal recognition sometimes accorded to the role of the Liberal and Labour Federation in policy-making. But Seddon himself, addressing the Federation's Conference in 1903, spoke rather bluntly. 'You will also, no doubt, in the course of the Conference, express your views upon the larger questions of policy which are now before the country. It is by meeting as you now meet, it is by discussing these questions, that we shall be able to arrive at

[1] Interview, Mr. A. H. Nordmeyer, Dec. 1958.
[2] *Newsletter*, 31 July 1926; Gardner, art. cit., vol. xiii, no. 2, pp. 22–23.

just and profitable conclusions.'[1] The contrast between the parts to be played by 'you' and 'we', respectively, imply that, under 'King Dick', the Federation was to function as a benevolent despotism, not as a democratic republic.

In the National Party it has never been claimed that resolutions of Conference on policy are binding on the leadership. Policy is made by the Leader along with the policy committee of the Dominion Council.[2] 'At most, remits are looked upon by the leadership as a guide that they [sic] should follow as much as possible. At worst, they are all but ignored completely.'[3] In Conference itself Holland stated that Conference was not the place to formulate election policy. But Conference is, nevertheless, important, because, representing a wide range of interests and people from all parts of the country, it exchanges and studies ideas that may be of advantage to the party and to New Zealand. The decisions of Conference have some degree of persuasive authority. Conference also has the important power of being able to alter the constitution or rules of the party. In 1939, for instance, it had to make the decision whether or not the Leader should be President *ex-officio* and should appoint the Chairman.[4]

The composition of Conference and the method of voting are simple compared with the Labour Party. Apart from members of the Dominion Council and National Party M.P.s,[5] each electorate is entitled to be represented by four delegates. These are chosen by the Electorate Committee, except that, where there is a Junior Section, one of the four must be a Junior, appointed by that section.[6] It is also usual for one of the four delegates to be a woman. In practice some electorates do not send their full complement of four delegates. The total number of delegates at an 'average' Conference (apart from Dominion Councillors and M.P.s) is therefore about 250. About thirty of these are juniors and almost a hundred are women. Consequently in the whole Conference almost two-fifths of all those attending are either juniors or women. Visually, in contrast to the Labour Party,

---

[1] *Report of Proceedings of the Conference of Delegates of the Liberal and Labour Federation of New Zealand*, p. 4.

[2] See pp. 176–9, above, also Robinson, *Oligarchy and Democracy*, pp. 37–38.

[3] Kelson, *Political Science*, vol. vi, no. 2, art. cit., p. 16.   [4] See p. 172, above.

[5] Apparently M.P.s and ministers used to sit apart from the delegates, but this arrangement ended in 1954 (*Evening Post*, 22 Aug. 1956).

[6] *Constitution and Rules (1963)*, rule 34.

there is a prevailing impression of women in white hats rather than of men with red ties. Each person at the Conference has one vote, and so there is no need for card votes. If a 'voice' vote is indecisive, then the matter is settled by a show of hands.

The proceedings of Conference, apart from remits, cover much the same ground as at the Labour Conference, but they are more routine and less likely to be debated or contested from the floor. The President's Address is short, the printed report of the Dominion Council is usually taken as read, and there is no serious questioning or debate on either of these items. The election of officers is usually without interest, because generally there is only one nominee for each position. One distinctive feature is that, when the party is in office, the proceedings are interrupted from time to time to enable ministers to give brief addresses.

In contrast to Labour Party procedure, by which remits are considered only at the Annual Conference, the remits which appear on the National Party Conference agenda have already been screened at divisional level. This screening amounts not merely to the rejection of some remits, but since the mid-1950's has included designating certain remits as 'priority' remits which will go before Dominion Conference. Other remits are referred to Dominion Council. Remits which call for administrative action and are not of nation-wide interest are also excluded at this stage. Present headquarters policy is to try to persuade the lower echelons of the party to keep such requests for administrative action out of the Conference remit-machinery altogether. It is pointed out that if they are sent to party headquarters for consideration by the Dominion Executive or the General Director (and, where relevant, for passing on to ministers if the party is in power) they will be dealt with more speedily.[1] Each division used to be allocated one remit for every two electorates in the division for consideration at Dominion Conference. The Dominion Executive may select additional remits for the consideration of Conference. The introduction of a committee system in 1963, however, meant that the total of remits to be considered could be raised from forty to forty-nine. There may be further increases in the number in future. Each remit consists of only one part; there are no lettered sections as there are in the Labour Party remits.

[1] Interview, Mr. Ralph Wilson, May 1964.

The remits to be discussed are circulated before the Conference, but not so far in advance as Labour Party remits. Remits will be received by Dominion Council up to four weeks before the Conference, and need be circulated to all electorates only three weeks before. Delegates may sometimes be 'pledged' to support particular remits, usually those from their own electorate or ones where a local interest is involved. Quite often delegates from an electorate may not all vote the same way.

Although the National Party Conference has fewer remits to deal with than its Labour counterpart, it also has less time at its disposal. The Conference lasts for only two days plus one evening, less than the period of the Labour Conference.

In 1963, for the first time, committees were used, as an experiment. The remits were divided into five groups. A few, of general interest, were reserved for full Conference, while the remainder, grouped according to their subject matter, were allocated to one of four committees. Each electorate, if sending its full quota of four delegates, assigns one to each committee. When the remits reach full Conference, they are accompanied by a stencilled sheet showing the relevant committee's recommendation on each, along with two or three lines summarizing the main arguments for and against. The use of the committees has increased the total time for comments, although the time for discussion in full Conference has been reduced. Future procedure will probably allow more debate in full Conference on remits which have been contentious enough to be pressed to a vote in committee.

Before the vote is taken there is often a 'ministerial comment' by a relevant minister, when the party is in power.[1] These point out the background of the matter contained in the remit and, most important, often give an estimate of what a proposal would cost. These ministerial comments seem to have developed from the practice, in operation before the party came to power in 1949, by which comments on remits from the Research Department were made available for use at Conference.[2] Apparently such comments were similar in content to the subsequent ministerial ones. This practice was resumed when the party was in

[1] On receipt of remits at Dominion Headquarters, regardless of whether they are to be discussed in Conference or Dominion Council, they are submitted to the relevant ministers for information and comment.
[2] Interview, Theo Hills, Oct. 1958.

opposition, 1957 to 1960. In 1963 the ministerial comments were made in committee except in the case of the remits which went direct to full Conference.

Some delegates are dissatisfied with the limitations on their speaking time, especially when this is contrasted with the larger amount of time given to ministers who may be speaking against them. Movers of remits have three minutes, other speakers two. Ministers have three originally, but are more likely to be granted extensions. At the 1963 Conference one minister had an extraordinary number of extensions. At a Conference some years ago one delegate said he wished to register his protest against the disparity in the allocation of time, which happened again and again at Conference. An ingenious attempt to 'expand' the time available was made by the supporters of a remit in favour of re-establishing a Second Chamber at the 1957 Conference of the party. As delegates entered the hall they were handed cyclostyled material in favour of the proposal in order to supplement the short time available for speaking from the floor. However, at the next meeting of Dominion Council it was ruled that the practice of circulating unofficial material would not be allowed at future Conferences.[1]

Usually more remits are carried than rejected, which perhaps indicates how carefully they have been screened at lower levels of the party. Some of the delegates get excited some of the time, particularly on traditionally controversial 'free enterprise' topics such as, until recently, compulsory unionism. But most of them are only too anxious to please all the time, especially when the party is in office, as is revealed in such statements as 'Conference should help the National Government, and not act as a pressure group'. They are usually soothed and satisfied by ministerial reassurances such as, 'I think you may safely leave it to the Government to . . .'.

Close voting is rarer than at Labour Party Conferences. Only three or four times at each Conference do hands have to be counted; otherwise a voice vote or an uncounted show of hands is enough. The proportion of Conference delegates casting a vote on resolutions nowadays seems to be rather higher than that described by Kelson for the 1954 Conference, perhaps because procedure has been changed since then.[2] The Platform—

[1] Ibid.　　[2] Kelson, art. cit., pp. 17–18.

that is the President of the party, who is chairman, and the Leader—do not often intervene or take sides in the discussion of remits. Sometimes the President may seem to be speaking on behalf of the parliamentary party. At other times he will comment on it, from outside as it were, in his capacity as head of the extra-parliamentary organization. At the 1957 Conference he stated, on tourism, 'Our Government needs prodding in this matter, and I hope the remit dealing with the tourist industry is passed, with a request that it be expedited.'[1] When the President, or the Leader, does intervene the intervention is almost invariably decisive. At more than one Conference Holland, when Leader, spoke against remits urging the immediate re-establishment of a Second Chamber, and on each occasion the proposal was blocked. Similarly, at one Conference during the period 1949–57, Sir William Sullivan, the former Minister of Labour, was called on to speak and lend the weight of his authority against remits to put an end to compulsory unionism.

An interesting argument was used by the Leader in 1963 to persuade Conference to drop a recommendation in favour of corporal punishment, thus reversing the stand taken by two previous Conferences. Mr. Holyoake argued that National M.P.s would have to be given a free vote in Parliament and that the Bill would therefore be defeated. 'I don't want to influence you', Mr. Holyoake said, causing laughter. But he added, 'You wouldn't expect me to put a bill forward, knowing that it would be defeated.'[2]

Sometimes, but less frequently than at the Labour Conference, a remit may be referred to another body, usually the Dominion Council.[3] This might conceivably be used as a means of 'shelving' a proposal, which, off the shelf, would lead to dissension within the party. An interesting technique was used in 1957 after the Prime Minister had spoken against immediate action on re-establishing a Second Chamber and the issue had been referred to the Dominion Council by a majority of 4 to 1. The Conference chairman (the party's President), after discussion with the Prime Minister, Deputy Prime Minister and the Attorney General, took an informal poll of the delegates for or

[1] *Evening Post*, 12 Aug. 1957. [2] Ibid., 23 July 1963.
[3] In 1954 25 remits were carried, 15 rejected, 11 referred to Dominion Council, 9 withdrawn, and 4 consolidated with other remits (*Freedom*, 14 July 1954).

against re-establishment, as an indication of opinion in the party. There was a majority of nine votes against, out of over 200 cast. This procedure was doubly revealing. It showed the large number of delegates who were in favour of re-establishment, but nevertheless had just been persuaded, on the Leader's advice, to delay action on it. It also showed that the Platform, in spite of the fact that Conference resolutions are not binding, did not want to be inhibited by even the persuasive authority of a formal resolution.

Another type of awkward remit is one concerning a topic which the party leadership plans to 'feature' at the next election. To disclose the party's intentions on this prematurely would possibly lead to the loss of secrecy and surprise at the election. If such a question is raised in a remit, the best tactic may be to say that it is already under study by the Dominion Council, and to hope that the proposer will be sufficiently perceptive not to press the point.

On one occasion the technique of re-committal was used to rescue the party from an awkward tangle. In 1954 a remit that the (National) Government should give serious consideration to 'the question of pay-as-you-earn taxation, with a view to having it included in the Party's election platform' was defeated, in spite of the fact that it had been commended to the Conference by the President and by the Associate Minister of Finance. The party's official organ *Freedom*[1] wrote, 'The first vote was close enough[2] to suggest that some who opposed it did not fully appreciate the implications or what the remit was designed to do. The Prime Minister, Mr. Holland, therefore explained fully what was in mind, and thereupon unanimously modified the first decision to the effect that the Dominion Executive in conjunction with representatives of the parliamentary party examine the matter with a view to what further action shall be taken to give effect to the conference's more maturely expressed decision.' The reason why additional 'maturity' was required was that the Government had already, in principle, decided to introduce a PAYE scheme, perhaps to be announced in detail at the 1954 election. The party would have lost face if it had gone ahead with such a scheme, if Conference had only recently condemned PAYE.

---

[1] *Freedom*, 14 July 1954.
[2] Kelson, p. 18, says the remit was originally defeated by a 'significant margin'.

Remits passed by Conference are sent to the policy committee,[1] and will be considered, along with the recommendations of Conference, for possible inclusion in the next election manifesto. As in the Labour Party, some delegates want to know what action is being taken to implement such remits and, if nothing is being done, what are the reasons forinaction. At the 1956 Conference, commenting on a remit asking that reasons be given in such cases, the Leader 'said the Government could not be answerable to a conference. The remit was finally amended to read that headquarters be advised of the results of Conference remits submitted to the Government.'[2]

Because of Conference's limited control over policy-making, a few important members of the party have sometimes expressed the view that the proceedings are a waste of time. But, apart from any social functions which it may perform, Conference 'provides an opportunity for the leaders to report in person to the rank and file and for the rank and file to question their Parliamentarians and leaders on performance and policy'.[3] More specifically, Conference has an educative function for those party members who are enabled to come and hear 'the answers'. And it is 'educative', in another sense, for the top people in the party, because the nature of the questions raised at Conference is a useful indication of what the mass membership is thinking and feeling.[4] Also, sometimes Conference actually does influence policy. To be sure, very few of the remits approved by Conference get into election policy in unaltered form. But the feelings expressed at successive Conferences against compulsory unionism undoubtedly contributed to the National Government's decision to 'abolish' it in 1962.

For two or three years before 1956 Conference was open to the Press with certain limitations; for example, it was open only to approved reporters or only at certain times—for instance when ministerial statements were being made.[5] Since 1956 it has been completely open to the Press, except in the unlikely event of its choosing to go into committee, and also to members

---

[1] So are 'non-priority' remits, which have gone to Dominion Council instead of Conference and have been approved by it.

[2] *Evening Post*, 20 Aug. 1956.

[3] Ibid., 17 Aug. 1956.

[4] Interview, Sir Alex. McKenzie, Feb. 1958.

[5] Kelson, *Political Science*, vol. vi, no. 2, art. cit., p. 19.

of the public who apply for admission.[1] Apart from newspaper
reports no account is published of the Conference proceedings.

Comparisons and Criticism

Both party Conferences are too unwieldy and too concerned
with ritual to be classified as 'Thought-organizations'.[2] But
neither are they exactly mass rallies or 'Will-organizations'.
The numbers attending are not as huge as in Britain, where
nowadays it is sometimes impossible to fit all the delegates into
one assembly hall. The New Zealand Conferences are small
enough to allow some intimacy of communication, as is evident
in the closing scenes of a Labour Conference when some of the
delegates have already left and the remaining hundred or two
link arms and sing 'Auld Lang Syne'. Conference activities
serve primarily to promote solidarity by building morale and
by affording opportunities for social contacts. To some extent
their importance as sources of policy has varied with time. It
could be argued that in the Labour Party, which began its life
outside Parliament, the role of Conference has declined in importance with the building up of a Labour Party *inside* Parliament. This decline was sharpest when the party assumed office
for the first time in the years immediately after 1935. Even
nowadays it is probably true that Conference has more influence
on the parliamentary party when the party is out of office.
At such times 'the Platform' cannot resist proposals for policy
changes from Conference by saying that it is bound by its pledges
to the electors for a three-year period. On the other hand, it
might be said that the National Party Conference, whose 'an-
cestors' in previous non-Labour parties were not held in any
great respect, has probably gained in importance as it has
become an established institution. If the party were in Opposition for a long period, its persuasive authority might increase,
because it might tend to become a forum and a rallying point
for the expression of discontent with an unsuccessful leadership.
Comparing the Conferences of the two parties today, the situation strongly resembles the corresponding one in Britain.[3] For
all the differences between the constitutions of the parties, which
seem to point to the Labour Conference as having a much more

[1] *Evening Post*, 11 Aug. 1956.   [2] Graham Wallas, *The Great Society*, pp. 238 ff.
[3] McKenzie, *Political Parties*, p. 488.

influential role in policy-making, in practice the Conferences perform surprisingly similar functions and exercise surprisingly similar limited, but useful, powers.

The working of the British Labour Party Conference has recently provoked criticism on two main counts, the role of the unions[1] and the conflict between the party's responsibility to Conference and its responsibility to the electors.[2] The first of these issues is hardly alive in New Zealand. Interest in it in Britain derives mainly from the fact that some of the large unions cast huge block votes, some of them amounting to over a million, and that the vote of three or four big unions can be decisive in passing or rejecting the policies of the party leadership. However, even in Britain, it is well to remember that the influence of the unions on party policy should not be credited simply to their voting power in Conference.[3] In New Zealand it is well known that the unions have great influence in the Labour Party. But this is not made obvious at the Party Conference. There is no huge union block vote, but only the card vote of the individual members representing the unions. In any case, making allowance for differences in scale, there are fewer 'very large' unions in New Zealand, and their vote is not proportionate to membership, but is somewhat 'scaled down'. Union influence is also obscured by the fact that a delegate may represent a branch or an LRC as well as a union—or may even represent more than one of each of these. Most important of all, perhaps, there is never any official record made, or announcement given, of which union, LRC or branch, voted for what. The strength of the unions at Conference is therefore neither overwhelming nor obtrusive.

There is, however, the same potential conflict of responsibility in the New Zealand Labour Party as there is in the British. Is the party bound by the wishes of Conference, or, especially when it is the Government, is it to act in accordance with its pledges to the electors and with what it thinks is best for the country? To

[1] M. Harrison, op. cit., ch. v.

[2] McKenzie, *Political Studies*, art. cit.; Ralph Miliband, *Political Studies*, art. cit.; Ivan Yates, 'Power in the Labour Party', *Political Quarterly*, vol. xxxi, no. 3 (1960). An attack on Conference domination of the New Zealand Labour Government (particularly on the conscription issue in 1949) is contained in H. E. Childs's *Quo Vadis, New Zealand?* (Wellington, 1949. Foreword by S. G. Holland).

[3] M. Harrison, op. cit., p. 255.

some extent this dilemma arises from the very nature of parties in a democracy. Parties

provide the bridge to connect the groupings of society with the institutions of the state. On the one side, society generates the clusters of interests which push their way into the political process. On the other side there stand the constitutional régime, the men and machinery of government, the institutional structures which compose the state. The state exists within society, and society permeates the state. But an intermediary is needed to provide a link between them—an intermediary which, to perform its role, must belong partly to both. Such are the political parties.[1]

If (as is the case in the British and New Zealand Labour Parties, but not in the Conservative or National Parties) it is further assumed that the party is in some sense *responsible* to certain interests, as well as to Parliament and the electors, then the dilemma is fully apparent. Until recently any conflict over party responsibility in the British Labour Party was left unresolved; it was generally agreed that Conference was regarded as the *ultimate* source of policy, but that, within the limits laid down by it, the Parliamentary Labour Party might use its discretion in interpretation and timing.[2] The situation in New Zealand might also be explained in rather similar terms. It is not enough to restrict changes of policy by Conference during a three-year period. This would not avoid, but would merely postpone, the brutal problem of a potential conflict of responsibility. It would still be possible for Conference to pass any policy resolution in election year, no matter how far-fetched or Utopian, and then claim that it 'ought' to go into the next election manifesto. If Labour were afterwards returned to power, presumably the policy resolution 'ought' then to be put into effect. If such a resolution were in fact passed, no doubt the policy committee would modify it, in the direction of practicability, when putting

[1] Leslie Lipson, 'Party Systems in the United Kingdom and the Older Commonwealth: Causes, Resemblances and Variations', *Political Studies*, vol. vii, no. 1 (1959), p. 12.

[2] This view approximates to that of Rose, op. cit. It lies between the extreme views of McKenzie, *Political Parties*, p. 488, and C. R. Attlee, *The Labour Party in Perspective* (London, 1937), p. 93. But note the difference in Attlee's account, after leaving office, in Francis Williams, *A Prime Minister Remembers* (London, 1961), p. 91. The conflict was brought into the open in 1960 when Mr. Gaitskell, at the Labour Party Conference, said that the PLP would not consider itself bound by Conference's decisions (McKenzie, op. cit., pp. 615–16).

it into the manifesto. But, although this would be a 'solution' of the problem from the politicians' point of view, it would still leave academic analysts intellectually unhappy about the exact role of the Labour Conference.

With good reason, Labour politicians do not care to dig too deeply into the issues involved. There may be advantages in having one compartment of the mind believe that Conference is supreme, while another compartment behaves on the principle that Governments are responsible to the electors. For one thing, if the 'myth' of Conference supremacy were destroyed, the interest and vitality of the delegates might decline.[1] Therefore, from the politicians' angle, the question is best left undebated and unresolved. When at a Conference an official on the Platform says that it would be 'embarrassing' for the Labour Government if an awkward mandatory resolution were passed, it would be tempting to ask 'why'? Would it be embarrassing because the Government would be *bound* to put it into effect? Or would it be embarrassing because, although the Government would *not* be bound to put it into effect, its endorsement by Conference would reveal 'disharmony' between different parts of the organization, just as rejection of PAYE by the 1954 National Party Conference would have disclosed 'disharmony' in the National Party?

Conference Procedures and Policy-making

Certainly the prevalent belief that Labour Conference decisions 'matter' is reflected in the Conference's procedures. The committee system for remits has been more efficient, at least in appearance, than National Party procedure. The intricate voting system can be justified only on the ground that the votes are on something important. This impression of a 'business-like' body meeting to transact weighty affairs is reinforced by the huge number of 'officers' at the Conference—doorkeepers, credentials committee, agenda committee, press committee, minute secretaries, time-keepers, tellers, returning officers, and scrutineers. Exclusion of the Press before 1963 may also have derived, not only from a general fear of 'distortion', but also from the feeling that there was 'real business' being transacted at the Conference which could be distorted. On the other hand, since the National

[1] Miliband, *Parliamentary Socialism*, p. 172.

Party Conference had, in theory, a less important part to play, there was less reason to exclude the Press. This is particularly true, because the 'wilder' remits had already been killed off at lower levels, and only the more 'sensible' ones remained.

Kelson was severe in his observations on the National Party Conference.[1] His criticism, that 'the situation of seeming to make policy when in fact it does not is a harmful one', is surely wide of the mark,[2] and might apply rather to the Labour Conference. Kelson thought one possibility would be 'to try to make Conference more responsible. More responsible delegates should be invited to attend.' He did not specify what a 'more responsible' National Party Conference would be responsible *for*, or to *whom* it would be responsible. By 'more responsible delegates' he possibly meant 'more knowledgeable' delegates, with a smaller proportion of women and juniors. Yet if it is conceded that Conference has an important educative function, then the education of the party's women and juniors, relatively 'underdeveloped' sectors of the party membership, might pay high dividends. He also suggested that remits might be weeded out and consolidated more than they were in 1954 and that a committee system could be used profitably. Changes of this kind have since been made. Paradoxically, however, by helping to convey the image of a 'business-like' Conference, such changes may have the effect of creating a distinct impression of a gap between appearance and reality in policy-making—a gap which Kelson, mistakenly, thought already existed.

[1] Kelson, *Political Science*, vol. vi, no. 2, art. cit., pp. 19–20.

[2] Although there was one delegate in 1963 who referred with approval to the view that Conference was the governing body of the National Party (*Evening Post*, 23 July 1963).

IX

CANDIDATE SELECTION

FOR the immediate purpose of winning an election the choice of a candidate hardly matters. In New Zealand and elsewhere electors have sometimes voted for candidates of the lowest calibre imaginable. They will continue to vote for such candidates, because in many countries with a fully developed party system the personal vote is now negligible, and most electors vote for the party, not the man. Nevertheless, the choice of parliamentary candidates is an important enough matter to deserve a short chapter to itself.

In the first place, although a party may be able to 'carry' some low-grade candidates who become Members of Parliament, there is a limit to the number it can support with safety. The quality of the men who represent a party in Parliament matters a great deal in the long run. If it is low, measured against the standards set by *other* parties, or by the expectations of the electors, the party's public image will deteriorate. Further, when the party becomes the Government, it will be without a sufficient reservoir of talent to fill the most important ministerial jobs. Even from the point of view of securing his own re-election, the work of a member *over a period* may make the difference between a lively organization in the electorate and a moribund one, which may in time be reflected in the votes cast for him and his party. As in the 1963 general election, assiduous attention to constituents by a sitting member may even be rewarded by an increased majority.

But candidate selection is also of importance, not just because it is necessary to obtain good candidates, but because it is also essential to devise good *methods* for choosing good candidates. This is relevant in order to secure party unity and ensure maximum participation by the members in party activities. If the methods of candidate selection are demonstrably fair and efficient, then non-successful aspirants to be candidates will be the more likely to accept their results. If party members are brought into the selection process, interest in all aspects of the party's work is stimulated. In one respect at least, proceedings within the party become more democratic and less oligarchical. 'A system for selecting candidates is, therefore, not a mere contrivance for preventing party dissensions, but an essential feature of matured democracy.'[1]

History of Candidate Selection

Before 1890, and very often after then, the parties had no regular procedures for candidate selection. In each electorate small groups of notables put forward a candidate. Some of these candidates announced that they supported a certain party or its Leader, or the Leader might announce that he supported them. The first attempt at imposing rules for selection came from the Liberals, and was stimulated by the large number of 'Liberal' candidates, sometimes several for one seat, who offered themselves at elections after 1890 in the hope that they could mount the Liberal bandwagon. To meet this threat an official list of Liberal candidates was published in the *New Zealand Times* and reproduced in other newspapers,[2] and candidates were required to pledge themselves to vote with the Government on all motions of no confidence.[3] The real choice between candidates and the real power of conferring the designation 'official' lay with Seddon.[4] A little-known story about Seddon concerns the method he once used for 'choosing' among six rivals for a Liberal nomination. Seddon arranged for the five who were intended to be *unsuccessful* to be present on the platform at a rally in the constituency. Without notice he called on all five to speak in succession. All were unprepared, and all gave a pitiful performance. Seddon then announced the choice of the *sixth*, who had been deliberately kept away from the meeting, as the official Liberal candidate.[5]

When the Liberal and Labour Federation was formed, the procedure was standardized. Branch meetings were held to vote for the parliamentary candidate. But the final decision was the

[1] Dr. Findlay, *Report of Proceedings of the Conference of Delegates of the Liberal and Labour Federation of New Zealand 1903*, p. 20, quoting Bryce.

[2] Foster, 'Development of Unity and Organization in the New Zealand Political Parties of the Liberal Era' (thesis), p. 83.   [3] Ibid., p. 109.

[4] Ibid., pp. 85-90; Burdon, *King Dick*, pp. 132-3. Ward continued this function; see Foster, op. cit., p. 240.

[5] Interview, Mr. T. E. Y. Seddon, Dec. 1958.

Executive's, in fact Seddon's. 'The Executive, after consultation with the Branch of each electorate, shall select the candidate for each such electorate.'[1] As the secretary of the Federation remarked, many 'branch meetings' had been 'packed' in the past, and were only candidate's committees using the Federation's name.[2] To prevent such abuses, some central control was necessary. In 1908 and 1911 the problem of multiple candidates was eased by the introduction of the Second Ballot.[3] But even then the Leader might have to intervene after the First Ballot to determine who should stand down at the Second.[4]

On candidate selection, as on many other aspects of organization, E. E. Vaile of the Reform Party favoured schemes to secure widespread participation by his party's supporters. He wished to end the 'system', prevalent in the early years of the century, by which a small party committee in the electorate selected the candidate. Vaile proposed that there should be a general meeting of all supporters to choose a committee, which would then choose the candidate. In this way there would be some weight of support behind a Reform Party candidate, whereas, at the time of writing, Vaile had met people who disputed that McLean was *the* Opposition candidate (for Parnell), and wanted to know who made up 'the party' that chose him. However, in Vaile's scheme, while there would be meetings to choose candidates, the final decision would be made by the Central Committee of the electorate 'in conjunction with the Provincial Executive and the Leader of the Party'.[5] There was no provision about the choice of candidates in the 1912 Reform Party Constitution, and Massey was apparently opposed to any moves to place the power of choice in the hands of the branches.[6]

Before 1914 Vaile's system of candidate selection was put into operation in the Waikato.[7] But the whole Reform organization

[1] *Constitution of the Liberal and Labour Federation of New Zealand, 1903,*
[2] *Report of Proceedings of the Conference of Delegates of the Liberal and Labour Federation of New Zealand, 1903,* p. 10.
[3] See p. 33, above.   [4] Foster, op. cit., p. 240.
[5] Vaile to Massey, 29 June 1905; Vaile to Massey, 14 Jan. 1906; 'Suggestions by E. E. Vaile', (Vaile MSS., Auckland Public Library). Details vary in these manuscripts. But two points are clear: large meetings were to be held to indicate preferences for a candidate; there was to be approval of the choice higher up in the hierarchy, either by the Leader or by the central executive.
[6] Gardner, *Political Science*, vol. xiii, no. 2, art. cit., p. 20.
[7] Graham, *Waikato Politics*, pp. 188 ff.

was disrupted during the war, and the attempts to build it up again afterwards, in accordance with Vaile's specifications, were not wholly successful. In the 1920's there seems to have been a considerable contrast between the method by which Reform candidates were *supposed* to be chosen and the way in which the choice was actually made. The *Newsletter* went to great lengths to describe the system, on the occasions when it operated. For instance, in 1924 in the Waikato the polling booths in the electorate were divided among twenty-one areas. Party organizers addressed previously advertised meetings in each of these areas, and the meetings elected delegates on the basis of one for every fifty votes cast for Reform at the previous election. The delegates then met in a selection conference, and chose the candidate after the contenders had signed a pledge to accept the choice and had each addressed the conference for ten minutes and answered questions.[1] Driven by the desire to avoid the vote being split by rival 'Reform' candidates, as it had been in 1922, the party laid great reliance on local 'democracy' in selection. The Chairman of the Party's Organization Committee said in one electorate, 'The finding of a suitable candidate is your job, not ours; and subject to certain pledges which our rules demand, the man or woman who will satisfy the electors will satisfy our party. When the day arrives that our party or any other party throws upon an electorate a candidate of an executive's choosing, then the days of constitutional Government, for which we stand, are gone.'[2]

These efforts were successful in preventing multiple Reform candidates at the 1925 elections. But the selection system did not always work 'democratically'. Sometimes complaints were made that meetings at which delegates were chosen were packed and had not been properly advertised.[3] Piecing together a number of accounts it seems to have been quite usual, even in the 1920's, for the candidate to be chosen by a small number of prominent local people. In at least one instance the new candidate was chosen by the retiring Reform M.P. and the provincial

[1] *Newsletter*, 31 July 1924, p. 11. The procedure is also described in *Hints and Instructions to Branch Secretaries and Committees* (Political Reform League, 1928), pp. 14 ff.; *Constitution and Rules of the Political Reform League*, p. 18.

[2] *Newsletter*, 31 July 1925, p. 12.

[3] Ibid., 29 Nov. 1924, 27 Mar. 1926, 30 June 1926; Robinson, *The Rise of the New Zealand National Party*, p. 44.

organizer of the party. Sometimes Massey may have influenced the choice of a candidate, but the stereotype of him as holding a series of one-man selection meetings on railway platforms does not seem to be justified. He was often obliged to choose some local notable, whose views he disliked, in order to avoid a Liberal or Labour victory.[1] Finally, in the Reform Party there was never any question of a sitting member having to submit himself for re-selection by a meeting of delegates.[2]

Chapman[3] has suggested that there was a difference between town and country in the use of the selective ballot. In the Reform Party in the country, where support was high, the selective ballot was likely to be used. But in the towns the Leader, or the Dominion Executive, was more likely to make the nomination. In the Liberal Party, on the other hand, where the party's strength was greater in the towns, it was there that 'democratic' selection was more widely practised.[4]

Selection in the National Party

Allowing for some exaggerated contrasts, the 'irregularities' of candidate selection in the Reform Party are confirmed by the National Party's subsequent criticism of the 'old' methods. In the new party there would be no more nominations by a small team in Wellington or elsewhere.[5] 'They had seen many mistakes made by a strong leader nominating a candidate.'[6] It is easy to discern a note of surprise in the Wellington Division's comment, in 1937, that the new rules on selection really had to be obeyed. 'Since the Party is governed by the Constitution adopted by the May Conference in 1936 it appears that the rule to advertise for nominations will have to be adhered to, and if there should be more than one nomination received a ballot will be necessary. The meeting confirmed by general consent that the rule would have to be carried out.'[7]

The main difference between candidate selection in the

---

[1] Gardner, *Political Science*, vol. xiii, no. 2, art. cit., p. 24.
[2] *Hints and Instructions to Branch Secretaries and Committees*, p. 14.
[3] Chapman, *The Significance of the 1928 General Election*, p. 32.
[4] Ibid.; interview, Mr. T. E. Y. Seddon, Dec. 1958.
[5] S. G. Holland, *Manawatu Standard*, 5 Mar. 1937.
[6] J. A. Hargest, *Southland Times*, 27 May 1938.
[7] Wellington Divisional Committee, *Minutes of second meeting*, 10 Mar. 1937. Even in 1931 and 1935 the Coalition did not have a standard procedure for selection (Robinson, *The Rise of the New Zealand National Party*, p. 44).

National Party and in the Reform Party apparently lay not in the existence of well drafted rules, but in the fact that the National Party rules were consistently applied. To some extent the leadership of the new party may have seen the 1935 election as a repetition of the 1905 and 1922 elections, with the Democrat candidates playing the disruptive role that unofficial Reform candidates had previously played in creating a 'split vote'. So after 1935 the aim was to gather all anti-Labour supporters and potential candidates into the one party. This was only a version of what Vaile had proposed, revised to meet the circumstances of the time. But there was one notable change. Vaile had wanted to link 'participation' and candidate selection together. But the National Party stressed the nature and the value of the link between the two constituted by *membership* of the party. Whereas the delegates for candidate selection in the Reform Party had been chosen by *supporters*, in the National Party only *members* could take part in the process.[1] Hence the emphasis on mass membership in the National Party.

The system for candidate selection is laid down in great detail in the National Party's *Constitution and Rules*.[2] Indeed the section on this is longer and more elaborate than that on any other topic. It is impossible to reproduce all the provisions, but a few may be mentioned. Selection is made locally, in the electorate, subject to there being 2,000 financial (paid-up) members. If there are not, Dominion Council's approval for local selection must be obtained. The Electorate Committee must give at least two weeks' notice for nominations to be handed in. It is not hard to be nominated; one need only be a financial member of the party (and not ineligible to be an M.P.) and be proposed by at least ten other financial members. The nomination form also contains the candidate's pledge to observe the party rules, be loyal to the organization and the Leader, work for the candidate selected, and, if unsuccessful in the selection, not to stand in the electorate in question or for any other electorate unless duly selected by the National Party. After the closing date for nominations candidates require the prior consent of the Electorate Committee or its executive before they attend and address

[1] Robinson, ibid., pp. 22–23.
[2] 97–129. For the evolution of the system since 1936, see Robinson, *Oligarchy and Democracy*, pp. 27–28.

meetings of the party or make use of any other form of publicity. The nomination papers are sent to Division along with biographical and other notes, and then to Dominion Council with Division's recommendations. Council then approves or (very rarely) disapproves of the nominations. It acts through an 'emergency committee' consisting of members of the Dominion Executive available in the Wellington area. 'The Selection Committee shall comprise the members for the time being of the Electorate Committee, together with such additional members, if any, as may be necessary to ensure that each Branch shall be represented on the Selection Committee by one member . . . for every complete 20 . . . qualified members and 1 further representative for a fraction thereof over 10.'[1] With permission from Division, a city electorate may choose all its delegates at a single general meeting. The selection committee is called together by the Electorate Committee, with provisions for a certain amount of notice. The chairman of the meeting is named by the Electorate Committee; often they choose the divisional chairman. All the contenders give an address, at least for ten minutes or longer as decided by the meeting, in an order determined by drawing lots. Voting is secret and by preferential ballot.[2] The delegates are to have a 'free hand' in exercising their votes, that is, they are not to come to the meeting already pledged.[3] But usually a 'little informal plugging' is done, and there is a natural tendency for delegates to support candidates from their own part of the electorate.

An alternative possibility is that the Electorate Committee, with the approval of Division, will choose to have a postal ballot. This is a more expensive procedure than the other, and is used in only two or three electorates at each general election. Sometimes a postal ballot is held in a large rural electorate, where it is difficult to assemble a selection committee. Another reason for using it might be the desire of the 'outlying' branches in an electorate which was dominated by a large town to prevent the

[1] *Constitution and Rules (1963)*, rule 114. The use of the Electorate Committee as a basis for the Selection Committee dates only from 1962.

[2] In the Reform Party the second ballot had been used (*Hints and Instructions to Branch Secretaries and Committees*, p. 17).

[3] *Constitution and Rules (1963)*, rule 121. For a comparison with different Australian methods of selection, see Overacker, *The Australian Party System*, pp. 251–5 and 102–7.

delegates from that town being 'captured' by one of the candidates.[1] A problem when the postal ballot is employed is to provide the members with some evidence about the ability of the candidates. One way of ensuring this is to hold meetings at central points in the electorate, at which all the candidates give an address. Instead of this, or in addition, biographical notes on all candidates may be circulated, along with photographs.

At some selection committee meetings four or five ballots may be necessary. In spite of local loyalties and preconceived ideas on voting, speeches can sometimes make a difference and may result in a win by an outsider. It is easier to give examples of how to make bad speeches than to say how to make good ones. It is a mistake to be 'too theatrical', to quote too many figures, or, with rare exceptions, to attempt humour. One candidate at a selection meeting, who had done some publicity work for the party, managed to convey the impression that he was being merely 'slick' when he 'dragged' religion into his speech. In fact he was deeply religious and an active church worker. At another meeting a candidate 'ranted', and addressed himself mainly to the people at the back of the hall. Unfortunately for him, they were not delegates but only 'observers' who did not have any vote to cast in the selection. In rural areas non-farmers, especially if they are 'foreigners' (that is are not local), have a hard row to hoe. In the last few years such rural electorates as Hauraki, Patea, and Wallace have selected men who were not farmers. But Duverger's generalization that in country areas lawyers are usually chosen as parliamentary representatives in preference to farmers[2] certainly does not apply to New Zealand. Indeed one lawyer, who had been selected for a rural seat and had been attacked as a non-farmer and an outsider, had to defend himself by saying that he had a distinct rural bias and had never lost touch with his birthplace in the electorate, although he had lived outside it for sixteen years.[3]

On the whole the system of selection has worked well, although occasionally there are disputes arising from allegations of faulty procedure, for instance in Mid-Canterbury in 1938[4] and Clutha

[1] Kelson, *Political Science*, vol. vi, no. 2, art. cit., p. 28.
[2] Duverger, op. cit., p. 158.
[3] Clifton Webb (*North Auckland Times*, 1 Sept. 1943).
[4] *Ashburton Guardian*, 2 July 1938 and 21 July 1938.

in 1957.[1] Another possible source of friction occurs when Dominion Council exercises its right to disapprove of a candidate. This does not often occur. When it does, the reason for disapproval is nearly always personal rather than ideological.[2] The National Party is strict on 'immorality', on those who have been in trouble with the police, or who are in trouble with the income-tax authorities. Disapproval need not be exercised formally; a candidate may be given, and will amost invariably take, a hint to withdraw. In one of the four cities a candidate was found to be living 'immorally' only after he had been selected, but at an interview he was still persuaded to withdraw. Usually candidates who are disapproved of 'go quietly'. Sometimes they do not. Mr. Vallance who had been selected for Marsden in 1954, but was then asked to withdraw because of his income-tax difficulties, stood for Marsden all the same as an Independent candidate. 'Local selection', therefore, really is *local*. There is hardly any interference from Dominion Council or any other part of the central organization. To say that in the National Party the choice of candidates is 'laid down from above' is ludicrously inaccurate.[3] On the contrary, a more reasonable complaint might be that there is *too little* central control, and that it is hard for 'the centre' to raise the quality of candidates (and consequently of M.P.s and ministers) without offending local susceptibilities. Something can be done along these lines, but it must not be attempted directly. For instance, if a President of the party were to make an open pronouncement in favour of a certain man as candidate for an electorate, there would be a tremendous uproar in the name of 'local autonomy'. But, if a President were to hear good reports about a possible candidate, he might encourage him, unofficially, to enter the selection ballot, and tell the local organization that, in his opinion, this was a man worth seeing and hearing. This would be as much as a President, or any other high official in the party, could do. From then on it would be up to the candidate himself to show what he was worth. There may also be *local* efforts to persuade men of high quality to enter the selection ballot, without any

[1] *Truth*, 3 Sept., 1957.
[2] Unlike the opposition by constituency associations to several British Conservative M.P.s after Suez. See Leon D. Epstein, 'British M.P.s and Their Local Parties: The Suez Cases', *American Political Science Review*, vol. liv, no. 2, 1960.
[3] Asubel, *The Fern and the Tiki*, p. 127.

guarantee that they will be successful. In some seats informal approaches on behalf of the Electorate Committee are made to possible candidates to ask them if they would like to be considered.

The selection procedure outlined above was not followed in any of the four Maori seats before 1948. Previously selection was made on an informal basis.[1] But since then the procedure has tended increasingly to follow the same lines as in the European electorates.[2] An exception occurred at the 1962 Eastern Maori by-election when the three intending candidates addressed a meeting of 300 Maoris,[3] and the winner was chosen by a group of elders.

In the National Party, unlike the Reform Party, there are constitutional provisions for removing a sitting member. Until 1962, if a meeting of the Electorate Committee (held after fourteen days' notice) did not confirm a sitting member in his candidature, then, subject to the consent of Division and the Dominion Council, he was bound to enter the selection process on the same basis as any other person who wanted to become the candidate.[4] This was in sharp contrast to previous procedures, particularly those employed in 1931 and 1935 when the sitting members were automatically endorsed,[5] as the simplest way of deciding whether the Coalition candidate should be ex-United or ex-Reform. Originally in the National Party the initiative for requiring the member to submit himself for re-selection lay with the Divisional Committee.[6] But in 1941 a change of rules transferred the initiative to the Electorate Committee.[7] Almost immediately there was a test case in Remuera, where there had been previous agitation that the M.P., Endean, should submit his name to a ballot.[8] Some of the 1941 proceedings in Remuera did not follow the rules very closely. The Leader, apparently without any constitutional basis, made a statement that he, the parliamentary party and the President of the party supported Endean.[9] It was then decided to hold a

[1] North, op. cit., p. 30.
[2] e.g. in Northern Maori in 1957 (*Otago Daily Times*, 25 Nov. 1957).
[3] *Evening Post*, 14 Oct. 1962.
[4] *Constitution and Rules (1960)*, rule 98.
[5] Robinson, *The Rise of the New Zealand National Party*, p. 43.
[6] Ibid., p. 41.   [7] Ibid., p. 228.
[8] *Auckland Star*, 22 July 1941.   [9] *Dominion*, 2 Aug. 1941.

ballot among the other five prospective candidates.[1] But this was then changed to a postal ballot simply giving members the choice of voting for or against Endean. In the event of his defeat, nominations were to be called for again. The result was that 2,068 postal ballots were sent out, and, in a 60 per cent. poll, Endean had a majority of 676–563.[2] Endean's victory, and candidature, were solemnly confirmed at a meeting of the electorate committee which was attended by the Leader and the President,[3] and the anti-Endean men on the Remuera committee resigned.[4] But, in spite of the procedural oddities, the new principle which ended the 'perpetual mortgage' of sitting members was established. It was also given practical expression in 1943. When Endean was overseas, nominations were called for and a National candidate was selected. Endean, on his return, rejected this candidate's offer to go to a ballot of party members in the electorate and announced that he would stand as an Independent, but withdrew before polling-day.[5]

Since then there has been a number of instances of sitting members having to face re-selection. The provision is invoked mostly against older members who 'hang on too long'. Its existence, even without its actually being applied, has to be taken into account by members when they consider their time of retirement. National Party electorate committees are regarded by Labour Party officials as being rather ruthless with the older members. Perhaps some toughness may be needed; there is now no upper house to which elderly members can be elevated. However, from the point of view of finance, the existence of a pension fund softens the blow of retirement for any member who has been long enough in Parliament to benefit substantially from it.

The decision to ask a sitting member to submit himself for re-selection was entirely the electorate's before 1962. Any interference 'from above' would have been strongly resented. In 1957 the Franklin electorate, after a ballot, decided to adopt a younger candidate instead of Mr. J. N. Massey, M.P., aged 72, son of a former Prime Minister, who had been a member for twenty-six years. The Prime Minister, Holland, expressed

[1] *Evening Post*, 15 Aug. 1941.   [2] *New Zealand Herald*, 3 Sept. 1941.
[3] *Dominion*, 8 Sept. 1941.   [4] Ibid., 2 Oct. 1941.
[5] Robinson, *The Rise of the New Zealand National Party*, p. 230.

personal regret at losing Massey as a colleague, but at the same
time said that the provision in the party's rules under which
Massey had been dropped 'was a big contribution to its large
voluntary membership for the reason that people felt that
membership gave them an intimate first-hand contact with the
running of the party'.[1]

On the occasion of boundary changes (normally every five
years), new electorate committees have to be chosen, and automatically, even before 1962, there had to be a selection ballot.
If the changes were minor, the sitting member for the old
electorate usually found it easy to be nominated for the new one.
Sometimes, however, the 'obvious choice' was outmanoeuvred,
as Mr. Sheat was for Egmont in 1954. The effects of redistribution could be very serious for individual members; and
especially for ministers, whose ministerial career could be
imperilled. Therefore redistribution may lead to jockeying for
position, especially in the towns where natural boundaries and
community of interest are not very clearly defined. The successful efforts of Mr. Watts, Minister of Finance, to move from St.
Albans (made distinctly unsafe by redistribution) to Fendalton
in 1957 are a good example of this.[2] From 1962 onwards the
rules removed the special provisions about the candidature of
a sitting member. Now he is in the same position as any other
contender, from the purely formal point of view. In practice,
it will continue to be comparatively rare for a sitting member
to be challenged, although he will probably still be especially
vulnerable when substantial boundary changes are made.

Another important change which followed the formation of
the National Party concerns a candidate's contributions to expenses. Before 1938 a Reform candidate was himself usually
responsible for the bulk of the election expenses,[3] although sometimes he might persuade one or two wealthy supporters to make
contributions. The average cost of fighting an election in the
1920's was perhaps between £200 and £300 per seat, an M.P.'s
pay at this time being £300 a year.[4] The situation did not change
immediately in the new National Party. Some candidates were

[1] *Evening Post*, 30 July 1957.   [2] Ibid., 23, 27, and 28 Aug. 1957.
[3] Robinson, *The Rise of the New Zealand National Party*, p. 67; interview, Theo
Hills, Oct. 1958. In the Liberal Party, however, some less well-off candidates received financial help regularly (interview, Mr. T. E. Y. Seddon, Dec. 1958).
[4] Lipson, *The Politics of Equality*, p. 328.

given financial help in 1938, but the National Party had not yet raised sufficient money to pay most of the expenses of all its candidates. According to a former National Party official who had been a divisional secretary, in 1935 nearly all the National candidates paid most of their expenses; in 1938 they still paid, except for a few who 'squealed'; by 1943 or 1946 only about 15 per cent. of the candidates in his division paid any substantial amount.[1] Even today, of course, candidates continue to pay, in loss of time, in use of their own car, and through hospitality, even when their expenses are 'paid'.

Selection in the Labour Party

By a curious contrast the Labour Party, which is committed to 'democracy' in the formulation of policy, has moved *away* from the democratic selection of candidates. Up to 1951 the general rule was that selection was made by postal ballot of the members of each LRC, although the names had to be taken from a list of persons who had satisfied the LRC of their suitability, and the names had to be approved by the national executive. The final choice made at the selection ballot could be reviewed and finally determined by the national executive, if it were appealed to by an LRC.[2] In rare cases the national executive exercised a veto; for example, because of a police record. But even during this period there were exceptions which constituted restrictions on local choice. For the 1935 election the national executive added 'a number of able younger men, many of whom were outside the trade union field', and Conference voted the executive 'full power' to determine selections not yet made.[3] In 1946, also, candidates were selected by the national executive after consultation with a selection committee of five from the LRC. This procedure was decided on because the late revision of the electoral boundaries for the 1946 election did not leave much time for the use of selection ballots.[4]

At by-elections selections were always made by the national

---

[1] Interview, Theo Hills, Oct. 1958. This change is confirmed by Mr. Alex. Gordon (interview, Oct. 1958) and by Robinson (*The Rise of the New Zealand National Party*, p. 67). However, Robinson believes that the main change took place in 1938 rather than later.

[2] *Constitution with LRC, Branch Rules and Standing Orders (1937)*, p. 24.

[3] Overacker, *American Political Science Review*, art. cit., p. 720.

[4] *Tribune*, 15 Dec. 1945.

executive, although only after the National Secretary or other persons from Labour headquarters had visited the electorate to consult the LRC, hear the opinions of party members expressed at meetings,[1] and sometimes even listen to addresses by the candidates.[2] After one selection by the national executive, an LRC fulsomely expressed 'its appreciation of the opportunity of consulting with the National Secretary as the representative of the National Executive'[3] on the selection. This expression of gratitude for having been listened to does not suggest that the LRC had any strong feelings in favour of local autonomy in selection.

Furthermore, final approval by the national executive was not a mere formality. After a minister had failed to secure re-nomination for his seat in 1941, a Labour spokesman explained that when a ballot was taken for a seat not held by Labour, it was usual for the national executive to endorse the LRC's choice. But this might not happen if a Labour minister held the seat. Headquarters might use its discretion in such a case on the ground that to disregard his claims would be to strike a blow at the party's prestige.[4]

So there were many exceptions to local autonomy in candidate selection even before 1951. The usual system was also criticized on several counts. The majority of the party members entitled to take part in the selection process were trade-unionists. But the records of the addresses of unionists were incomplete and inaccurate. Consequently voting figures were low. In one postal ballot (a procedure that was used quite often) only 378 members out of about 2,000 cast their votes.[5] The system was therefore not outstandingly 'democratic', in view of the low proportion of members voting and the opportunities it offered for strong and active trade-union secretaries to mobilize the vote of their unions and so determine the results. A further defect which was often complained of was that not all the trade-unionists who had a vote in making selections were Labour Party supporters. After

[1] At the Christchurch South by-election, 1939 (*Press*, 8 May 1939; *Standard*, 11 May 1939).
[2] *New Zealand Herald*, 12 Apr. 1940 and 22 Apr. 1940.
[3] *Standard*, 11 May 1939.
[4] *Auckland Star*, 27 June 1941. The minister in question was renominated for the 1943 election, the '1941 election' having been postponed.
[5] Overacker, *American Political Science Review*, art. cit., p. 719.

compulsory unionism was introduced many unionists were non-political or even right-wing. On the other hand, some were Communists or fellow travellers. This defect may easily be exaggerated. It would have required a considerable degree of organization by non-Labour Party trade-unionists for them to determine a result, and their efforts would probably have been sufficiently obvious for successful counter measures to have been taken.

After 1951 the system was that nominations could be made by any six party members within the electorate. Any person nominated had to sign a pledge to support duly elected party candidates, not to withdraw, if selected, without the consent of the national executive, and, if elected, to vote as the majority of the members of the Parliamentary Labour Party decides. The choice of the candidate is made by a committee of six, three members of the national executive and three appointed by the LRC. Since 1956 in multiple LRCs the three LRC appointees have been chosen by delegates from the electorate concerned.[1] For the 1963 election the latter were chosen at a meeting of the LRC held immediately before the selection meeting. The three from the national executive almost always include the President and the Secretary. In 1957 the third, where practicable, was the Divisional Area Representative, with the Vice-President acting as a 'reserve' in case one of the three were not available. In choosing the candidate the selection committee is not limited to persons who have been nominated. In two instances in 1951 the committee made a choice from outside this list.[2] If the committee cannot agree, the national executive decides on the candidate. At particular elections the committee of six has adopted different procedures. In 1951 and 1954 the persons nominated were interviewed by the selection committee of six and questions were put to them. In 1957 and since then all the prospective candidates, in succession, give a brief address to a meeting of members of the LRC.[3] The selection committee attends, and, after the addresses, its members retire and choose the candidate. Usually the choice is announced to the meeting. If there is a 3–3

[1] *Constitution and Rules* (*1955*), 21 (e), as amended at the Fortieth Annual Conference, 1956.

[2] Overacker, *American Political Science Review*, art. cit., p. 720.

[3] *Constitution and Rules* (*1955*), 21 (f), as amended at the Fortieth Annual Conference, 1956. A similar system had been tried in some seats in 1954.

split, a secret ballot is taken of those present at the meeting to guide the committee in its choice. If there is still a deadlock, the committee refers the matter to the national executive which makes the final decision. This present system takes a long time. It is also 'less searching' than the previous system of interview, because some prospective candidates have their addresses written for them. However, there is often some informal vetting, on the day of the meeting, when the selection committee meet the prospective candidates for a drink. This gives a good opportunity for 'dropping questions on them', and seeing how they talk without a prepared script. Members of the committee are also often approached, or 'phoned up, by people who want to give information, usually unfavourable, about one of the candidates. 'If something is wrong with one of the candidates someone will tell you pretty soon.'[1]

Some alterations in the system were approved at the 1963 Conference. Basically they consisted in having a pool of candidates and in the division of seats into two categories: seats capable of being won by Labour together with those already held by Labour; and the remainder. The intention was that candidates for the former category of seats would be selected first—over a year before the election. Candidates could be drawn from the pool to fight these 'winnable seats' and must be prepared to work in the electorate for a period of at least twelve months before the election. However, the scheme was not put into effect in 1963.

Criticism is most often heard, not of changes since 1957, but of the major change in 1951, by which the national executive was given such a prominent voice in selection. Certainly, in talking of candidate selection, members of the national executive who have taken part in it have sometimes used phrases such as 'I offered seat X to A', or 'We moved B to seat Y'. From time to time remits come up at Labour Party Conferences aimed at diminishing the power of the national executive in this respect, for instance, by increasing the number of LRC representatives to four or by providing that in case of a split between the three national executive members and the three LRC members, the decision should be made by the LRC and the branches and not by the national executive.

[1] Interview, Mr. M. Moohan, Oct. 1958.

More specifically, discontent has been expressed in some electorates on the ground that the national executive representatives can 'impose their man' if they want to, and that they have sometimes 'shoved in' their organizers. A related complaint is that national executive representatives in selecting candidates try to keep out vital or unorthodox personalities who might be difficult for the executive or the parliamentary party to handle. Certainly the procedure will not work well if either group of three has its mind made up rigidly in advance. More cynically, an alternative rule might be that the national executive representatives should not *appear* to have their minds made up in advance. Splits of 3–3, with the national executive representatives aligned against the LRC representatives, are very rare. In one case where such a split occurred all six members of the selection committee went before the national executive (less the three members who were on the committee) and were heard one by one over a period of several hours. The final decision upheld the view of the three national executive members of the committee. But the decision does not always go that way. A rather strange case occurred in 1960. After a 3–3 split (LRC representatives on one side, national executive members on the other) the audience at the meeting voted in favour of the same candidate as the national executive members. But, although one might have thought that this vote would have had considerable persuasive authority, the *full* national executive decided in favour of the LRC representatives' choice.

The extent of the changes caused by the new procedure since 1951 should not be exaggerated. The type of candidate chosen is much the same. Nor has the role of the national executive greatly altered, because even before 1951 it had considerable influence over selections. The story is told, for example, that when H. E. Holland died in 1933 his son, who had been active in the Labour Party, was informed at the funeral, by his father's colleagues, that he could have a safe seat any time he wanted one. Indeed, from some aspects, it is desirable that the national executive should play some part in selection. On some occasions *none* of the candidates nominated locally is of even the minimum calibre necessary, and someone has to be found from outside. But, if the decision were left to the LRC, for reasons of local pride or from lack of knowledge of what outside people were available, it might insist on putting forward its 'best' man. National executive intervention and co-ordination is also helpful in dealing with the problems resulting from multiple candidacies. Some people, including organizers, may be nominated for more than one seat. If the executive has a say in selections it may be able to produce a better pattern of nominations than if the LRCs were left to make uncoordinated free choices.

It was remarked above that the party had no official policy of attempting to 'place' its organizers in Parliament with a view to raising the quality of its M.P.s.[1] However, if it recognizes a promising man the national executive can make suggestions to him about likely routes to Parliament. A Labour candidate who was defeated a few years ago, says that he had the following proposals put to him. He was offered a headquarters organizer's job, which would be an avenue to finding a seat; he could move to a particular city and let the LRC consider him for one of the likely seats in that city; he could move to one of three towns, all marginally held by the National Party, with the prospect of receiving the national executive's backing when the time for selection came.

It is very unusual for a sitting member not to be re-selected. The Labour Party is more tender towards its veterans than the National Party, possibly because they are more likely to be completely dependent on their parliamentary salary or pension. While he was Prime Minister Fraser denied an allegation that the party was considering ousting some of the older parliamentary members. 'It would be a scandalous thing, alien to the Labour movement and its idealism and spirit, if we were to say that some person who had given his whole life to it and helped to lay the foundations of its success should be thrown aside solely because of old age. I should never be a party to that—never.'[2] Sometimes the party does put its foot down, although not in a brutal way. A few years ago, after the introduction of the '1951 system', there were some doubts about the re-selection of a member, partly on grounds of age (with the possibility of a by-election in a marginal seat if he died suddenly), partly because he had not been very active. However, the national executive sympathetically decided that he could stay 'until he got a few more bob in the pension fund', but made him sign a pledge that he

[1] See pp. 188–90, above. [2] Thorn, *Peter Fraser*, p. 229.

would not stand again in three years' time. After the three years were up the pledge was enforced.

As in the National Party, boundary changes may result in a sitting member's not being reselected. Sometimes the loss may not be too deeply felt by the party. An obvious example of this was the non-selection of Mr. Kearins for the 'new' version of his 'old' electorate after the boundary changes in 1954.[1] On the other hand, boundary changes may result in a game of 'musical chairs' in which an unobjectionable M.P. may find himself without a seat. A situation of this type was resolved in the Auckland area in 1963 only by the death of Mr. Hackett shortly before the election, thus creating one more vacancy.

It is quite common for a Labour candidate who has lost an election to be offered a second, or even a third, chance, sometimes for a 'better' seat. Six out of the ten Labour members elected for the first time in 1954, had fought and lost previous elections. It is comparatively rare for a National candidate to 'progress' from a hopeless seat to a safe seat at a later election. But Labour members who have lost their seats are not often reselected for safe seats, although Mr. Nordmeyer, who lost Oamaru in 1949 and returned to Parliament as a member for Brooklyn in 1951, is an outstanding exception. Dr. A. M. Finlay had to wait from 1949 until 1963.

The New Zealand Labour Party, which in its early days was almost exclusively a working-class and trade-union movement, has now become more middle-class. The proportion of its votes which come from trade-unionists has declined, although financially it is still largely dependent on the unions. As was seen in Chapter I, this shift has been accompanied by a decline in the proportion of Labour M.P.s who may be classified under the headings of 'workman' or 'trade-union secretary'. Although no statistical calculations have been made on the subject, it is evident that there has also been a drop in the proportion of trade-union *candidates* over the last thirty or forty years. There was some reaction against this in the late 1940's and early 1950's, just as there has been against corresponding trends in Britain.[2] The National Council of the Federation of Labour in 1947 had urged the nomination and selection of Parliamentary Labour candi-

[1] See p. 142, above.
[2] M. Harrison, *Trade Unions and the Labour Party since 1945*, p. 270.

dates 'with a Trade Union background and a working-class understanding.'[1] At the Federation of Labour Conference of 1951, held while the industrial dispute of '151 days' was in existence, affiliates were requested to give support in the selection of parliamentary candidates to those who had co-operated in furthering the policy of the New Zealand FOL. It was explained by the FOL Secretary that in the waterfront dispute some representatives of the Parliamentary Labour Party had not co-operated with the FOL.[2] Later in 1951 there was even some possibility of 'industrial' candidates being put forward in competition with ordinary Labour Party candidates. Trade-union grievances, according to 'a group of trade unionists', were that trade-unionists as such had no voice in the selection; the quality of the candidates selected was unsatisfactory, and most were business men; the attitude of Labour politicians to the Federation of Labour and those industrial leaders loyal to the FOL was disliked; Labour was not vigorous enough against the Communists.[3] The timing of the discontent is significant. It occurred when the Labour Party leadership, in the opinion of the FOL and the right-wing unions, was not willing to provide sufficiently determined opposition to the militants. After the militants were smashed by the National Government in 1951, the discontent, and the agitation that more industrialists should be chosen as candidates, died down. An intelligent view of the situation was expressed in conversation by a leading trade-unionist. Direct union representation in Parliament is not so important. Maybe it is necessary to have new types of Labour members in the House in order to attract middle-class votes, although some trade-unionists may feel envious towards others who have the chance of leading the glamorous life of an M.P. But, in general, the trade-union leaders are willing to accept the existing situation, so long as the Labour Party's policy is agreeable to them. Trade-union sponsorship of candidates at constituency level has raised acute problems in Britain.[4] Some candidates have been selected principally because of the financial backing given them by wealthy unions. But in New Zealand this type of influence is less evident at constituency level. At the national level,

[1] *Minutes and Report of the Fourteenth Annual Conference of the New Zealand Federation of Labour*, 1951, p. 9. [2] Dick Scott, *151 Days*, pp. 126–7. [3] *Evening Post*, 25 July 1951. [4] M. Harrison, op. cit., ch. vi.

trade-union campaign contributions make up by far the greatest part of the funds available for fighting elections. But, at electorate level, a prospective candidate sponsored by a union which may make a large contribution does not seem, *ipso facto*, to obtain a great advantage over his rivals. The power which the national executive wields in the selection process may be one important reason why pressures at the local level are less important.

The Labour alliance with Ratana did not stipulate that all Labour candidates for Maori seats must belong to the Ratana Church, although some Ratana leaders have insisted that it did. There is, however, a strong presumption that these candidates will be Ratana. It is said that on the death of M. Ratana (Western Maori) in 1949 the Labour Party decided to select a non-Ratana candidate. But his widow, Mrs. I. M. Ratana, threatened to stand as a Ratana Independent, and she was given the nomination.[1] In 1963 for the election in Eastern Maori, Mr. S. Watene, a non-Ratana candidate was chosen.[2] The nomination would probably have gone to a Ratana candidate, but Mr. Omana's announcement of his intention to resign apparently took the obvious Ratana choice to succeed him by surprise, and he failed to fulfil the constitutional requirements for nomination. Ratana did not fight this decision as fiercely as it might have done. At the by-election for Northern Maori, which occurred shortly afterwards, a Ratana candidate, Mr. M. Rata, was selected.

Local Autonomy and Central Direction

'Local autonomy' and 'central direction' in candidate selection both have their advantages and defects. Local autonomy helps to arouse interest and enthusiasm and a sense of democratic participation. In New Zealand the electorates are small enough for the number of delegates not to be minute in comparison with the number of electors. At the selection meeting the proportion of delegates to electors is much closer to one to a hundred than to one to a thousand.[3] But local choice may

[1] Henderson, *Ratana*, p. 95.
[2] *Evening Post*, 24 Jan. 1963; *Dominion*, 4 Feb. 1963.
[3] One of the complaints of Mr. Nigel Nicolson (*People and Parliament* (London, 1958), p. 45), who lost his seat over Suez, was that only one in a thousand electors could attend the selection interview.

result in low-calibre candidates, chosen with only parochial considerations in mind.[1] Perhaps because of the small size of the electorates there is strong prejudice against non-resident members, especially in the country seats. Therefore the National Party, which relies on a system of almost complete local autonomy, has one great problem. Since it has so few urban seats, a number of 'safe' seats, where the party is dominated by farmers, should choose, in the interests of the party as a whole, not farmers but business or professional men as candidates. This has happened in several seats during the last few years, but it may not continue to happen on a sufficient scale to produce the necessary number of non-farmers to give the party balanced representation in Parliament and a sufficient supply of talent to fill the most important ministerial posts when in office. Central direction, on the other hand, provides an opportunity for raising the calibre of candidates,[2] although there is no guarantee that the opportunity to do so will always be taken. But any measure of central direction is liable to diminish local enthusiasm and to provoke resentment and charges of domination from headquarters. The New Zealand Labour Party, having failed to find a system of local choice which was truly 'democratic' from the point of view of the proportion of members voting, has therefore settled for a system embodying some degree of central direction.

The Candidates' Conferences

Each party now holds a candidates' conference before each election. The idea is to brief the candidates on the party's election policy and also to give new candidates some political and social background and pointers on how to fight an election. Labour appears to have held its first conference in 1943, National in 1938. Each party has attempted a degree of 'specialization' in these conferences. Labour has sometimes held more than one conference, in different parts of New Zealand. In 1963 it held three, and each candidate could choose which one he would attend. National in 1960 and 1963 held two each year, one for

[1] See L. C. Webb, 'Politics and Administration' in Belshaw (ed.), *New Zealand*, p. 264.

[2] See the suggestion that the quality of British Labour Party candidates should be raised through having them vetted by a sub-committee of the national executive (John Cole, *Manchester Guardian Weekly*, 26 Nov. 1959).

the new candidates only, on the coast near Wellington, and another at which the manifesto was explained to all candidates;[1] extensive changes in wording, although not of content, were made in the light of the questions and observations made at the latter meeting in 1963.[2]

[1] Chapman, Jackson, and Mitchell, op. cit., pp. 155–6; Weeks, *Political Party Personnel in New Zealand*, pp. 15 and 51–52.

[2] Interview, Mr. Ralph Wilson, May 1964.

X

CONCLUSION

I F political systems are classified into types, New Zealand is
clearly 'Western' and 'democratic'. There is a high degree of
consensus, and social and political divisions are not too intense
to be resolved by bargaining and compromise. Power is exercised peacefully, and changes of government take place without
incident.[1] The individual feels loyalty directly to the political
system as such, not just via the medium of 'particularistic sub-
systems', for instance the family or the tribe.[2] But it is impossible
to look at New Zealand closely without being made aware of
the limitations of typology. Study of Duverger must be tempered
by the warning of Lavau that the anatomy of political parties in
any country cannot be understood irrespective of its economic
and social conditions and its history.[3]

Obviously, a special feature which moulds New Zealand's
political life is the smallness of the population and, with the
exception of the Maoris, its homogeneity. Correspondingly,
New Zealand is 'more unitary' and less complex in its political
structure even than the United Kingdom,[4] and decidedly less
complex than federal countries. This simplicity of structure is
reflected in the number of parties[4] and also in their anatomy.
Since the government of New Zealand is not federal, the parties
are not 'federal' either, with consequential effects on struggles
for power within the parties. By virtue of the federal system
a rebel faction of the Australian Labor Party in New South
Wales (Lang Labor) maintained itself as the strongest *state* wing
of the party for several years in the late 30's and early 40's. But,
because of the difference in structure, this situation could not
be reproduced in New Zealand.

It is true that in New Zealand there is a certain degree of

---

[1] S. M. Lipset, *Political Man* (London, 1960), chs. 1 and 2.
[2] Almond and Coleman, *The Politics of the Developing Areas*, p. 30.
[3] G. E. Lavau, *Partis politiques et réalités sociales* (Paris, 1953), pp. 7–8.
[4] Lipson, *Political Studies*, pp. 19–20.

political differentiation, as there is in other 'Western' systems, and as there is *not* in some non-Western systems. Political control is highly differentiated from other social control systems, such as the family.[1] And political functions are relatively specialized and marked off from each other, according to whether they are mainly rule making (legislative), rule application (executive) or rule adjudication (judicial).[2] But in a country the size of New Zealand differentiation does not exist to the same degree as in larger 'Western' countries. This is true *socially*. Many observers have remarked that New Zealanders look alike and speak alike. Lack of a clear distinction between 'town' and 'country' has partly been responsible for the absence of a specifically 'Country' Party. And the low proportion of Catholics may have been one reason why there is no equivalent of the Australian 'Democratic Labor Party'. Politically, specialization is absent, in the sense that there is no 'governing class' from which a high proportion of politicians has been drawn. In the operation of government there is also a low degree of differentiation and specialization. Since 1950 there has been no second chamber. And, traditionally, ministers have been inclined to concern themselves with the minutiae of administration to a greater degree than would be possible in larger countries. In 1963–4 this probably contributed to three ministers suffering heart attacks within six months. Even the Prime Minister is expected to concern himself with local issues. 'Resentment and dissatisfaction were expressed by Tawa Borough councillors last night at the suggestion of the Prime Minister [Mr. Holyoake] that if the council had any further proposals about the Linden rail crossing, it should submit them to the Minister of Railways . . .'.[3] In the party structure and party procedures there is also less differentiation than in a country the size of the United Kingdom. For instance, the Parliamentary Labour Party, when out of office, has no need of an executive committee, and in each party the headquarters staff is less elaborate, and party organization in the field is more rudimentary.

Another feature of New Zealand life which has political implications is that, although its population is mostly 'Westernized', the country is a dependent economy, reliant on the export

[1] Almond and Coleman, op. cit., p. 10.   [2] Ibid., pp. 17–18.
[3] *Evening Post*, 23 Mar. 1964.

of primary produce. This is a feature usually associated with developing, non-Western, countries, although, paradoxically, in its egalitarianism and emphasis on social welfare, New Zealand is *more* 'developed' than the majority of Western societies. Some rural New Zealanders have the same distrust of the big city, and the big city financier, as the farmers in the West of the United States and in the Prairie Provinces of Canada used to have.[1] Only, because New Zealand cities and financiers are relatively 'small', much of the animosity is directed towards financiers *outside* New Zealand. Such feelings have also contributed to the strength of social credit ideas, to support for 'insulation', and to opposition to joining the International Monetary Fund or the World Bank. These attitudes, combined with the persistence of the pragmatic spirit appropriate to the era of the frontier, have strengthened distrust of ideas and intellectuals, and help to explain such odd phenomena as, in some rural areas, the addiction to belief in colour therapy (for animals as well as for human beings).

Comparing New Zealand's political institutions with the corresponding institutions in Britain, there is clearly a greater emphasis on democracy and equality, while the elements of authority and tradition have been diluted. Particularly in the Labour Party, caucus plays a more important role *vis-à-vis* the Leader; the procedure for the choice of a new National Party Prime Minister is less dependent on the discretion of the Governor-General than is the choice of a new Conservative Prime Minister on the discretion of the monarch; on some issues the use of the referendum enables the people to pronounce their views directly. More important, a kind of 'dualism' is apparent in the working of the system. In some respects it does not operate with the same impartiality and fairness as in Britain. The conventions of Parliamentary debate have not been observed so scrupulously, and sometimes parliamentary time has been wasted by members who have tried to 'explain away' expressions that are unparliamentary or to argue the point with the Speaker in a way which would rarely occur, and would certainly not long be tolerated, at Westminster. Other examples of ways in which canons of fair play have been infringed—in civil-liberties legislation, in war-time censorship, in the allocation of radio time at

[1] Cf. Russel B. Nye, *Midwestern Progressive Politics* (East Lansing, 1959), pp. 43 ff.

elections—have already been cited. The point to notice is the obvious one that New Zealanders *do* observe the traditions of fair play where they *think* that they are relevant and important; by and large they are observed in the fields of business, in the materialistic aspects of politics (Who gets What, When, How?), and, obviously, in sport. But where 'liberty' or 'correct behaviour' is at issue, most New Zealanders do not believe that these really matter.

The New Zealand parties possess most of the classic virtues of a stable two-party system.[1] They provide for control over the executive; they are recruiting agents for political office; they are brokers of interests, in other words performers of the aggregation function. Two reservations may be ventured. Perhaps in the past the parties have aggregated reasonably efficiently where material felt needs have been concerned, but have failed to lead public opinion in the non-material sphere. Also, in the last few years the similarities of the parties' policies, although perhaps largely attributable to the nature of New Zealand society and its high level of prosperity, have resulted in a growing lack of interest in politics.

New Zealand possesses to a high degree the necessary 'conditions' for democracy stipulated in a schematic diagram by Lipset—an open class-system, economic wealth, an egalitarian value-system, a capitalist economy, literacy, high participation in voluntary organizations.[2] But it also possesses one of the characteristics, fostered by democracy, which may in the long run have the effect of *undermining* democracy. Two of these characteristics, mentioned by Lipset, 'bureaucracy' and 'mass society', are not prominent in New Zealand, perhaps because of its small size. But the third characteristic, 'political apathy', is obviously present. It was argued earlier that much of the apparent interest in New Zealand 'politics' may not be strictly 'political' at all. As Attlee remarked of Britain twenty-five years ago, 'One has to remember that there is only a small proportion of people who are continually interested and active in politics . . . They are on the political side strengthened by many who are interested in

---

[1] For example, as recently stated in H. Eckstein and D. E. Apter, *Comparative Politics: A Reader* (Glencoe, Illinois, 1963): D. E. Apter, 'Introduction' to Part V, and S. Neumann, 'Toward a Comparative Study of Political Parties'.

[2] Lipset, op. cit., pp. 72–75.

the fight just as they are interested in other forms of sport.'¹ This observation is even more applicable to New Zealand today. For example, in the branches in both parties, it is only by offering opportunities for social life and entertainment that 'interest' can be stimulated. But the number of active workers is small; the political effects on others who attend branch meetings can be only of the 'rub-off' variety.²

The Objects and Policies of the Parties

If attention is directed only towards the militants in a party, then it may be useful to divide them into 'Utopians' and 'Fabians',³ or, alternatively, into 'Anarchists' and 'Bureaucrats'.⁴ But in the National and Labour parties, most members do not fit into either of these categories. They are simply members, and for many this means no more than that a membership fee has been paid on their behalf. A certain amount of apathy may be necessary for the functioning of democracy. Possibly in New Zealand there is too much apathy.⁵ Perhaps, in contrast to many developing countries with ethnic and linguistic divisions, there is even *too much consensus* in New Zealand. The existence of consensus is illustrated by Chapman's finding that movements of opinion, for or against a party, tend to take place, in parallel fashion, in all groups of districts in European electorates from the richest to the poorest.⁶ It could be argued that this 'parallelism of opinion' would make it unprofitable for a party to present obviously sectional policies or platforms. On the other hand, it might be worth while considering the hypothesis that,

¹ Attlee, *The Labour Party in Perspective*, p. 103.

² B. R. Berelson *et al.*, *Voting*, p. 244.

³ Michael Shanks, 'Labour Philosophy and the Current Position', *Political Quarterly*, vol. xxxi, no. 2 (1960), p. 243.

⁴ G. D. H. Cole (following the Webbs) 'What Next?', *Fabian Journal*, Apr. 1954.

⁵ On apathy and the functioning of democracy see Berelson *et al.*, op. cit., ch. 14. Increasing attention has recently been given to the concept of 'depoliticization': Ulf Himmelstrand, 'A theoretical and empirical approach to the study of de-politicization' and Ulf Torgersen, 'The trend towards political consensus: the case of Norway' in Stein Rokkan (ed.), *Approaches to the Study of Political Participation* (Bergen, 1962); G. Vedel (ed.), *La Dépolitisation, mythe ou réalité?* (Paris, 1962). The concept of 'depoliticization' is ambiguous, as Himmelstrand points out. But in New Zealand there has certainly been depoliticization in one sense at least, that of decreasing differences between the policies of the parties.

⁶ Robert Chapman, 'The Response to Labour and the Question of Parallelism of Opinion, 1928–1960', in R. Chapman and K. Sinclair (eds.), op. cit. Note that Maori voting does not move 'parallel' to the rest (p. 249).

over the last few elections, parallelism of opinion has existed, partly because party policies have in fact been so similar that 'class' reactions would not have been provoked even if sectional differences had existed. What is undoubtedly true is that the differences in the ideologies and programmes of the major parties are slight. There are no striking contrasts between the objects of the parties, as given in the party constitutions. The first four objects of the National Party[1] would be acceptable to almost any New Zealander. Object number 5, 'To formulate and carry out policies designed to benefit the community as a whole, irrespective of sectional interests, to foster the growth of goodwill between all sections of the community and particularly to bring about co-operation between country and city interests, and between employers and employees', is indirectly a criticism of the 'sectional' Labour Party as well as a statement of the National Party's difficulties in constructing a policy to please all interests. But it is still unexceptionable, almost to the point of being platitudinous; it simply amounts to saying that a party ought to 'aggregate' interests rather than merely 'articulate' them.[2] It is a pity, perhaps, that the National Party lost the curious distinction of enshrining Benthamism in its constitution by dropping an object of its predecessor, the Reform Party—to secure 'the greatest happiness of the greatest number'.[3]

The Labour Party's objects are also rather general. Before 1951 the party had a permanent 'platform', which contained the awkward 'socialization' objective and which had fallen into disuse. In any case it was held that this was not a sufficiently flexible arrangement, and that the party should not be tied to a rigid platform at a time when conditions were changing rapidly.[4] The platform was therefore dropped. Consequently, since 1951, the party has 'aims': 'to educate the public in the principles of Co-operation and Socialism, to elect competent men and women to Parliament and Local Authorities, and to ensure the just distribution of the production and services of New Zealand'. It also has an objective—'To promote and protect the freedom of the people and their . . . welfare.'[5] But there

---

[1] *Constitution and Rules of the New Zealand National Party (1963)*, rules 2–5.

[2] See pp. 129–30, above.

[3] *Constitution and Rules of the Political Reform League*, p. 1.

[4] Interview, Mr. A. H. Nordmeyer, Oct. 1958.

[5] Overacker, *American Political Science Review*, art. cit., p. 711. A motion to reinstate

is no more specific 'policy' of the party, except the most recently issued Election Manifesto. So, it has been said that, 'when candidates pledge themselves faithfully to observe the "policy" of the party they are, in a sense, signing a blank cheque'.[1]

From time to time repetition of the 'old guard' emphasis on the class struggle and the need for 'working-class understanding' is reminiscent of Labour's sectional role in the past. Whatever its stated objectives, the Labour Party was never socialist when it was the Government. Liberal–Labour movements and Governments 'have not been socialist governments. Or, if you insist on calling them socialist, their socialism has been of a very practical kind dealing only with individual issues. A real socialist attack on capitalism would aim at the sources of power, not at the broken sectors.'[2] Certainly some possible justifications for nationalization in Britain, such as promoting equality and achieving full employment,[3] are less cogent when applied to New Zealand. It is not surprising that in Mr. Nash's book, *New Zealand, a Working Democracy*, there is no explicit mention of socialism in his account of the Labour Party's philosophy.[4] Mr. John A. Lee's conceptions of 'socialism' are not necessarily authoritative, and at times he seems to have equated 'being left-wing' with adherence to his own theories on credit and borrowing. But, even with this qualification, the criticism in a song sung by him and other M.P.s on the Wellington–Auckland express in the later 1930's has point:

> The people's flag is palest pink,
> It's not so red as you might think.
> We've been to see and now we know
> That they have changed its colour so.[5]

The problem of the Labour Party is that, having achieved its major 'reformist' and 'humanitarian' objectives, there are

the original socialization objective was lost, 359 to 149. Note the relative lack of opposition to the removal of the socialization objective compared with the more substantial opposition faced by Gaitskell in Britain (McKenzie, *British Political Parties*, pp. 607 ff.).

[1] Overacker, *Political Science*, vol. ix, no. 2, art. cit., p. 27.
[2] Ormond Wilson, 'New Zealand's Political and Economical Future', *Journal of Political Science*, vol. i, no. 1 (1949), p. 52.
[3] H. T. N. Gaitskell, *Socialism and Nationalization* (Fabian Tract 300, 1956).
[4] Walter Nash, *New Zealand, a Working Democracy* (New York, 1943), p. 27.
[5] John A. Lee, *Evening Post*, 2 June 1959.

no policies remaining to distinguish it from its opponents, except a 'socialist' programme, which would have little general appeal. This has been described as the 'suicide-through-success' line of argument,[1] or the 'paradoxical performance of securing defeat through victory'.[2] It applies particularly to left-wing parties which are perpetually *expected* to produce novel and aggressive policies.[3] The fact that the Labour Party has run short of acceptable reforms is not the only reason why the policies of the parties have come to resemble each other more closely. Both parties have 'shaded' their policy to avoid losing electoral support. Labour 'toned down' its land policy in the 1920's and also seems to have slowed down its programme of controls and nationalization, 1945–9, because war-time restrictions had made the electors hostile to such proposals.[4] The National Party accepted Labour's Social Security legislation, once it was convinced that the legislation was too popular to be repealed.

Whatever the exact processes by which the parties' policies have come together,[5] there is little doubt about the fact that they have done so. To adapt Mr. Innes's phrase, in so far as they are not bound to the *status quo* they are bound for the same *terminus ad quem*.

The evidence of election surveys suggests that quite a number of electors may not think it makes much difference which party wins,[6] and only about 40 per cent. of those who vote for a party support it strongly.[7] Such conclusions actually fail to convey the slender differences between the parties' policies today. Many electors may be strong party supporters from tradition or habit, without knowing much about politics and may greatly exaggerate the gap between the parties. Some time ago Professor Beer drew attention to the close agreement on policy between the major

[1] Mayer, *Historical Studies*, art. cit., p. 259.
[2] H. H. Innes, *The Status Quo Seekers* (Wellington, 1963), p. 9.
[3] Mayer, art. cit.
[4] Interview, Mr. A. H. Nordmeyer, Dec. 1958.
[5] It is not suggested that this tendency to 'convergence' under a two-party system is more than a special case of the rule that 'every party under every competitive political system is concerned to maximize its electoral support' (S. R. Davis, 'Introduction', S. R. Davis et al., *The Australian Political Party System* (Sydney, 1954), pp. 21 ff.).
[6] This is an interpretation of Donald, *Political Science*, art. cit.; 70 per cent. of those questioned said it made a great difference which party was in office, but a much smaller number were able to say *what* the difference would be.
[7] Milne, *Political Science*, art. cit., p. 39.

parties in Britain,[1] and, indeed, Maine predicted, in the 1880's, that a wide suffrage combined with 'the Wire-puller' (party organization) would lead to the parties' having similar policies.[2]

The *rapprochement* of the parties has, of course, brought forth bitter expressions of disgust from the militants in each. At National Party Conferences the right wing has stigmatized the proposals of the centre as arguments of mere expediency, involving a sacrifice of principle. And at one Labour Conference in the late 1950's a delegate denounced the moderation of the leadership by saying that the party 'should be more than just an alternative to government by the National Party'. As early as 1937 it was pointed out that, in trying to make capitalism work in New Zealand, the party might lose sight of socialism as an objective.[3] And, according to one source, after the 1938 election the party had 'sufficient confidence from the electorate' to have introduced additional measures for public ownership, but the leaders of the party seemed reluctant to go ahead.[4] This could be explained in various ways. The leaders might have believed that they would be in power for ever, so that there was no need to be in a hurry with legislation. Alternatively, according to Mr. Lee, Fraser foresaw the dangers of success being followed by suicide. 'Jack, . . . if we go at the rate you want us to travel we'll have nothing left to do.'[5] Within the Labour Party resentment has sometimes extended to personalities. In 1950 a left-wing article complained that Labour Party leaders had sacrificed their principles in order to retain the leadership.[6] A few old-timers in the movement do not see much idealism in some of the younger men in the party, and suspect that they merely want the job of being an M.P. This attack is not completely convincing. Even in the past the Labour movement did not consist entirely of idealists, nor did all its members work entirely without hope of reward. One is reminded of Curtin's reply,

[1] 'Democratic One-Party Government for Britain?', *Political Quarterly*, vol. xxxii, no. 2 (1961).
[2] Sir Henry Maine, *Popular Government* (London, 1886), pp. 31 and 33. See also G. P. Murdock, 'Political Moieties', in L. D. White (ed.), *The State of the Social Sciences* (Chicago, 1956); D. E. Stokes, 'Spatial Models of Party Competition', *American Political Science Review*, vol. lvii, no. 2 (1963).
[3] *Tomorrow*, 14 Apr. 1937.
[4] Milburn, *Political Science*, vol. xii, no. 2, art. cit., p. 182, quoting Mr. A. H. Nordmeyer.   [5] Lee, *Simple on a Soapbox*, p. 76.
[6] T. M. Lees, 'The Crisis in Social Democracy', *Landfall*, vol. iv, no. 3 (1950).

when Prime Minister of Australia, to a politician who asked him for a diplomatic post in recognition of his long service to the party: '*Your* service to the party. If it hadn't been for the party's service to you, you'd still be on the basic wage.'[1] Also, many critics of the younger men forget that an M.P.'s salary, which seems princely to them in their retirement when compared with what members' salaries used to be, is not so very high today, relative to what is paid in some other jobs.

The similarity between the party's policies has not stimulated them to think out many novel lines of approach. It has simply resulted in a 'devaluation' of the word, policy. 'Policy' in New Zealand has been 'short-term election policy' or 'fighting policy'. In each party 'policy' is generally taken to mean simply the programme on which the previous election was fought. In some democratic countries the 'policy' of a party is taken as consisting of its 'stand' on a number of issues, as revealed, for example, in the case of the British Labour Party, in Conference decisions, resolutions of the National Executive Committee, motions of the Parliamentary Labour Party, declarations by official spokesmen in Parliament, and public statements by the Leader or Deputy-leader.[2] But in New Zealand in neither party has there been much attempt to sort out, discuss, and co-ordinate the policies implicit in such sources, except to the extent that they are used as a quarry in which to dig for material for the Election Manifesto. This is perhaps a more serious weakness when a party is in opposition, for, without the responsibility of governing, a party may not even have elaborated a set of coherent proposals, let alone proposals which are related to its principles and to the needs of New Zealand. Neither New Zealand party (particularly when in opposition) has been exempt from the criticism made of the Australian Labor Party; that when it is in opposition 'policy' is the last-minute concoction of two or three party leaders wanting to attract votes.[3] The fact is that the New Zealand parties, since they lack any clearly thought-out body of middle-range policy, have no alternative but to offer a mixed bag of *ad hoc* proposals to the voter. Naturally, if the contents of the 'bag' are not linked with an appeal to any great principle

[1] Whitington, *The House Will Divide*, p. 138.
[2] S. Rose, *Political Studies*, art. cit., pp. 128–9.
[3] A. Davies and G. Serle (eds.), *Policies for Progress* (Melbourne, 1954), pp. 170–1.

or cause, the voters prefer attractive items to repulsive ones. Policy then degenerates into promises. As a former Finance Minister is reputed to have asked a journalist, 'when yet has a New Zealand election been won by promises of blood, toil, tears and sweat?'

New Zealand politicians have sometimes succumbed to the temptation to offer 'bribes' in election years by promising increases in social service benefits, remissions of taxation and, more recently, relaxations in import controls. However, in 1928[1] and 1935[2] the election-year budgets were 'tough'—and, incidentally, on each occasion the Government lost the election. Anyway, British critics should not be too self-righteous on this score. In 1874 the upright Mr. Gladstone 'offered a really juicy "carrot", the repeal of the income tax, in his own election address'.[3] In 1955 the Conservatives raised old-age pensions shortly before the election, and also made taxation reductions, which were followed by an emergency anti-inflationary budget soon after the election. But, especially since the influence of Keynes has sapped the rigidity of 'orthodox finance', 'electoral bribery' has been more pronounced in New Zealand than in Britain. Its importance is seen in the extraordinary insistence, in both parties, on keeping the details of election policy *secret*. Each party is mortally afraid that the other will steal its clothing, mainly because the clothing is not distinctively marked with the party's name. If election policy were more closely related to party long-range policy, there would be no need for each party to spend hours working out whether the other could meet its election offers by more attractive counter-offers. There would not have been the same secrecy about party Conferences in the past, in case they should give away indications of what offers might be forthcoming. Another evil consequence of a lack of long-range policies has been the effect on the Opposition. Without firmly established policies, an Opposition will tend to make instinctive and indiscriminate attacks on government proposals, which may be quoted against it as a proof of inconsistency if it returns to power and then decides to carry on the policies of the previous Government.

[1] *Round Table*, vol. xix (1928–9), p. 218.
[2] Rollo, 'The Election of 1935 in New Zealand', p. 57.
[3] Jennings, *Party Politics*: vol. ii, *The Growth of the Parties*, p. 160.

Lately there have been a few signs of improvement in both parties. The policy resolutions at the 1952 Labour Conference were perhaps a first step towards evolving a longer-term policy. By about 1958 the National Party was also becoming aware of the 'gap' between detailed election proposals, on the one hand, and the very general 'objects' of the other. With a view to filling this gap one or two party meetings were held, at which spokesmen for various interests, such as farmers, manufacturers, retailers, and consumers put their point of view, and an attempt was made to work out a policy on such matters as the conditions under which manufacturing should be encouraged in New Zealand. Early in 1960 the interesting step was taken of publicizing some items of the party's policy some months before the time when a general election was due.[1] The Labour Party also came out with some broad outlines of its policy before the 1963 general election. But in neither case was the policy released early by the opposition party a truly long-range policy. At best, each was perhaps a 'lower-middle range' policy.

To argue that the parties would do well to formulate longer-range policies is not to say that they should 'create' issues. Shannon has said that it is issues that create parties, not parties issues.[2] But it is misleading to talk of 'creating' issues. The problem is rather for a party to find issues which are in accordance with its own broad principles, which can be expressed in more detail in the form of middle-range policy, and at elections can be translated into still more concrete terms as election proposals. The issues must express the party's own ideals and also be in accord with the individual values of electors and with the changes taking part in the social environment.[3] The issues chosen must bear some relation to the party aims, or to put it differently they must be in accordance with the 'party image' or the 'party myth'.[4] Images and myths change only slowly. 'A democratic party can very rarely be persuaded to give up even one of its traditional principles, and can never afford to scrap its central myth. The job of the party leaders is often to persuade their followers that the traditional policy is still being carried out

[1] *N.Z.P.D.*, vol. cccxix, pp. 88–89 (1 July 1959).

[2] Shannon, *The Decline and Fall of the Liberal Government*, p. 248.

[3] Richard Rose in Abrams, *et al.*, *Must Labour Lose?* p. 71.

[4] R. H. S. Crossman, letter to *Encounter*, quoted by Mark Arnold-Foster, 'The Future of Labour, VII—Some Party Myths', *Manchester Guardian*, 20 Dec. 1954.

even when this is demonstrably not true.' This was the task faced by Mr. Nordmeyer in 1963 when dealing with 'old guard' Labour supporters who still cherished the class struggle and socialization. Whether a party has only *one* central myth or image, or whether it has several, is arguable;[1] the essential point is that the 'core' of a party's principles changes only very slowly and that the issues taken up by a party, and eventually put forward at elections, must be easily and closely related to that core. Thus, if a New Zealand party takes up the middle-range issue of consumer protection,[2] it should be related to the party's principles—to some familiar facet of its myth or image. The National Party should link it with the image of the party as being opposed to controls and liberal in its import policy. The Labour Party should put the issue forward as an aspect of its traditional opposition to monopoly and 'price rings'. Social Credit could relate it to its criticisms of the monetary system, which would make it necessary for the purchasing power of consumers to be increased.

Issues, to be successful, must also be in accord with the values of individuals. At the end of the Second World War few New Zealand electors were in a mood to support policies which would entail the continuance of controls. Social changes must also be taken into account. The New Zealand parties, like New Zealand herself, must be quick to adjust themselves to changing conditions. In 1900 it was possible (with the help of the country quota) for a party to hold power almost entirely through possessing rural support. Now this is no longer feasible, and the selection of issues must be modified accordingly. Similarly, the changing age-composition of the electorate[3] should lead the parties to put more weight on issues likely to appeal to youth. From the tactical point of view, it takes at least months, possibly years, to 'convey' a new issue to the electors. Issues of the type just discussed should be launched *between* elections. They should not make their first appearance in an election manifesto. Similarly the attempt at the 1963 election to create a new image of the Labour Leader, Mr. Nordmeyer,[4] was launched far too late for any hope of success.

It is not self-evident that the New Zealand National Party

[1] J. J. de Jong, *Overheid En Onderdaan* (Wageningen, 1956).
[2] See pp. 287–8, below.   [3] Dickinson, *The Younging of Electorates*.
[4] e.g. *Dunedin Star*, 9 Nov. 1963.

(or the Australian Liberal Party) has been a truer expression of the country's culture and sentiment than any other party.[1] But it is certainly correct to say that it has been, until recently, slower to make substantial policy proposals than the New Zealand Labour Party, both because it represents a wider range of interests, and also because, on the whole, it has been satisfied with the existing pattern of society. To this extent it has been a party of resistance,[2] 'a party of the *status quo*'.[3] Also, by contriving to identify itself more closely than the Labour Party with the Commonwealth, national defence, and opposition to strikes and Communism, it has managed to represent itself successfully as the 'patriotic' party. It is also looked upon as the party which keeps law and order, and deals capably with strikes. To quote a person interviewed in a public opinion survey:[4] 'One good thing old Holland done was the time the strikes was on.' What are missing, for the National Party as for the Australian right-wing parties, are the symbols of 'permanence, authority and stability',[5] which reinforce the image and the appeal of the Conservative Party in Britain.

It is a temptation for a right-wing party to rest on its platform of defence of the country and the *status quo*, and, even when out of power, to believe that 'a few strong planks and one or two cries is all an Opposition wants'.[6] Alternatively, its leaders may be tempted to speak as if public relations were a substitute for policy. 'Politics are, after all, only a matter of salesmanship. Maybe our goods were not quite so attractive as some others eighteen months ago, but I can assure you that the position is going to be reversed eighteen months hence (interruption by laughter). Our goods will not only be more attractive, but they will be wrapped in cellophane.'[7]

Prominent in the image of the National Party is its belief in free, or private, enterprise and its opposition to socialism and controls. But, although the Nationalists may have 'inherited'

[1] Eggleston, op. cit., pp. 38–39 and 155.

[2] Mayer, op. cit., pp. 254 ff.   [3] Innes, op. cit., p. 18.

[4] Wellington Central, 1957.

[5] J. D. B. Miller, 'Aspects of the Party System in Australia', *Parliamentary Affairs*, vol. vi, no. 4 (1953), p. 329.

[6] Vaile to Massey, 14 Jan. 1906.

[7] S. G. Holland, *Standard*, 29 July 1937 (some descriptive material has been omitted). The approach may have been influenced partly by the nature of the audience, the Canterbury Commercial Travellers' Association.

laissez-faire from the Liberals,[1] it has been greatly qualified by the New Zealand atmosphere, and by the desire not to be 'outbid' by the Labour Party. By 1959 the President of the National Party was definite on this point:

Some wanted to resurrect the theory of 'laissez-faire'—the doctrine of non-interference by Governments in matters which might be of vital concern to the great mass of the people. In Mr. Mc-Kenzie's view any attempt to apply such doctrines today would be repudiated by the public. Even in non-Socialist countries, the over-riding responsibility of the State to intervene in matters which might affect the welfare of large groups of people was no longer seriously challenged. The trend towards more Government control, of co-operation in non-Socialist countries, was generally brought about by economic circumstances, international competition, the benefit of co-ordination and guarantee by a central authority, and through the development of the Welfare State.[2]

'Free enterprise', then, does not mean *completely* free enterprise. But, while accepting some controls and restrictions, the party draws the line before the Labour Party does. 'I cannot say too often that the National Party believes in a property-owning democracy.... We believe in the maximum degree of personal freedom and the maximum degree of individual choice for our people. We believe in the least interference necessary with individual rights, and the least possible degree of State inter-ference.'[3] The National Party is thus able to take up a position which is not completely identifiable with *laissez-faire*, but which, analytically at least, may be distinguished from the approach of the Labour Party. It has related its policies of relatively lenient import controls to this general concept of freedom. In abolishing compulsory unionism it was guided by the principle of freedom; although by choosing a close substitute to 'replace' compulsion, it avoided antagonizing the unions. What the National Party cannot do is to secure electoral support for 'freedom' as such, without linking the concept to some concrete issue or proposal which is of interest to the electors. It was a

[1] Ormond Wilson, 'Conservatism and the National Party', *Here and Now*, vol. iii, no. 1 (1952).
[2] *Freedom*, 28 July 1959, reporting Sir Alex. McKenzie's presidential address at the Annual Party Conference.
[3] K. J. Holyoake, *N.Z.P.D.*, vol. cccxix, pp. 405–6 (14 July 1959). For an earlier statement of the basis of a National Party 'philosophy' see J. R. Marshall, 'The Faith of a Liberal', *Journal of Political Science*, vol. i, no. 1 (1949).

decisive stage in Mr. Algie's education, and in his graduation
from professor to politician, when, as executive officer of the
Freedom Association, he made the discovery that few people
were interested in freedom in general as opposed to particular
advantages of economic freedom.[1] In the terminology of the
authors of *Voting*, New Zealanders may show interest in 'position'[2]
(largely economic) issues; they are unlikely to get very excited
over most, non-economic, 'style' issues, such as a Second Chamber, civil liberties, a written constitution, the reform of the state
services or penal reforms. Of recent years the National Party
has concentrated to a large extent on legislation in the field of
style issues of this kind. It may be doubted whether the electors
are much moved by most style issues, and some which do interest
them, such as liquor licensing or capital punishment, are ultimately determined by referenda or by a free vote in Parliament.
However, during the past few years, the National Party has
introduced legislation to relax the licensing laws, particularly
in the direction of making it easier to have a drink along with a
meal outside normal drinking hours. This issue, as well as being
related to the general concept of freedom, is probably also in
tune with the changes which are taking place in individual
values and the social environment in New Zealand.

Apart from any effects from changes in the social environment,[3] the New Zealand Labour Party has reason to be afraid of
changes in individual values. The proportion of the electors who
have suffered in the great depression of the 1930's has declined.
And, for a party whose voters are probably less likely to rate
themselves as working-class than as middle-class, it is ominous
that so many of them have an image of the party as 'for the
working class'.[4] The party is also regarded by some voters, both
National and Labour, as too much dominated by the trade
unions.[5] From the electoral or party image point of view, although not organizationally or financially, it may be a handicap
to the party to be so closely associated with the unions.[6]

[1] *Truth*, 26 Oct. 1938.
[2] On style and position issues, see Berelson *et al.*, op. cit., pp. 184 ff.
[3] See pp. 89–92, above.
[4] Milne, *Political Science*, art. cit., tabs. i and x.
[5] Ibid., tab. x. See also the Victoria University survey of the 1963 election (to
be published).
[6] See M. Harrison, op. cit., p. 350; Abrams, op. cit., pp. 38–41.

It has been remarked that the New Zealand Labour Party is handicapped by the very fact that so many of its humanitarian proposals have now been adopted. Because the number of possible issues is relatively limited, the road to 'suicide-through-success' has been shorter than in most other countries. Perhaps this point may be illustrated by referring to the critical topical issues not yet 'in the gateway'[1] (i.e. not already fully discussed and debated) which a few years ago Mr. C. A. R. Crosland thought the British Labour Party should take up and annex:

1. The creation of genuine and equal educational opportunity.
2. Urban planning to save both town and countryside.
3. Greater social investment to reduce the present unbalance between public and private spending.
4. Protection of the consumer against large-scale producing interests.
5. World disarmament and the control of nuclear weapons.[2]

It is obvious that comparable proposals by the New Zealand Labour Party would not be nearly as attractive or effective. New Zealand has already almost achieved Number 1, and has gone far along the road to Number 3. There is little New Zealand can do about Number 5 except to raise her small voice in favour. Because the density of population is relatively low, as is concern for aesthetic considerations, Number 2 might not have much appeal in spite of the cogent case that has been made out for it.[3] Consumer protection is a possible issue. When Labour was last in office it set up a Consumer Council, retained by the National Government, to give consumers factual information about products and prices. But, from the short-term point of view, the New Zealand consumer needs protection not so much against large-scale producers as against small-scale manufacturers who are taking part in the drive for the industrialization of New Zealand. And, quite apart from considerations of possible effects on the votes of the manufacturers and their employees, such manufacturers do not dominate the economy to

[1] Berelson *et al.*, op. cit., pp. 209 ff.
[2] Anthony Crosland, *Can Labour Win?* (Fabian Tract 324, 1960), p. 19.
[3] R. H. Brookes, 'Wellington', in W. A. Robson (ed.), *Great Cities of the World* (London, 1954).

such a degree that Labour could represent limitation of their profits as a crusade for the taming of economic power.[1]

At the time of the great economic depression, issues were relatively uncomplicated for Labour politicians. Unemployment, with its attendant evils, was the great enemy. In fighting it any means which were moral were justified and any opponents who stood in Labour's way were wicked. The older Labour leaders had faith in the righteousness of their cause. Their spirit is well expressed by Mr. Nash's paraphrase of Browning at a Party Conference, when he said that the movement would

> Never turn but march breast forward,
> Never doubt clouds would break,
> Never dream, though right were worsted, wrong
> would triumph,
> Hold we fall to rise, are baffled to fight better,
> Sleep to wake.

But now there has been no substantial unemployment for twenty-five years, and the National Party has accepted the bulk of Labour's reforms and has largely succeeded in changing its own image. The Labour Party has almost exhausted its ideas, and its difficulties in finding new ones are intensified by its distrust of intellectuals and also, perhaps, by the emphasis on the authority of the leadership after the Lee 'rebellion'. Criticism of the party for being anti-intellectual, though largely justified, may have been pressed a little too far. The number of intellectuals in New Zealand is so limited that there is a tendency for them to be inbred and to be very very intellectual indeed. The non-intellectuals in the party might possibly argue that, if it is new middle-range policies which are required, the intellectuals should come part of the way, out of the clouds, to meet them.

During the 1950's, and particularly after the 1957 election, the Labour Party made much of the import control issue and the extravagance of the National Government in having allowed too much importing. This issue linked up very well with the pro-full-employment aspect of Labour's image and with the party's encouragement of New Zealand manufacturing in the late 1930's. As was observed in 1940, import control 'is a step which gives much greater control of the capitalist system, and

---

[1] R. H. S. Crossman, *Labour in the Affluent Society* (Fabian Tract 325, 1960).

it has given the government means of rapidly extending manufacturing within New Zealand and of maintaining full employment and a New Zealand level of wages'.[1] By denouncing some imported items as 'luxuries' Labour also took advantage of the 'pro-equality' features of its image. However, there are few obvious new issues waiting for the Labour Party to annex. The abolition of Compulsory Military Training was an effective issue at the 1957 election in that it agreed with the party's fundamental principles, was not obviously contrary to the interests of New Zealand, and was perhaps instrumental in gaining votes. Closer links with Asia and more generous contributions in foreign aid would be an issue in keeping with New Zealand's humanitarian traditions. But at present there seems to be little difference in the actual policies of the two major parties on this issue, and it is hard to see many votes being won on it. Labour's problem is essentially to channel the enthusiasm generated in attacking the old evils into the fight against the evils of today. The attacks on these old evils were successful. 'No government today, whatever might be the individual belief of its members, would dare to interfere substantially with the structure of society erected by Labour . . . .' But must success be followed by suicide? When Labour is in office must it 'keep on flogging the dead horse'[2] by sticking to old unreconstructed policies? Labour must steer a course somewhere between rigidly applying an out-of-date ideology and having no distinctive ideology at all. To the 'old guard' of the movement Dr. Finlay's approach is anathema. Yet there is some truth in the view that most of the present Labour M.P.s 'know nothing of capitalism or socialism. They have never read a tract on the capitalist crisis. Their loyalty is not to an idea, but to a machine, to a job as an M.P.'[3]

One suggested source of new policies is that some British Labour Party proposals, for instance on partial 'nationalization' by buying a proportion of the shares in private companies, or schemes for retirement pensions proportional to income, should be circulated within the New Zealand Labour Party with a view to their possible adoption in a form suitable to local

[1] W. B. Sutch, *New Zealand's Labour Government at Work* (New York, 1940), p. 28.
[2] *Report of the Forty-fifth Annual Conference* (1961), 'Dr. Finlay's Presidential Address', p. 4. See also the 'Statement of Aims and Objectives' presented by him a year later, *Report of the Forty-sixth Annual Conference*, pp. 18–20.
[3] Lee, *Simple on a Soapbox*, p. 276.

conditions.[1] Several themes for new policy were suggested in Dr. Finlay's 1961 Presidential Address.[2] The only one which he worked out in any depth was defence, but among the others he mentioned were race relations, the cost of professional services, problems of the West Coast, urban development and town planning, immigration, delinquency, and the use of leisure. Labour's 'new look' 1963 election policy also laid a new emphasis on growth and development. It remains for Labour to elaborate these themes and link them closely to its existing party image.

Organization and Tendencies to Oligarchy

Turning to the organization of the parties, it is clear that each of them has to satisfy the claims of several different groups or sections. To put it in the simplest form, each must take into consideration the claims of those who support the party financially, of the militants, of members who are not militants, of voters who are not members. Within each of these sections, of course, satisfying some individuals or groups may mean alienating others. Analysis of the way in which the parties try to deal with various claims may be obscured by invariably making distinctions among (a) the party in Parliament; (b) the party outside Parliament; (c) interests outside the party which nevertheless usually support the party. Such distinctions are necessary in certain contexts. For instance, it has been observed that (a), unlike (b), must take account of the responsibility of the ministry to Parliament and the electors when the party is in power. And the very fact that most trade unions explicitly play a role in (b) in the Labour Party, while farming groups fall under heading (c) in relation to the National Party, alters the nature and significance of the relationship. It puts a 'for better or for worse' seal on what otherwise might be a close, but conceivably temporary, friendship. But, from the point of view of process, the parties' activities consist of bargaining and compromise. In this regard the relations between (a) and (b), and those between (a) and (b) taken together and (c), are not very different. In both cases the flow is two-way. At times the balance which exists between the various forces is criticized. It is often alleged that a party

---

[1] Interview, Dr. A. M. Finlay, Feb. 1958.   [2] Op. cit., pp. 4–5.

is being dominated by 'outside interests'. Alternatively, trade unionists sometimes think that the Labour Party is becoming weighted against the unions, and demand that more unionists be put forward as candidates; or occasionally certain business groups, believing that the National Party has moved too far to the left, may toy with the notion of reviving the equivalent of the 1935 Democrat Party under a new name.

In an extreme case the allegations of 'outside domination' might be justified—namely if either party became so closely tied to one or more groups that, when in power, it simply articulated, and translated into law, the interests of these groups without making any attempt at 'aggregating' all interests. This situation does not seem to have occurred in New Zealand, at least not since 1890. Of course voters may *fear* outside domination, or approximations to it, and this will condition their images of the parties and their vote. Some see the National Party as 'too sectional', while others see the Labour Party as dominated by the trade unions. Thus, to some extent, the voters have a defence against outside domination—in voting for the other party, provided that the parties are not both equally dominated from outside.

R. T. McKenzie's book, *British Political Parties*, has raised once again the question of oligarchy or democracy inside parties, and recently Robinson has made a study of it in the New Zealand National Party.[1] Robinson is informative on some aspects of decision-making in the party up to 1949, but comparable material is lacking for the period after 1949 and for the Labour Party. There is also an absence of information on the origins and occupations, education, and so on of the non-parliamentary *élites* in both parties. The problem of oligarchy is, plainly, less simple than Michels thought.[2] Michels did not actually *define* oligarchy, although he described its symptoms and causes. A modern commentator, after examining possible definitions, has put forward the following: 'An oligarchy is an organization characterised by the fact that part of the activities of which it consists, viz., the activities having the highest degree of authority (which have been called "leadership" or "executive"

[1] Robinson, *Oligarchy and Democracy*. On Britain see Richard Rose, 'Complexities of Party Leadership', *Parliamentary Affairs*, vol. xvi, no. 3 (1963).
[2] Michels, *Political Parties*.

activities), are free from control by any of the remainder of the organizational activities.'[1] As Robinson points out, a further refinement might be to make the law 'dynamic' rather than 'static'—that is to reformulate it in terms of *tendencies* towards inequality of power which may result in oligarchy.[2] Michels himself, although pessimistic in his conclusions, did not see a steady tendency towards oligarchy in the organizations he studied, but rather an ebb and flow between 'oligarchy' and 'democracy'.[3] To this extent a 'dynamic' concept of oligarchy would seem to be more relevant than a static concept. But perhaps one should go further. There must be very few, if any, organizations in which the leaders are completely 'free from control' by the led. Perhaps it would be preferable to follow the approach of G. C. Field[4] when defining 'democracy', and say that an organization is oligarchical *in so far as* the leaders are free from control by the led. This approach seems desirable, because 'pure' oligarchy is unlikely to exist, just as is 'pure' democracy. The 'classical' theory of democracy by which the people express their 'will' on a large number of issues, and their representatives are thus given a mandate to carry out that will, just does not apply in those countries which are usually described as democracies.[5] It is inapplicable largely for the same reasons, the lack of interest of the governed, the prestige of leaders, the complex subject-matter of government, which Michels summed up as the psychological and technical causes of oligarchy.[6] To expect a high degree of democracy in political parties is doubly naïve. Such an expectation ignores the tendencies away from democracy, and towards oligarchy, in all large organizations. It also fails to take any account of R. T. McKenzie's contention that, at least when it is in power, a party cannot be under the

[1] C. W. Cassinelli, 'The Law of Oligarchy', *American Political Science Review*, vol. xlvii, no. 3, 1953, pp. 773–84.
[2] *Oligarchy and Democracy*, pp. 4–5.
[3] Michels, op. cit., Part Six, ch. iv; A. W. Gouldner, 'Metaphysical Pathos and the Theory of Bureaucracy', *American Political Science Review*, vol. xlix, no. 2 (1955).
[4] *Political Theory* (London, 1956), p. 43; cf. the concept of 'reciprocity' developed in R. A. Dahl and C. A. Lindblom, *Politics Economics and Welfare* (New York, 1953).
[5] Berelson *et al.*, op. cit., ch. xiv; Milne and Mackenzie, *Marginal Seat, 1955*, op. cit., ch. 13; J. A. Schumpeter, *Capitalism, Socialism and Democracy* (London, 1952), pp. 250 ff.; J. Plamenatz, 'Electoral Studies and Democratic Theory, I: a British View', *Political Studies*, vol. vi, no. 1 (1958).
[6] Michels, op. cit., pp. 25 ff.

control of its members beyond a certain point without damage to its responsibility to Parliament and the electors as a whole.

Robinson has pointed to the existence of several factors which operated against oligarchy in the National Party, 1936–49. Among them were the democratic system of values which prevails in New Zealand; the diversity of the interests which had to be united in opposition to the Labour Party; the local feeling in certain areas resulting from geography; and the party's large membership, system of election to committees, and decentralization of organizing activities and candidate selection.[1] Some of these, such as the New Zealand value system and 'local feeling', would apply to the Labour Party as well. From general considerations of this kind it might be possible to say that the National Party was relatively 'democratic' during this period. But it is difficult to be much more precise. In considering 'freedom from control' what activities, what areas of decision-making, are to be considered? Robinson chooses six: general policy and election policy; the selection of leaders; relations with other political parties; parliamentary tactics; decisions made by the party as a fighting machine; decisions on changes in the party structure.[2] But opinions may differ on the weight to be given to each of the areas. The first, policy-making, is clearly of outstanding importance. The selection of leaders also seems to be decidedly more important than the remaining four. But it is difficult to go beyond that. As regards policy-making, Robinson concludes that, on policy decisions, 'while the Policy Committee and the Leader had the final say, the necessity of bargaining with so many divergent interests and viewpoints left little in actual fact to the discretion of the committee'.[3] In the second area he cites the removal of Forbes and Hamilton, when 'the goods were not delivered', as examples of a high degree of control being exercised over the leaders.[4]

Robinson also asked the question whether there was a ruling *élite* in the National Party. Taking Dahl's criterion, was there a 'minority of individuals whose preferences regularly prevail in cases of differences in preferences on key political issues'?[5]

[1] *Oligarchy and Democracy*, op. cit., p. 88. [2] Ibid., pp. 32–79.
[3] Ibid., p. 42. [4] Ibid., pp. 52–53.
[5] R. A. Dahl, 'A Critique of the Ruling Elite Model', *American Political Science Review*, vol. lii, no. 2 (1958).

Robinson found that no single group within the party was pre-dominant, not even the parliamentary party and the Leader: '. . . tendencies operated in the direction of concentration of power in the hands of a few at each level of the party's structure, Branch, Electorate, Division, Council and parliamentary party. There was a tendency toward increasing inequality of power but this did not lead to the dominance of a single group.'[1] The analysis is suggestive, but comparisons are difficult. Clearly the New Zealand National Party during this period was far removed from 'pure' oligarchy. And it might be possible to argue, on account of the difference in size, New Zealand values such as the absence of an aristocratic tradition, and other factors, that the party was less oligarchical than the British Conservative Party. But what would be the result of a comparison between the two New Zealand parties? As regards policy-making, in appearance the Labour Party is the more democratic in that, by its constitution, policy is supposed to come from the Annual Conference. However, partly because of the Labour leadership's need to have a free hand on policy when Labour forms the Government, it uses its 'defences in depth' to resist Conference resolutions which are inconvenient. The difference between the parties on this point is therefore smaller than might appear at first glance.

If only the parliamentary parties are considered, the Labour Party is more 'democratic', at least in form; for example, in having regular elections for Leader. Nevertheless, as in Britain, the right-wing party Leader has not as much job-security as he might appear to have, especially when the party is out of office. The choice of the Cabinet by caucus is another obviously demo-cratic feature of the PLP.

Of course it is debatable whether the parliamentary party should be considered in isolation when the matter of 'democracy' is discussed. To meet the needs of government, caucus, especially when the party is in power, requires some freedom of action. But how much? In the late 1930's, when Savage—with the back-ing of the national executive, the big union leaders, and Con-ference—defied a majority of caucus on several occasions, was he acting 'democratically' or not? If the PLP is regarded as a closed system, he was not. If the unions are accorded the special

[1] *Oligarchy and Democracy*, pp. 84 and 85.

weight given to them in the Labour Party constitution, then
he was.

In the selection of parliamentary candidates, at least since
1951, the Labour Party has been less democratic than its rival,
and National Members of Parliament are more dependent on
local support than Labour members. In making policy the
National Party has had to consult a wider range of interests
than Labour, although this does not amount to saying that the
main decisions are made by a larger number of persons. An
important feature is the prominence given to *regional* interests
in policy-making. As in the Labour Party, the need has been
felt for a small executive body which meets frequently. But,
while in the Labour Party this is a body composed of persons
based on Wellington, in the National Party the divisional chairmen are included in the Dominion Executive to represent
regional interests.[1]

With reference to the concentration of power inside the
Labour Party as a whole, Overacker thinks that the concentration is in a 'small interlocking directorate of leaders of the PLP,
N.E.C. and trade unions centred in Wellington'.[2] She does not
specify in detail what the composition of the group is. Any
attempt to give a list of names would probably be countered by
quoting other names, not in the list, of men who exercised great
power in the movement. Without necessarily agreeing with
Overacker, there are several reasons why it might be easier to
point to a single power group in the Labour Party than in the
National Party. The party is based on the concept of solidarity,
is more disciplined and represents more homogeneous interests.
Its use of a Wellington committee of the national executive
might also contribute to the development of a single power
group. Furthermore its lack of fully developed divisional or
regional bodies would indicate a lack of strong, *potentially opposing*, power centres;[3] even the city LRCs are perhaps not strong
enough to play such a role. The setting-up of a Regional Advisory Council in Auckland, the activity of one or two younger
Auckland M.P.s, and the success of the *Statesman* published there

[1] See p. 174, above.
[2] Overacker, *Political Science*, art. cit. p. 27.
[3] For a comparison with the Australian Labor Party on this point see G. M.
Carter, 'The Commonwealth Overseas: Variations on a British Theme', in
S. Neumann (ed.) *Modern Political Parties* (Chicago, 1956), pp. 92 ff.

after the official *Standard* had to cease publication in Wellington, alter the picture somewhat. In time Auckland might become an important additional power centre. At present Overacker's thesis is plausible, although not proven.

Organization and Ideology

The doctrine and social basis of a party clearly influence the working of the formal organization. This is, roughly, the basis of Margaret Cole's main criticism of McKenzie's book on the British parties. 'McKenzie says that ideology is outside his scope. But this is surely an enormous omission, and one which seriously affects any evaluation of the history, even the organisational history, of the Labour Party'.[1] In New Zealand organization and ideology clearly react on each other. The belief that Labour is a fighting voluntary movement has persisted into an era when it is increasingly difficult to find Labour volunteers for party work, and has had the effect of slowing down professionalization of the party. Much of the early enthusiasm has been lost, without the party having yet made and acted on a careful scrutiny of its organization, as the British Labour Party did in the 'Wilson' Report.[2] The appeal of the early leaders, notably Savage, has gone, but it has not yet been replaced by efficient routines. The party's ideology, in the widest sense, is also influenced by its organization. Its constitutional relation with the trade unions sets a limit to its advocacy of new policies which might have little appeal to union leaders. Viewed from one angle the emphasis on loyalty to the leadership during the Savage–Lee battle and during the war curbed deviations. But, seen from another aspect, it also discouraged the expression and development of ideas. The limitations on Conference's policy-making power, which are at times necessary for Labour to function properly as a *government*, injure it as a *party*; delegates see their remits defeated after intervention by the leadership, or, what is even more frustrating, passed and then quietly shelved. In these ways, and in others, organizational arrangements can dampen the ardour of the militants, who may sometimes also be the most

[1] Margaret Cole, 'Political Leadership and Organization', *Fabian Journal*, Mar. 1955, pp. 14–15. McKenzie's comment in the Preface to his second edition, pp. ix–x, does not quite meet the point.
[2] R. T. McKenzie, 'The Wilson Report and the Future of the Labour Party Organization', *Political Studies*, vol. iv, no. 1 (1956).

active workers in the constituencies. To list these problems is not to say that there is an easy answer, 'if only Labour would...'. For instance the 'simple' tactic that Labour should be more receptive to the ideas of intellectuals would probably have unfavourable consequences in arousing the suspicion and resentment of the trade unionists; 'one would have to ask whether there are not permanent forces within the movement giving it an anti-intellectual character. If this were so, one could not simply graft intellectuals on to the movement, since it would lead to the loss of support by other forces.'[1]

The National Party's problems are different. 'Ideology' has never been important in inspiring many people to work for the party. The motive power of its few really active members has been non-intellectual anti-socialism. The inspiration of the other members has been largely 'social', in a broad sense. The numerous elections within the party, including the choice of parliamentary candidates, with their 'sporting' overtones, also stimulate 'social' interest. Some concern with policy exists, as is shown by the attention given to the remit system, but not to the same degree as in the Labour Party. Also, to the extent that National proposals on policy have been reactions against Labour measures or proposals, when the stimulus decreases so will the reaction. Especially in the rural areas the social attraction of the National Party may soon decrease, now that an obvious rival, television, has come to New Zealand.

A Country without Issues?

New Zealand is fortunate in having solved most of its big political problems, always excepting those that can be determined only externally. But it is probable that, although its party organizations will become increasingly elaborate and effective, the subjects with which they deal will become increasingly uncontentious and unexciting. Is the tendency towards greater tranquillity in New Zealand politics to be deplored? Probably not—the *raison d'être* of political activity must surely be that it helps to solve political problems or that it satisfies the desire for social, rather than specifically political, activity. But in New Zealand most major political problems have been solved, and it is likely

---

[1] Henry Mayer, 'Some Conceptions of the Australian Party System, 1910–1950', *Historical Studies, Australia and New Zealand*, vol. vii, no. 27 (1956), p. 268.

that the spread of television will reduce the number of people who engage in politics mainly for social reasons. Possibly, of course, New Zealanders' notions of what is 'political' will broaden, and the encouragement of the arts and the aesthetic aspects of town planning will constitute fresh issues for political controversy. But, otherwise, the stuff of New Zealand politics will continue increasingly to fall into two categories. It will consist partly of large-scale 'parochial' issues, such as motor-ways, harbour bridges, hydro-electric and other public works schemes, and universities. It will also consist of issues forced upon New Zealand's attention by the remaining 99·9 per cent. of the world's population. Of these the problems which might result from Britain's joining the European Economic Community would be an obvious example. New Zealand governments may contrive to soften or modify the impact of these issues on particular groups, but against their general effects the country can never be securely insulated.

NOTE

THE SOCIAL CREDIT POLITICAL LEAGUE

THE origins, election policies, and voting strength of the Social
Credit Political League have already been indicated.[1] Until 1953
Social Crediters in New Zealand had tried to work through existing
parties, except for a few who stood as Independents.[2] The aim was to
brng persuasion and pressure to bear on existing parties in order to
secure the realization of Major Douglas's proposals. But this aim was
not realized, and Social Crediters came to feel that the major parties
had helped themselves into office by putting Social Credit ideas into
their platform, but had subsequently failed to carry them out. It was
believed that this had happened in 1935 when Social Credit ideas
had been appropriated, but not applied, by Labour. Less obviously
in 1949 the National Party 'made large scale propaganda of its policy
to stabilize currency and restrict its issue to equate with productivity.
This policy was widely acclaimed and offered hope of economic
stability. Very little time, however, was to elapse before it became
evident that this government too had used its false promise of reform
as a stepping stone to the treasury benches.'[3] By 1953, also, New
Zealand Social Crediters were on the whole convinced that the argument that the teachings of Major Douglas forbade the founding of
Social Credit parties was incorrect. So in 1953 a group of Social
Crediters decided to form the Social Credit Political League.

In 1954 the League did very well for a new party, collecting 11 per
cent. of the vote. In 1957 the proportion fell to 7 per cent. This may
have been partly the result of the publication of the *Report* of the
Royal Commission on Monetary, Banking, and Credit Systems

[1] See the references in Ch. II, pp. 49 and 63–67; Ch. III, p. 77.

[2] The exception was the Real Democracy Movement, which 'holds the distinction of being the first national political movement organised to promote Social
Credit principles in New Zealand' (Daniels, op. cit., p. 187). On the non-political
side the Social Credit organization had different names at different times. At about
the same time as the League was formally registered the 'educational' side of the
movement changed its name to the New Zealand Social Credit Association. It still
exists, but at a reduced level of activity.

[3] John O'Brien, 'Social Credit and Politics', *Comment*, July 1962, p. 30; *Vote for
Honest Money* (National Party, 1946); *Real Prosperity—the National Way* (National
Party, 1949); Robinson, *The Rise of the New Zealand National Party*, op. cit., pp.
181–2. A rejoinder to the O'Brien article by Martin Nestor appeared in *Comment*,
January 1963, p. 28.

(1956), which the League believed had been set up specifically to *discredit* Social Credit. At the elections of 1960 and 1963 there was a slight variation in the vote, to 9 per cent. and 8 per cent. respectively. These figures might suggest relative stability in the support for Social Credit. But on inspection this impression is shown to be incorrect. In 1954 the League was relatively successful in the South Island, including Christchurch and Dunedin, less successful in the rural areas of the North Island and least successful in Auckland and Wellington. But from 1957 onwards the pattern altered perceptibly. There was a big drop in support for the League all over the South Island, but the drop in the North Island was not nearly so steep. The main strength of the League is now in the rural areas in the centre and the extreme North of the North Island. This is precisely where the strongest support existed for the Country Party thirty years ago. It is significant that the seat nearly won by Social Credit in 1963 was Hobson, which under the name of Bay of Islands was held by Captain Rushworth, a Social Credit follower inside the Country Party, in the 1930's. Both then and now this constituency could be termed 'under-developed'. During his tenure of the seat Rushworth was not opposed by Labour, and there are reports that some local Labour Party officials in Hobson did not want to oppose the Social Credit candidate in 1963 so that he might have a 'clear run' against National.

Informed guesses may be made about where Social Credit votes come from. Outside its main areas of strength in the North Island it may draw more protest votes than ideological votes.[1] But where its vote is highest a larger *proportion* of it is probably cast in support of its policy of monetary reform.[2]

The League's long-term policy is to implement Douglas Credit proposals. But to draw up shorter-term statements of policy for particular elections is a more difficult matter. The active members of the League have not always agreed on the technical details of their proposals, and in the period 1958–9 there appear to have been divisions in the League on basic ideology. Even when agreement exists, there is the problem of presenting technical matters to electors who are not interested in intricacies of technique. So the League must try to avoid two extremes which are equally undesirable from the point of view of appealing to the public successfully—incomprehensibility through the too free use of Social Credit 'jargon',

[1] See R. S. Milne, *Political Science*, art. cit. p. 58.
[2] A voting survey of some 'strong' Social Credit constituencies was carried out at the 1963 election (by mail) by the members of the School of Political Science of the Victoria University of Wellington. It is intended to publish an analysis of the results.

and generalities which fail to impress because of their vagueness. The *Official Policy for 1963 Election* tried to meet this by giving a few 'basic principles underlying Social Credit Policy'; by putting the Financial Policy very simply ('A distribution system which allows the goods they produce and the services they provide TO BE AVAILABLE TO THE PEOPLE. That means as much money and credit available as there are goods and services. That means Social Credit'); by listing 'Our First Steps'. The tone of the *Official Policy* was decidedly reasonable and non-alarmist. The Financial Policy section ended by saying that the 'introduction of Social Credit involves the acceptance of a principle and would not upset the day by day workings of banks, trading concerns, importers, or anything else. Just as New Zealand accepted overnight the principle of Social Security which meant more money to those in need, so the acceptance of Social Credit in principle would allow an up to date, efficient and intelligent monetary system to start operating the day after the election.'

Another question concerns the extent to which the League should introduce proposals about matters other than finance into its appeals to the electors. In 1954 the platform for the election was largely financial. Since then election platforms have broadened and have included items on education, on liquor licensing, and quite detailed proposals on defence.

The League has always been strongly individualist and pro-free enterprise. This aspect has become fully emphasized in its election policies, and in 1963 the first of 'Our First Steps' in the *Official Policy* was, 'We will introduce a Bill of Rights for New Zealand to limit the powers of Government and safeguard the individual against the invasion of Rights and Liberties.' These attitudes and recommendations are much more in line with National Party policy, and Constitutional Society policy, than with Labour Party policy. Other attitudes seem to be discernible in some members of the League, but no statistical study has yet been made of them. It might be guessed that a higher than random number of keen Social Crediters would be opposed to fluoridation of water. Based on hatred of orthodox finance there is fierce opposition to the World Bank and the International Monetary Fund, which in turn sometimes finds expression in extreme insular and 'pro-Empire' attitudes. Opposition to orthodox finance in a few isolated instances may give rise to anti-Semitic utterances (by individual Social Crediters, not officers of the League) on the ground that 'the Jews' are at the heart of an international financial conspiracy.

The *Constitution and Rules* of the League describe a structure which is in some respects reminiscent of the National Party, and which contains electoral branches, a Regional Organization and a Dominion

Council. The provisions on 'The Parliamentary Section', especially
the one providing that Dominion Conference may resolve that 'there
shall be two Deputy-Leaders', show that the League has written its
optimism about its electoral prospects into its constitution. In practice the League has been sadly perplexed by organizational problems.
Originally it had a Leader, as distinct from a Dominion President,
who 'was involved in both administrative and political questions'[1]
both at elections and between them. However, apparently this led
to too much emphasis being placed on the Leader's role and too
little on branch organization membership. Consequently since the
resignation of Mr. Owen as Leader in 1958, a Leader has been
chosen only in election years; Mr. P. H. Matthews in 1960 and
Mr. V. F. Cracknell in 1963. This arrangement will probably be
altered if and when the League gains some seats in the House. Mr.
Owen's resignation was largely the result of his doctrinal differences
with other prominent members of the League. However, for parties
which are not in office, the greatest sin is consistent electoral failure,
and the drop in the Social Credit vote, 1954–7, may have been
responsible for his resignation.

Organization in general is weak, because the number of dedicated
Social Credit voluntary workers is small, and because the League is
too poor to employ much paid labour. Unlike the major parties, it
does not receive large donations from farming, business, or labour
organizations. Apart from a few clerical workers there has been a
paid Secretary-Treasurer since 1962; previously the corresponding
position was called Secretary-Organizer and, before that, Secretary.
There are now one or two full-time area organizers working in the
field, and others are employed for short periods during elections. Many
of the branches have a very small membership. The weakness of the
organization may be judged from the fact that at the 1963 election
three of the eighty candidates failed to present their nomination
papers in time. Recently there have been some improvements. It
was decided that at the 1963 election there should be a concentration
of effort on about sixteen of the most promising electorates and
particularly on Hobson. Unfortunately this decision was taken
rather too late to be completely effective. From 1960 the League has
had an official monthly journal, *The New Zealand Guardian*. Since
1959 professional public relations counsel have been employed, who
have helped in Press and radio contacts and research. They conducted a 'poll' in the Hobson electorate in 1963, which was useful
in indicating what support existed for the League and also in putting
before those interviewed in a striking way the possibility that the
candidate, Mr. Cracknell, had a good chance of being elected.

[1] O'Brien, op. cit., p. 32.

Discipline in the League has been rather chaotic. This is partly because the party is a new one and perhaps also because the intricacy of Social Credit doctrine has produced varying interpretations which have made it difficult for some enthusiasts to conform to official policy. This tendency may be reinforced by the emphasis on individualism and personal freedom among Social Crediters. Conferences are now more 'structured' and more orderly than they used to be. But, if the League ever returns members to Parliament in substantial numbers a new conception of party discipline might need to be worked out. The major parties' system of a party line enforced by Whips has often been denounced by Social Crediters. 'The Social Credit League is so designed as to break up this control. It is a league of independents. Its candidates for parliament pledge no allegiance to a party "boss" or to any detailed policy other than the Social Credit monetary technique. It has no party Whips, the parliamentary members have restricted powers at Dominion conferences, and are quite free to serve their electors and to act according to their own consciences.'[1] Whether this concept of the functioning of a parliamentary party would work remains to be seen. It is interesting that the *Constitution and Rules* say that membership in the League will be terminated by a member 'becoming a member of any political party'. The inference is that the League is *not* a party.

As regards future prospects, the League has better chances than most previous third parties in New Zealand. It appears to have not only a secure base, in certain areas of the North Island, but also potentialities of expansion throughout New Zealand, which the Country Party, for instance, never had. But it is difficult to see how these chances might develop favourably, failing a change in the voting system, which the established parties would be unwilling to concede. It would take a major economic depression or the disastrous consequences of rapid and unplanned automation to provide the conditions for a breakthrough by Social Credit. And even then both the Government and the other major party would have to be extraordinarily inept in handling the situation to enable Social Credit to reap any decisive advantage.[2]

[1] C. W. Elvidge, quoted in *New Zealand Social Crediter*, 15 May 1957.
[2] Except for the above references and those given on the last four general elections in Ch. II, very little has been published on the political aspects of Social Credit in New Zealand. Most of the publications in existence, including those of the League, refer to the economic aspects.

BOOK LIST

Bruce Brown, 'The Labour Campaign', *Political Science*, vol. x, no. 1 (1958).

——, *The Rise of New Zealand Labour* (Wellington, 1962).

Lord Bryce, *Modern Democracies* (New York, 1924), vol. ii, pp. 265–332.

P. Campbell, 'Politicians, Public Servants, and the People in New Zealand', *Political Studies*, vol. iii, no. 3 (1955) and vol. iv, no. 1 (1956).

R. M. Chapman (ed.), *Ends and Means in New Zealand Politics* (Auckland, 1961).

——, W. K. Jackson, and A. V. Mitchell, *New Zealand Politics In Action* (Oxford, 1962).

—— and K. Sinclair (eds.), *Studies of a Small Democracy* (Auckland, 1963).

J. E. Colechin, 'The Social Credit Campaign', *Political Science*, vol. x, no. 1 (1958).

J. B. Condliffe, *New Zealand in the Making* (London, 1959).

W. J. Gardner, 'The Rise of W. F. Massey, 1891–1912', *Political Science*, vol. xiii, no. 1 (1961) and 'W. F. Massey in Power', ibid., vol. xiii, no. 2 (1961).

R. N. Kelson, 'The New Zealand National Party', *Political Science*, vol. vi, no. 2 (1954).

——, 'Voting in the New Zealand House of Representatives, 1947–1954', ibid., vol. vii, no. 2 (1955).

——, *The Private Member of Parliament and the Formation of Public Policy: A New Zealand Case Study* (University of Toronto, 1964).

John A. Lee, 'Psychopathology in Politics', *Tomorrow*, 6 Dec. 1939.

——, *Simple on a Soapbox* (Auckland, 1963).

——, *A Letter which every New Zealander should Read* (Auckland, n.d.).

Leslie Lipson, *The Politics of Equality* (Chicago, 1948).

——, 'Party Systems in the United Kingdom and the Older Commonwealth: Causes, Resemblances and Variations', *Political Studies*, vol. vii, no. 1 (1959).

R. S. Milne, 'Citizen Participation in Political Life, New Zealand', *International Social Science Journal*, vol. xii, no. 1 (1960).

——, 'Voting in Wellington Central, 1957', *Political Science*, vol. ii, no. 2 (1959).

Austin Mitchell, 'Dunedin Central', *Political Science*, vol. xiv, no. 2 (1962).

——, *Waitaki Votes* (Dunedin, 1962).

P. J. O'Farrell, 'The Formation of the New Zealand Labour Party', *Historical Studies, Australia and New Zealand*, vol. x, no. 38 (1962).

W. H. Oliver, *The Story of New Zealand* (London, 1960).

Louise Overacker, 'The New Zealand Labor Party', *American Political Science Review*, vol. xlix, no. 3 (1955).

J. T. Paul, *Humanism in Politics* (Wellington, 1946).

Political Science, vol. xv, no. 2 (1963), special issue, 'Politics in New Zealand—a Symposium'.

W. P. REEVES, *The Long White Cloud* (London, 4th edn., 1950).

A. D. ROBINSON, 'The National Campaign', *Political Science*, vol. x, no. 1 (1958).

——, *Oligarchy and Democracy: the Distribution of Power in the New Zealand National Party, 1936–1949* (The Hague, 1959 (mimeo.)).

ALAN ROBINSON, 'Class-Voting in New Zealand', S. M. Lipset and Stein Rokkan (eds.), *Party Systems and Voter Alignments: An Approach to Comparative Politics* (Glencoe, Ill., to be published).

J. L. ROBSON (ed.), *New Zealand—the Development of its Laws and Constitution* (London, 1954).

K. J. SCOTT, *The New Zealand Constitution* (Oxford, 1962).

A. SIEGFRIED, *Democracy in New Zealand* (London, 1914).

K. SINCLAIR, *A History of New Zealand* (London, 1959).

F. L. W. WOOD, *The New Zealand People at War* (Wellington, 1958).

N. S. WOODS, *Industrial Conciliation and Arbitration* (Wellington, 1963).

INDEX

Committee, 148, 174–7, 183, 237, 241, 254, 295; Dominion Treasurer, 173, 174, 175; electorate organization, 192, 193, 206, 207–10, 218, 236, 253, 257, 258; farming groups, relations with, 85, 114–15, 119, 120, 121, 176, 282; finance, 85, 123, 175–6, 193, 195–6, 204–5, 208–9, 259–60; general director, 179; headquarters organization, 179–80; juniors' organization, 192–3, 196–7, 236–7, 247; Leader, 174, 175; Leader and candidate selection, 253, 257; Leader and caucus, 158, 159; Leader, choice of, 146–50, 170, 181; Leader and Conference, 239, 240, 241, 242; Leader and Dominion Council, 173, 174, 175; Leader and policy formulation, 176–8, 236, 293; Leader, powers of, 171, 172; Leader and President, 172, 236; Maori organization, 92, 173, 210, 257; membership, 204–6, 207, 209; ministers, choice of, 152; organizers, 194–5, 206, 208–10; origins of, 53; parliamentary party, relations with extra-parliamentary party, 146–9, 165, 171, 172, 173–4, 176, 178, 180; party discipline, 136, 138–44, 160, 240; policy, 57–58, 65–66, 120, 276–88, 297, 301, policy committee, 176–7, 179, 180, 236, 242, 293; President, 172, 173; President and candidate selection, 256, 257; President and Conference, 239, 240, 241; President, election of, 172; President and Dominion Council, 174, 175; President and Leader, 172, 173, 236; President and policy committee, 176; publicity department, 180; remits, 178, 179, 197–9, 207, 208, 220, 237–42, 246–7, 297; research department, 180, 198, 238; Secretary, 179; sub-divisional organization, 199; trade unions and, 62–63, 109, 129, 130, 284; womens' organization, 173, 196, 236–7, 247.

National Political Federation, 47, 146, 170.

National Research Organization, 129.

nationalization, 14, 15, 38, 53, 61, 108, 111–12, 276–9; of Bank of New Zealand, 14, 51, 59, 61, 124–5, 135, 161, 163, 232, 289; of Reserve Bank,

51, 59, 61; proposals for a State Bank, 38, 41, 48, 59.

Nash, W. (Sir Walter), 144, 151, 160, 186, 277, 288; and Conference, 223, 232; elected as Leader, 145–6; financial policy of, 51, 52, 56, 161, 163, 226, 232; and guaranteed price, 54; and party discipline, 142; and party organization, 189, 191; qualities as a politician, 23; and trade unions, 62, 110, 145–6; and trade-union relations with Labour Party, 114.

Nelson, 76, 84, 90, 95.

New Plymouth, 94, 174.

New Zealand, authoritarianism in, 11–12; economy of, 5–6, 272–3; equality in, 6–8, 23; external relations, 4–5; insulation of, 10–11, 298; interest groups in, 15, 98–101, 284, 290–1; interest in politics in, 2–3; minorities in, 18–19; origins and ties of population, 3–5; political system in, 12–14, 270, 272; sensitivity to public opinion in, 18; similarity of party policies in, 276, 278–9, 297–8; social conservatism in, 8–11.

New Zealand Alliance, 121, 202.

New Zealand Amalgamated Society of Railway Servants, 230.

New Zealand Co-operative Dairy Company, 47.

New Zealand Guardian, see newspapers, party.

New Zealand Liberal, see newspapers, party.

newspapers, party: *Freedom*, 180, 241; *Maoriland Worker*, 17, 39; *New Zealand Guardian*, 302; *New Zealand Liberal*, 123; *Southern Cross*, 17; *Standard*, 17, 88, 295; *Statesman*, 17, 295.

1951 strike, 18, 62, 102, 109, 129, 145, 234, 267.

Nordmeyer, A. H., vi, 144, 155, 266, 283; elected as Leader, 146, 151; and 'new look', 66, 110–12; as party President, 184.

North Island, the, 2, 29, 33, 34, 35, 42, 55, 67, 78, 80, 85, 87, 90, 116, 146, 155, 300, 303.

Northern Maori, 210, 268.

Oamaru, 266.

oligarchy, party, 3, 183, 249, 290–6.

PRINTED IN GREAT BRITAIN
AT THE UNIVERSITY PRESS, OXFORD
BY VIVIAN RIDLER
PRINTER TO THE UNIVERSITY